China and the West to 1600

China and the West to 1600

Empire, Philosophy, and the
Paradox of Culture

Steven Wallech

WILEY Blackwell

This edition first published 2016
© 2016 John Wiley & Sons, Inc.

Registered Office
John Wiley & Sons, Ltd, The Atrium, Southern Gate, Chichester, West Sussex, PO19 8SQ, UK

Editorial Offices
350 Main Street, Malden, MA 02148-5020, USA
9600 Garsington Road, Oxford, OX4 2DQ, UK
The Atrium, Southern Gate, Chichester, West Sussex, PO19 8SQ, UK

For details of our global editorial offices, for customer services, and for information about how to apply for permission to reuse the copyright material in this book please see our website at www.wiley.com/wiley-blackwell.

The right of Steven Wallech to be identified as the author of this work has been asserted in accordance with the UK Copyright, Designs and Patents Act 1988.

Library of Congress Cataloging-in-Publication Data

Names: Wallech, Steven, author.
Title: China and the west to 1600 : empire, philosophy, and the paradox of culture / Steven Wallech.
Description: Chichester, UK ; Malden, MA : John Wiley & Sons, 2016. | Includes bibliographical references and index.
Identifiers: LCCN 2015035753 (print) | LCCN 2015041226 (ebook) | ISBN 9781118879993 (cloth) | ISBN 9781118880074 (pbk.) | ISBN 9781118879962 (pdf) | ISBN 9781118880067 (epub)
Subjects: LCSH: China–History–To 221 B.C. | China–History–221 B.C.-960 A.D. | China–History–960-1644. | Europe–History–To 476. | Europe–History–476-1492. | Europe–History–1492-1648.
Classification: LCC DS741.5 .W23 2016 (print) | LCC DS741.5 (ebook) | DDC 303.48/25104–dc23
LC record available at http://lccn.loc.gov/2015035753

A catalogue record for this book is available from the British Library.

Cover image: Corbis @iStockphoto / yangphoto @ GettyImages

Set in 10/12.5pt Galliard by SPi Global, Pondicherry, India
Printed and bound in Malaysia by Vivar Printing Sdn Bhd

1   2016

Contents

Acknowledgements

The author would like to thank SuShuan Chen, Matthew Jaffe, and a third anonymous critic for the valuable suggestions and corrections they made to the draft manuscript of this book. Furthermore, the author would like to extend a special thank you to his editor, Andrew J. Davidson.

Preface

Teaching and studying world history at the college level is a uniquely challenging endeavor, the subject so immense that it can at times overwhelm the novice—first-time instructors and students alike—with its wealth of details.

Nearly all other college or university courses in history tend to focus on a single culture or region, distinguishing it from all other human communities. As a result, such courses tend to highlight differences. To teach world history, however, the instructor must reverse this emphasis. Theme or themes must be found to explain the common problems faced by humanity, and then explore how each culture did or did not find solutions. In this manner, the instructor deals with the commonality of our shared humanity, from which certain patterns over time, or themes, emerge.

This text uses one such theme to consider the comparative histories presented. This is the artificial relationship between humans and the plants they grow, and the animals they raise, to feed their population. This theme sets the material limits that confront a culture: how many people it can feed, how much geographic space it can command, and how effectively it can use it resources. In addition, this theme reveals how the nature of the relationship between humans and their food supply produces a continuous paradox, one that every civilization must face: an abundance of food generated by agriculture feeds a growing population that soon outstrips the food surpluses generated and threatens famine, epidemic disease, and exhaustion of the land that in the extreme can lead to ecocide, or the collapse of the ecosystem. Two subordinate themes are also useful in explaining how this paradox unfolds in world history: 1) the beliefs (religions and philosophies) that the production of surplus food supplies supports as civilization tries to address the central paradox cited above, and 2) the consequences of the close association between farmers and herders as they compete for use of the land.

Two civilizations are singled out in the pages that follow to facilitate this study: China and Western civilization. These two make good case studies because they were the richest and most powerful civilizations in world history during the ancient era. They produced material features that were remarkably similar. They faced the same internal problems at roughly the same time. They generated great philosophies in an attempt to find solutions to common problems. And they both faced the threat of invasion by a nomadic enemy as they spiraled into collapse at the end of the ancient era.

Post-Han Empire China and post-Roman Empire Western civilization diverged during the course of the Middle Ages. This divergence, the different paths China and "the West" took after the fall of their respective ancient empires, was in part a reflection of the varying degree of success they achieved in implementing the different philosophies they had developed to try to address the central paradox of culture. This divergence also reflects their levels of success and failure in dealing with nomads, ever present on their frontiers.

Furthermore, as the paradox of agriculture unfolds, subordinate paradoxes appear. The most important one to the study of world history is that the success China achieved in maintaining its ancient traditions ended up trapping Chinese culture in these traditions. In contrast, medieval Europe failed to recover the unity of Rome. Also, institutional contradictions emerged as a result of trying to mix surviving features of Greco-Roman culture with Christian practices and values and Germanic (and nomadic) customs. This created a dysfunctional feudalism that failed so spectacularly that Europe broke with tradition and modernized, making Western civilization the first to do so. Hence, the original paradox of culture, agriculture, spawned a series of subordinate ones considered by this study. The subordinate paradoxes reveal the great complexity of a great civilization in a simple, and, we hope, engaging way.

One still might ask: Why compare the ancient civilizations of China and Western civilization? The answer rests on the brilliance of both. Since these two civilizations achieved the pinnacle of material success in the ancient world, both examples can be used by the student of world history to study other human communities. An understanding of how both China and Western civilization struggled with the paradox of agriculture also provides a useful method of historical analysis.

Finally, this text can serve as supplemental reading for both halves of the world history survey. In ancient and medieval world history, it explains the complex consequences caused by humanity's choice to abandon a natural way of making a living and adopt the artificial lifestyle that agriculture created. This book also provides a complete treatment of the tensions between nomads and sedentary farmers that persisted throughout most of ancient and medieval Eurasian history. Finally, this book explains why modernization began in Europe and not in China, which might relieve the instructor of a course on the history of the modern world from having to spend a great deal of time laying a foundation for the course.

Introduction

The paradox of culture refers to the inescapable contradictions that marked civilizations throughout world history. The oldest and most significant paradox surfaced with the agricultural revolution. Once discovered and mastered sometime near the end of the last Ice Age, agriculture, a reliable method of producing food, gave rise to civilization, but at the same time trapped humans in a cycle of unwelcome consequences. When ancient farmers began to cultivate specific plants and raise specific animals to support sedentary communities, they deviated from nature, creating an artificial setting for human survival. By giving up a nomadic lifestyle and cultivating these organisms, the first agriculturalists not only produced their own food, but generated the first food surpluses in world history, launching a human population explosion. People began to settle down in ever-greater numbers, organizing and then reorganizing their methods and systems of food production. In so doing they changed the landscape.

The increasing numbers of people who had adopted agricultural and permanent living sites soon began to place pressures on the local environment. One consequence of adopting a sedentary lifestyle to cultivate food was the attraction of parasites, not only insects and rodents that wished to feed on humans or their food supplies, but pathogens that spread easily among concentrated populations of people and their domesticated plants and animals. Periodically these pathogens devastated local populations in the form of epidemic disease. In addition, this new, artificial relationship called "agriculture" set in motion periodic episodes of "ecocide." In other words, the very methods the early farming communities employed to generate food eventually ended up undercutting their capacity to produce

China and the West to 1600: Empire, Philosophy, and the Paradox of Culture,
First Edition. Steven Wallech.
© 2016 John Wiley & Sons, Inc. Published 2016 by John Wiley & Sons, Inc.

sufficient supplies of food by causing soil erosion, soil exhaustion, defor-estation, or all three simultaneously. The end result was that the agricul-tural revolution created a fundamental paradox: the more successful the society is in producing plenty of food, the more potential there was for ecological disasters, whether biological or environmental.

In an attempt to defeat this fundamental paradox, each ancient civiliza-tion developed its own system of beliefs and practices, known collectively as its *culture*, designed to try to increase its control over the natural world. The various cultures attempted to integrate human actions, expectations, and agriculture, with the end goal of creating a steady flow of food to feed the ever-increasing needs of their ever-increasing populations. Nonetheless, none of these early cultivating communities could escape the consequences of its actions, as the artificial conditions under which they lived generated ever-greater distances between human civilizations and the natural envi-ronment.

Two such societies, China and the Western world, provide excellent examples of human culture's struggle with the fundamental paradox agri-culture created. Singling out China and the West for a comparative study is instructive, for both civilizations experienced striking similarities during the ancient era, and then dramatically diverged during the Middle Ages. Both societies matured roughly at the same time and at the same rate. Both grew to roughly the same size in terms of the number of people and amount of land under political control. And both suffered similar fates at the end of the ancient era for roughly the same reasons. Yet, with the beginning of the medieval era, China managed to hold the center, recover, and keep its ancient, classical institutions intact, while the post-Roman West collapsed and splintered into the eclectic European cultures of the Middle Ages. Furthermore, once the medieval era began, China entered a golden age of traditional practices that set it apart as the richest culture in Eurasia. In contrast, Western civilization lurched from one institutional design to another, from the Early to the High and then to the Late Middle Ages (500–1500 CE). Ultimately, and ironically, China's great success in maintaining its traditional culture throughout the upheaval of the Middle Ages trapped its society in stasis, even as Europe's stunning failure to maintain its traditional society set in motion great upheaval and change, a process that, ultimately and ironically, led to modernization, leaving China "behind" for centuries.

To accomplish the task of comparing and contrasting the paradoxes embedded in China and the West, we will consider three major themes: agriculture, philosophy, and the threat of and interaction with nomads. Agriculture is an obvious choice since the central paradox under study in this book springs from the singular event of humans selecting and planting specific domesticated plants. Chinese and Western philosophy is not as obvious a choice as agriculture, but one that nonetheless reflects the cultural paradoxes derived from changes in agricultural production. Finally, responses to, and interaction with, nomads serve as the third choice. The nomadic lifestyle required the breeding, raising, and herding of livestock and the ability to continually pick up and move in order to find fresh pastures. In contrast, cultivating domesticated plants required the adoption of a sedentary lifestyle: staying in one place, building fences, maintaining borders, and excluding intruders. These major differences in food production and lifestyles led to open conflicts between farmers and herders, struggles that played out over the entire course of ancient and medieval world history.

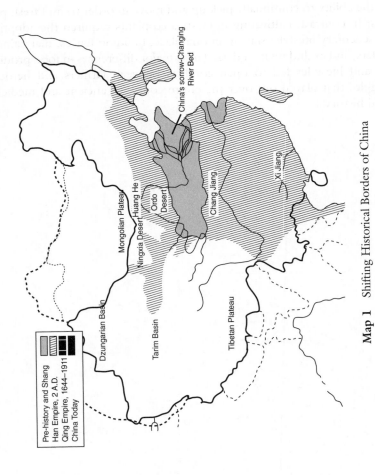

Map 1 Shifting Historical Borders of China

Legend:
- Pre-history and Shang
- Han Empire, 2 A.D.
- Qing Empire, 1644–1911
- China Today

Labels on map: Mongolian Plateau, Huang He, Ningxia Desert, Ordo Desert, China's sorrow-Changing River Bed, Chang Jiang, Xi Jiang, Dzungarian Basin, Tarim Basin, Tibetan Plateau

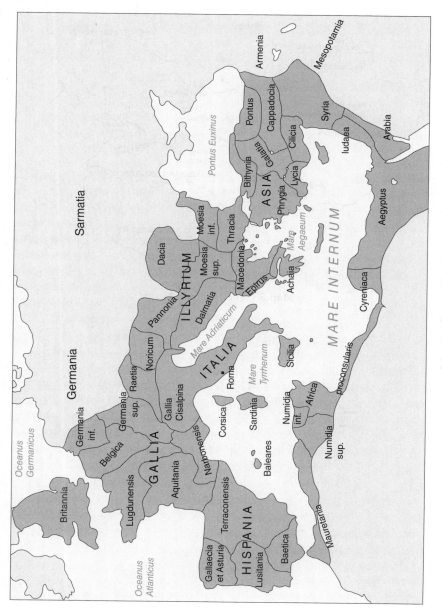

Map 2 Roman Empire

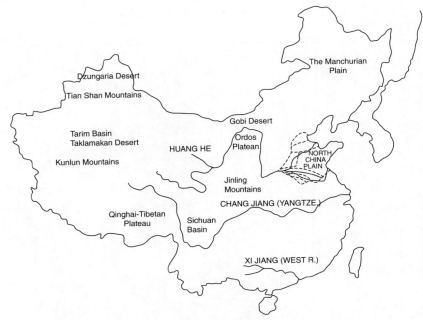

Map 3   The Nomadic Steppe

CIVILIZATIONS OF THE ANCIENT WORLD
CHINA AND THE WEST

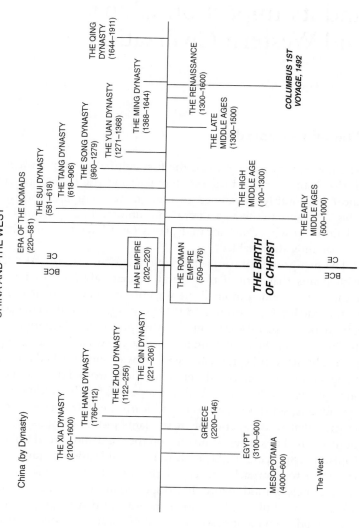

China (by Dynasty)

THE XIA DYNASTY
(2100–1600)

THE HANG DYNASTY
(1766–112)

THE ZHOU DYNASTY
(1122–256)

THE QIN DYNASTY
(221–206)

HAN EMPIRE
(202–220)

ERA OF THE NOMADS
(220–581)

THE SUI DYNASTY
(581–618)

THE TANG DYNASTY
(618–906)

THE SONG DYNASTY
(960–1279)

THE YUAN DYNASTY
(1271–1368)

THE MING DYNASTY
(1368–1644)

THE QING DYNASTY
(1644–1911)

BCE
CE

CE
BCE

THE BIRTH
OF CHRIST

The West

MESOPOTAMIA
(4000–600)

EGYPT
(3100–900)

GREECE
(2200–146)

THE ROMAN
EMPIRE
(509–476)

THE EARLY
MIDDLE AGES
(500–1000)

THE HIGH
MIDDLE AGE
(100–1300)

THE LATE
MIDDLE AGES
(1300–1500)

THE RENAISSANCE
(1300–1600)

COLUMBUS 1ST
VOYAGE, 1492

1

The Paradox of Agriculture and its Impact on China and Western Civilization

The Oldest Paradox

The use of agriculture created the first cultural paradox in world history, in that it both enabled the development and rise of the first civilizations and continuously threatened to undermine them and lead to their fall. This is because in the ancient era, they unintentionally created an artificial relationship with domesticated plants (and later animals) that was not permanently sustainable.

The first groups of people working in agriculture created a relationship with plants that proved to be quite unnatural. The circumstances that created this bond combined the warmth of a new climatic era at the end of the last Ice Age (around 18,000 years ago) with the appearance of an abundance of seed-bearing grasses that promised a bounty of new foods. In this new setting of melting ice, exposed new lands, and seed producing plants, hunters and gatherers began a new economy called foraging. These foragers collected seeds in different locations around the world by studying such plants as wild wheat, barley, rice, corn, lentils, chickpeas, peas, flax, rye, millets, sorghum, and so on, to learn their life cycles. These foragers learned that wild varieties of these plants produced pods that spontaneously opened to scatter their seeds on the wind and spread throughout the landscape. Studying the life cycle of these wild varieties taught these foragers when to approach clusters of these seed-bearing plants and harvest their kernels of food before they dispersed in the wind. Learning so much about the wild plants, these foragers noticed that every once in a while a rare genetic mutant appeared that did not scatter its seeds. This rare plant

China and the West to 1600: Empire, Philosophy, and the Paradox of Culture,
First Edition. Steven Wallech.
© 2016 John Wiley & Sons, Inc. Published 2016 by John Wiley & Sons, Inc.

(one mutant in every two to four million wild plants) stood out because its pod did not open, its seeds grew to an unusually large size, and these seeds remained trapped with the parent plant.[1] The large seeds in these unopened pods promised to provide a very rich diet if more of these plants could be found. But these plants did not reproduce.

Having learned a great deal about wild seed producing grasses, these foragers collected these mutant seeds whenever they appeared and sowed them rather than ate them. Very quickly, the number of mutant plants increased each year, changing fields of wild, seed-bearing plants into this rare mutant variety. By eating some of the large seeds, and planting the rest, these foragers unintentionally became farmers and rapidly began raising fields of mutant plants that could not reproduce on their own. A new bond had been forged: the first farmers in world history perpetuated the existence of plants that could not generate their numbers without human intervention.

Not surprisingly, this artificial bond between humans and their mutant plants led to a dramatic increase in the population of both. In a relatively short time this mutually beneficial relationship, which biologists call a "symbiosis," changed the landscape. Wild varieties of seed-producing grasses gave way to human cultivators planting their mutant food sources. But this new symbiosis was not a natural relationship because these ancient farmers had sowed the seeds of plants that should have disappeared after one growing season.

Biologists refer to individual organisms that do not reproduce in the wild as *omegas*. The mutant plants that ancient farmers chose to cultivate certainly belonged to this category of life form. In contrast, biologists call successful organisms that do reproduce in the wild *alphas*. The wild variety of seed-producing grasses that scatter their seeds, sending them flying on the wind far away from the parent plant certainly belong to this category. These proved the most successful in the process Charles Darwin called "Natural Selection," while planting mutant *omega* grasses required human intervention, or what biologists called "artificial selection." All agricultural communities used artificial selection.

By selecting *omega* plants, the first farmers secured a reliable food source. The predictability of producing seeds from single *omega* parent plants provided offspring that matured at the same time and at the same rate. Also, since grasses are hermaphrodites, the male and female sex organs on the same mutant parent plant produced seeds with a very stable DNA. Such an abundance of food from a stable gene pool fed growing numbers of people and soon ancient farmers and their *omega* plants thrived together. The result was the rapid increase in the number of *omega* plants, as well as the number of those groups of people who had turned to agriculture (and by extension a sedentary lifestyle). As the number of humans and *omega* plants linked in the symbiotic relationship we know as agriculture continued to increase, these groups began to move aside the once widespread *alpha* plants, changed the physical landscape, and (unintentionally) narrowed the range of food sources available for human consumption. Soon thereafter, unintended consequences followed.

These consequences played out following a long and tortuous scenario, one repeated in more or less the same order in all long-lasting agricultural communities:

1   The earliest form of agriculture, known as "slash and burn," involved the killing of large forests of trees by stripping off their bark, burning the dead trees, and using the ash as fertilizer to grow *omega* plants.
2   The human-*omega* plant symbiosis supported by slash and burn agriculture increased the total population of both groups of organisms.
3   Continuous growth in the populations of sedentary human farmers and *omega* plants resulted in deforestation and altered the local landscape.
4   Deforestation exposed the land under cultivation to soil depletion and erosion, making it particularly vulnerable to changes in climate, which could in turn lead to great ecological damage and even the collapse of the local ecosystem, the latter known as ecocide.
5   Great ecological damage forced farmers to abandon exhausted fields and seek new locations in which they could settle and grow the crops upon which they had grown dependent for sustenance.
6   The most desirable locations for permanent fields in which to grow crops were near rivers that could provide season after season of fresh soil and water thanks to annual floods of the river valleys and their nearby floodplains.
7   In order to avoid drowning during these annual floods, local farmers began irrigation projects in attempt to both bring the water of the river closer to their fields and regulate the impact of the floods.
8   Long periods of successful growing seasons and increased human numbers soon required farmers to devise methods to count their seeds, store them, and ration their supply in order to ensure a continuous supply of food to eat from harvest to harvest, year after year.
9   The need to count seeds, measure time, and ration food supplies led to the development of mathematics, writing, and calendars by the people living in the successful farming communities.

10 Those individuals who developed numbers, letters, characters, and concepts of time held specialized occupations, did not spend their days farming, and lived near one another in towns. These were near but separate from the fields and those individuals who remained tied to the land and had to tend to the crops on a daily basis.

11 As human numbers continued to grow, towns became cities and the urban centers became the foundations of civilizations.

12 As a civilization expanded, more and more of the surrounding local landscape fell under human control, causing nature to continue to retreat.

Eventually, however, nature always seemed to rebel. The increasingly large human imprint on the local ecology upset the delicate balance between ancient farmers, their *omega* plants, and the conditions that both needed to exist. This apparent natural rebellion could take the form of droughts, soil exhaustion, increased local aridity, violent floods, the sudden eruption of epidemic disease (whether in the human, or domesticated plant, or domesticated animal populations), or, most destructive of all, complete ecocide, or collapse of the power of the ecosystem to sustain life. Any and all of the unpleasant consequences of agriculture that inflicted damage on the natural environment could and usually did disrupt the human organization needed to continue to cultivate the local landscape. Such disruptions could cause a very high death rate among farmers and threaten the very foundations of a given civilization. Sometimes the inhabitants of the ancient farming community would find a way to recover from the disruption and continue to develop; sometimes the community would unravel and simply cease to exist. In either case, any surviving farmers found themselves still caught up in the incessant struggle to exist, but now sustenance by agricultural was the only way they knew how to feed themselves, so all who could do so moved to a new location, inevitably altering the landscape wherever they settled.

As agriculture developed in the ancient world, two very successful human communities that followed the above-mentioned scenario of humanity's struggle with food production, its ecological impact, and its mounting population pressures, were China and the Western world. Within Chinese and Western civilizations' long histories, Han China and Imperial Rome managed to produce the richest empires of the world's ancient era and maintain a remarkably long period of command over their respective domains. Han China rose to power in 202 BCE and fell in CE 220. The Roman Republic began in 509 BCE, with the Roman Empire officially coming to an end in CE 476. During these long periods of rule, and within their respective parts of Eurasia, these civilizations were unrivaled in the number of people they could feed, the size of the geographic area they commanded, the amount of wealth that they produced and amassed, and the length of time they managed to secure their borders from nomadic raiders.

To understand the conditions that underpinned such major imperial successes requires an analysis of two central themes of world history: cultural diffusion and geographic isolation. The history of Eurasia, and the adjacent lands of North Africa, is one of frequent intercultural contacts, or much cultural diffusion. This is because an east-west land axis dominates the geography of Eurasia and North Africa, a physical alignment that allowed the many different peoples of Europe, North Africa, and Asia to range far and wide and engage in considerable cultural interaction. Frequent cultural exchanges resulted in the transference of all manner of domesticated plants and animals, tools, ideas, and commercial goods, from one end of this large portion of the world to the other. It also accelerated the development of civilizations throughout the entire geographic zone. For this reason, the ancient civilizations of Eurasia and North Africa developed more quickly than did those of sub-Saharan Africa or the Americas. Still, of all the ancient civilizations of Eurasia, none achieved as great a material success as did Han China and the Roman Empire.

In contrast, geographic isolation, which of course limits cultural diffusion, dominated the history of the Americas and sub-Saharan Africa. In the Americas, the land axis runs north to south, which precludes the easy movement of domesticated plants and animals due to dramatic changes in climatic zones and habitats as one moves farther north or south of the equator. In addition, the Atlantic and the Pacific Oceans virtually quarantined the peoples of the Americas from those of Eurasia and Africa, effectively denying almost all forms of cultural and even biological contact.

Finally, and unlike the Americas or Eurasia, the land axis of sub-Saharan Africa runs both north and south and east and west. The Sahara Desert, however, dominates most of the east-to-west axis. This means that this massive desert, one of the largest in the world, undid most of the advantages an east-west land axis might otherwise have afforded the peoples who inhabited the zone. Climate and habitat remained similar along this east-west axis, but sand dominates much of the landscape. The only area where humans could thrive was the grasslands just below the Sahara, but until the arrival of the camel, an animal not native to the area, foreigners had no way to reach the grasslands. Therefore, the grasslands of sub-Saharan Africa would go undeveloped until the rise of Islam and the use of the Arabian camel to cross the Sahara in large numbers and open trade routes during the Middle Ages (CE 500–1500). The only exception to this condition of severe isolation was sub-Saharan cultures situated on or near the Nile River. Ancient Kush (1700 BCE– CE 350) had a history anchored in its contact with Egypt situated to the north, and along the Red Sea coast a later civilization called Axum (CE 100–700) thrived after the beginning of the Common Era. But south of Kush and Axum, climate denied further cultural penetration into sub-Saharan Africa because summer rains drowned Egypt winter grass crops.[2] This helps explain why no civilization in the Americas or sub-Saharan Africa ever matched the material successes found in Eurasia and North Africa during the ancient era.

Even though both Han China and the Roman Empire were unrivaled in the ancient world, neither was immune to the trappings of the paradox of agriculture. The strain on the local ecology of increasing human and *omega* plant numbers resulted in periods of decay in both. In addition, the success of China and Western civilization increased the distance between their human populations and the natural setting in which these people lived. Ultimately, the more both cultures succeeded, the more population pressures they created. And the more population pressures they created, the more likely they were to face massive failures. These continuous issues of human numbers and the spread of *omega* plants required constant adjustments to maintain order in both civilizations. Finally, the Han Dynasty and the Roman Empire represent the most complex cultural developments of ancient Chinese and Western civilizations.

This chapter explores the paradox of agriculture, ties it to the biology and geography of cultivation in these two cultures, and considers the developmental adaptations of both. Below is the history of this paradox as it unfolded in the ancient era in both China and Western civilization. Each responded by continually adjusting institutions to the organizational needs of food production as they teetered between order and chaos.

Chinese Agriculture

For much of world history, China maintained the globe's most dynamic culture. Chinese wealth and power enjoyed pre-eminence from the Han Dynasty (202 BCE– CE 220) to the beginning of the modern age (*c.* CE 1500). Each ruling dynasty, or imperial family, that governed China, did so with absolute power. That power, however, was tempered by the necessity to delegate authority to highly trained bureaucrats who administered the emperor's will. Chinese emperors selected these officials from individuals who had passed the rigorous Confucian examination system, which promoted the most talented men of each generation. These Chinese scholar-bureaucrats then rose in rank, based on their interpersonal skills and bureaucratic cunning. This system of centralized authority allowed each imperial family to rule China for centuries. The end result was the creation of the Chinese dynastic cycle: the ability of traditional China to regenerate its political organization century after century despite the fact that each ruling family eventually fell from power.

Through their dynastic cycle, the Chinese developed and maintained a highly successful political organization. Despite periodic disruptions due to internal rebellions or nomadic invasions, the Chinese managed to return to their well-tested system. In short, China exhibited an ancient form of internal coherence that the cultures of India, Europe, the Middle East, the Americas, and Africa never equaled. A critical underpinning of this successful rule lay in the Chinese system of agriculture.

The history of Chinese civilization began on the northern plain, situated around the massive Huang He (Yellow River). This is an area rich in a fine-grained yellow soil called loess, a wind-deposited dust comprised of lime derived from the decomposition of tiny organisms. The fertility of loess is without equal, and it served to support a style of cultivation that was distinctly Chinese.[3] In short, the Yellow River carried loess to its floodplain and thereby offered rich rewards to ancient Chinese farmers. This offering, however, came at a big price. Due to periodic and often violent flooding, the Yellow River also bears another name: "China's sorrow."[4] The Yellow River gained this second name because it drew Chinese farmers to its rich soils, and regularly drowned them with disastrous floods. The Chinese soon learned to work together in specialized tasks and on a large scale to develop systems of irrigation to produce their crops and prevent these ruinous floods.[5]

Most of China is unproductive agriculturally. Only relatively thin bands of land support crops. These thin bands are concentrated in river valleys, or across acreage found on local floodplains, and along coastal plains. These few areas attracted the Chinese, who figured out how to use them by building an irrigation system that permitted the development of ever-wider bands of arable acreage than those offered by nature.[6] At the dawn of Chinese civilization, during the Xia Dynasty (*c.* 2207–1766 BCE), the Chinese mastered the techniques of irrigation necessary to harness the waters of the Yellow River to increase food production, indeed to create food surpluses, and see their culture expand. The entire length of the Yellow River came under human control by the start of the Han Dynasty (202 BCE– CE 220). But the Chinese never fully mastered the continued violent flooding of the Yellow River. This river produced such disastrous floods because it was a waterway that carried more silt than the Amazon, the Mississippi, and the Nile combined. This silt fell in the Yellow River's riverbed, forcing the Chinese continually to build up their irrigation levees, the embankments they used to prevent the water from inundating the surrounding land. Eventually, the silt in the Yellow River raised the riverbed until it towered as high as 50 feet above the floodplain in several locations. At those locations where the river levees reached their greatest height, weaknesses in the irrigation system led to massive breeches in the levees. This led to massive floods that spread across the landscape and swept across the North China Plain. Sometimes this extended hundreds of miles from the river's banks, killing all the farmers in its path. Such colossal disasters reminded the Chinese people time and again that they needed a strong centralized political system, one that could marshal the resources of capital and labor necessary to build projects to manage the water supply of the great Yellow River and try to keep its murderous waters at bay. These reminders led to the central theses of Chinese history: political unity, highly organized divisions of labor, specialized tasks, and numerous large-scale enterprises worked best to produce food.

Origins of Chinese Agriculture

The earliest Chinese farmers who used their domesticated plants as food unwittingly unleashed population pressures, but had taken the first steps toward the process of a developing a civilization. In so doing China followed the common historical scenario laid out above, taking on increased institutional complexity as more and more people came to depend on agriculture for food. In China's case, ancient cultivation began when a set of farmers domesticated millets on the loess plains along the Yellow River. This domestication occurred sometime around 5000 BCE. These farmers, situated in northern China, were the first to begin to change China's countryside in order to meet their needs and provided the staple crop that gave life to the first Chinese dynasties. Attributing social order to Hou Ji ("Lord Millets," a Chinese name praising the value of millets), the agricultural sites these farmers founded laid a foundation for the first Chinese cities. But long before any cities appeared, the early Chinese farmers practiced slash and burn agriculture to clear forests for crops, secure ash to enrich the soil, and plant their millet seeds. Whenever soil exhaustion reduced their crop yields, the farmers, who belonged to the prehistoric Yangshao culture (c.5100–2950 BCE), were forced to relocate and clear land for new fields.

Archaeologists have uncovered several hundred Yangshao culture village sites widely scattered across the central Yellow River basin, from Henan to

Shaanxi and Shanxi. Collectively, the artifacts unearthed at these sites provide evidence that these peoples lived a semi-sedentary lifestyle common to all those who practiced slash and burn agriculture. It also tells us that they had domesticated different varieties of millets, supplementing the grains these plants yielded by hunting and fishing. The evidence does not, however, indicate any sort of central government that would have united the many villages.

Following the peoples of the Yangshao culture, were the Dawenkou people (*c.*4700–3600 BCE). This new culture, which also cultivated millets, developed later than the Yangshao and lived in village sites farther to the east, on the Shandong Peninsula on the north-eastern coast of China. Exploiting the resources of the mouth of the Yellow River, Dawenkou farmers left evidence that suggests that they had abandoned slash and burn cultivation. They built semi-permanent villages, taking advantage of the rich loess soils deposits of the Yellow River's delta to grow their crops. It also appears that they engaged in small-scale irrigation projects. The artifacts left by these semi-permanent agricultural villages suggest a more highly developed culture, one on the verge of city building. Typically, archaeologists have found that as any given farming population grew, and its villages became more permanent, a central village ultimately emerged as an administrative center. Dawenkou culture exhibited such developmental signs.[7]

The Longshan people were the next group to produce farming communities in northern China (*c.*3000–1900 BCE). Longshan farmers lived in far more permanent settlements than those of the Dawenkou culture, although they, too, lived on the Shandong Peninsula. Longshan cultures improved upon earlier millet-cultivating techniques and spread out to cover a much broader area than the Yangshao and Dawenkou peoples combined. Longshan farmers used different soil-renewing methods prior to gaining control over the Yellow River's flood cycle through irrigation. The Longshan people spread fertilizers based on animal waste, as opposed to ash, and left some of their fields "fallow," letting the field rest for a year, giving the land a chance to recover from agricultural use. The permanence of Longshan sites supported a steady increase in human numbers that, in turn, caused significant population pressures. Longshan villages spread from their original location on the Shandong Peninsula both north and west, making them, in the eyes of most Chinese scholars, the founders of the first Chinese civilization.

A look at the artifacts of each of these early Chinese peoples reveals a steady development of Chinese technique in cultivation. The increasing level of permanence in farming settlements from the Yangshao to the

Longshan cultures points to a growing need for sedentary agriculture on sites where the Yellow river's floods regularly renewed soil fertility. The early farming communities did not endure, but they did lay the foundation for Chinese civilization, as well as a legacy of domesticated plants that would continue to feed a growing Chinese population dependent on well-established farming practices.

China's Domesticated Animals

Along with the domestication of millets, northern Chinese farmers added domesticated dogs, pigs, water buffalo, cattle, sheep, goats, horses, chickens, geese, ducks, and silk worms to their agricultural resource base. These ancient farmers acquired their animals by domesticating certain native species and, in time, importing others. Archaeologists have determined which of the animals listed above were actually domesticated by the Chinese by looking at skeletal remains. Did the remains of these animals indicate a transition from wild *alphas* to domestic *omega* species, or did they indicate only the domesticated skeletons of beasts belonging to some other local culture? The first animal to exhibit evidence of domestication was the dog, although since dogs played no role in agriculture they are of little relevance here.[8]

Sometime around 6200 BCE the Chinese domesticated the pig, the first useful beast as a food source in an agricultural community. Archaeologists found the remains of the earliest domesticated pigs at Kuahuqiao in Zhejiang province, near the mouth of the Yangzi River (the great waterway that dominated the southern half of China and its history). The remains indicate that the wild variety of pig had given way to the domesticated version in much the same way *omega* plants had replaced *alpha* grasses. The evidence of these changes lies in the skeletal size and the teeth of the pigs. In comparison to wild pigs, domesticated pigs are larger and also have distorted teeth, because they are breed to have teeth capable of chewing cast-off food, which tended to be quite coarse. Chinese pigs came under human control gradually, as the skeletal remains reveal, and in time the domesticated varieties became a standard food source, one celebrated in later Chinese literature.[9]

Archaeologists also found cattle remains in a cave at a Shantaisi site near modern Lizhuang in Henan province in central China. These remains date back to 2500 BCE, but the spread of cattle continued westward until 2200 BCE. The archaeologists who found these cattle bones in the Shantaisi cave could not determine if they were native to China or imported from abroad because they found too few specimens to examine.

Nevertheless, the bones indicated that the animals lived in the middle and lower reaches of the Yellow River, the same region in which millet cultivation was commonly practiced, suggesting that cattle might have become useful as draft animals to pull the ancient Chinese plow.[10] The way that agriculturalists actually used cattle, however, depended on the tools they had.

Ancient Chinese Tools

The oldest agricultural tools in China were stone axes, machetes, and hoes used in seasonal farming. These are tools common to slash and burn cultivation and indicate that the Yangshao people used this farming technique. Later, the inhabitants of Dawenkou and Longshan villages augmented stone axes, machetes, and hoes with spades that eventually became Chinese plows. All of these tools belong to the "Neolithic Age."* This is marked in the archaeological record by the finds of polished rather than chipped stone tools. Polished stone axe blades, for example, can be used to strip bark from trees, whereas chipped-stone axes would break on impact. Chipped stones tools, however, did make excellent blades, which is why they were common, and are found where there were hunting and gathering communities. Hence, chipped stone tools belong to the "Paleolithic" Era, or "Old Stone" Age. The development of Neolithic tools indicates the start of agriculture in northern China.[11]

The First Chinese Plow

All three early Chinese cultures started with the same Neolithic technology. All of the early farmers used polished stone axes, wooden and stone shovels, machetes, and hoes common to slash and burn cultivation. When the more permanent villages developed in the north, open fields with renewable soil techniques required a shift in technology, at which point the spade became the chief tool. Spades date back to 6000 BCE. Archaeologists found spades in Hubei and Henan provinces located along the central Yellow River floodplain, where the ancient Chinese farmers used them in an unusual fashion. The Chinese Neolithic farmers used spades as proto-plows by stamping them into the ground with their feet and then pulling them along in a straight line. Ancient spade heads changed shape over time, from square to triangular, and eventually evolved into the plowshare. Neolithic farmers originally fashioned spade heads from wood,

---

* The Neolithic Age (or New Stone Age) marks a new technology, where polished agricultural tools replaced sharpened chipped tools used in hunting.

but in time they began to craft the blades from bone and stone. The plowshares that emerged from the spade were all made of stone, the first plow appearing in China sometime around 3000 BCE.[12]

Archaeologists, however, have only found the stone plowshares themselves, not the bodies of the plows. This means that the total design of the first Chinese plow remains unknown, which makes understanding exactly how people used it difficult. Nonetheless, Chinese experts speculate that the first plows consisted of a converted spade head pulled through the ground, in the manner mentioned above. The widespread finds of these ancient plowshares suggests that Chinese everywhere, both in the north and the south, used them, so their use could not have been limited to just one Neolithic culture.[13]

How China's Dawenkou and Longshan cultures pulled these plows through the earth becomes a major question because this tool came into use before they acquired cattle. Therefore, most scholars believe that Chinese men served as the original draft animals. This is not unreasonable, given that Egyptian farmers, who did have oxen, also built a smaller plow to be pulled by men (see below). Furthermore, Egyptian black earth (deposited by the Nile in each flood cycle) and Chinese loess soils share a common feature: both forms of soil are very fine, soft, and non-stratified. This makes them easier to cut through with a blade than the types of soil found in Mesopotamia (also see below). Finally, man-pulled plows are still in use in China, in Guizhou province of Inner Mongolia and the Gansu and Shanxi provinces of northern China. Cattle were first used as draft animals quite late in Chinese history, during the Spring and Autumn Era (771– 403 BCE), but we will return to this part of the story below.[14]

The First Chinese Dynasties

The Xia Dynasty (2205–1766 BCE)

While the aforementioned tools and animals had been available since the emergence of the Dawenkou culture, it was the Longshan people who generated the first traditional Chinese dynasty: the Xia. Scholars noted that the Longshan agricultural villages in northern China far outnumbered similar Dawenkou agricultural sites. This means that the population of the Longshan people reached the critical mass that caused the formation of first towns, and later cities. It is from these first urban sites that the Xia Dynasty, which officially launched China's Dynastic Cycle, emerged.

One of the difficulties of studying Chinese history is the way that legend can become fact with each new archaeological discovery. While the Xia and the following Shang Dynasties were long shrouded in legend, the Shang Dynasty (1766–1046 BCE) emerged from myth in the 1920s. During that decade, archaeologists discovered ancient Shang sites that verified the actual existence of the dynasty's ruling family. Today, many scholars claim that the same type of discovery has verified the existence of the even older Xia. The key archaeological site in question is Erlitou, found in 1959.

Erlitou is situated in the junction between the Wei and the Yellow Rivers, ten miles southwest of Yanshi City in Henan Province. Artifacts discovered at Erlitou date back to somewhere between 2100 and 1800 BCE. These dates put this site beyond the traditional years credited to the Shang Dynasty. As a result, more and more scholars now argue that Erlitou proves the existence of the Xia.

According to legend, King Yu (*c.*2200–2100 BCE) founded the Xia. Yu was purported to be the last in a long line of figures selected to rule because of their remarkable talents. He was also the first monarch in Chinese history to transfer royal power to his son. Then, when King Yu's son inherited the throne, a line of succession followed that became China's first ruling dynasty. Also, King Yu is the first Chinese king of lore to qualify as a real historical figure because he is credited with achieving the impossible: he was the monarch that tamed the Yellow River.

According to Chinese legend, King Yu devised a method of controlling this violent river by digging canals and channels instead of simply building dams. These canals and channels distributed necessary supplies of water and new soil to the millet fields. To organize the labor needed for the massive task of digging a series of irrigation canals and channels, and to better rule his realm, King Yu divided his people into nine groups and dispatched them into nine different regions. Under his leadership, the Yellow River's floodwaters flowed to the sea through a network of nine newly dredged irrigation channels. After ten years of intense labor, he could claim victory over a river whose floods had regularly caused disaster. This reputation for having tamed the Yellow River and organizing the people into a well-planned society made King Yu the personification of the selfless, benevolent Chinese king. His image as a ruler, and his devotion to duty, also made him a model for other kings. He helped to shape the ethics of authority that later became "the Way" of Chinese philosophy. Finally, the fact that Yu was the first ruler to impose his will on the Yellow River supports the thesis that civilization in China required some centralized form of government to exploit the limited arable land available for cultivation. At any rate, Yu is probably the first generally recognized historical figure in Chinese history.

The Shang Dynasty (1766–1046 BCE)

The Xia Dynasty lasted from 2205 to 1766 BCE and commanded huge swathes of land along the Yellow River, some three hundred miles long and one hundred miles wide. The Xia followed a pattern of rise and fall that became known as the dynastic cycle. King Yu, the model monarch, characterized the energy and devotion to duty that brought a ruling family to power. Seventeen generations later, the last of the Xia kings, King Jie (reigned *c.*1818–1783 BCE), became a model of the corrupt ruler. His selfish ways, self-indulgent quest for pleasure, and neglect of his people caused a man named Shang Tang to rebel (reigned *c.*1783–1753 BCE). He defeated King Jie, restored order to China, and became the founder of the Shang Dynasty (1766–1046 BCE). Shang Tang possessed all the virtues of an ethical monarch.

Ancient Chinese scholars noted the fall of what had over time become a corrupt dynasty and its replacement by one that restored order and virtue, and from this created the traditional Chinese model of the rise and fall—or succession—of dynasties. They based their explanation of the rise of a ruling family on the virtuous ruler, one whose talents, intelligence, and compassion served his people well. They explained the eventual fall of the same dynasty on the vile practices of a corrupt king, one whose egotistical quest for pleasure and indifference toward his people caused them to suffer. And once the people were suffering, it was only a matter of time before the overthrow of the old dynasty and the rise of a new one occurred. This model outlined the traditional history of the Xia, and it would become a central theme in the Chinese vision of the natural order of things, as will be discussed further in chapter two.[15]

The territory controlled by the Shang connected the eastern half of the Yellow River valley with the Yangzi valley and comprised a realm about a thousand miles long by a thousand miles wide, making it about three times larger than the Xia's realm. This increase in size meant a comparable increase in agricultural complexity. To administer such a massive expansion in cultivation under the control of the new regime required literacy. It is no surprise, then, that the Shang developed Chinese writing. This development facilitated the use of rationing, the allocation of resources, and the conscription of the labor needed to serve the ruler. The Shang rulers also implemented a system of feudalism, with local lords overseeing the work of peasant farmers to try to maximize crop yields and produce food surpluses.

Each of these developments reveals the increased complexity of life under the Shang. And such complexity indicates the growing distance between Chinese agriculture and the natural setting from which it first sprang.

Life in the Bronze Age placed significant limitations on the efficiency of agricultural production. Bronze is a hard metal made up of two softer metals: copper and tin. Copper and tin ores were scarce compared to iron, making bronze technology highly prized. In Bronze Age cultures everywhere, only the urban elite could afford to own objects made of precious bronze, so Chinese farmers continued to rely on stone and wooden tools. This effectively kept Chinese agriculture in the Stone Age, which restricted food production and resulted only in limited surpluses. In addition, because Shang kings had chosen to rely on feudal lords to ensure sufficient attention to local food production, they had to devise a way to ensure the loyalty of the lords, as well as that of the peasant farmers under them.[16] In time, the Shang rulers came to rely on religious authority to justify their rule.

The Shang claimed the right to rule by linking the ruling family to Shang Di, the ancestral deity of Shang Tang, who now became the supreme god of all the Shang Dynasty. The creation of a divine ancestry— the blurring of the line between emperor and god—filled China's nobility and farmers with awe, a sense of amazement, and respect that combined with fear to inspire loyalty among all of the Shang's subjects. And it was this strong devotion that allowed the Shang to develop a military system that could field an army of 13,000 soldiers if pressed with a crisis. Such numbers were very impressive for the Bronze Age, given the limitation on available metal weapons. Normally, however, the Shang mounted wars against raiding nomads with forces numbering no more than around 5000 men.

In time the Shang rulers combined religious with political and military authority. They performed religious ceremonies, administered the state, appointed subordinates to specialized offices, and commanded aristocratic clan leaders and their men. Once possessed of a mighty military the Shang rulers began to engage in offensive warfare to expand their domain, consolidating their control of the land by building new towns and opening new fields for cultivation. As mentioned, the Shang rulers devised the earliest form of Chinese ideograms (i.e. written characters) that would evolve into the modern Chinese language. Finally, the Shang rulers transformed China's climate and landscape by cutting down the forests that once dominated the North China plain to clear land for cultivation. Deforestation reduced the humidity of the region as an unintended consequence of expanding food production.[17]

The Shang rulers wished to convert as much of China's landscape into arable field as they could. This massive assault on the countryside required conscripted laborers engaged in all manner of complex projects, which included clearing land, building new cities, constructing defensive walls, and digging new series of irrigation canals. The Shang kings continually had to expand agricultural production to meet the needs of a continually growing population, and in so doing continually increased the complexity of life in China.[18]

Meanwhile, nomads living north of the Yellow River posed a constant threat to Shang farmers because there were no topographic barriers separating cultivated fields from pastureland. The threat to every Chinese dynasty posed by the nomads came to the fore whenever these pastoralists ventured into farming regions on raiding expeditions (see chapter three for the role of nomads in Chinese history). The Shang kings responded to these raids with warfare, using the chariot as their principal weapon, which helped them retain control of their newly open farms along the frontier line.[19]

The religion the Shang rulers had created to help them command the loyalty of the people relied heavily on the family to maintain obligations to both the living and the dead. For this reason the family came to form the core labor unit necessary to keep the dynasty running. Since the Chinese dynasties that followed the Shang counted their populations by the number of hearths around which families assembled, the hearth, or household fireplace, represented the basic labor unit. The importance of the family as the link between Heaven and Earth tied this fundamental labor unit back to Chinese religion.

Shang religion assigned the role of high priest to the Shang kings. In order to communicate with their ancestors in Heaven, the kings would write a question on the thigh or shoulder bone of a sheep, place the bone in a fire, and then "read" the cracks in the bone caused by the heat. They believed that their interpretations of the cracks would impart the insights of their dead ancestors to whom they had sent their questions. The Shang believed that if they properly honored the wishes of their ancestors, they might avoid natural disasters.[20] When natural disasters did occur, they typically took the form of floods, famines, droughts, or plagues, any of which signaled Heaven's displeasure with the ruler by killing mass numbers of people. Sequences of such disasters indicated the need for rebellion.

The history of the Shang Dynasty paralleled that of the Xia. The first Shang kings exemplified the moral, compassionate, and talented ruler, but the last Shang kings exhibited selfish desires, petty jealousies, and indifference to their people. In 1046 BCE, the last Shang king fell to rebellion, giving rise to a new dynasty, just as the first Shang king had overthrown the last Xia ruler. The last Shang king, Zi Xin (reigned *c.*1075–1046 BCE), was a tyrant who lost the respect and support of his people.[†]

By the thirteenth century BCE, the Shang had expanded into Gansu province, the region once occupied by the Xia Dynasty at the junction of the Wei and Yellow Rivers. The Shang assigned this region to the Zhou people. The Zhou sub-kings guarded the Shang's western flank from raiding bands of nomads and provided security to the Shang's seat of power in the east. Ji Chang (1152–1056 BCE) was a ruler of the Zhou and a vassal of the Shang Dynasty. King Zi Xin grew fearful of the highly competent Ji Chang's growing regional power and popularity. Known to his people as King Wen, Ji Chang possessed charismatic qualities that allowed him to expand his power within his own domain. Eventually a wary Zi Xin decided to put Ji Chang in prison, where he perished. Outraged by the harsh treatment his father had received, Ji Chang's son, Ji Fa, engineered a rebellion, raising armies in the west of Gansu to face the Shang. Ji Fa, later known as King Wu (reigned *c.*1046–1043 BCE), defeated those men loyal to Zi Xin in the Battle of Muye (1046 BCE), thus launching a new dynasty and era, the Zhou.

The Zhou Dynasty (1046–256 BCE)

The Zhou Dynasty justified its victory against the Shang by introducing a central theory of power to Chinese civilization: the Mandate of Heaven. The Mandate stated that Heaven supported all of China's rulers who worked to secure the prosperity of the people. Heaven smiled upon virtuous kings and punished wicked ones. Heaven provided good weather, fertile lands, and rich agricultural yields to hard-working peasants who served benevolent kings. And Heaven caused famine, plague, warfare, and rebellion to punish depraved kings who failed to sustain their people. The Zhou used this theory to supplant Shang Di, the supreme god of the Shang Dynasty. The Mandate reassigned the awe needed by a Bronze Age ruler from the Shang to the Zhou. Hence, the legitimacy of the new Zhou Dynasty was sanctioned by Heaven in its victory over a worthless Shang monarch.

Having acquired the realm through divine sanctions, the Zhou replaced the Shang and gained control over its domain, and the realm the Zhou

---

[†] During the Bronze Age, kings ruled China. The term "emperor" did not come into use until the Iron Age, when an agricultural revolution supplied the ruler with enough food surpluses to unify China and forego feudalism.

commanded was impressive. Its lands drew water from both the Yellow and Yangzi Rivers; the size and dimensions of the Zhou's domain was roughly the same as the Shang's, but the Zhou developed a system of cultivation that tilled the soil more thoroughly. This superior methodology that made better use of the land relied on an important change in Chinese feudalism.

Unlike the Shang kings, the Zhou rulers assigned their nobles to semi-independent realms, meaning that each of the subordinate rulers had sufficient authority to refine agricultural production to achieve maximum crop yields. In addition, each of the assigned rulers received a walled capital city and the power to hand their titles and estates down to their sons. Subordinate to the Zhou king, these great nobles supplied the monarch with the warriors (armies raised locally) needed to defend the entire realm against a constant nomadic threat (see chapter three). Supporting and subordinate to the warriors were the Chinese peasants, the backbone of agriculture. At the very bottom of Zhou society were the slaves, who performed the least desirable tasks in the Zhou kingdom. The only major flaw in the structure of Zhou feudalism was that the degree of autonomy offered to the Zhou nobles encouraged these men to become more independent over time. This form of decentralization slowly began to erode the Zhou king's power.

It was the Zhou who introduced the well-field system to Chinese agriculture, a model of food production that later Confucian philosophers would praise. The well-field system allotted 100 *mu* of land to each adult male in a family (one ancient *mu* being one pace wide and one hundred paces long).‡ Eight families received eight plots of land comprised of as many *mu* as adult males in the family. These eight family farms were situated around a central communal field, making the pattern of all such fields resemble the shape of the mouth of a well. Since the Chinese ideogram for "well" looks very much like the English ideogram for number, "#," this is how the "well"-field system got its name. Each peasant family worked the outside farms that ringed the common inner plot, that which supported the local aristocrat. The peasants who worked the outer plots did not own their land. Instead, it was the aristocratic families of the Zhou Dynasty who owned all of the fields.[21]

The millet yield per ancient *mu* was 12–13 *dou* per harvest. A *dou* was a measurement of food, the amount of which varied widely until the Qin Dynasty (221–206 BCE) standardized the weights and measures of China (see below). The Qin *dou* provides a sense of how much a Zhou *dou* produced in terms of crops yielded. The value of a *dou* for the Qin was two meals served to an adult male engaged in heavy labor on a government

---

‡The modern *mu* is much larger: 0.6667 of an acre.

project. This means that an adult male working his 100 *mu* of land could expect to yield from 2400 to 2600 meals of grain per harvest or ($[2 \times 12$ to 13 dou] $\times$ [1mu] $\times$ [100 mu]). Such a high yield illustrates the rewards for the intensity of family labor units involved in producing food all along the course of the mighty Yellow River.

Over the length of an almost eight-century reign, the Zhou's well-field system eroded in a manner similar to Zhou feudalism. Zhou feudalism, as mentioned, began to erode because the practice of inheritance of estates had slowly undercut the loyalty between the Zhou rulers and their subordinate regional noble aristocrats. The sons of these Zhou aristocrats came to perceive that they owned their estates because they had received their land from their fathers and not the Zhou king. The breakdown of these feudal bonds then began to influence the way the Zhou nobility felt they could use their lands. Between 1046 and 403 BCE, feudal lords of the Zhou Dynasty discovered that peasant-owned plots were more productive than the small farms allotted to family units in the well-field system. Peasant-owned plots led to larger farms worked by several peasant families with a will to succeed. As royal power disintegrated with time, the aristocracy found that agricultural reforms linked to the peasant's will to produce food increased the nobility's wealth. Higher yields on peasant-owned acreage allowed the lord to tax the larger harvests instead of receiving a fixed income from one-ninth of a communally cultivated collective farm.[22]

These changes in agricultural labor came just as China entered the Iron Age, sometime around 600 BCE. Unlike bronze, iron was plentiful. The greater availability of this abundant hard metal allowed for the development of a new farm technology, releasing Chinese farmers from the Stone Age and permitting them to cultivate with the most efficient metal technology available. Iron-bladed plows, iron scythes, and iron rings and sickles replaced wood and stone farm equipment. The efficiency of such tools encouraged the growth of larger and larger farms, which came to supplant the tiny plots common to the well-field system. In the Iron Age, China experienced an agricultural revolution.[23]

This agricultural revolution caused by iron plows in China combined with the disintegration of royal authority due to Zhou feudalism to unleash a wave of political chaos that led to the fall of the Zhou. In 770 BCE, partially assimilated nomadic warriors on the Zhou's northwestern frontier, as well as two former Zhou vassals, rose up in rebellion. The rebel forces killed the Zhou king and forced the remnants of the Zhou family to flee east. From their new eastern headquarters, the weakened Zhou monarchy claimed to rule what remained of their realm, from 770 to 256 BCE. With the move east, however, the Zhou kings effectively forfeited political and military control over their nobles, the Zhou aristocracy now feeling free to function as potential kings. Added to the rise of these petty monarchs was the sudden increase in food surpluses generated by the development of iron plowshares and the use of oxen as draft animals. The timing of the agricultural revolution and newly liberated—and competing—kings drove China into political turmoil. The Zhou's ex-nobles decided to use their windfall harvests to draft peasants, train them as soldiers, and place them in Iron Age armies.

Scholars call the times that followed "the Eastern Zhou" (770–221 BCE), during which the agricultural revolution continued to spread rapidly. In addition, the development of large-scale irrigation projects and expansion of cultivated fields brought the Yellow and Yangzi River valleys under tillage. Engineers such as Sunshu Ao (*c.*630–593 BCE), Ximen Bao (*c.*445–396 BCE), and Li Bing (governor of Sichuan *c.*277–250 BCE) built the largest irrigation systems located in China during the fall of the Zhou.[24]

The first half of the Eastern Zhou era produced what Chinese scholars call the Spring and Autumn Period (770–481 BCE). During this time, the Zhou nobility used their expanded farms to feed private armies that they raised and maintained to invade neighboring non-Chinese realms. The result of this was that Chinese-controlled territories begin to expand beyond the old Zhou kingdom. As addition of new territories to the Chinese realm increased, the ethnic diversity of China also began to change. Furthermore, as the Zhou nobility changed into petty kings, they selectively incorporated practices from their newly acquired non-Chinese subjects. One of these non-Chinese practices was the use of cavalry in warfare. With this new tactical force at their disposal, the power (and heads) of the newly minted petty kings began to swell, and they began to turn on one another. This launched the second half of the Eastern Zhou, the Era of the Warring States (403–221 BCE). By 403 BCE, a state of anarchy swept across the land.

The struggle that unfolded during the Era of the Warring States caused so much chaos that it inspired Chinese philosophy (see chapter two). At the same time, the agricultural revolution (mentioned above) that led to competing kingdoms, spread beyond what was once Zhou China. Finally, one kingdom destroyed all its rivals and ended the wars. This kingdom, the Qin, presented China with its first emperor.

The Qin Dynasty (221–206 BCE)

The Qin victory completely changed China. The Zhou originally ruled lands stretching from the loess plateau in the west, through the Yellow River floodplain, and onto the ocean in the east. The Zhou also expanded south, incorporating large portions of the Yangzi River basin. As mentioned above, the Zhou built a feudal system that ultimately unraveled due to decentralization. By the end of the civil war in 221 BCE, the Qin began building a new China. In so doing they abandoned the feudalism of the Zhou era. Qin China was a fully integrated empire with an iron-based agriculture. And thanks to Iron Age surpluses of food, the Qin could rule this empire without having to carve their state into petty feudal estates ruled by nobles. The food surpluses fed the labor force as well as the armies the Qin used to assimilate all of China's lands politically. The Qin also linked the peoples of the Yangzi River basin to those of the Yellow River basin, bringing much of what is modern China under the authority of one imperial office. This new arrangement combined the agricultural resources of these two major rivers into one community. Through a process of cultural assimilation, the Qin created a style of absorbing foreign peoples into the mainstream culture that became known as *sinicization* (transforming non-Chinese cultures into Chinese civilization).[25]

The territories controlled by the Qin eventually included the entire Yellow River basin and a new realm in Southern China called the kingdom of Qu, the people of which had ruled an area more than a thousand miles long and a thousand miles wide that encompassed a multi-ethnic population of non-Chinese. From the Qin's perspective, the problem they faced—continually as it turned out—was how to integrate the holdings in the north with the new lands in the south. Interestingly, the Qin never completely solved this problem, nor would their successors, the Han (202 BCE– CE 220).[26]

The main drive of the Qin south saw them expand toward the headwaters of the Yangzi, pushing south and then west, in the process acquiring fertile lands occupied by tribal peoples who farmed rice. Next, they moved toward Zhejiang and Fujian on the south-west coast of China. The Qin also added Lingnan, which is today modern Quangdong and Quangxi on the southernmost coast of China. Once they had conquered this area, the Qin divided it into three military commands that served as buffers for northern China from rebellion in the south. Thereafter these newly acquired southern provinces became a colonial zone that the Qin settled with banished criminals and political exiles. The southern tribal peoples naturally resisted this type of expansion, prompting the Qin to send a series of expeditionary forces into the region to pacify the various peoples of the land. This military exercise ended up taking seven years (221–214 BCE), and only partially succeeded.[27] Soon after the death of the first Qin Emperor, Qin Sui Huangdi (221–210 BCE), portions of this southern region broke free under the rule of rebel Qin generals.[28]

Despite the vast additions of lands acquired by the Qin Dynasty, the amount of arable acreage available to agriculture did not exceed more than 11 percent of the entire empire. Due to this shortage of arable land, farming in China remained labor-intensive, which required a further increase in the level of centralized authority. This remained the case well after the fall of the Qin, continuing as an economic reality for all the Chinese regimes that followed. The Qin, however, was the first to confront this fact as they tried to pull together the vast new lands that they had conquered. They tried to achieve too much too quickly, however, and pushed their people to the brink of rebellion.[29]

For example, the Qin overtaxed its people with the great costs associated with the construction of the first Great Wall of China, the standardization of all weights, measures, coins, and written scripts, and the conquests and assimilation of new lands. Within four years of the first emperor's death in 210 BCE, the Chinese people rebelled and the great Han Dynasty captured power in 202 BCE. From this moment forward a pattern of political, economic, and cultural controls transformed the Chinese people into the "Han" people. In addition the Han Dynasty (202 BCE– CE 220) set the pattern for the dynastic cycle and imperial rule that dominated Chinese history for more than two thousand years, all the way up to the year CE 1911.

The Rise of the Han Dynasty (202 BCE– CE 220)

Han agriculture consolidated all the developments of previous dynasties from the Bronze Age Xia to the Shang and Zhou and through the Iron Age Qin. The agricultural surpluses offered by the iron-based revolution that led to the rise of the Qin then fed the Han. And the Han spread this Iron Age agriculture as they conquered vast new lands. The Han Dynasty successfully built a stable system of power and economic integration that became the hallmark of China's enormous wealth during the ancient and medieval times. Using the philosophies generated during the Era of the Warring States (see chapter two), the Han developed a political ideology that allowed them to control their expanding empire. The spectacular success of the Han Dynasty overshadowed all that came before and set the pattern for all that would follow. Hence, the remainder of Chinese history involved the expansion, consolidation, and refinement of Han practices, coupled with numerous innovations that enhanced centralized authority throughout Chinese ancient and medieval history.

Roman Agriculture

When considering Western civilization, one notes immediately that the Roman Empire relied on a highly diversified economy when compared to that of China. The Roman economy, centered on the lands surrounding the Mediterranean Sea, comprised numerous and varied provinces organized to feed and service the people of Rome through food production, manufacturing, and trade. In contrast, Han China depended on managing the waters of a particularly volatile river, and later the other major river in the land. The "control" of the Yellow River required the implementation of a centralized political authority to administer what would become a vast and complex system of irrigation. This irrigation system, in turn, fed an expanding political society. At the same time, countless nomads, amassed on the frontiers of the empire, posed a constant military threat to the security of China, one that only reinforced the need for a powerful and highly centralized imperial rule (see chapter three). In contrast, the Roman Empire, the basis of what would become known as Western civilization, engaged in a pattern of conquests that periodically added new provinces to an expanding political base. As Rome continued to expand, the number of military challengers to Roman rule seemed to diminish, and each new province added to the empire provided a unique economic stamp that served to feed Roman society.

The genius of the Roman Empire was that it managed to combine military prowess with a highly pragmatic political system that allowed its inventive culture to conquer, incorporate, and consolidate an empire equal to that of Han China to the east. Indeed, each newly conquered Roman province seemed to enhance the ability of the empire to continue to survive on its own economically. In terms of food production, each of the new local provinces had already developed its own system of agriculture, manufacturing capability, and trade networks—all of which Rome simply absorbed. As a result, however, the Roman Empire never really achieved the same level of internal coherence throughout its vast domain as did Han China.

Unlike China, Rome was actually a cultural consumer of Greek civilization rather than an exporter of its own traditions. As a Hellenized civilization, Rome found it much more difficult to Romanize other civilizations than China. Also, Rome conquered other sedentary cultures rather than absorb nomadic peoples into its civilization. Rome expanded against well-established civilizations, while nomads surrounded China. Only the Celts north and west of Italy and some of the Berber tribes of North Africa consumed Roman practices, while all other sedentary foreign communities maintained their well-established agricultural habits. This meant that Rome allowed most conquered local peoples to continue with their original traditions so long as these traditions did not interfere with Roman rule. Accordingly, local agricultural production continued along the earlier lines of those people that founded the regional system of food production in the empire's various provinces. In contrast, China *sinicized* nearly every foreign population that ventured into Chinese territory, with perhaps the Mongols being the only exception (see chapters four and six).

To study Roman agriculture, then, one needs to consider this vast economic diversity of the empire's regional food production. To try to impart a working understanding of Roman food production, this text will feature several key provincial economies to show how the empire fed itself. One of these provinces, of course, must be Italy, for this is the peninsula on which Rome was based and fed in its formative years. A second province must be Egypt, because this ancient culture, eventually absorbed by Rome, supplied the latter the wheat and barley it needed to continue to feed the vast and growing population of Rome itself. A third province (actually a set of provinces) includes the Levant Coast and Mesopotamia, which made up the Fertile Crescent. It was the peoples of this region that domesticated the first plants and animals that would feed Western civilization. A fourth and final province is Greece. The Greeks occupied a unique geographic region, one with landforms that encouraged the formation of a system of independent city-states. This same region also had soil conditions—a rocky terrain with mostly thin and nutrient-poor soils that discouraged local food production. Instead, the peoples of the Greek city-states turned to the development of sailing technology and the development of sophisticated trade networks. These so-called network cities survived on the export of olive and grape products in exchange for the import of foreign-grown wheat and barley. This saw the major Greek city-states develop a highly urbanized population that helped shape the very influential Greek worldview, one that Rome consumed (see chapter two). Finally, an overview of the Roman economy is necessary, one that will explain how the Roman Empire actually worked. To begin, we turn to a consideration of the Italian peninsula.

Italian Agriculture

Throughout the first half of Roman history, known as the Roman Republic (509–30 BCE), land use on the Italian peninsula evolved from tiny family farms to massive commercial plantations. Over the course of five centuries, the Italian landscape provided not only level plains for cultivation, but also the slopes of the Apennine Mountains, where the Romans developed a system of terraced agriculture. To plow their fields, the Romans used an ard, a simple plow only capable of breaking the soil by scratching the earth with an iron blade. With use of this crude tool, the Romans plowed their fields in two directions set at right angles, to create an even, flat surface. Since the soils of Italy tended to be heavy, and contain a good many roots and vines, the Romans used powerful oxen to draw two different types of plowshares, one with a curved, knife-like blade to cut into thick soil, and the other with a broad, flat blade useful for breaking up looser soils. The Romans attached both types of plowshares to a frame with two small wheels to reduce traction as the plows cut into the ground. To help them prepare the land for agricultural use, the Romans also built dams and reservoirs for irrigation, lining their reservoirs with a form of waterproof cement. Their development of such extensive sophisticated irrigation systems was essential in light of the increasing size of the empire and the attendant demand for ever more food.

Rome expanded slowly throughout the Italian Peninsula from 509 to 265 BCE, the slow pace of this initial expansion giving the Romans time to link their agriculture to an expanding political system that could maintain an internal balance. As Rome continued to grow, so, too, did the number of its citizens who doubled as farmers and soldiers. Rome added significantly to its citizenship on two occasions: the Latin Wars (340–338 BCE) and the Social Wars (91–88 BCE). In both conflicts, the peoples of the defeated cities (Latin and Italian) became part of Rome when the Romans granted either Roman citizenship or associated citizenships to its former foes. Full Roman citizenship permitted an ally to marry a Roman, vote, and hold office in Rome; associated citizenship granted the right to marry Romans but not to vote or hold office. Both types of citizenship, however, required citizens to fight alongside Rome in its various wars. Hence, the people of these former enemy states joined Rome's citizen-farmer-soldiers in the dangers of and shared with them the spoils of war. From the combination of Roman and allied citizens, as well as the Roman citizen-farmer-soldier, one can see that the early Republic had linked agriculture to its political and military system. As a result, Rome's initial slow growth over two and a half centuries gave the Romans time to integrate systems of food production with a successful and expanding military and a constitutional-republican system of governance.[30]

The Roman citizen-farmer-soldier engaged in a wide variety of seasonal activities, from planting and harvesting, to fighting and voting. Each activity had its season and, if done correctly, ensured high crop yields per acre, a secure realm, and stable politics. Considering agriculture alone, the Romans practiced hoeing and weeding in much the same way as those of traditional rural communities do today. They also understood that by growing a certain variety of crops concurrently, they could reduce the number of weeds in their fields. Furthermore, they recognized the benefits of the use of animal wastes as fertilizer, and they often used fallow fields as grazing land for their cattle. During the harvest, the Romans replaced the straight handle on a sickle with one set at an angle, to reduce back pain. They also developed a mowing scythe for fields of greater size. For milling their grain, the Romans used a waterwheel that produced the rotary motion needed to grind wheat into flour. Eventually these waterwheels developed into the watermill, around 20 BCE. The Romans built their largest known set of watermills around CE 300, which had two rows of eight wheels each placed one below the other as the water cascaded down a long canal to turn each wheel. The Romans developed different milling processes to produce different grades of flour.

The Romans domesticated several different species of animals. They used oxen, mules, and donkeys for work, and sheep and cattle for their milk, wool, hides, meat, and manure. They raised pigs and goats, and they fancied birds, such as ducks and peacocks, for gourmet meals. The Romans developed saltwater fish farms as early as 95 BCE to satisfy their taste for fresh fish. Lucius Licinius Murena, a Roman Consul (chief magistrate) in the year 65 BCE, expanded the idea of fish farms by drawing seawater onto his estates using channels dug to the sea. Soon these types of farms became common, and they effectively allowed even those Romans who lived far from the coast to enjoy fresh fish. Control of the fish populations joined with a system of breeding animals to supply food early in Roman history. Together, livestock and fish allowed for a diet rich in protein for many citizens of Rome.

Farms during the Roman Republic varied sharply in size, so much so that historians have divided them into three different categories. First came the small farms that ranged from 18 to 108 *iugera*. (One *iugerum* is equal to about 0.65 acres, so the small farms varied in size from 11.7 to 70.2 acres.) The next level comprised medium-sized farms ranging from 80 to 500 *iugera* (52 to 325 acres). Finally, came the large estates called *latifundia*, which exceeded 500 *iugera* (more than 325 acres).[31]

Over the course of the Republic's history, farms increased in size. Early on, most farms fell into the first two categories: small and medium. In the Late Republican Era (265–30 BCE), latifundia began to dominate Roman agriculture. This shift from small and medium-sized farms to large estates began in earnest after 265 BCE. From 265 to 202 BCE, Rome defeated

Carthage, a Phoenician colony, and added the lands and wealth of the Western Mediterranean to the empire. This rapid expansion of the empire pumped riches into the hands of Rome's wealthiest citizens. After 202 BCE, these wealthy Romans began buying up farms from Italian planters who could no longer make a living in agriculture. The reason behind the failure of the small and medium-sized farms was a new war policy the Romans initiated after 202 BCE. This policy drew the Roman citizen-farmer-soldiers away from the land to fight in the military. In short, Rome's poor and middle-class citizens could not farm and fight at the same time. The land of the many failed farms then became available for sale, and latifundia increased in number. A secondary consequence of the increasing number of latifundia was a major change in Roman politics—one that led to civil war.

Part of this change entailed a social bond known as the patron-client relationship. Poor Roman citizens often sought legal and financial support by seeking out wealthy Roman benefactors. The benefactor gave his support in return for expected political backing. These benefactors typically belonged to Rome's aristocracy, the *patricians*, but they could also be among the rich *plebeians*, the commoners. Rich Romans of either class seeking a political career enlisted as many clients as possible. As more and more Roman farmers lost their farms, more of them sought out patrons. These increasingly powerful patrons became political rivals who competed for office. Eventually the competition increased in violence until, finally, only civil war could resolve the issue.

The Roman civil war erupted in 131 BCE and lasted until 30 BCE. The conflict pitted rival combinations of poor citizens and their rich patrons against one another. Spanning four generations, the civil war began when the wealthy leaders of the poor devised a land reform program to restore small and medium-sized farms to the plebeians. This led to the creation of the Popular Party, the goal of which was to break up the growing numbers of latifundia (owned by aristocratic rivals) and grant the land to the farmer-soldiers who had originally built up the Roman Empire. This threat to the owners of the latifundia, in turn, led to the formation of an opposition party, the Optimates, comprised mostly of the aristocrats and their clients. Violence followed.[32]

Using and abusing the Roman constitution, the Popular Party fought the Optimates without either side winning a decisive victory. In the second generation, Gaius Marius (155–86 BCE) shifted the direction of the Popular Party's land reform program by recruiting Roman soldiers directly from Rome's lowest economic and social stratum and equipping them with armor. This undercut the link between the farmer and his duty as a soldier, which justified his citizenship. Marius' military reform created a professional army and linked it to a general's military and political career. After 20 years of service in the army, Marius secured a farm for each of his soldiers as a form of retirement program, which further eroded the citizen-farmer-soldier bond. Finally, these reforms made the civil war worse: now rival politicians could rely on their own armies to settle their differences.[33]

In the third generation of the conflict, a leader of the Popular Party, Julius Caesar (*c.*102–44 BCE), launched a political and military career that saw him defeat all of his rivals. He rose to power linking success in public office with conducting winning military commands. He then used these military commands to win higher offices. His genius as a politician and soldier was unequalled. Finally, his rivals threatened his future in politics as his command over his army in Gaul, site of his latest military victory, neared its end. He decided on open warfare to resolve the issue. He destroyed the Optimate Party in battle and prepared to rule Rome as a dictator for life. Not long after assassination ended Julius Caesar's political career, but ended up transferring his wealth and prestige to his great-nephew, Octavius Caesar (63 BCE– CE 14). Octavius ultimately realized Julius' political goals as a member of the fourth and final generation of the civil war. Octavius defeated his rival Mark Antony (83–30 BCE), one of Julius Caesar's generals, at the Battle of Actium in 31 BCE. This victory secured Octavius' command over Rome. Then, between 30 BCE and CE 14, Octavius Caesar established the Roman imperial system.[34] While Octavius Caesar won the contest for command of the state, citizenship died in the process. Octavius Caesar, every bit the dictator, maintained the façade of the Republic to avoid assassination, as befell his great uncle Julius, but Roman citizenship had become a sham (see chapter two for the consequences).

The Imperial Era (30 BCE– CE 476), or the second half of Roman history, dominated the remainder of Rome's political existence. The imperial era produced a regime that brought Roman history in line with the Han Dynasty of China. By this time, both of the new and mighty empires had reduced all their people to mere subjects. Even though Rome continued to call some of its people "citizens," they were no longer the politically active individuals who had run the Roman Republic.[35]

Originally farm size, military service, and political responsibility went hand in hand in Roman society. The shift of the bulk of Rome's population from active citizens to passive subjects, however, destroyed a vital aspect of the Roman constitution. This shift had eliminated the political-economic-ideological bond that had held society together. Initially, as mentioned, the early Roman Republic had relied on citizen-farmer-soldiers to supply the men needed to serve in the infantry as well as raise food to feed a growing population. The concept of the citizen-farmer-soldier was a vital part of the pact laid out in the constitution because he used his own income to outfit himself for war and play his role in politics. Also, the original small number of latifundia supplied the officers of the army with its cavalry and the men who served as the city's magistrates. Again, farm size and political responsibility went hand in hand. During the Late Republic, however, Marius' military reforms broke up the farmer's responsibilities to the state as a soldier and a citizen. Thus, the professional soldier had replaced the citizen-farmer-soldier, which broke the link between self-reliant farmers, citizenship, and military duty.[36]

Considering the role played by the farmer in the Rome's military, focuses attention on the availability of farmland in the Roman system. The amount of arable soil in the Roman Empire stands in sharp contrast to the limited fertile acreage found within the Chinese Empire. The fact that the size of a Roman farmer's holdings defined his role as a citizen and a soldier was necessarily based on a large supply of farmland in the Italian Peninsula. In contrast, the relatively small supply of arable land in China imposed intense labor requirements on families working very small farms. Simultaneously, the danger posed by the unpredictability of the Yellow River also imposed the need for a strong centralized authority, in order to organize labor and funds to build and maintain an extensive irrigation and levee system.

The various sizes of early Republican farms generally exceeded those of Chinese peasant families. Even the small and medium-sized farms of the early Roman Republic were larger than the average Zhou family farm.[§] The amount of income a Roman farmer derived from a small farm supplied him with the light weapons needed to serve as a skirmisher. A medium-sized farm provided enough income to equip him as a heavy infantryman. In contrast, Chinese peasants served as draftees in the Zhou and later the Qin and Han armies; the ruler simply imposed both military service and a labor tax on the Chinese people. Chinese peasants' labor belonged to the state, which compelled them to maintain the irrigation systems, construct such massive state projects as the Great Wall, and build canals, roads, palaces, and defend the empire. Chinese peasants did not have a choice in the matter because the state used their labor for the common good—and however it liked. So long as China's peasants believed that their efforts did serve the common good, they worked willingly.

However, to limit the history of Roman agriculture to the Italian peninsula is to misunderstand the complexity of food production in imperial

---

[§] The only exception to this issue of comparative farm size was Rome's smallest farms. These were smaller than Zhou farms, but Romans that worked so few acres could not buy the armor needed to be soldiers or serve as citizens.

Rome. Much of the livestock and the domesticated plants that fueled the Roman army, government, and economy came from conquered lands. Rome added numerous provinces to its empire between 509 and 30 BCE. The acquisition of these lands opened Rome to diverse agricultural practices. For example, the domesticated plants and animals consumed by the Romans came primarily from the earliest agricultural sites of Mesopotamia and Egypt. Both regions became part of the Roman Empire, as did every other culture whose shores touched the Mediterranean and much of the Black Sea. To begin to understand the scope of the vast wealth of the agricultural lands available to Rome, one must start with Egypt, the Levant Coast, and Mesopotamia. This is where the domestication of plants and animals, as well as the formation of the first cities of Western civilization, began.

Egypt

When considering Egypt's contribution to the Roman economy, it is necessary to go back to the Bronze Age (3000–1200 BCE). This is because the domesticated plants, animals, and tools that helped form the bases of Western civilization were developed by peoples living in the Ancient Near East (i.e. Egypt and Mesopotamia). Also, once cultural traditions were fixed in an ancient culture like that of Egypt, patterns of life rarely changed. Finally, when the Iron Age began in 1200 BCE, Egypt was one of the few cultures in which an agricultural revolution did not occur. Egypt's methods of cultivation remained unchanged because so little land was fertile in this desert domain that the introduction of new and better iron tools changed little. Only the acreage that was watered by the Nile River produced food, though the amount of food generated by Egyptians working the Nile's floodplain was staggering. Hence, this text must travel back in time the see how the ancient culture of Egypt ended up feeding the people of Rome.

It was Egypt and Mesopotamia that contributed the oxen that pulled the Roman plow, the sheep, goats, and pigs that fed and clothed Romans, and the wheat and barley that Romans baked into bread or cooked into soup. Egypt itself became Rome's granary toward the end of the Roman Republic. In 31 BCE, Octavius Caesar defeated Mark Antony as well as the Egyptian Queen Cleopatra VII at the Battle of Actium and ended the Roman civil war. This victory gave Octavius control of Egypt as his personal domain. Now Octavius could use the fertility of the floodplains of the Nile River to feed even the poorest Roman citizens for free, so long as they came to Rome to eat.[37] In effect, the acquisition of Egypt made Octavius the patron of Rome, with all its citizens his clients.

The bounty of the Nile Valley approximately matched that of the Yellow River, but the Nile was a far gentler river then the Huang He. The first Western historian, Herodotus (*c*.484–425 BCE), aptly called Egypt, "the gift of the Nile." Surrounded by harsh deserts on the Libyan and Arabian sides of the river, the Egyptians needed the Nile to survive. As Egypt lies in a region that receives only one inch of rain per year, the Nile was the vital source of water and fresh mud that renewed Egyptian fields each year. To understand the limited amount of soil available for cultivation in ancient Egypt, one must learn a little bit more about the Nile itself.

The Nile is a remarkable river that flows from south to north, out into the Mediterranean. It headwaters are over 4000 miles away, near Lake Victoria. Lake Victoria is the largest body of fresh water in Africa, one whose shores are shared between modern Uganda, Kenya, and Tanzania. Supplied by the monsoon rains of eastern Africa, the Nile fills a deep riverbed with water that has cut a narrow crevasse on its trip to the sea. This narrow crevasse is also the fertile floodplain of Upper Egypt in the south. Emptying into the eastern Mediterranean, the mouth of the Nile has built up a massive river delta that offers more arable land to the Egyptian people. The delta is called Lower Egypt. Taken together, Upper and Lower Egypt represents 2.92 percent of all the land available to Egypt: approximately 11,675 square miles. This ribbon of fertile earth created the acreage used to feed the ancient Egyptian culture.

The Nile draws its water from very stable monsoonal rains. The abundance of moisture that these rains bring to eastern Africa fill Egypt's riverbed and cause a slowly rising and overflowing flood pattern. Given the relative gentleness of the Nile's flood cycle, Egyptian farmers never faced the Chinese farmers' central dilemma: the best land for cultivation also proved to be the most dangerous to work. On the contrary, Egyptians cultivated fields that seemed already prepared by nature for human use. Due to the annual monsoons, the Nile increases its water volume by fiftyfold during its flood cycle, and then retreats back into its deep riverbed, saturating the floodplain along its banks with moisture and fresh soil. In other words, the annual rise and fall of the Nile permitted a single, very long growing season on a very narrow ribbon of land with relatively little demands on labor.

The Egyptians formed a central government very early in their history. This central government arose from two key facts. First, the Nile's deep riverbed, gentle currents, and stable floods made this river an excellent highway. And second, the winds in Egypt blow steadily from north to south at a rate stronger than the south-to-north current of the Nile. Hence, a ruler could unify the country through travel. He could send a ship north by lowering his vessel's sail and moving with the current. Then, to make a voyage south, all he had to do was raise the ship's sail and catch the prevailing winds. This permitted a royal presence throughout Egypt so that by 3100 BCE the country came under one king's rule.

Even though Egypt developed a central government very early in its history, the king never controlled the entire realm, as did the first Qin and Han Chinese emperors. Along the course of the waterway, local administrators managed the waters of the Nile for the Egyptian king. These officials governed *nomes*, or administrative divisions of the Nile, and thus were called *nomarchs*. They represented royal authority in their districts and built the dams that regulated the Nile's water and the soil. The laborers these nomarchs oversaw did not have to work very hard to maintain the irrigation system. They only had to move an estimated thirty cubic meters of soil each year, which only amounted to about ten days of labor.

In contrast, silt carried by the waters of the Yellow River continually clogged the riverbed, as well as the irrigation canals and channels. Compared to the Nile, the Yellow River carried 6.3 times the amount of silt in just over three-quarters the length.**

In hard numbers, the Yellow River carried 1.764 billion tons of silt each year as compared to the Nile's 280 million tons. This made the accumulation of mud in the Yellow River's irrigation system a constant problem. Every year, the Chinese had to mobilize thousands of peasants from many different provinces to dredge the Yellow River's mud deposits.

Unlike their Chinese counterparts, Egyptian *nomarchs* simply organized local peasant labor to build dams to irrigate portions of the Nile's floodplain. Constructed at right angles to the river's flow, these dams cut Upper Egypt into agricultural basins. Each basin varied in size from the smallest at 990 acres to the largest at 4200 acres. Within each basin, Egyptians carefully leveled the land so that the flood saturated every square inch of available earth. The annual flood began in June and ended in October, with the high-water level reached by September. At its peak, the Nile covered most of the river valley within Upper Egypt's crevasse. Towns and villages obviously had to be built on ground sitting above this water line, lest they be flooded, too, or mired in fresh mud. The moisture of the flood penetrated about one to two meters beneath the soil, which meant that farmers had enough water on the land to plant and grow their crops without the need to water the plants many more

---

** The Yellow River carries 57 pounds of silt per cubic yard, and the Nile carries 9 pounds in the same volume of water. This is a difference of 6.3 times the silt in the Nile. Also, the length of the Yellow River is 3395 miles, and the Nile is 4258 miles.

times as the plants matured. Hence, cultivation began in October, when the standing water had gone but the soil was still moist. This aligned Egypt's cultivation pattern with the winter planting cycle of the *omega* grasses of the Fertile Crescent: wheat, barley, lentils, peas, chickpeas, bitter vetch, and flax.

With the amount of labor needed to prepare for cultivation at a minimum, nearly all of Egypt's farmers focused their energies on planting, weeding, and harvesting after the flood. In addition, Egyptian soil was easy to work because the mud was fresh and simply laying on the surface of the floodplain. Rapid field preparation and generous harvests made Egypt a very rich country. Also, since the June to October flood cycle left the Egyptians idle, they were free to develop a type of peasant-cottage industry. This free time also liberated labor to build the land's spectacular monuments that made their civilization so famous.

Due to the soft mud deposited regularly by the Nile, Egyptian farm tools reflected the light demands of the agricultural workers. Put simply, they did not need to use heavy plows. The Egyptian plow was lightly built and harnessed to oxen by the animals' horns. The Egyptians shared with the Chinese the non-stratified soils of loose earth that made plowing easy. When draft animals were not available, Egyptian farmers simply harnessed themselves to a smaller and lighter version of the ox-pulled plow. They worked the land in a manner similar to the Stone and Bronze Age Chinese farmers.

In addition to the plow, Egyptian farmers also used a short-handled hoe with a very long blade. Farmers developed the latter early in Egyptian history, when they first started digging the earth along the Nile. The design of the hoes did not change with time, as the Egyptians continued to find them adequate for weeding and excavating the land. Because of the very short handles, however, these hoes required farmers to bend over quite close to the land, making the work they performed very hard on their backs.

Using the domesticated grains, pulses, and animals of the Ancient Near East to plant their fields, the Egyptians produced spectacular harvests on their fertile soil. The total harvest for any given year in Egypt depended on the amount of land covered by the Nile's flood. On average, the acreage ranged from 8 million to 14.7 million square acres per year, from which an Egyptian farmer could anticipate an average yield of 165 bushels of wheat for every 2.2 acres. This meant that harvest ranged from 600 million to 1.103 billion bushels per year. Scholars estimate that the subsistence requirements to feed an Egyptian farming family of six came to about 132 bushels per year, meaning that an Egyptian harvest could produce the bare minimum of food to feed some 27.2 to 50.1 million farmers.[††] In other words, each year Egypt alone could have fed anywhere from 40 to 83 percent of the entire Chinese population during height of the Han Dynasty. Since Rome fed as many people as did Han China, Egypt must have been the Roman breadbasket.

Compared to other agricultural zones of the Levant, Anatolia, Greece, and Rome, Egyptian arable land was extremely productive. As a result, Egyptian farmers produced three to four times the yield of their counterparts in Greece or Italy. Also, while the river valleys of China were as fertile as Nile Valley, the quality of the Nile's soft water and natural tendency to irrigate the land eliminated the need for extra labor. Also, the Nile watered its floodplain without ravaging the land with periodic floods; but the Yellow River flooding often killed thousands of Chinese peasants. Such a stable supply of food as found in Egypt fuelled the political unity that helped to make Rome the ruler of the West.

The Levant and Mesopotamia

Turning back the historical clock to see how Egyptians worked the land revealed practices that survived into Roman times and belong to Western civilization. This is also required to understand how farmers cultivated the Fertile Crescent, which became part of the Roman Empire during the Roman civil war. Gnaeus Pompeius Magnus (106–48 BCE), also known as Pompey the Great, was a rival of Julius Caesar. Pompey was a talented general who oversaw successful military campaigns that added Turkey, Syria, and Palestine to the Roman Empire between 67 and 62 BCE. Caesar, however, defeated Pompey at the Battle of Pharsalius in 48 BCE, and Pompey suffered assassination in Egypt while trying to raise a second army to rechallenge Caesar. Pompey's death eliminated Caesar's last great rival to power, and Caesar went on to defeat what was left of his political opposition by 46 BCE. Mesopotamia fell under Roman rule during Trajan's reign (CE 98–117), but never fully remained in the hands of the Romans due to military threats from the Persians under the rising Parthian Dynasty (250 BCE–CE 226). Nonetheless, the addition of the lands of the Fertile Crescent to the Roman Empire set the stage for agriculture in Western civilization.

[††] I developed these population figures by using 132 bushels per year to feed a family of six as a base number. Then I used a yield of 165 bushels for every 2.2 acres. Next, I divided 8,000,000 cultivated acres by 2.2 to get 3,636,363, and multiplied this number by 165 bushels to obtain a harvest of 600,000,000 bushels. The next step was to divide 600,000,000 bushels by 132, giving 4,545,454 bushels that fed a family of six. And finally, I multiplied 6 times 4,545,454, giving a total of 27,272,727 people. I repeated this process with 14,700,000 cultivated acres and obtained 50,113,636 people.

Two varieties of wheat, emmer and einkorn, barley, peas, chickpeas, lentils, bitter vetch, and flax, plus pigs, goats, and sheep all come from the Fertile Crescent. Slash and burn farmers domesticated these plants and animals at beginning of agricultural revolution in 9600 BCE. Ecocide caused by deforestation drove these first farmers to rivers in quest for permanent fields. The Tigris and Euphrates rivers supplied the water and fresh soil these early farmers needed, and they chose the marshes at the mouth of the Persian Gulf, where the Tigris and Euphrates empty into the sea, as the most desirable place to grow their crops and found the most ancient of all the farms of Western civilization.

Interestingly, the *omega* plants and animals from the Fertile Crescent did not include cattle. Archaeologists have recently traced the domestication of cattle to the eastern Sahara with a very high level of certainty. In light of this find, the primacy long given to the Fertile Crescent as the region responsible for the most varied and generous supply of domesticated plants and animals to find their way into Western civilization needs at least slight modification. Nonetheless, the remainder of the original *omega* plants and animals produced on the floodplains of the Nile, Tigris and Euphrates, and Indus Rivers still belong to the Levant and Mesopotamia.

Modern world historians have long called the Fertile Crescent the "Cradle of Civilization." Surrounded by desert, the Fertile Crescent's lands enjoyed a Mediterranean climate that provided the perfect conditions for the earliest foragers to decipher the secrets of cultivation. Warm dry summers and mild wet winters produced an abundance of wild seed-producing grasses. From the knowledge they gained from gathering these seeds, the foragers developed the first *omega* varieties of grains and pulses. Also, the geographic location of this crescent-shaped region, spanning, as it does, a land bridge, provided a natural conduit for the transference of the Fertile Crescent's discoveries to three continents: Europe, Asia, and North Africa. The end result was the development of the oldest cities in world history.[38]

The phrase "Fertile Crescent" comes from James Henry Breasted (1865–1935), a nineteenth-century archaeologist from the University of Chicago. He was one of the most widely known scholars of antiquity and the founder of the field of Egyptology in the United States.[39] The region he described for its fertility comprised territories that span from modern Iraq to Syria, Lebanon, Israel, and Palestine. Also included is the southern fringe of Turkey. These lands were home to the Natifin people, foragers from the Neolithic era (16000–5000 BCE). They built tiny hamlets, spreading from the Levant Coast (Syria, Lebanon, and Israel) to the Tigris and Euphrates Rivers. During the Younger Dryas (10,400 and 9,600 BCE), a bitterly cold millennium, some of the Natufin people domesticated several of the key crops that helped them to survive this violent shift in climate. These crops made up the food base of the Fertile Crescent. After 9600 BCE, heirs to the Natufin legacy took up residence in the Shot-al-Arab region (marshes near the Persian Gulf) and produced the food that fed the world's first civilization, Sumeria.[40]

As a geographic site, the Fertile Crescent is a product of plate tectonics. This crescent shaped land bridge is a place where the African and Arabian continental plates collided with the Eurasian plate to produce a complex topography filled with broad alluvial basins (water-based floodplains rich in river sediments). Powerful rivers created marshlands that allowed the Fertile Crescent to support a long history of ancient cities. Starting with Sumer (4000–2200 BCE) at the mouth of the Tigris and Euphrates Rivers, civilization marched upstream. Akkad, Babylon, and Assyria followed, from 2800 to 600 BCE.

The Fertile Crescent also played host to invading chariot cultures: the Kassites who conquered Babylon, the Hittites who occupied Turkey, and the Mitanni who captured Syria from 1800 to 1200 BCE. Finally, the region supported the Phoenicians of Lebanon and Israelites of Palestine during the late Bronze and early Iron Ages (1200–500 BCE). From all these many cultures came the original artifacts of Western civilization: the first written scripts (which later became alphabets), legal codes, empires, agricultural tools, the oldest bronze and iron metallurgy in world history, the first monotheism, and the first plants and animals that fed the West and India.

It was the Fertile Crescent that set the stage for the development of Western civilization. Although its agriculture did not play a critical role in feeding the Roman Empire directly, it was the peoples of the Fertile Crescent who taught the founders of Rome what to grow, what animals to use, and what tools to adapt to their fields. Besides the material foundations of Western civilization, the cultures that began in the Fertile Crescent also supplied the Western civilization's first calendars, written scripts, and system of mathematics, something crucial for the efficient management of an agricultural system. Finally, it was a tiny sliver of the Fertile Crescent, Palestine, which provided the religious concepts that came to dominate Western civilization's cultural imagination. Hence, knowledge instead of food proved to be the key contribution of this "cradle of civilization."

Greece

The legacy of the Fertile Crescent, and the bounty of Egypt, made those two cultural zones highly valuable districts within the burgeoning Roman Empire. Less generous in terms of agricultural production, but more valuable in terms of economic development, was Greece. A study of ancient Greek agriculture, however, reveals a set of problems that produced some completely unexpected consequences. Some of these consequences were negative and others positive, but all of them were factors that shaped the Greek economy and ended up playing a major role in the development of the Mediterranean world and Rome (and therefore Western civilization).

Greece first became a province of the Roman Empire in 146 BCE, when a Consul (chief magistrate) of Rome, Lucius Mummius (*c*.175–126 BCE), crushed the Achaean League at the Battle of Leucopetra on the Isthmus of Corinth and ended Greek independence.[41] The addition of Greece to the Roman Empire inspired Quintus Horatius Flaccus (65–8 BCE), otherwise known as Horace, to utter the phrase "*Graecia Capta ferum victorem cepit, et artes intulit agresti Latio*," which translates as: "Greece, once conquered, in turn conquered its uncivilized conqueror, and brought the arts to rustic Latium." Taken together, both the conquest and the addition of the highly influential, cultural and intellectual Greece to Rome's growing empire changed the economy and creative imagination of the Roman people. How Greece made these changes to the Roman world reflects the way Greek geography influenced Greek culture.

The geography and climate of Greece created the setting for the development of a unique economic culture. The effects of plate tectonics made the Greek peninsula what geographers call a "shatter belt zone," meaning a region featuring chaotic, or irregular mountain patterns. The Greek mainland formed from a collision between the African, the Eurasian, and the Aegean Plates. The jagged mountains formed in this land were always prone to frequent earthquakes and volcanic activity. Sharp earth trimmers and massive lava flows further shaped a complex landscape. With the land's many valleys isolated from one another by the nearly impassable mountain ranges, the development of overland travel was discouraged, but the many natural harbors and easy access to the sea fostered sea travel and soon maritime trade. The climate offered hot, dry summers, temperate springs and autumns, and mild and wet winters. In the isolated valleys the people undertook agriculture.[42]

Greece's unique geographic setting and climate encouraged the integration of ancient Greek farming with trade so that soon these two economic activities became inseparable. Farmers had access to fertile fields in their various valleys so long as they were willing to invest the time and labor in clearing the land. Such activity, however, also caused significant erosion when the winter rains hit the open landscape. As a result, all ancient Greek communities soon became aware of the precarious balance between plowed fields, sharp variation in seasonal rains, and soil erosion, all three of which determined the year's food supply. Because of the uncertainty of water volume during the rainy season and the limited spaces in which to practice cultivation, each ancient Greek community developed a strong possessiveness of their locality. These conditions combined with a reliance on sea travel to shape Greek religion, social organization, law, government, commerce, and immigration. The end result was the formation of the Greek city-state as the dominant political system and the spread of their sophisticated network of commerce throughout all of Greece, as well as all the lands along the Mediterranean and Black Sea coastlines.[43]

Many of the features and conditions of ancient Greek agriculture matched those found in Italy. The use of ards, oxen, sickles and scythes, the valleys, the plains, and the terrace cultivation patterns were similar, but the availability of space in Greece was far more limited compared to Rome. Jealous protection of these isolated fields led to constant warfare between the city-states, which aligned the defense of a town's lands with the concept of citizenship. The perfection of defensive body armor, helmets, and shields, along with offensive weapons such as spears and swords, encouraged infantry formations that aligned able-bodied farmers with the defense of their city's food source. The inability to support a large population of horses on the limited grazing lands of Greece restricted military engagements to combat on foot. The result was the formation of a city-state system that encouraged a union of military action, politics, and agriculture.[44]

The relative poverty of Greek agriculture compared to that of Egypt, the Fertile Crescent, and Italy set the tone for a spectacular event that unfolded in Greece, one that profoundly shaped Western civilization. Between 750 and 550 BCE, a population explosion on the Greek peninsula quickly outstripped the land's capacity to feed the increased number of people. The end result was an exodus of citizens on a quest for new land that took members of different city-states, first east to the Aegean Islands, then to the Turkish Coast, and finally into the Black Sea. Soon after, there were further migrations westwards to southern Italy, Sicily, the southern coast of France, the eastern coast of Spain, and south to North Africa. The Greek colonies in North Africa and Sicily soon encountered, clashed, and then fought the earlier settlers, which led to a long history of conflict. Each of these new Greek colonies brought the institutions of their founder city with them, but all of them were independent economic and political experiments. All these Greek ventures looked for several qualities in a site on which to establish a colony: good soil, plentiful natural resources, defensible land, and a good location for trade. Once they had firmly established themselves, the new colonies soon formed commercial networks with the Greek mainland, making agriculture and trade even more inseparable. The end result was the formation of so-called network cities.[45]

A network city is one that lives by trade more than by local food production, a profile that numerous Greek city-states fit. Among the most prominent of these Greek network cities of the ancient world were Athens and Corinth. Their commercial design and their colonies allowed both network cities to import food from abroad and specialize in grape and olive production for export—a type of commercial design that made food production and commercial exchange nearly the same activity. Although both cities developed powerful trade networks, local politics still followed independent lines of evolution. Athens became famous for its democratic institutions, and Corinth was a notable oligarchy.[46] Both cities also engaged in independent political decisions, diplomacy, and military campaigns. But it was Athens that stood out as an intellectual center, so much so that it was soon distinguished from all other cities in Greek history.

It is this intellectual tradition that was the most important to Western civilization. Greek philosophy and science blossomed as a result of the linking of trade and agriculture. All the cities that contributed to the Greek philosophical tradition belonged to the network of commercial activity that colonization stimulated. Situated all across the Mediterranean basin, these various cities made contact with many different and contradictory cultural practices. These contradictions led the Greeks to question their own traditions. Doubt undermined the Greek religious worldview and opened the Western mind to explanations of nature that did not necessarily include the gods. This was a unique approach to an understanding of the natural world that only the Chinese would match. These new philosophical beliefs that functioned without a visible role for the gods emerged in China and the West at roughly the same time. This is the subject of chapter two.

Soon after Rome conquered the Greek colonies of Italy, the Romans began to imitate the Greeks. When the Romans conquered Carthage, Macedonia, and Greece, Rome added trade to its agricultural base. As Rome expanded to gain control of the entire Mediterranean, the Romans became completely Hellenized. The end result is that a new and powerful culture emerged in Western civilization: the Greco-Roman culture. This is the civilization that statistically matched China in size, number of people, and administrative structure. Yet, all the different elements that went into the Roman Empire still made it much more diverse in design than China.

Overview of the Roman Economy

Diversity defined the geographic composition of Rome's conquests. Each new province that Rome acquired went through a process of economic assimilation, a process that followed a common pattern.

Wherever the Romans added a new province, they engaged in vast deforestation projects that served as a general method of clearing the land for agriculture. Each new province they acquired became part of a growing, complex economy. From this complexity emerged three broad economic spheres between 200 BCE and CE 400. The first of these spheres, the inner sphere, comprised Rome and Italy; this sphere functioned as a consumer magnet that drew in wealth from all Roman provinces, as well as the trade that went beyond Rome's frontiers. The second sphere was a ring of rich provinces comprised of Spain, Syria, Greece, Gaul, North Africa, and West Asia that generated a wide variety of goods and products that matched the economic model first established by Greek commercial network cities. The third sphere included the border provinces that took up defensive stations to protect the inner workings of the Roman Empire.[47]

By the first century CE, the Roman Empire fed some 50 to 60 million people, which required a highly elaborate infrastructure. To reach inland territories, the Romans built a primary system of roads that eventually comprised 56,000 miles of paved highways. These roads remained unrivaled in design until the macadam roads of nineteenth-century Europe. To these highways the Romans added another 200,000 miles of secondary roads that supported a widely dispersed and regionally specialized economy. This vast overland commercial network sustained a wide variety of inland urban centers; these were the cities that trade and travel by sea could not reach. Among these cities were some 900 towns in Rome's eastern provinces, over 300 in North Africa, and another 300 on the Iberian and Italian peninsulas. These cities made up the urban areas of the first and second economic spheres and served them as the richest provinces of the Roman Empire. They ranged in size from 500 to 1000 acres, or between just under 1–2 square miles. Rome itself covered 3500 acres, or 5½ square miles, and housed 750,000 people. The towns of the third economic sphere were frontier fortresses, such as the now modern cities of Cologne, Strasbourg, Vienna, Belgrade, and Mainz and sustained major concentrations of legionaries. These cities grew into major manufacturing centers, and served a well-equipped standing army estimated at 350,000 strong.[48]

Within this urban landscape, the distribution of the Roman population placed 23 million people in Europe, 20 million in Rome's Asian provinces, and another 11.5 million along North Africa's shores. Among Rome's provinces, Syria, Egypt, Cyrenaica, and Cyprus maintained the most densely populated zones, with as many as 45,600 people per square mile. Italy came in second, with populations ranging from 2400 to 22,800 per square mile. With such heavily concentrated urban centers and rural zones to support, Roman agriculture and overland transport had to be very effective.[49]

Roman trade routes crisscrossed the Mediterranean and its surrounding lands in every direction by the end of the first century CE. All these trade routes placed Rome at the center and then expanded outwards across Asia Minor, the Levant coast, the Red Sea, and the Persian Gulf, reaching as far east as China and India. In time the Roman Empire became highly dependent on imports such as grain, natural resources, spices, animals, ores, gems, exotic birds, gold, silver, copper, lead, and other essential materials, from well beyond its borders. Such an elaborate internal system, which matched and relied on an equally elaborate external commercial network, took over five hundred years to build. The trade routes themselves linked Rome to the Eurasian and African worlds. The items exchanged within the Roman Empire, and between the Roman world and Eurasia and Africa, emphasized the differences between a highly urbanized civilization and far less technologically developed regions found within Asia and Africa. From the first century CE, Rome imported at least 15 million bushels of grain from North Africa and Egypt per year. The western trade routes brought great quantities of gold and silver into Rome, which it needed to balance its payments with China and India. Gold, silver, tin, and other metals were brought to Rome from mines in Spain, Gaul, and Great Britain. Wine and oil traveled from Spain, Gaul, and Greece. As a result of this elaborate system of trade, Rome ran a deficit in its exchange of goods with China, India, and Africa. Nonetheless, this complex system represented an elaborate economy that the Romans built, and medieval Europe would not be able to duplicate Rome's achievements[50]

Because of the complexity of its economy, the Roman world denied ancient Western civilization the economic and political focus found in China. Unlike the model of political organization created by the Han Dynasty that demonstrated to the Chinese people how to organize the vast terrain of their enormous empire, the Roman system was simply far more diverse. The Han imperial example taught the Chinese how to manage their agricultural resources and tame their violent rivers. This model also included the development of a workable philosophy that served as a successful political ideology to remind the Chinese how to conduct the state's business (see chapter two). This meant that when the Han Dynasty fell, the circumstances for the successful reorganization of a replacement state still existed. Western civilization did not share these same attributes and, as we shall see in chapter two, Western philosophy and political history never successfully integrated. Finally, the diversity and variation in Western agriculture denied a similar economic focus as found in China. When Rome fell, no good economic or philosophical system existed to facilitate reunification in the West. This made the post-Rome splintering of Western civilization into localized, separate political systems both possible and likely. This, however, will be the subject of chapter three.

Notes

1   Steven Mithen. *After the Ice: A Global Human History 20,000–5000 BC*, p. 37.
2   Jared Diamond. *Guns, Germs, and Steel: The Fate of Human Societies*, pp. 186–187.
3   For an excellent description of China's loess deposit see: *The Secret of China's Vast Loess Plateau*. Biot Report no. 357, May 7, 2006. http://www.semp. us/publications/biot_reader.php?BiotID=357 and http://news.stanford. edu/news/2011/june/china-reap-part3-061511
4   For a cross section of the Yellow River's riverbed and flood patterns see John K. Fairbank and Edwin O. Reischauer. *China: Tradition and Transformation*, p. 10.
5   Paul S. Ropp. *China in World History*, p. xv.
6   For a description of ancient Chinese agriculture see: *Chinese Geography and Maps*. Ronald Knapp consultant. http://afe.easia.columbia.edu/china/geog/maps.htm
7   See Neolithic Tomb at Dawenkou. http://depts.washington.edu/chinaciv/ archae/2dwkmain.htm
8   Jing Yuan. *Livestock in Ancient China: An Archaeological Perspective.* http:// anthro.unige.ch. p. 84.
9   *Ibid.* pp. 87–89.
10 *Ibid.* p. 89.
11 *Ibid.* p. 89.
12 Yin Shaoting. *The Source, Types and Distribution of Chinese Plows.* Sessions III. The Folk Implements and Folk Techniques. pp. 103–104 http://www.himoji.jp
13 *Ibid.* p. 104.
14 *Ibid.* p. 107.
15 Dun J. Li. *The Ageless China: A History*, pp. 333–337.
16 Steven Wallech *et al. World History: A Concise Thematic Analysis*, 45–46; The Bronze Age. http://mygeologypage.ucdavis.edu/cowen/~gell15/115ch4. html and The Great Bronze Age of China. http://afe.easia.columbia.edu/ special/china_4000bce_bronze.htm
17 J.A.G. Roberts. *A History of China*, pp. 4–8; Paul S. Ropp. *China in World History*, pp. 6–9.
18 J.A.G. Roberts. *A History of China*, pp. 4–8; Paul S. Ropp. *China in World History*, pp. 6–9.
19 *The Shang Dynasty, 1600–1050 BCE.* The Spice Digest. Freeman Spogli Institute for International Studies. Stanford University. http://iis-db.stanford.edu. Fall 2007.
20 *Ibid.*
21 Dun J. Li. *The Ageless China: A History*, p. 32.
22 See a description of Qin agriculture in Paul S. Ropp. *China in World History*, p. 13.

23   J.A.G. Roberts. *A History of China*, pp. 13–14.
24   Joseph Needham. *Science and Civilization in China*, p. 271.
25   See John A. Harrison. *The Chinese Empire: A Short History of China from Neolithic Times to the End of the Eighteenth Century*, pp. 90–92; J.A.G. Roberts. *A History of China*, pp. 23–26.
26   See John A. Harrison. *The Chinese Empire: A Short History of China from Neolithic Times to the End of the Eighteenth Century*, pp. 90–92; J.A.G. Roberts. *A History of China*, pp. 23–26.
27   See John A. Harrison. *The Chinese Empire*, pp. 90–92; J.A.G. Roberts. *A History of China*, pp. 23–26.
28   J.A.G. Roberts. *A History of China*, pp. 23–26; Paul S. Ropp. *China in World History*, pp. 21–24.
29   Ye Jianping, Zhang Zhengfeng, and Wu Zhenghong. *Current use of Arable Land in China, Problems and Perspectives*. http://www.agter.asso.fr. Dun J. Li. *The Ageless Chinese: A History*, p. 4 and pp. 97–103; John K. Fairbank and Edwin O. Reischauer. *China: Tradition and Transformation*, p. 9 and pp. 55–59; Jacques Gernet. *A History of Chinese Civilization*, p. 3 and pp. 103–110.
30   See Steven Wallech *et al*, *World History: A Concise Thematic Analysis*. Volume I. p. 171.
31   Michael Rostovtzeff. *Rome*, pp. 95–183; Charles Freeman. *Egypt, Greece, and Rome: Civilization of the Ancient Mediterranean*, pp. 400–401.
32   Anthony Everitt. *The Rise of Rome: The Making of the World's Greatest Empire*, pp. 351–403.
33   Anthony Everitt. *The Rise of Rome*, pp. 375–376; Charles Freeman. *Egypt, Greece, and Rome: Civilizations of the Ancient Mediterranean*, pp. 406–407.
34   Robert B. Kebric. *The Roman People*, pp. 70–103; Michael Rostovtzeff. *Rome*, pp. 95–183; Charles Freeman. *Egypt, Greece, and Rome: Civilization of the Ancient Mediterranean*, pp. 403–444 and 450–464.
35   Robert B. Kebric. *The Roman People*, pp. 70–103; Michael Rostovtzeff. *Rome*, pp. 95–183; Charles Freeman. *Egypt, Greece, and Rome: Civilization of the Ancient Mediterranean*, pp. 403–444 and 450–464.
36   Michael Rostovtzeff. *Rome*, pp. 24–84; Charles Freeman. *Egypt, Greece, and Rome: Civilization of the Ancient Mediterranean*, pp. 372–382.
37   Michael Rostovtzeff. *Rome*, p. 178; Charles Freeman. *Egypt, Greece, and Rome: Civilization of the Ancient Mediterranean*, pp. 500–504.
38   Jared Diamond. *Guns, Germs, and Steel: the Fate of Human Societies*, pp. 125–128.
39   James H. Breasted: the University of Chicago Faculty, *A Centennial View*. http://www.lib.uchicago.edu/e/spcl/centcat/fac/facch10_01.html
40   Steven Mithen. *After the Ice: a Global Human History 20,000–5000 BC*, pp. 30–31, 34–35, 35–36, 37–39, 46–49, and 50–54.
41   Charles Freeman. *Egypt, Greece, and Rome: Civilizations of the Ancient Mediterranean*, p. 393; Anthony Everitt. *The Rise of Rome: The Making of the World's Greatest Empire*, pp. 344–345.

42 Frank J. Frost. *Greek Society*, p. 19; *Greek Tectonics and Seismicity.* http://geophysics.geol.uca.gr

43 Frank J. Frost. *Greek Society*, p. 20; John Boardman, Jasper Griffin, and Oswyn Murray, editors. *The Oxford History of the Classical World*, pp 23–26; Charles Freeman. *Egypt, Greece, and Rome: Civilizations of the Ancient Mediterranean*, pp. 220–222.

44 Frank J. Frost. *Greek Society*, pp. 19–22 and 39–47; Charles Freeman. *Egypt, Greece, and Rome*, pp. 140–142; Nicholas Geoffrey Lemprière Hammond. *The History of Greece to 322 BCE*, pp. 135–169.

45 *Ancient Greek Colonization and Trade and their Influence on Greek Art.* http://www.metmuseum.org/toah/hd/angk/hd_angk.htm; Frank J. Frost. *Greek Society*, pp. 30–32; Charles Freeman. *Egypt, Greece, and Rome*, pp. 147–154; Nicholas Geoffrey Lemprière Hammond. *The History of Greece to 322 BCE*, pp. 109–121; Michael Rostovtzeff. *Greece*, 49–72; John Boardman, Jasper Griffin, and Oswyn Murray, editors. *The Oxford History of the Classical World*, pp. 23–26.

46 Frank J. Frost. *Greek Society*, pp. 39–85; Charles Freeman. *Egypt, Greece, and Rome*, pp. 247–256; Nicholas Geoffrey Lemprière Hammond. *The History of Greece to 322 BCE*, pp. 140–168; Michael Rostovtzeff. *Greece*, pp. 72–98; John Boardman, Jasper Griffin, and Oswyn Murray, editors. *The Oxford History of the Classical World*, pp. 124–156.

47 Keith Hopkins. "Taxes and Trade in the Roman Empire 200 BC–AD 400." *Journal of Roman Studies*, pp. 101–25; Sing C. Chew. *World Ecological Degradation: Accumulation, Urbanization, and Deforestation 3000 BC–AD 2000*, p. 81.

48 Keith Hopkins. "Roman Trade, Industry, and Labor." *Civilizations of the Ancient Mediterranean: Greece and Rome*, pp. 753–778; Keith Hopkins. "Economic Growth and Towns in Classical Antiquity." *Towns in Societies*, pp. 35–79; Sing C. Chew. *World Ecological Degradation: Accumulation, Urbanization, and Deforestation 3000 BC–AD 2000*, p. 86; Klavs Randsborg. *The First Millennium AD in Europe and the Mediterranean*, pp. 41–114; William K. Klingaman. *The First Century: Emperors, Gods, and Everyman*, pp. 18–20.

49 Keith Hopkins. "Roman Trade, Industry, and Labor." *Civilizations of the Ancient Mediterranean: Greece and Rome*, pp. 753–778; Sing C. Chew. *World Ecological Degradation: Accumulation, Urbanization, and Deforestation 3000 BC–AD 2000*, p. 86.

50 Lionel Casson. "Trade in the Ancient World." *Scientific American*, pp. 98–104; Michael Fulford, "Territorial Expansion in the Roman Empire." *World Archaeology*, pp. 294–305; Daphne Nash. "Imperial Expansion under the Roman Republic." In *Centre and Periphery in the Ancient World*, pp. 89–102; J.M. Blazquez. "The Latest Work on the Export of Baetican Olive Oil in Rome and the Army." *Greece and Rome*, pp. 173–188; Sing C. Chew. *World Ecological Degradation: Accumulation, Urbanization, and Deforestation 3000 BC–AD 2000*, pp. 78–80.

2

Ancient Philosophy: Chinese versus Western

After the study of the impact of agriculture on Chinese and Western civilizations in chapter one, the focus now shifts to philosophy and political ideology. But this is still linked to agriculture. Periodically agricultural communities experience internal dislocations caused by nature, such as changes in the ecology, epidemic diseases, climate shifts, or increasing population pressures. Sometimes these dislocations are products of human institutions, such as internal political decay, rebellions, the introduction of new technologies, or new land-use policies. Occasionally institutional contradictions within a seemingly successful culture undercut its success when human numbers overburden the established order and unleash chaos. In this chapter, the text will focus on three such episodes of chaos and the philosophical responses to them. These three episodes link local developments in agriculture to failing human institutions and reveal how the need for order grew exponentially within the context of mounting anarchy.

Answering this need for order is human creativity. Every civilization responds to the problems posed by the paradox of agriculture with a genius to innovate. Sometimes this genius produces positive results; sometimes it does not. The tension between population pressures and potential ecocide caused by the artificial consequences of agriculture compels people to respond. In addition, the internal contradictions within a well-established civilization compel cultural adaptations. Philosophy, religion, and science lie at the center of this human capacity to solve such problems. The greater the problem, the more creative the response.

The first episode of chaos addressed by creativity occurred in China. When the institutions of the Zhou Dynasty (1046–256 BCE) ultimately

China and the West to 1600: Empire, Philosophy, and the Paradox of Culture,
First Edition. Steven Wallech.
© 2016 John Wiley & Sons, Inc. Published 2016 by John Wiley & Sons, Inc.

failed and spiraled downward into a period of violence that lasted 182 years, a time known as the Era of the Warring States (403–221 BCE) erupted. As mentioned in chapter one, the wars of this period reflected the consequences of political decentralization, combined with agricultural developments near the end of the Zhou Dynasty. These wars began when the use of a new, iron-bladed plow drawn by oxen caused an agricultural revolution that coincided with the collapse of the Zhou's royal authority. This new-found wealth (the result of great new surpluses of food) encouraged local noble lords to raise private armies, which they now had no problem feeding. These newly empowered nobles then proceeded to fight one another, with China eventually embroiled in a devastating form of civil war. This episode of apparent cultural suicide, however, inspired and set in motion magnificent philosophical innovations that would provide the Chinese with a functional—and remarkably durable—political ideology.

The second such episode began in Greece, when the Greeks saw the collapse of their city-state system during a series of wars between 431 and 338 BCE. Also mentioned in chapter one, this episode of conflict reflected the Greeks' cultural responses to their geography, soil conditions, and trade networks. For the Greeks, the complexity of these conditions and their climate encouraged olive and grape cultivation over that of grain in several of the major city-states. The choice of olives and grapes over wheat and barley transformed these cities into unique designs that geographers call "network cities." These network cities relied more on trade than domestic food production to feed its people. Rivalry between such network city-states in their quest to control expanding commercial empires, plus hostility toward cities that opposed trade in favor of local food production, unleashed unprecedented violence. In addition, the Greek practice of linking military service to citizenship predisposed the most powerful of these city-states to use warfare as the primary means of solving their differences. The result was another episode of cultural suicide that also inspired magnificent philosophical development.

The story of Western philosophy, however, does not end with a link between philosophical conclusions and political action, as so clearly drawn in China. Instead, Western philosophy shifts its focus after Macedonia conquered the Greek city-state system and destroyed the role of the citizen in autonomous cities. This shift redirected discussions concerning the citizen (*polite*) in the city-state (*polis*) to the *kosmopolite*, or citizen of the universe. This shift away from *politics*, that is, the proper conduct of the citizen within the city-state, focused attention on how to lead a good life. What was lost in this shift was the purpose of the individual, who now felt "… shorn of his customary network of political, social, economic, and religious relationships that constituted him as *polites*…."[1]

The third episode occurred in Rome. As also mentioned in chapter one, the Romans revitalized the role of the citizen and offered him a promising future in the Roman constitution. Rome expanded the Greek concept of citizenship beyond simply men born of Roman parents within Roman territory. Roman citizenship evolved by providing methods of political assimilation that extended Roman citizen privileges to Latin and Italian allies willing to share in the burdens of military service. Changes in Roman politics combined with agriculture, however, to undercut the link between the citizen, the farmer, and the soldier, which precipitated the Roman civil war. The result of this four-generation-old bloody struggle witnessed the demise of Western citizenship for a second time. This second rise and fall of the *polite* coincided with Rome's absorption of Greek philosophy. As a result, the *kosmopolite* replaced the *polite* once more, and Western civilization lost its link between the individual and his political rights and duties. Furthermore, the *kosmopolite* later linked with a new religion, Christianity, which stated: "render unto Caesar that which is Caesar's and unto God that which is God's." This separation of one's commitment to God from his commitment to the Roman state allowed Christians within the Roman Empire to invest their loyalty in Heaven rather than government. In short, Western civilization did not forge a link between philosophical beliefs and political action as the Chinese did so successfully. Hence, the history of Chinese and Western philosophy pushed the two cultures in opposite directions, causing the two greatest civilizations of the ancient world to follow different paths of development. For China, civil war forged a link between political ideology and state formation; for Rome, no such linked developed.

The Chinese Quest for Stability

The increasing disintegration of any literate civilization will galvanize an unprecedented hunger for order among that culture's best thinkers, so as to inspire philosophical or religious inquiries. Numerous Chinese schools of philosophy emerged from just such a period of cultural collapse. The Era of the Warring States (403–221 BCE) trapped China in a period of cultural suicide that they describe in such horrifying terms as to justify the order the Han Dynasty achieved in its wake (see chapter one). The degree of anarchy that hit China during this destructive era spurred extraordinary wisdom among ancient China's best philosophers.

Ultimately, the Chinese fused portions of three disparate theories to explain their understanding of the ordering principles embedded in nature. They then used these principles to form the basis for political conduct that created the longest period of cultural unity in world history (202 BCE–CE 1911). Paradoxically, however, the success they achieved in their hunger for order trapped them in practices that subtly denied any alternative. Hence, the Chinese achieved a philosophical solution to their ancient cultural crisis that trapped their medieval and modern behavior within the limitations of their ancient imagination.

At the dawn of classical Chinese history, warfare destroyed the Bronze Age Zhou Dynasty (1046–256 BCE). As mentioned in chapter one, this era of conflict began slowly, in 771 BCE; thereafter it mushroomed into a clash that proved desperate for the Chinese people after 403 BCE. From 403 to 221 BCE, this emerging suicidal struggle spanned nearly two centuries and coincided with the beginning of the Iron Age in China (600–400 BCE). The increasing number of armed conflicts waged between the petty kings that began this period remained largely small-scale and aristocratic so long as the traditional rules of warfare held. But as the conflict matured, these rules disintegrated. Stronger kings absorbed the realms of their weaker, smaller rivals. The size of kingdoms grew, as well as the size of armies. The agricultural revolution caused by an Iron Age technology fed and armed new military formations. Unrestricted total warfare became the norm.

This evolution in the intensity of violence began as the Spring and Autumn Era (771–481 BCE) drew to an end. The use of new Iron Age weapons, such as the crossbow and the halberd, coincided with the development of new military tactics such as use of the cavalry and vast infantry formations. The rival kings that instituted Iron Age changes first tended to dominate the battlefield. The growing absence of restraint in military actions led to enormous casualty rates and completely changed the political landscape of China. At the beginning of the Spring and Autumn Era, there had been roughly 25 major states and hundreds of minor ones. By 403 BCE, only seven major realms remained, and it was these realms that began the struggle known as the Era of the Warring States.[2]

During this incredibly violent era, each of the seven kingdoms hoped to replace the Zhou Dynasty. The number of fortified cities each king ruled increased, the number of specialized occupations within their respective realms proliferated, and the commercial practices needed to support their armies mushroomed. Privately owned farms replaced the well-field system, and innovative farmers joined their lords in efforts to accelerate food production. The internal coherence of each competing realm determined the survival of its king, so that, here and there, numerous theories of political power received royal support. The chaos of the era spawned the rise of intellectuals such as Sunzi, who wrote *The Art of War* (*c.* the fifth century BCE) as a manual for military victory, while other theorists sought an end to war itself. In other words, this long era of warfare and division inspired a great hunger for order that generated numerous schools of philosophy competing for royal patronage.[3]

Where, one might well ask, did all these theorists come from? And why did so many of them seemingly come onto the historical stage at once? To answer these questions, a quick look at the contrasts between European and Chinese feudalism should prove helpful, even essential, since world historiography assigns the term "feudalism" to both cultures. Nonetheless, the two systems are definitely not the same, even if they share a common name.

European feudalism was strictly rural, based on vast estates and castles, and did not recognize the legitimacy of any other form of property besides land (see chapters four and five). In addition, European feudalism distributed its rural estates between the church and the monarchy, so that the two became separate but parallel institutions in the service of God. Finally, European feudalism supported a nobility comprised of knights engaged in the physical tasks of warfare, as well as ennobled priests who served as guardians of the spirit. In contrast, Chinese feudalism (*fengjian*) centered on major cities that served as the capitals of semi-independent realms. Chinese feudalism favored rural wealth, but recognized the legitimacy of urban riches as well. Also, the Chinese form of feudalism held that the king possessed (and ruled by) the Mandate of Heaven, which made him both a priest and a monarch. He combined both religious and political authority in one body. Finally, Chinese feudalism sustained a status of *shi* nobles who derived their income not from land but from their acumen as scholars. They continually sought more knowledge, served as administrators, and aligned themselves with the petty kings who broke away from the central Zhou authority after 771 BCE. In short, the *shi* nobles were the intellectuals who developed the theories of government and nature inspired by the great era of instability and warfare. These same theories were based on key documents that had come down to the *shi* nobles from Chinese antiquity.[4]

These documents, direct conduits of culture in a sense, served as the embodiment of the venerable heritage of China's past. Offered as the orthodox sources of a sacred legacy, these documents explain the obligations, rights, and ethics of proper conduct in a civilized society. Assembled in a collection of writings that the Chinese call *Jing* (the classics), they were compiled around or before 200 BCE. The oldest of these texts are the *Wujing*; they provide the Chinese philosophical version of existence, politics, poetics, society, and history. They combine historical commentaries on past events with poetic expressions of sacrificial ceremonies and ritualized court practices that helped to define moral conduct. From these venerable sources, numerous Chinese philosophers sought to uncover the truths about the natural world and how they governed ethics, society, and government.[5]

The *Wujing* included five works: *The Book of Changes (Yijing),* a text on divination; *The Book of Documents (Shujing),* a collection of writing and speeches ascribed to mythical kings and actual Shang and early Zhou rulers; *The Book of Poetry (Shijing),* an anthology of folksongs and odes; and the *Spring and Autumn Annals,* a history of the tiny state of Lu. Added later was a compilation of writings in *The Book of Rites (Liji),* which commented on the changes taking place in society due to the increasing level of violence in warfare. These five works comprised natural theories about *yin* and *yang,* the masculine and feminine forces in nature that serve as a dynamic dualism, and which join with the five elements—wood, metal, fire, water, and earth—to explain the material agencies of nature. Taken together, *yin* and *yang* plus the five elements became the source of a naturalistic cosmology derived from the Chinese worldview. All together, these five books dealt with the rituals and practices that guided filial piety and kept heaven and earth content and in sync.[6]

Using these venerable documents, a philosopher named Kong Fuzi (552–479 BCE) founded what Western scholars came to know as Confucianism. Kong Fuzi's goal was to return China to "the Way," an unstated understanding of how to balance the rhythms of nature with human conduct to produce order in any system, including politics. The Way appears in all variations of Chinese philosophy as a given condition that these philosophers expected everyone to understand. It speaks of a dynamic relationship between people, heaven, and earth that links human conduct with natural consequences and vice versa. It also describes the cycles of nature as unchanging principles, very much like natural laws to which people must adhere. Finally, the Way defines a reciprocal relationship between humanity and the universe, indefinable yet constant, that people cannot afford to ignore.[7]

Confucianism: The First Generation

The first philosophical system seeking order through the Way came from a *shi* noble named Kong Fuzi. He proposed that social order required that everyone conform to an assigned station in accordance with China's traditional past. He proposed a vision of social order as a fixed set of statuses and responsibilities that derived from one's occupational name. From a collection of answers offered by Kong Fuzi to questions posed by his students, he states: "let the ruler be the ruler and the subject the subject; let the father be the father and the son be the son."[8]

By this, Kong Fuzi meant two things. First, that the king alone is the king; he is not the subject. The father alone is the father; he is not the son. Second, that although both sets of relationships include an authority figure and one or more subordinates, the bonds differ in nature. The king governed a vast number of subjects in a political relationship that was a distant one. The father ruled a limited number of sons in a familial relationship that was a close one. While the father *loved* his sons and nurtured them through instructions in the Way, the king *empathized* with his subjects and nurtured them through benevolence in accordance to the Way. The sons, in turn, obeyed their fathers in harmony with the Way so that their behavior shaped their future. And the subject supported the king as required by the Way because his leadership provided support for all those living in society.[9]

Kong Fuzi's reference to roles and names speaks to the chaos of his day and is not simply a conservative's desire to preserve the order of society. Kong Fuzi felt that the chaos caused by the increasing violence he saw all around him derived from the subject having forgotten his role in society. At the time, a number of feudal lords were trying to assume the position of the one true king. Simultaneously, numerous sons sought to usurp the authority of their fathers and abandoned the order of the family. Conversely, the "king" no longer acted like a king and drove his subjects into rebellion, and the father failed to educate his sons properly, so the latter failed to understand and execute their duties. In short Kong Fuzi believed that the people had forgotten the ethical principles embedded in the Way, and this had caused society to fall out of line with the natural order of things. To solve this problem and restore order, he became a teacher and looked to education as the key to the restoration of society. Referencing the *classics* as the sources that conveyed the Way, he hoped to teach ethical conduct to a select few. Once these few had grasped the natural order of things as embedded in the Way, they would gain employment as state officials. As such their task would be to guide kings back to benevolent conduct, thus restoring order and securing prosperity for the people.[10]

These few enlightened men Kong Fuzi called *junzi*, "gentlemen." Gentlemen fully understood integrity and righteousness, and they had the courage to express both. They could guide others through conscious activity and recover social order. Their manners and fortitude served to inspire others and preserve the elegance of China. They grasped the reasons behind proper conduct as embedded in the rituals that expressed social etiquette. And they understood the balance between inner virtue and the external order.[11]

Daoism: A New Vision of the Way

While Kong Fuzi sought a recovery of social order, a competing philosophy looked away from great kingdoms and mighty empires and sought a return to nature. Called Daoism, this rival philosophy found expression in a complex text called the *Dao De Jing*, reputedly written by Laozi.* This text proposed a worldview that rejected the existing social order in China as a solution to the current problems. Instead, the *Dao De Jing* called for a retreat from society and a return to nature based on the *Dao* (the Way). This retreat back to nature would eliminate the artificial distinctions and practices of a great civilization that distanced humanity from the natural world. In effect, the *Dao De Jing* sought a utopian setting in which people enjoyed the simple life of small agrarian farmers and villagers. Living in simple communities allowed humanity and the *Dao* to work in harmony with one another, freeing the people from the pitfalls of wealth and power.

As mentioned, the *Dao* also means "the Way," but the concept of the Way in the *Dao* is used in a manner quite different from Confucianism. This means that one must be careful not to confuse the two. The Way of the *Dao De Jing* is nameless, formless, transcendental, and universal. It is an agency that unifies all natural processes and humanity into a harmonious whole. As the *Dao*, the Way resolves the contradictions that human consciousness creates. Every human being experiences these contradictions, as they are an inescapable part of being alive, but the *Dao* resolves them all.[12]

Being alive confronts every human with such ideas as authority and freedom, good and evil, beauty and ugliness, and so on. These ideas are fixed in words, and words, of course, populate languages. Languages, therefore, by their very construct confine consciousness to the realm of contradictions, denying conscious access to the *Dao*. Words support the artificial human construct of civilization and separate us from nature and the *Dao*. In contrast, the *Dao* supersedes these contradictions and civilization, for it works as an ineffable and natural agency beyond words,

---

* "Laozi" means old master and refers to a historical figure that reputedly met Kong Fuzi and gave him instruction. Laozi may or may not have existed. Some say he is an invention of the Daoists to place him in King Fuzi's generation.

beyond language, and beyond the rules and laws of society. The *Dao* is the hidden, transcendental order found in nature that governed finite lives.[13]

At the moment of birth, our consciousness separates us from the *Dao*. We enter an artificial world filled with contradictory ideas and practices conveyed from one generation to the next by language. We live amid these contradictions until we die. Our death then dissolves our consciousness, and we return to the *Dao*. While we live, however, the *Dao* still governs us, even if we are not conscious of it. Therefore, the solution to China's problems is to retreat from the consciousness of civilization and return to the rhythms of nature. Once there, the people must align themselves with the mystery of the *Dao*.[14]

While Confucianism obsesses over the need for social order and stability, Daoism focuses on the hidden, mysterious forces of constant change that governs our lives. Daoism argues that people can only live in peace when they return to the *Dao*, which unveils the hidden rhythms of our lives. Daoism states that when people become obsessed with virtue, as did Confucianism, they automatically distinguish it from evil, and, in so doing, create evil. Daoism contends that organized governments, and the artificial order of society they create, only strengthen such distinctions as good and evil, wealth and poverty, power and helplessness, and freedom and slavery. In so doing, evil, poverty, slavery, and powerlessness all become part of "civilized" life.[15]

In effect, then, the Daoism of the *Dao De Jing* opposed civilized society, the organized learning that it requires, and the acquisitive nature that naturally follows. In their place, *Laozi* recommended that the main principle of one's life should be the recognition of the natural cycles of change that life represents. One can see these rhythms in the cycles of the moon, the seasons, and one's own life and death. The *Dao* governs these rhythms, and suggests that we should avoid trying to build a permanent and powerful kingdom. After all, "permanence" simply does not exist. In the place, then, of permanence, we should seek a small and insignificant realm wherein one's inconspicuous existence might increase one's chances of living in harmony with nature.[16]

Confucianism's Second Generation: Mengzi

A second generation of philosophers added greater dimensions to both Confucianism and Daoism. This generation included Mengzi (*c.*372–279 BCE) and Zhuangzi (*c.*369–286 BCE). Both men lived a century after the masters whose schools of thought they reputedly followed.[17] Mengzi revived Confucianism, and Zhuangzi did the same for Daoism.

Mengzi provided Confucianism with a new depth and coherence that Kong Fuzi did not produce. Mengzi's philosophy comes to us through a text entitled *The Book of Mencius*.[18] This book reveals a coherent vision of Confucianism that the sayings of Kong Fuzi could not possibly achieve. Mengzi's book revitalized and systematized Kong Fuzi's teachings so that Chinese scholars could grasp the depth of Master Kong's vision. Mengzi did for his intellectual mentor, what Plato did for his master, Socrates, in the parallel philosophical developments in the war torn Greek city-state system (see below).

To understand Mengzi, one must first turn to his thesis. This thesis was a simple one: humanity is good by nature. By this, Mengzi meant that at birth humans have a natural tendency to care for one another and seek the well-being of their neighbors. To preserve this original nature, therefore, was to serve Heaven. To serve Heaven was every person's duty. Mengzi stated: "To fully develop the kindness of the heart is to understand human nature. To understand human nature is to understand the mandate of Heaven. And to preserve one's kind heart and one's nature is to serve Heaven."[19]

Humanity's inherent goodness had to be nurtured by a good education based on the *classics*, lest it dissipate. If the king, the father, and the teacher provide such an education to the subject, the son, and the student, the people would be capable of creating a prosperous, well-ordered society. But Mengzi also acknowledged the existence of evil, the result of a bad education. If the subject, the son, and the student received a bad education, the king, was not a good king, the father not a good father, and the teacher not a good teacher. In this scenario chaos will ensue. Heaven would signal this chaos through a series of natural disasters and warfare. Mengzi agreed with Kong Fuzi that the king was ultimately responsible for the well-being of the people, but Mengzi went one step further than his master. While Kong Fuzi accepted the existing order of society and offered no solution to living under the rule of a bad king, Mengzi boldly stated, "Heaven hears as the people hear. Heaven sees as the people see,"[20] which ultimately meant that Heaven authorized rebellion against bad kings.[21]

Mengzi's advocacy of a justified rebellion seems to contradict the Confucian commitment to a traditional, hierarchical society. Yet, Mengzi's brand of Confucianism clearly supported tradition, and he was fundamentally a conservative. Like that of Kong Fuzi, Mengzi's Confucianism looks to the *classics* as the model for the natural order of things. Unlike Kong Fuzi, however, Mengzi found more in the *classics* than his master. For Mengzi, the *classics* provided the guidance needed to achieve the correct conceptualization of political power as articulated by the principle of "the Mandate of Heaven."

As mentioned in chapter one, the doctrine of the Mandate of Heaven emerged during the Zhou Dynasty (1046–221 BCE) as the justification for a ruler's authority. Turning back the historical clock to 1042 BCE, consider this ancient doctrine. The Duke of Zhou served as the regent to the heir to the Zhou Dynasty's throne, his three-year-old nephew King Cheng (reigned 1045–1021 BCE). To forestall rebellion against such a young king, the Duke of Zhou established the Mandate of Heaven as the divine principle that justified Zhou rule. He argued that any dynasty's rise to power was the will of Heaven, which explained why the Zhou's rebellion against the corrupt practices of the last Shang king had received Heaven's sanction (in other words, had succeeded). In making this claim to divine authority, the Duke argued that any subject could rebel against a corrupt ruler because the actions of such a bad king naturally would enrage Heaven.

Seven and a half centuries later, Mengzi resurrected this model as an example of an ethical rebellion. Using the Duke of Zhou's vision, Mengzi argued that when chaos befell the realm, the king had lost the Mandate. Signs of disorder in society were Heaven's way of declaring the need for a righteous and moral successor. When such a rebellion occurred, Mengzi argued that Heaven would appoint the new king by identifying the victor. Once the victor defeated a bad king, Heaven would sanction the new ruler's conduct only so long as he followed the Way. In this manner, Heaven guided events on Earth using the rhythms of nature to instruct the Chinese people in creating the proper order to their society.[22]

Daoism's Second Generation: Zhuangzi

Turning now to Daoism, Mengzi had an intellectual opponent in the person of Zhuangzi. Zhuangzi presented his counter vision to Confucianism in a text entitled *The Book of Zhuangzi*, and rejected both Kong Fuzi's and Mengzi's view of Heaven, society, and political power. Zhuangzi wrote at the same time as Mengzi and performed the same services for Daoism that Mengzi had done for Confucianism. In short, Zhuangzi was the theorist who consolidated early Daoism.

Zhuangzi was a gifted writer with a biting and humorous style rich in irony and paradox. To illustrate this point, consider one of his essays on Confucian morality. He argued that Confucianism satisfied only those who were already happy with what they had. He claimed that Confucianism justified the status quo for the benefit of those at the top of society and ignored those on the bottom. He then added that Confucianism sanctified the worst forms of theft, while punishing the lowly robber. Which, he asked his readers, was worse: the rebel who steals a kingdom, or the thief who steals food? On the one hand, Confucianism glorifies a rebel leader who kills thousands of people in order to take the crown. If this thief ends up toppling the old kingdom, he is said to have won the Mandate of Heaven and is meant to rule. On the other hand, Confucianism punishes the thief who takes food to satisfy his hunger, despite the fact that the act will preserve a human life. Both persons are thieves in both thought and deed, yet one is praised for his actions, the other executed for his pains.[23]

In addition to his biting political wit, Zhuangzi had a lively imagination. To illustrate this point, one might ponder his famous anecdote about the butterfly. He stated that once he dreamed he was a butterfly. As such he fluttered about, enjoying himself greatly until he suddenly awoke. Then he realized that he was actually Zhuangzi. But next the question arose: was Zhuangzi dreaming he was a butterfly, or was the butterfly dreaming he was Zhuangzi? Caught in the dual state of illusionary awareness, neither the butterfly nor Zhuangzi could be certain as to who was dreaming and who was awake.[24] This anecdote reveals the Daoist contention that life in this world might easily be an illusion fostered by desires, while the ineffable truth of the *Dao*, which appears to us as a dream, is in fact the reality.

Legalism: Xunzi

Half a century after Mengzi's and Zhuangzi's contributions to Confucianism and Daoism, respectively, another major philosopher, Xunzi (298–238 BCE), broke new ground. His contribution to Chinese philosophy, however, is complex because he writes in the Confucian tradition but is also known for a new theory called Legalism. He speaks of the gentleman, the *classics*, and social organization in a manner unquestionably familiar: Xunzi's voice is an echo of Kong Fuzi and Mengzi. Yet, he explicitly rejects Mengzi's thesis that humans are good by nature. Xunzi stated:

> Mencius [the Latinized name for Mengzi] states that man is capable of learning because his nature is good, but I say that this is wrong. It indicates that he has not really understood man's nature nor distinguished properly between the basic nature and conscious activity [i.e. the capacity to acquire knowledge from the *classics* and act on it]. The nature is that which is given by Heaven, you cannot learn it, you cannot acquire it by effort. Ritual principles, on the other hand are created by sages; you can learn to apply them, you can work to bring them to completion.[25]

Why did Xunzi take this new point of view?

During the intervening fifty years between Mengzi and Xunzi, the scale of violence in Chinese society had greatly increased. For example, the Qin General Bo Qi (died 257 BCE) led a brilliant campaign against the armies of Han, Zhao, and Wei between the years 264 and 260 BCE. Over the course of those four years, he took no prisoners. Han sources claimed that Bo Qi killed 240,000 men from the Kingdoms of Han and Wei, and 450,000 men from the Kingdom of Zhao.[†] The instability of human life in ancient Chinese society had reached a fever pitch, which led Xunzi to reject Mengzi's claim that humans were good by nature. Xunzi simply stated, "Man's nature is evil; goodness is the result of conscious activity."[26] And by conscious activity, Xunzi meant the conscious application of the wisdom gained from a lifetime of studying the *classics*.

Xunzi was the most organized of those writing in the Confucian tradition. He systematically compiled his philosophy into a cohesive text, one that constituted a primary source of his school of thought. A highly practical man, Xunzi well understood the nature of political power and the steps one must take to wield it effectively. His central argument states that since humans are evil by nature, they cannot be left to their own devices. They must instead be ruled by a set of laws handed down by kings who understand the Way. Since an appreciation of the Way comes only from understanding the *classics*, these venerable documents had to hold a basic truth. This truth was simply: the rhythms of Heaven are constant. An example of what he meant is shown in the calendar: a calendar outlines the year, and the seasons never vary from their sequence. Humans had to conform to this natural pattern of daily life or suffer the consequences.[27]

According to Xunzi, in the distant past, the creators of the Way, China's sage kings, studied the rhythms of Heaven and developed a set of rituals that taught how to establish social order. Implementing these rituals involved studying the wisdom of the sage kings embedded in the *classics* and then applying this learning as a lifelong endeavor. In a person's study, he had to analyze the *classics*, ingest their teaching, and transform his original, evil nature into something good. These efforts converted the "petty man" (those evil at birth) into the gentleman (those who transformed their nature through learning). A person who had assimilated the wisdom of the *classics* now infused this learning into his consciousness and applied it to the actions of everyday life. These trained men next had to support an ethical king in order that the essential rituals from the *classics* become standardized into an official, royal language. Then the kings had

---

[†] These are probably exaggerated figures to condemn the Qin for its bloodthirsty nature.

to convert this standardized language into a system of laws that govern the conduct of his people, remembering that they are evil by nature. Through ritual, language, and law, the conduct of humanity would conform to the Way, the rhythms of nature, and create social order. Hence Xunzi's reliance on law created Legalism, for only properly standardized laws could reflect the constant ways of Heaven.[28]

Legalism develops a worldview that relies on the authoritarian tendencies embedded in Xunzi's writings. If human beings are evil by nature, and very few people receive an education in the *classics*, then people cannot be allowed to govern themselves. This state of affairs cries out for a set of standardized laws derived from the development of a royal language that must serve as the foundation of an autocratic state.

Legalism's Second Generation: Han Feizi

While accepting Xunzi's basic principles, one of his students, Han Feizi (*c.*280–233 BCE), rejected his teacher's reliance on the past and the *classics*. Instead, Han Feizi argued that the state could only function in the present. This meant that the state had to devise a system of laws focused solely on its current needs. To meet these needs, the state had to act in the most efficient way possible. Since the most efficient way possible was through authoritative rule, Han Feizi posited that the king had to impose a set of objective, universal laws. He then set about creating the necessary legal tools. He also added a new twist: since people were evil by nature, the application of standardized laws must include harsh punishments.

For Han Feizi, the people were like headstrong children who failed to understand what was good for them. Since they could not be relied upon to regulate themselves, laws had to make the state strong enough to guide its subjects in the manner of a strict parent. In this model, whatever the king needed to do to create a strong state was justified. In effect, the people were merely the means to achieving the king's goals. Finally this vision had now created a state as harsh as the times.[29]

Implementing Legalism: Li Si and the Qin Dynasty

While Han Feizi was a theorist, another student of Xunzi's, Li Si (*c.*280–208 BCE), was a practical politician who worked for the Qin state. Having won a position in the employ of King Zheng (259–210 BCE), Li Si worked diligently to strengthen the Qin's administration and army. With these new political tools, King Zheng began a series of successful military campaigns after 230 BCE. By 221 BCE, he had completed the conquest of China and brought the Era of the Warring States to a close. Taking the name Qin Shi Huangdi, King Zheng became China's first emperor. Many of his advisors suggested that he continue the feudal system, but Li Si argued in favor of implementing a great many of Xunzi's ideas. Having persuaded Qin Shi Huangdi to follow his advice, Li Si began a Legalist program that converted Xunzi's theory of government into a working reality.[30]

Li Si instituted a series of measures that transformed China from a set of feudal states into an empire. He standardized China's weights and measures, built a network of roads and bridges, and even fixed the size of wheels on carts and set the lengths of their axles. He created a common system of coins that had a square hole in the middle so that they could be strung together into bands of equal value. He set the norm for the written language, requiring that Chinese characters conform to a common set of images, sizes, strokes, and meanings. And he began a program of standardization of thought wherein he persuaded Qin Shi Huangdi to require all contemporary scholars to turn over all of their historical texts. These he had burned, save for the ones already in the Qin's possession.‡

Then he persuaded his emperor to divide the realm into 36 military districts and prefectures (civil administrations) controlled by Qin officials. He created a supervisory board as another branch of government to assess and punish any officials deemed disloyal to the state. In the end, the purpose to Li Si's political methods was to make his emperor the true ruler of all of China.[31]

Li Si succeeded in empowering the emperor but caused intense suffering among the Chinese people. Li Si and Qin Shi Huangdi imposed reforms that moved far too quickly and imposed such severe punishments that the Qin Dynasty teetered on failure. Only absolute fear of Qin Shi Huangdi's vengeance kept the people's anger in check.

Li Si and Qin Shi Huangdi simply alienated every walk of life in Chinese society. The aristocracy longed for the feudal past that Li Si had crushed. The scholars condemned Li Si and Qin Shi Huangdi for the destruction of so many of their precious books. The peasants bridled at the unreasonable demands on their labor. For example, Qin Shi Huangdi relentlessly drafted peasant laborers to complete the Great Wall of China within his lifetime. He also constructed lavish palaces, built a vast number of roads, dug new canals, and constructed a massive tomb for his eventual burial. Furthermore, he forcibly drafted peasants into military service. These men fought a seemingly

‡The Han described the horror of these burned books, and stated that the Qin buried alive those scholars who refused to conform. These, too, are exaggerations.

endless series of military campaigns that produced a paradoxical consequence: the Qin captured more land than the dynasty could effectively hold. Rebellion quickly dismembered many of the Qin gains. In short, Qin Shi Huangdi simply exhausted his people.[32]

Despite all this relentless and heartless activity, the Qin did accomplish one thing: Li Si and Qin Shi Huangdi produced a united China. The legacy of the Qin was the creation of a great empire. Before the Qin, China was hopelessly divided. After Li Si and Qin Shi Huangdi's intense and brutal policies, China was unmistakably united. Yet, upon Qin Shi Huangdi's death, the Chinese people struck back.

Qin Shi Huangdi died in 210 BCE. A court rival imprisoned and executed Li Si in 208 BCE. In 207, Qin Shi Huangdi's weak heir was poisoned. In 206 BCE a rebellion erupted and the Qin surrendered power. From 206 to 202 BCE Xiang Yu (232–202 BCE), a nobleman from the state of Chu, and Liu Bang (*c.*256–195 BCE), a peasant, worked together to defeat the remnant of the Qin. Soon after their victory in 202 BCE, Xiang Yu tried re-impose feudalism, but Liu Bang objected and the two fought. Liu Bang defeated Xiang Yu, who then committed suicide. Liu Bang finished the conflict by establishing the Han Dynasty (202 BCE–CE 220) and China entered a long era of political stability.[33]

The Han Dynasty

The Han Dynasty lasted for over four centuries and laid a foundation for imperial rule that the Chinese would repeat for the next two millennia. In the process of building this new regime, the Han's most militant and authoritative emperor, Han Wudi (reigned 141–87 BCE), asked a scholar named Dong Zhongshu (*c.*179–104 BCE) to develop an official state ideology. Dong did so by blending Confucianism, Legalism, and Daoism into an official belief system, but called this new state-run philosophy only "Confucianism." In this new synthesis (for the actual mixture, see below), Dong defined three fundamental obligations of the ruler. The first was to serve Heaven by following the correct ancestral rites and setting the correct moral example for the people. The second was to serve the land by encouraging agriculture. And the third was to serve humanity by creating an educational system that would enlighten the people according to the *classics*. To these three duties, Dong added a new view of the natural world that comprised three parts: Heaven, the emperor, and the people. These three components formed a hierarchic entity that became the "grand unity." Heaven presided from above, the emperor ruled the earth, and the people obeyed. Given this view of things, Dong proposed the fundamental rules for all social behavior: the emperor would dominate the minister, the father would dominate the son, and the husband would dominate the wife. Dong also put forth the doctrine that divinity and humanity belonged to a common union. He argued that the interaction between Heaven and humanity was unmistakable. He claimed that Heaven sent omens to inform the emperor about his performance as the son of Heaven and that these signs must be translated into political action. In short, Dong managed to transform the so-called official Confucianism into a philosophy and a state religion.[34]

With Dong's help, Han Wudi made this new brand of "Confucianism" the official voice of the state. To pave the way for Dong's new ideology, Wudi dismissed from the Board of Erudites (the agency that guaranteed and transmitted ancient learning) all the non-Confucian scholars. Within five years, only Confucian intellectuals practicing the new "Confucianism" filled all the vacancies Han Wudi had created. Led by Gongsun Hong (*c.*200–121 BCE), the official keeper of the state's ideology, Han Wudi established an imperial university that taught the new brand of Confucianism in Chang'an, the Han capital. The emperor then handed his Confucian scholars their first great victory. He made them the official keepers of the state's dogma.[35]

Dong's teachings did, however, impose some restraints on the emperor. As mentioned, he maintained that Heaven was the ultimate judge of the conduct of a ruler. Omens from nature expressed the will of Heaven and served as a guide to evaluating existing policy. These omens were part of the Mandate of Heaven that drove Confucianism. The omens also included the transcendental agency of the *Dao* (from Daoism) as a hidden force in nature to guide the emperor. The interpretation of these omens empowered the Confucian officials of the Han Dynasty to warn the emperor of potential dangers. This made heavenly portents a powerful political weapon and enhanced the authority of men like Han Wudi's imperial secretary, Gongsun.

Yet, the pragmatic nature of Dong's approach in constructing a semi-Daoist/Confucian picture of Heaven and Earth also placed more power in the hands of the ruler than ever before. Within Dong's doctrine was Xunzi's voice, along with his version of Confucianism mixed with Legalism. Together, Confucianism, Daoism, and Legalism became completely intertwined as a single political ideology focused entirely on the emperor's will. Ultimately, the union of these three belief systems spread across China by an official Confucian education system. Wudi used this official Confucian educational system to recruit state administrators charged with ensuring that the state's ideology permeated all walks of Chinese life.[36]

Dong's doctrine also changed the very conception of the emperor, making him more than a man but less than a god. Since the emperor linked Heaven to Earth through state policy, the people were expected to hold him in awe. This created a style of implicit worship that Western civilization's kings and emperors also sought. But unlike his Western counterparts, the Han emperor was bound by the new state ideology to maintain his filial obligations to his ancestors, and therefore run a moral and benevolent government on Earth. If he did so, he deserved the full cooperation of the Chinese people. If Heaven signaled its approval of the emperor by visiting prosperity on the Chinese people, then the people should continue to see the emperor not only as the agent of Heaven but also its true son. In this sense, as long as the Chinese people prospered, the emperor possessed a sacred nature that all had no choice but to fully accept.

By the end Han Wudi's reign, the link between belief and action had come to firmly define imperial authority, this union having a number of positive consequences. The success achieved by the Han Dynasty demonstrated the efficacy of unifying a common political vision with traditional Chinese teachings. In addition, the Han Dynasty had established strong links between the educational system, the civil service, the ruling elite, the emperor, and the people—a system that worked well as long as the people prospered. Over time, this system saw China become the wealthiest culture in Eurasia. In addition, those people who lived on Han China's borders found themselves overawed by the brilliance of their powerful neighbor's political system. Therefore, sinicization, or the adoption of Chinese ways by other cultures that came into contact with China, became a common experience; in short, no other contemporary system of rule save for Rome, could equal the Han system in terms of economic productivity. China, however, achieved a form of internal coherence that Rome failed to establish (see below). Later Chinese dynasties harkened back to the Han Dynasty as the starting point for creating their own pattern of rule. Each one would, in succession, try to improve on the Han legacy, a pattern that served continually to reinforce the Han model through new refinements.

The Greek Worldview: Part One—the Problem

As mentioned above, the apparent disintegration of any literate civilization will galvanize an unprecedented hunger for order among that culture's best thinkers. These thinkers will launch an inquiry seeking a solution to the crumbling edifice they call their society. Just as China faced cultural chaos during the Era of the Warring States, so the Greeks confronted the same problem first launched by the Peloponnesian Wars (431–404 BCE). Numerous schools of Greek philosophy emerged, seeking a solution to their growing cultural problems. But the era of warfare continued to engulf the Greeks and lasted until 338 BCE, when Macedonia conquered Greece. During this 93-year period, conflict trapped the Greek city-state system in a form of cultural suicide that the Greeks hoped to resolve without losing each city's autonomy, citizenship, and social order. The degree of anarchy that descended upon Greece, therefore, spurred an extraordinary search for wisdom that matched that of the Chinese.

From the Greek perspective, however, divergent philosophies did not become one organized belief system as happened in China under the authority of Emperor Han Wudi and the creativity of Dong Zhongshu. Rather, competing philosophical traditions emerged in Greece. One of the most powerful of these systems became known in Western Civilization as the Socratic school. Although founded by Socrates (469–399 BCE), it was his student, Plato (429–347 BCE) who actually wrote down and systemized the Socratic method. Plato gave this school its literary legacy.

A century and a half before Plato's literary achievement, and the wars that inspired a quest for cultural order, Greek philosophical speculation had already begun. Competing schools of thought emerged from the scattered city-states situated throughout the Mediterranean Basin. These various philosophical inquiries focused on the world from two different perspectives. One line of inquiry started with Thales (636–546 BCE) and looked at nature (*physis*) by studying objects in the world. This approach led to what eventually became known as "physics." The other line of inquiry started with Pythagoras (c.570–495 BCE) and rejected things as an evidentiary source of reality; instead, this approach proposed reconstructing the natural order by seeking transcendental ideas buried within things. This line of inquiry led to the development of math and logic.

Both styles of speculation would continue into the era of warfare that enmeshed Greece in seemingly suicidal destruction, but did inspire the Greeks to seek out a more global system of inquiry. The problems that led to this more global search belonged to what this text calls the "Greek Paradox." This paradox emerged from Greek citizenship, the autonomy of each city-state, and the ambitions of the most successful of these cities. Greek citizenship rested on military service. Citizens of a city-state risked their lives defending their city's autonomy, and therefore earned the right to vote and participate in politics. Successful Greek city-states expanded their command over the world's wealth by displacing other rival cities and building empires. But an empire denied the autonomy of neighboring Greek city-states. A successful city, therefore, became a common enemy to its neighbors and inspired them to band together in defense of their independence. The net result was constant, destructive warfare. This cultural paradox pointed more and more to a new logical principle: the law of contradiction. Greek city-states seemed to contradict each other's existence.

The classic example of this paradox launched the era of warfare that threatened to destroy the city-state system. The two cities involved in the first of these wars, Sparta and Athens, led other cities into a struggle that seemed to have no end. This first war, known collectively as the Peloponnesian Wars (431–404 BCE), began as a result of the growing power and wealth of Athens. This developed out of the Greek victory over Persia that occurred a mere 48 years earlier: between 499 and 479 BCE. Athens had played a central role in this previous war and developed an alliance that became an empire, based on this Persian conflict.

Athenian leaders guided their allies in the fight against the Persian Empire after 479 BCE. Victory in this fight elevated Athens into a great power, commanding trade routes in both the Aegean and Black Seas. Vast amounts of wealth poured into Athens, raising fear and jealously among the other Greek city-states. One of these cities, Sparta, used its military prowess to form an opposing alliance against Athens. The two cities launched a long cycle of wars much like those in China during the Era of the Warring States. The Peloponnesian Wars (431–404 BCE) ended with Sparta's victory, after which the Greeks began to fear Sparta. An alliance formed against Sparta and led to the Corinthian War (394–386 BCE), the War of Liberation (379–374 BCE), and the Overthrow of Sparta (374–369 BCE). Finally, the rise of competing powers, Athens and Thebes (369–338 BCE), saw warfare continue until Macedonia defeated both cities at the Battle of Chaeronea in 338 BCE.[37]

The Greek Worldview: Part Two—the Quest for a Solution

The wars that engulfed the Greek city-states did not result in the unity that China achieved at the end of its long period of conflict. For Greece, a foreign power conquered the city-states and imposed royal authority over all of the Greek mainland. The demise of the city-state system brought to an end an era known as "Classical Greece." The era that followed was one of great monarchies that undercut the ideals of citizenship, the city-state, and politics.

While no single city-state won an ultimate victory in the conflicts that ensued between 431 and 338 BCE, these wars did inspire a magnificent intellectual response: the Socratic School. In its formation, the Socratic school presented Western civilization with three brilliant men who stepped forward to create a philosophical synthesis of the previous centuries. This new philosophical synthesis ended up establishing a powerful worldview. This, in turn, would come to dominate the secular imagination of the Western world well into the modern era after CE 1500. Indeed, the thinking of these three men define the parameters of Western philosophy even to this day. The first of these men was Socrates (469–399 BCE).

One can think of Socrates as Western civilization's equivalent to Kong Fuzi, because both men responded to similar circumstances: a sharp increase in military and political chaos inspired a quest for order. In addition, both thinkers produced a philosophical worldview that addressed their culture's major questions, and both failed to leave a written legacy. Furthermore, it was the students of each man who ended up conveying an understanding of their teacher's achievements to a wider audience. In the last comparison, however, Socrates had the advantage of having several highly accomplished pupils, men who portrayed the thinking of their teacher most ably in the immediate generation that followed his life. In contrast, the teachings of King Fuzi had to wait nearly a century before Mengzi revitalized his school of thought. Of those who followed Socrates, the most exceptional student was Plato.

Socratic Thought

It is from Plato that we discover that Socrates did not have a set of traditional texts to which he could refer, as did Kong Fuzi. Rather, Socrates inherited the speculative conclusions of early Greek philosophers that imposed reason, or reason and observation, on the world to define reality and truth. Those early philosophers who relied on reason alone (*a priori* thought) postulated a form of reality that violated common sense; they declared that the transcendental agencies of math or logic operated to shape human experience. These thinkers had formulated compelling arguments that could not be denied, but they could not be verified. In contrast, those who relied on both reason and observation (*a posteriori* thought) linked common sense to the hidden world of natural law to explain change. This vision of reality conformed to the world of experience, but it, too, could not be proven with certainty. What Socrates sought to achieve was a working and compelling synthesis of these two philosophical strategies.

From Plato, we know with certainty that Socrates proffered a simple fact: "no one knows anything." By this Socrates meant that knowledge did not come from humans; instead, it existed outside humanity and was embedded in nature. To demonstrate this point of view, Socrates developed a form of logic based on dialogue (dialectic logic) that tested the veracity of anyone's thinking. Using logic, he asked questions of his fellow Athenians, and determined that their answers violated the law of contradiction. Everyone Socrates questioned gave a series of answers that started with a thesis but ended with an antithetical statement. In other words, the last answer contradicted the first one. Having concluded this exercise, Socrates came to see that the truth did not come from people, but from an objective realm outside human beings. In other words, the truth existed in impartial, universal sentences untainted by personal (the individual), local (his city), or a cultural (Greek) perspective. Therefore, the truth found in any objective sentence applied to everyone and everything the same way all the time. But where did such sentences exist? His answer was in a joining of natural processes and human purposes. In other words, if an individual understands the rational, objective laws that govern nature, that person can design actions beneficial to himself or other human beings. Socrates concluded: if something exists (natural processes), it does so for a good reason (universal, objective purposes useful to humans).[38]

Socrates' discovery of objective reality and knowledge never found expression in Athenian politics. Instead, the Athenians executed Socrates in 399 BCE after charging him with corrupting the youth of the city and undermining the state religion. None of these accusations constituted a capital crime. But the year in which Socrates went on trial came only four years after Athens' defeat at the hand of Sparta.

Athens had lost the Peloponnesian Wars and soon thereafter suffered through a period of bloodshed imposed by a violent band of oligarchs led by Critias (died 403 BCE). Critias and his fellow oligarchs imposed a form of tyrannical rule that destroyed democracy in Athens. Called the "Thirty Tyrants," this band held power in Athens briefly with Spartan support, but their excessive executions and exiles led to their undoing. The Athenian democrats, with the support of Thebes, defeated Critias and his bloodthirsty partners. The democrats restored the old constitution. Meanwhile, at Socrates' trial, the Athenians remembered that Critias was once one of Socrates' students. They therefore used the trial as an opportunity to seek revenge, and Athens ended up destroying one of the voices trying to save the Greeks from their own paradoxical behavior.[39]

Plato

After Socrates' death, another of his former students, Plato, duplicated for Greek thought what Mengzi achieved in the service of Confucianism: Plato preserved Socratic thought, developed Socrates' discovery of objectivity, and produced the first thorough analysis of reality (ontology), knowledge (epistemology), ethics (axiology), and beauty (aesthetics). Plato integrated these four branches of philosophy into a coherent system of ideas and left a complete literary legacy of his achievements. To summarize his worldview requires viewing Plato's work as a synthesis of corresponding ideas. In other words, for Plato, if something is real, we can state the truth about it, and then use this truth to engage in ethical conduct so that our actions will be beautiful.

To begin analyzing Plato, let us consider the central problem posed by Socrates: if knowledge exists in an objective realm independent of human perspective, what is truly knowable? Plato answers with an illustration of the discovery of certainty. When one studies geometry for the first time, ignorance of proofs concerning points, lines, angles, curves, surfaces, and solids is the general state of mind. But as the student becomes more thoroughly trained in geometric thinking, moments of complete realization take hold. The certainties of proofs become unmistakable, irrefutable. As one comes to realize that these proofs will always produce the same results, and continue to do so forever, this awareness demonstrates the transcendental nature of certainty. In other words, the student discovers that geometry's answers will remain fixed for eternity, exist independently of human experience, and yet are still within the range of human knowledge. This realization further awakens in a person's mind an innate consciousness of both the orderliness of human thinking and the orderliness of the world. This grasp of the transcendental nature of objective reason opens us to the discovery of a rational, transcendental order in the universe. And this transcendental order became the basis of Plato's ontology.[40]

Plato's vision of reality divides the universe into two parts. One part is the transcendental realm, one filled with ideas that function as eternal forms that give shape to what we see in the world around us and that which we convert into words. These ideas are perfect in a manner similar to the world Pythagoras described: a hidden, perfect mathematical and logical realm. The other realm comprises the objects we see, are made of matter, and are always changing—very much like the world described by physics. Plato then links these two worlds together. For Plato, the realm of ideas provides the rational, objective, and transcendental forms (*ontos*) that mold the world of material objects into what we see. These transcendental ideas also become the concepts we develop into words and sentences governed by logic (i.e. *logos*). For Plato, knowledge (*episteme*) derives from this rational, transcendental order and allows us to interact with all material things through *logos*: that is, words, speech, and logic. In this fashion, when we name things, we link the things we see with the transcendental forms (*ontos*) that exist in the universe. For example, the word "desk" matches the transcendental *desk* that governs the reality of what a carpenter thinks when he makes a desk.[41]

This transcendental realm comprises eternal, objective forms and provides us with the means to know reality (i.e. *epistemology* corresponds with *ontology*). It also gives shape to matter to produce the things we see, hear, smell, touch, and taste. Plato then asserts that the material world of our senses is inherently chaotic, but, if understood by the transcendental world of forms (*ontos*), it will generate certainty. He goes on to state that every rational human trained in philosophy must allow his understanding of the transcendental realm to govern his actions in the material world. Very few of us, however, can do this. The reason why most of us cannot do so is because common sense leads us into the world of matter and error. We allow our senses to govern our minds when we should be allowing our mind to rule our senses. If we allow our minds to govern our senses, our actions would become rational. If our actions were rational, we could become ethical (*axia*) in our conduct. If we could conduct ourselves ethically on a regular basis, we could achieve the true meaning of the word "citizen." Once we grasp what is true, we achieve real citizenship. For example, we would understand the meaning behind the term "justice." If we really understood justice, we could govern a stable and peaceful city-state for the benefit of everyone living within the *polis*. In effect, Plato linked an understanding of objective knowledge, *episteme*, with a grasp of reality, *ontos*, which, in turn, revealed the true meaning of ethics, *axia*. The correspondence of all three made a stable and effective city-state possible.[42] Such a correspondence would make our actions beautiful, and with this internal beauty attained, we could strive for physical excellence, in art, architecture, and athletics. This last step, of aesthetics, completes the Platonic system of philosophy.

Plato argued that most people, however, fall victim to matter, their senses, and their desires. Therefore, he rejected Athenian democracy. In its place, he proposed a system of government wherein rational guardians ruled; their command of reason would place them above desire and in the realm of objectivity. They would command the soldiers who defended the city; the soldiers, therefore, would prove more valuable than merchants, artisans, and farmers because the military's dedication to the city would place the love of the *polis* above the desire to survive. At the bottom of Plato's society would be the merchants, artisans, and farmers because desire rules their lives; while their labor might be essential, their existence followed their cravings.

Plato believed that if this recipe for objectivity and politics was not followed then the world of corrupt matter would rule. If the senses are allowed to overwhelm reason, desire becomes the master of actions. Plato condemned giving into desire because it would then drive a person's will, make him compete for material things, and ultimately leave him unsatisfied. Conflict would result, and violence would follow. When desire triumphs over reason, Plato argued that the world would look very much like Greece during his lifetime: a world filled with constant warfare and strife in which might determines right.

Plato's solutions to the problems of the city-state, however, never found expression in the Greek world. Instead, during Plato's lifespan, he witnessed the disastrous after-effects of Sparta's triumph over Athens (in 404 BCE). In the fourth century BCE, Sparta tried to impose its will on Greece in a manner similar to the command Athens had tried to force on its growing empire in the fifth century BCE. This caused a cycle of wars between Sparta and Thebes that ultimately led to a Spartan defeat. The slow decline of Sparta during the fourth century BCE proved once again that Greek philosophy could not yet heal the broken city-state system. Consequently, the link between personal ethics and political action achieved in China eluded the Greeks.[43]

Aristotle

Plato's most brilliant student, Aristotle (384–322 BCE), made a third attempt at saving citizenship in his efforts to explain reality. In his endeavor to spell out the conduct of the *polite* (citizen) within the *polis* (city-state), and outline politics, Aristotle approached philosophy in a very practical manner, very much as had Xunzi. Also like Xunzi, Aristotle wrote in a well-established tradition, but one of math, logic, and physics, rather than *classical* texts. Unlike Xunzi, Aristotle did not see humanity as basically evil. And unlike the work of Xunzi, Aristotle's efforts did not bear fruit politically.

During his inquiry into the key questions of his day, Aristotle saw himself as the culmination of a train of philosophical thought that stretched back to the seventh century BCE. Aristotle's goal was to press the frontiers of knowledge further than any generation of Greek thinkers before him, even if the political circumstances of his day revealed factors that made the preservation of citizenship impossible. He came from the city of Stagira in northern Greece, and his father served as a physician in Philip of Macedon's court. Aristotle even tutored Alexander the Great in his youth, yet Aristotle's service to a king did not dissuade him from still seeking to preserve the city-state. This may seem ironic given that, as mentioned above, Philip of Macedon destroyed the city-state system at the Battle of Chaeronea in 338 BCE.[44]

Nonetheless, Aristotle pressed ahead. In his physics, ethics, and politics, he dealt with the material world and defined what he termed "the good," as well as justice that is required of citizenship. He did not deny the significance of common sense and sensation, nor did he dismiss the importance of understanding *phenomena* (events that we sense and seek to understand). He did, however, define the limits of common sense, positing that knowledge derives primarily from reason, which must govern sensation. According to Aristotle, substance defines objects, and Plato's transcendental realm of eternal forms are an integral part of substance. For Aristotle, Plato's forms work through causation to set the transcendental destination of every natural process. For example an acorn has an oak tree as its universal, transcendental destination. Plant the acorn, watch it grow, follow the logic of its steps of development, and see it arrive at its destination: an oak tree. In other words, the form "oak tree" determined the acorn's path of development. But since the "oak tree" was a transcendental form, no acorn could evolve into anything else; this means speciation (the evolution of new biological species) was impossible. With this explanation of change in the real world determined by the transcendental destination of all things, Aristotle then moved into ethics and politics.[45]

Aristotle's politics focused on an explanation of justice through his understanding of ethics. His ethics laid a foundation for proper conduct by defining "the good" as the objective purpose behind human decisions. The "good" should direct our actions to produce results that are positive for us as well as everyone else. One became good by making the best choice for an action in any given situation and then acting accordingly. One also had to perform these actions in a proper manner, that is, a manner based on a stable disposition. Acquiring a stable disposition (*hexis*) amounted to developing moral virtue (*ethike arête*), which produced the practical wisdom that allows one to act ethically. But attaining a stable disposition in the first place required finding an internal equilibrium within our personality. This internal balance was "the golden mean:" the desirable middle ground between two extremes, for example between cowardice and rashness was courage, or between envy and maliciousness was righteousness.[46] The golden mean led to *sophrosyne*, that is, a steadiness in character that permitted wisdom to guide our decisions. With *sophrosyne*, we could be moral. Aristotle asserted that everyone sensed this need to be moral, but not everyone was strong enough or intelligent enough to do that which was required. To be a citizen, however, necessitated both this strength of character and rational intelligence to permit the individual to act with courage and rational purpose in every situation.[47]

In terms of politics, Aristotle expanded on the Greek concept of *ethike arête*. *Arête* is Greek for excellence. *Ethike* is virtue and manly courage (i.e. the strength to act on one's convictions).[§] By excellent virtue, Aristotle meant the capacity for a citizen to reach within himself and act solely on behalf of the state to achieve the common good. Aristotle acknowledged that in every Greek city-state, the citizen held office. At the lowest level, they were members of the popular assembly. In this legislative body, the citizens made the laws. Political constitutions, however, varied from city to city. Of the various forms a government could take, Aristotle recognized three as legitimate: the polity, the aristocracy, and the monarchy. A polity assigned citizenship to every able bodied man. An aristocracy assigned citizenship to a few outstanding men. And a monarchy assigned citizenship to only one exceptional man. These three forms of government, however, had their corrupt counterparts: democracies, oligarchies, and tyrannies. What distinguished a legitimate form of government from a corrupt one were the motives of the citizens. If each citizen used *ethike arête* to guide his political decisions, justice prevailed. In the corrupt forms of the government, however, only the well-being of the citizens themselves defined the purpose of the state. Democracies only served the majority and ignored the rest. Oligarchies served only the few. And tyrannies served only the interests of the ruler. True justice enacted by a legitimate constitution used *ethike arête* as its moral and intellectual guide. Under a just system, the citizen became the ruler who ruled himself with *sophrosyne* so that *ethike arête* served the interest of the entire body politic. *Ethike arête* defined a citizen's action; collectively all the citizens within the state became a means to an end. The end was simply the common good.

Aristotle's physics, ethics, and politics, mixed the transcendental realm of reason with the physical world of sensation to create a compelling teleology. Teleology is the study of ultimate or final goals. Teleology infused nature with a universal purpose for every natural process. Every universal purpose was one of Plato's transcendental forms. These forms served as Aristotle's final destination, or ultimate effect, for every causal series. The final cause

[§] Greeks excluded females from public life, creating two homo-social realms: one male and the other female.

for humanity became the ethical agency within will that guided moral decisions. And *ethike arête* became Aristotle's final cause for all political action. The universal nature of the common good defined humanity and directed political decisions. Together, all the variations on final cause defined the *telos* (end/goal) of the individual and the world.

Had the Greeks implemented Aristotle's political philosophy, he might have saved the Greek city-state system. But by the time Aristotle developed this philosophy, Macedonia had already destroyed Greek citizenship. Only Aristotle's corrupt forms of politics seemed to remain. For people living in Greece, a vital part of their lives came to an end. Now Greek philosophy shifted in an effort to rethink its goals. The philosopher had to abandon his: "presumptions that personal ethics was subordinate to the master science of politics. The Hellenistic Age [i.e. Greece after the Battle of Chaeronea in 338 BCE] brought into sharp focus the plight of the individual shorn of his customary political... relationships that constituted him as a *polite*."[48]

Yet, the brilliance of Socrates, Plato, and Aristotle could not be denied. Hence, embedded in the Western belief system was an inspired ethical code and political philosophy that spoke to ideals that had no possibility of implementation. In effect, a paradoxical split had begun between Western philosophical ideals and actual political action. This unfortunate state of affairs infused Hellenistic culture with an unmistakable sense of permanent loss.[49]

The Roman Worldview

The Roman paradox contrasted sharply with the problems that confronted the Greeks. As mentioned above, the Greek paradox stemmed from the link between citizenship, military service, and individual city-states struggling to maintain their independence, while absorbing their Greek neighbors into empires. Simultaneously, this was a paradox exacerbated by commercial wars fought between competing network cities such as Athens or Corinth. Also, the Greek paradox included wars between network cities and city-states that grew their own food and feared trade as a source of power as well as corruption. Sparta was such a city. Unlike the complex combination of rival cities found in Greece, the Roman paradox emerged from within Rome itself.

Rome was a center-place city. A center-place city is the hub of a vast system of other cities integrated into a single economy and political system, in this case, an empire. Yet, paradoxically Rome still tried to retain a city-state constitution. Nonetheless, as Rome expanded and assimilated new citizens from its allied city-states in Italy, the Roman constitution became overburdened with men who could not find a place to express their political agendas. They shared the risks of warfare with Roman native-born citizens, but these allied citizens had no means to travel to Rome to voice their objections to policies with which they disagreed. Also, the poor Roman citizen found his political interests subordinated to those of his wealthy and powerful neighbors. Therefore power tended to accrue into the hands of a relatively few Roman men with great wealth who lived in Rome, could manipulate elections, and make decisions that served only their interests. Eventually these men became jealous of one another, fought over power, and civil war erupted. They feared the rise of any reformer who might redirect Roman politics to make power more equitably distributed to serve purposes much like the excellence (*arête*) and virtue (*ethike*) that Aristotle's politics recommended. Nonetheless, the possibility of salvaging citizenship remained so long as Rome assimilated new citizens and struggled to achieve a new and effective political balance.

The Roman paradox now raises the question: how did the Roman Constitution actually work? The Roman Republic (509–30 BCE) offered a complex political system that used a moral code based on moderation. Moderation balanced the various features of Rome's constitution with the willingness of Roman citizens to limit their ambitions for personal gain to achieve the common good. Moderation curbed the ambitions of the Roman aristocracy that might seek too much power for personal gain. Moderation also bridled the impulse to riot and urged acceptance of political decisions, even unpopular ones, among Rome's massive numbers of poor. Finally, moderation served as the primary ethical principle that drove the Roman constitution and served to check and balance the ambitions of Rome's various magistrates and assemblies.

The Roman Constitution

The Roman constitution outlines the increasingly cumbersome structure of power in Rome. This constitution offered numerous, complex, and overlapping features that pitted the magistrates against one another and the legislative bodies. The constitution also allowed wealthy men to obstruct and obfuscate the political process. A major piece of legislation might pass one year, only to be undone the next, as a reformer's term in office ended and that of another, and perhaps less honest, politician began. The increasingly violent rivalries at the end of the republican era attest to the inability of the Romans to remember the value of moderation and save their government from self-destruction.

The Roman constitution imposed an organic legal system that adjusted haphazardly to the realities of the expansion of Rome. One author likened the Roman constitution to a building site that did not dispose of its institutional debris as it changed.[50] It began as a kinship system comprising 126 *gentes* (clans) led by patrician aristocrats who possessed *genius*, the personification of a divine power designed to preserve the life of the clan's lineage. This aristocracy comprised the urban elite of Rome, who enjoyed great wealth as absentee landlords, while being served by a farming population comprised of the plebeians. The majority of plebeians comprised Rome's poor and middle-class farmers who lived in the countryside, produced food for Rome, and served in Roman armies as citizen-soldiers. There were a few plebeians, however, who came to match the patricians in wealth. They were called the equestrians (cavalrymen). The equestrians joined their patrician neighbors as commanders in the army and also served as magistrates in politics.

The magistracy was a multilayered set of offices with overlapping power. This body of city officials ran the republic and commanded its armies. Of the many sets of officers that made up the magistracy only three will be discussed here: the censors, the consuls, and the tribunes. The censors oversaw public morals, dispersed state funds, took the census, and reviewed the qualifications of the senators. The consuls were the chief civilian and military leaders who presided over the senate and assembled its agenda. The tribunes were plebeian magistrates who proposed laws, presided over the popular assemblies, and possessed the powers of *veto* and *secessio*. The veto could halt any action taking place in the senate, and the secessio declared a general strike against the patricians that withdrew the rural support of the city when the aristocracy overstepped its bounds.

Aside from the magistrates were the legislative bodies: the senate and popular assemblies. The senate's functions were complex: it set the city's finances, presided over the provincial administration, defined foreign policy, assigned military commands, served as an advisory body to the magistrates, administered public lands, and, on rare occasions, declared a state of emergency and appointed a dictator for a term of six months. The senate comprised 300 members who served for life, met a property requirement of one million *sesterces*, were at least 32 years old, and received the moral blessings of the censors. The counterbalance to the senate were the plebeian assembles. There were three of them, but only one will be discussed here because it was the only one that spoke with the unchecked voice of the Roman people. This legislature was actually called "the popular assembly."

It comprised all the male citizens, elected the tribunes, and passed all of Rome's laws by a *plebiscita*, or the will of the majority.[51] It required the assemblage of the citizenry, which took a very long time, and, once assembled, each voter present had to be counted to reveal a decision.

Roman citizenship was equally complex. As mentioned above, the key years in the history of Roman citizenship were 338 BCE and 91 BCE. Both years changed the composition of Rome's citizenry by extending it to the populations of various allied city-states. As Rome expanded, it encompassed many allied subject-people living in *provencia* (i.e. the Roman senate's sphere of influence). The number of *provencia* grew through Roman conquests until many of the subject peoples began to demand an equal share in the spoils of Roman wars. As allies, they took on the same risks as Romans, and now these allies demanded equal access to political power. First, the local Latin allies won either full or partial citizenship in 338 BCE, and second, all the Italian allies did the same in 91 BCE. This meant that Rome had created an expanding system of participation in Roman politics. Citizenship now embraced a general Italian population, linked them to military service and farming, and functioned in a manner similar to that which had taken place in Rome itself. But as the Roman system of citizenship grew, so did the complexity of Roman politics. The republic grew into a single expanding political system filled with an increasing number of voters. Those who lived in Rome, however, had the advantage of direct access public office and the assemblies. Those who lived in Italy in general did not. Therefore, wealthy Roman men could win office and pass laws that served only their interests.[52]

Corruption

The way in which the Roman system ultimately failed has already been mentioned in chapter one. As Rome expanded against Carthage (265–202 BCE), victory changed the practices associated with assimilating allied subject states. From 509 to 265 BCE, Rome grew at a slow pace, which gave its defeated foes plenty of time to grow accustomed to their new masters. During these two and a half centuries, a process of cultural assimilation occurred that made the once defeated Latin and Italian cities true allies of Rome who shared in the city's military destiny. Moderation in growth matched moderation in the political ambitions of Rome's magistrates, who managed to keep the balance between the empire and its subject states, as well as that between the patricians and plebeians. After 265 BCE, however, Rome defeated Carthage and began to grow at a rapid rate. Rome captured the western half of the Mediterranean world in only two generations, conquests that ultimately undid the moderation of the past. Assimilating so much wealth so quickly under the organic structure of the Roman constitution offered politicians of all stripes too many opportunities for corruption. The link between warfare and rapid gains in wealth so intoxicated the Roman magistracy and senate that a war policy followed. This was the policy that set in motion the farm failures mentioned in chapter one and led to the devastating civil war. As this war policy unfolded, the generals in command of Rome's armies ceased fighting for the good of the city and began fighting for their own gain. The end result was the victory of Octavius Caesar and the creation of imperial rule. As with Greece, citizenship had once again failed in Western civilization.[53]

This second failure continued the split between philosophical ideals and political action that had started in Greece, where Socratic philosophy and Macedonian power never integrated into a coherent system. Now the Romans had experienced the same type of political failure as Greece: an emperor had replaced the republic. Since the Romans consumed Greek culture to such a degree that all historians refer to Rome as a Hellenized society, this second failure of citizenship exacerbated the sense of loss already mentioned concerning the Greek people: "The Hellenistic Age [i.e. now a Greek and Roman experience] brought into sharp focus the plight of the individual shorn of his customary political... relationships that constituted him as a *polite*."[54]

Roman philosophy began to reflect the same displaced vision found in the Greek worldview after the collapse of the city-state system there. Now a new culture emerged, one called Greco-Roman. The new Greco-Roman culture followed the Greek example as Roman philosophies sought expression outside the bounds of the republic. What emerged was a desire to replace the emotional void caused by the loss of citizenship within the city-state with a vision of human conduct within the world in general.

The *Kosmopolite*

The quest for a way to replace the loss of justice and ethics so vital to Greek and Roman citizenship redirected Greco-Roman attention away from politics and into the universe. This shift of focus centered attention on the *kosmopolite*. Since *polite* meant "citizen" in Greek, and *kosmos* defined the "universe," the new quest in Greco-Roman philosophy was to make the individual a citizen of the universe. To do so, focused attention on the Greek concept of *logos*. As mentioned above, an appreciation of what *logos* means requires an understanding of three words: word, speech, and logic. "Word" matched Plato's *ontos*, or Aristotle's final cause: the ideal, transcendental form of all objects that shared a common name and directed its physical development—the "soul" of an object, so to speak. "Speech" linked "words" together using "logic" to capture objective truth: the transcendental concepts (*episteme*) that corresponded with how nature operated. *Logos*, therefore, permitted the individual to discover "natural law," that is, the objective, transcendental principles that governed all events in nature. If one could no longer be a citizen within the city-state, then that person could be a citizen within the universe and conform to nature's laws. In this way the individual could at least find his place in the surrounding world and obey its transcendental, objective principles.[55]

Greco-Roman ethics also shed its political ambitions and sought solace in several new explanations of natural law. These explanations took four major forms: three originated in Greece, and the Greek cities of the east, and migrated to Rome, and the last developed in the Roman Empire. They were: Epicureanism, Stoicism, Neo-Platonism, and foreign religions. Epicureanism focused on pleasure as a measure of goodness, but required moderation in all things to allow a person to mature intellectually, develop physically, and live as long as possible. Stoicism suppressed pleasure and the emotions in favor of dispassionate reason (*logos*) so that a person could think with a clear head, make good decisions, and live by the natural laws in the universe. Neo-Platonism resurrected Plato's *ontos* (i.e. transcendental form or soul) as the creative element of the universe; this ultimate cause served as a hidden, rational force that directed all things. Foreign religions introduced Rome to exotic faiths, the most powerful and successful of which was Christianity. These new philosophical orientations to the wider, external world ultimately created the perfect seedbed for the rise of Christianity and its spread throughout the Roman world.[56]

Christianity

Christianity combined the monotheism of the Jews with the ministry of Jesus, to which it added Stoic and Neo-Platonic expressions of Greco-Roman philosophy. At the heart of this emerging new faith, however, was Jesus, the son of Mary and Joseph, born in Bethlehem, a town in the Roman vassal state of Judea. He began life during the reign of Augustus (30 BCE–CE 14) and died during the reign of Emperor Tiberius (CE 14–37).

Jesus' ministry involved the task of preparing the Jews for the Kingdom of God. This preparation required that each person offer his/her life unreservedly to God, which compelled the individual to abandon the material world in favor of salvation. Jesus rejected any attempt at seeking a political solution in this quest because the world of politics belonged to the world of sin. Therefore, the pursuit of redemption trumped politics, for the latter compelled people to dwell on the very material concerns that Jesus condemned: wealth, status, career, and even family. The sacrifices Jesus imposed on himself and his followers required that they be willing to abandon all worldly possessions and even life itself.

Jesus taught that wealth, status, career, and family are all material things, and all such things were perishable. In contrast, the world of God transcended these temporal obsessions, offered life after death, and opened the way to the Kingdom of God. Yet, those who followed Jesus, and even his apostles, repeatedly misunderstood these strict requirements. Their continued misunderstanding of Jesus' ministry ultimately led to the "crime" that, in turn, led to his trial and crucifixion.

This alleged "crime" occurred during the Passover celebration in Jerusalem in CE 33. Jesus traveled from Galilee to Jerusalem, riding into the city on an ass. Riding a donkey into Jerusalem symbolized the prophecy of Zechariah, which declared that "the king of peace" would enter the city on such an animal. Shortly after his arrival, however, Jesus repeatedly offended the Sadducees (the priests of the Temple). First, he told the story of the "good Samaritan." The Jews of Jerusalem viewed their northern neighbors, the Samaritans, with disdain. Jesus recounted to his audience that the Samaritan had aided a victim of robbery after a Levite and a Temple priest had walked past the robbed and assaulted man. The Levite and the priest had feared that the blood of the wounded man might pollute them prior to their entry into Jerusalem, where both had official duties to perform at the Temple. This story echoed Jesus' ministry. First, it revealed that a lowly person often proved purer and more worthy than the rich and powerful, and second, the concerns of this world distracted people from their duty to God and their fellow human beings in the next one. Also, nothing would infuriate a Sadducee more than being outdone by a "filthy" Samaritan.[57]

Second, Jesus attacked the merchants and moneychangers at the Temple. He insisted on the purity of "his house of worship." Moneychanging was a transaction that took place in Jerusalem at the time in order for priests to collect their taxes. Pilgrims arriving in Jerusalem carried different currencies from abroad, and the moneychangers offered the going exchange rates. Jesus knew this, but he nevertheless objected to the nepotism and corruption that linked the priests to the practice. Moreover, the moneychangers of the city had gained a monopoly in the Temple by bribing the Sadducees.[58]

Third, when the Sadducees tried to trick Jesus into making anti-Roman statements, he outwitted them in each instance by turning their words against them. For example, when asked if Jews should pay their taxes, Jesus replied, "Give to Caesar what is Caesar's and to God what is God's."[59] This declaration reminded his audience that Jesus was interested in saving souls, not participating in politics. Also, this statement separated the Kingdom of God from the state by offering salvation for loyalty to the former over the latter. Finally, by practicing Jesus' message, his followers could become citizens of the ultimate realm, the Kingdom of God.

Fourth, the Sadducees tried to ridicule Jesus' claims of the resurrection. Again he outsmarted them by turning their words against them and by using Scripture.[60] But even Jesus' apostles did not understand him fully, for when they marveled at the beauty of the Temple, Jesus chastised them, saying, "As for what you see here, the time will come when not one stone will be left on another; every one of them will be thrown down."[61] What Jesus meant was that the Temple was made by people and as such was perishable. In contrast, the Kingdom of God was crafted by transcendental hands and therefore eternal. But the way in which the Sadducees interpreted Jesus' description of the Temple was that God's House would perish. Now they brought him up on charges of blasphemy.

Not having the power to inflict capital punishment during Passover, the Sadducees referred the case to Pontius Pilate, the Roman procurator (administrator) of Judea from CE 26 to 36. Pilate had already caused considerable trouble in Jerusalem with his arrogance by insisting on importing the symbols of Roman power onto Temple grounds. These symbols had included religious Roman images, their presence there having precipitated several Jewish riots. Fearing more bloodshed, Pilate tried to avoid hearing Jesus' case. But the Sadducees threatened that they might appeal directly to Emperor Tiberius, naming Jesus, in their charges, as "a king of the Jews." Wishing to avoid Tiberius' ire and antagonizing the local population, Pilate turned Jesus over to Herod Antipas, claiming Jesus was a Galilean. As the ruling Tetrarch** of Galilee and Perea (reigned 4 BCE–CE 39), Herod, a client of Rome, had to receive Jesus initially. But Herod had recently executed John the Baptist, and now Herod refused to judge another popular, radical rabbi. Therefore he sent Jesus back to Pilate, who again tried to avoid hearing the case. The Sadducees,

---

** A tetrarch is a ruler of a fourth part of a realm.

however, insisted on a final judgment. The only grounds that could be used to execute Jesus lay in his acceptance of the title: King of the Jews. But this title was completely alien to Jesus' ministry and, in any case, Jesus refused to answer any charges leveled against him. Instead, he claimed that the title his accusers tried to impose on him was their idea, not his own. Eventually, however, Pilate decided to accept responsibility for the case and have Jesus executed.[62]

One can find a description of these proceedings in the Gospels, documents that combine history with religious passion in their revelation of the beginning of a new age. They also document the separation of Christianity from Judaism, as major differences in belief developed between the two faiths. Meanwhile, the Jewish community that Jesus sought to instruct was also a divided one. First, there were the Temple priests, the Sadducees, keepers of the order that Jesus condemned. Second, there were the Pharisees, a Jewish sect dedicated to strict observance of Jewish rites and ceremonies. Third, there were the Zealots, yet another Jewish sect that fought against Roman rule as incompatible with strict monotheism. And, finally, there were the Essenes, a separatist and ascetic group caught up in apocalyptic visions that sought a monastic life in the wilderness. Jesus spoke with an Essene voice and confronted the Sadducees with an indictment of all their worldly ways. Such internal divisions reveal the lack of unity among the Jews and placed the onus of Jesus' execution squarely on the shoulders of the Sadducees and the Romans.

The divide between the Sadducees and Jesus that led to his execution, however, began to widen and spread into the larger Jewish community, despite the fact that the earliest Christians were also Jews themselves. These first-generation Christians differed from the wider Jewish community because these first Christians believed that Jesus was the Messiah. Nonetheless, they still went to the Temple and adhered to Jewish law, as did other non-Christian Jews. Then the missionary work of people like Paul of Tarsus (CE 10–69) increased the division between the two faiths. Paul argued that salvation must be made available to all, including both Gentiles and Jews. This widening of the Christian audience exacerbated the differences between Judaism and Christianity because Paul sought to facilitate the entry of the Gentiles into the Christian community by reducing the importance of Jewish law. Paul reduced the emphasis placed on the Torah (the first five books of the Bible) and spoke of an "eschaton" (i.e. a break in time, or end of an era). In this case, the birth of Jesus represented a break in the human calendar and forecasted a final eschaton: the end of the world. For evangelists like Paul, Jesus' birth launched a new age, an age of redemption that made salvation available to all, in preparation for the end of time. These challenges to Jewish law grew, as the Gentiles who converted to Christianity soon outnumbered the original Jewish Christians. These challenges further expanded the separation of Christianity from Judaism.[63]

By the third generation after Jesus' execution, at the end of the first century, the divide between the Jews and the new Gentile Christians became clear. A growing number of Gentile Christians in this third generation began explicitly calling Jesus "God" instead of the Messiah (i.e. the anointed king who would lead the Jews back to Israel and establish justice in the world). This major step in the separation of Judaism from Christianity is visible in the Gospel according to John with his opening sentence: "In the beginning was the Word, the Word was with God and the Word was God."[64] Written in *koine* Greek, the language of the eastern half of the Roman Empire, John used the Greek term *logos* (Λογος) for Word. His use of *logos* as an interchangeable term with God opened up Christianity to more Greek concepts. He also assigned *logos* to Jesus in this same line: the Word (Jesus) was with God and the Word was God (God and Jesus). This use of *logos* linked Christianity to such ideas as the *ontos* from Plato and final cause from Aristotle. In both cases, that is, *ontos* and final cause, Jesus and God were the same: they were the all powerful, creative, and transcendental force in the universe. Finally, this use of *logos* differed widely from the Jewish use of "word" in the Old Testament.

The use of "word" in Scripture belonged to a well-established tradition in the Old Testament. God's word in Jewish Scripture was an active, creative, and dynamic agency. One can see its power in the passage, "By the word of the Lord, the heavens were made."[65] The same sense of power is found in the passage, "He sends forth his commands to the earth; his word runs swiftly."[66] Finally, there is the passage, "Is not my word like fire, says the Lord, and like a hammer which breaks the rock in pieces."[67] The use of "word" in the above three citations, however, exists as an extension of God and is not equated with his Being. But John's use of "Word" as *logos* follows the Greek meaning and signals a new link between the Greek intellectual tradition and the new Christian faith. The Greek meaning of *logos* in John 1: 1 joined Jesus and God as transcendental Being and the ultimate cause of all things in nature. Thus, as Christianity entered the second century CE, the divide between the Jewish faith and the offspring faith of Christianity widened to the point where a rupture occurred. At the same time, a new state of maturity began in Christianity that used Greek philosophical concepts to create theology.

Perhaps the first theologian, Justin, marks the beginning of this new welding of Greek philosophy and Christianity's God. Born a pagan in

Palestine, Justin (*c.* CE 100–165) converted to Christianity in CE 132. He spent the remainder of his life as a traveling preacher and teacher. An energetic writer, Justin expanded on the connection between the Greek concept of *logos* and God linked in John 1: 1. Justin made Jesus the rationale for *logos* that was now let loose in the universe. Justin was the first to blend Greek philosophy and Christian doctrine in several major works. In his two *Apologies* written to Emperors Antonius Pius and Marcus Aurelius, Justin claimed that Christianity and Greek philosophy were deeply connected to one another. He declared that Christianity was simply a purer form of the truth buried in Greek learning. According to Justin, Christianity fulfilled the highest aspiration of Platonic philosophy, and he also recommended reading Pythagorean literature, Aristotle's works, and that of the Stoics. Furthermore, he spent enormous energy dispelling myths surrounding the earliest form of the Eucharist as an act of cannibalism (i.e. eating the bread and drinking wine that symbolized the flesh and blood of Christ in the Catholic mass.[tt] Justin's main contribution to Christianity was to transform the new faith into a true philosophy.[68]

A student of Justin's, Titian (CE 110–180), added a fiery temperament to theology by attacking pagan faiths, Roman law, and imperial rule. He expanded the linking of Greek philosophy and Christianity by making God the divine agency that used *logos* to shape matter into all of the objects found in the world around us. *Logos* sprang from God's divine will, caused creation, and continued to direct all natural events. In the new age of Christ, Jesus himself also became *logos*, having existed on earth as the power of his Father in the act of salvation. Titian added an increasing emphasis on austerity and self-denial to Christianity—especially for himself; he rejected wealth, meat, and marriage. When he retreated into Gnosticism, however, he broke with Christianity and became known as a heretic. Gnosticism was an esoteric faith in salvation based on an intuitive sense of the divine but incorporating pagan concepts of creation, good, and evil that Christianity rejected.[69]

In the transition from the second to the third century CE, Clement of Alexandria (*c.* CE 150–215) continued to take ideas from Greek philosophy and use them to build a stronger theological foundation for Christianity. Set out in a trilogy designed to convert pagans to Christianity, Clement's theology sought to distinguish further the new faith from Gnosticism. Clement was deeply concerned with issues raised by the Gnostics that might blend Christianity with a demiurge (i.e. a very strong force in nature that causes change in local events). In Gnosticism, a demiurge supplanted God as the

[tt] The Eucharist is the ritual converting bread and wine into the body and blood of Christ.

sole source of creation. For the Gnostics, this demiurge varied. Sometimes it was Adam, or Kadmon, Ahriman, El, Saklas, Samael, Satan, Yaldabaoth, and/ or Yahweh. For the Gnostics, the demiurge was the imperfect intermediary that created the universe alongside God. Clement rejected this demiurge and wanted to make sure that faith and knowledge blended together accurately. He focused on the correct link between Greek philosophy, God, and Jesus. For Clement, then, Greek philosophy was an initial foundation laid down by God to prepare the world for the coming of Christ.[70]

The slow synthesis of Greek concepts and Christian theology continued through the third century CE with the work of Clement's student, Origen (c.185–254). Then Emperor Constantine (reigned CE 312–337) legalized Christianity with the Edict of Milan in CE 313 and generated the first orthodox theology at the Council of Nicaea in CE 325. An unmistakable eclectic blend of the Greek worldview and the Christian faith took place in the doctrine of consubstantiation (i.e. Jesus and God are the same) issued by the Council. Athanasius was the author of consubstantiation. He argued that God's inner life and His action were not one and the same. The former was an extension of Gods nature, and the latter an expression of His will. This meant that God did not deliberate within Himself about His nature or existence, and goodness and mercy sprang naturally from His Being. In this sense, Jesus, as the offspring of God's nature, sprang spontaneously from that nature, and, therefore, was the same substance as God Himself. Hence, God and Jesus were the same. This meant that although two names existed for God, there was only one divine substance.

As Christianity absorbed Greek philosophy into its theology, the loyalty Christians felt toward God far outweighed their commitment to the state. This union of Christianity with Greek philosophy reinforced the philosophical break between ethics and political action that occurred with the end of the city-state and the rise of monarchy. The demise of citizen rule both in Greece and Rome crushed a vital part of a Greek or a Roman's identity. Greek philosophy, and later Roman variations, acknowledged this loss by redirecting its attention away from the city-state and into the universe. This relocation of the focus of philosophy saw the end of the *polite* and the rise of the *Kosmopolite* (mentioned above). Christianity joined this redefinition of the individual's personal loyalty but added a commitment to God over the state.

The failure of Roman citizenship encouraged the assimilation of Greek Stoicism, Epicureanism, Neo-Platonism, and ultimately Western civilization's Christianity into Roman culture. Ironically, Christianity became the legitimate faith of the Roman Empire, but its central message remained:

"Give to Caesar what is Caesar's and to God what is God's."[71] This pronouncement, as mentioned, hinted at a separation of church and state in declaring that the temporal world was not the same as the spiritual one. Hence, true loyalty to God required the type of dedication to the church that Jesus Himself was willing to make: abandon everything in the secular world in the service of the Lord.

Centuries after Jesus' crucifixion, the last theologian of Western antiquity, Augustine of Hippo (CE 354–430) helped to explain the fall of Rome. He wrote in *City of God* that two great cities exist in the world: the City of God and the city of man. The City of God was the church because it carried Jesus' message to the world, welcoming everyone as its citizens. The City of God offered redemption through Jesus so that those who chose to dwell there would reside eternally with God. The City of God was available to all, even to the "barbarians," who were at that time conquering Rome. The city of man lived off the blood of other men, ruled by lust and power, and would always dwell in darkness. The city of man was the city of the flesh that God fed with rain and crops, but this city would perish without the light of God. Rome was one of the cities belonging to the city of man; Rome would perish, but not before it helped to build the City of God within its domain. The City of God would survive the fall of Rome and continue to serve humanity.

Such a division between the City of God and the city of man confirmed a basic principle of what would be Western civilization's medieval worldview after the fall of Rome: the separation of church and state. This political vision would gradually become a central, spiritual theme of Europe during the Middle Ages as the fall of Rome divided the Roman Empire into three cultural zones. The first was the surviving Eastern Roman Empire. The second was the rise of Islam's Middle East. And the third was the emergence of medieval Europe.

At the end of the ancient era, then, the focus of Christianity had drawn Western imagination away from politics and towards Heaven. In contrast, the Chinese had managed to fuse their Confucian-Daoist-Legalist philosophy into a political ideology that functioned admirably for the state. The Chinese did not exhibit any doubt in this political ideology until the fall of the Han Dynasty (CE 220) when Buddhism made an entry into China. At that moment, loyalty to the Han Emperor failed temporarily (see chapter three), yet the Chinese retained a vested interest in resurrecting imperial rule based on the strength of their vested interest in Confucian-Daoist-Legalist ideology (see chapter four and five). Again and again this vested interest would restore the Chinese to their imperial system.

In contrast, Europeans living during the Middle Ages, after the fall of Rome, would completely drift away from the ethical and political goals originally set by the great thinkers of Western civilization—Socrates, Plato, and Aristotle. What became medieval Europe had lost its commitment to self-rule by citizens, the concept that had so clearly distinguished the Greek city-states and the Roman Republic from the new "barbaric" states. Only the network cities of medieval Italy would continue to exhibit any signs of citizenship (see chapters four and seven). Meanwhile, prior to the advent of the Middle Ages, the development of imperial rule in both the Hellenistic world of the Macedonians and the Roman Empire completely robbed Western civilization of the vital link between an individual's ethics and his dedication to the state. In the end, this division deprived the ancient Western world of its political spirit and set it up for what was to transpire in the Early Middle Ages (CE 500–1000), a time that saw the loss of most of the teachings of Western antiquity as Western civilization splintered into a myriad of fiefdoms. Meanwhile, China never lost touch with its intellectual heritage, centralized rule, and comparative prosperity. It was just a matter of time, therefore, before a new Chinese dynasty in the ancient imperial mode would rise again.

Notes

1   F.E. Peters. *The Harvest of Hellenism: A History of the Near East from Alexander the Great to the Triumph of Christianity*, p. 119.

2   See John A. Harrison. *The Chinese Empire: A Short History of China from Neolithic Times to the End of the Eighteenth Century*, pp. 46–47; J.A.G. Roberts. *A History of China*, pp. 13–14.

3   See John A. Harrison. *The Chinese Empire: A Short History of China from Neolithic Times to the End of the Eighteenth Century*, pp. 46–52; J.A.G. Roberts. *A History of China*, pp. 14–20.

4   J.A.G. Roberts. *A History of China*, pp. 10–11; John K. Fairbank and Edwin O. Reischauer. *China: Tradition and Transformation*, pp. 31–32.

5   Jacques Gernet. *The History of Chinese Civilization*, pp. 83–85.

6   John K. Fairbank and Edwin O. Reischauer. *China: Tradition and Transformation*. pp. 41–43; Jacques Gernet. *The History of Chinese Civilization*, pp. 83–86.

7   An excellent description of the power of the Way can be seen in Dun J. Li's description of the Dynastic Cycle. Dun J. Li. *The Ageless Chinese: A History*, pp. 333–337.

8   The *Analects* as quoted in John K. Fairbank and Edwin O. Reischauer. *China: Tradition and Transformation*, p. 44; John A. Harrison. *The Chinese Empire*, pp. 55.

9   John K. Fairbank and Edwin O. Reischauer. *China: Tradition and Transformation*, pp. 44–46; J.A.G. Roberts. *A History of China*, pp. 14–16; John A. Harrison. *The Chinese Empire*, pp. 52–60.

10 Dun J. Li. *The Ageless Chinese: A History*, pp. 71–79, Jacques Genet. *A History of Chinese Civilization*, pp. 87–88; John K. Fairbank and Edwin O. Reischauer. *China: Tradition and Transformation*, pp. 44–46; J.A.G. Roberts. *A History of China*, pp. 14–16, John A. Harrison. *The Chinese Empire*, pp. 52–60.

11 John K. Fairbank and Edwin O. Reischauer. *China: Tradition and Transformation*, p. 46.

12 *Laozi* is also known as the *Dao De Qing*. See Dun J. Li. *The Ageless Chinese: A History*, pp. 83–89; Jacques Gernet. *A History of Chinese Civilization*, pp. 93–95; John K. Fairbank and Edwin O. Reischauer. *China: Tradition and Transformation*, pp. 46–49; J.A.G. Roberts. *A History of China*, pp. 17–18; John A. Harrison. *The Chinese Empire*, pp. 64–68.

13 *Laozi* is also known as the *Dao De Qing*. See Dun J. Li. *The Ageless Chinese: A History*, pp. 83–89; Jacques Gernet. *A History of Chinese Civilization*, pp. 93–95; John K. Fairbank and Edwin O. Reischauer. *China: Tradition and Transformation*, pp. 46–49; J.A.G. Roberts. *A History of China*, pp. 17–18; John A. Harrison. *The Chinese Empire*, pp. 64–68.

14 *Laozi* is also known as the *Dao De Qing*. See Dun J. Li. *The Ageless Chinese: A History*, pp. 83–89; Jacques Gernet. *A History of Chinese Civilization*, pp. 93–95; John K. Fairbank and Edwin O. Reischauer. *China: Tradition and Transformation*, pp. 46–49; J.A.G. Roberts. *A History of China*, pp. 17–18; John A. Harrison. *The Chinese Empire*, pp. 64–68.

15 John A. Harrison. *The Chinese Empire*, pp. 64–67.

16 John A. Harrison. *The Chinese Empire*, pp. 67–68; Paul S. Ropp. *China in World History*, pp. 16–17.

17 Some contend that Zhuang Zhou is the master that created Daoism. Others claim he followed Laozi, the author of the mysterious text *The Laozi*.

18 Mencius and Confucius are Latinized names coined by Catholic Priests for Kong Fuzi and Mengzi.

19 Zhao Zengtao, Zhang Winting, and Zhou Dingzhi (trans). *Mencius*, p. 467.

20 James Legge. *The Works of Mencius: the Chinese Classics*, p. 357.

21 Jacques Gernet. *A History of Chinese Civilization*, pp. 95–96; John K. Fairbank and Edwin O. Reischauer. *China: Tradition and Transformation*, pp. 51–52; J.A.G. *A History of China*, p. 18; John A. Harrison. *The Chinese Empire*, pp. 60–61.

22 Jacques Gernet. *A History of Chinese Civilization*, pp. 95–96; John K. Fairbank and Edwin O. Reischauer. *China: Tradition and Transformation*, pp. 51–52; J.A.G. Roberts. *A History of China*, p. 18, John A. Harrison. *The Chinese Empire*, pp. 60–61.

23 Dun J. Li. *The Ageless Chinese: A History*, pp. 83–89; Jacques Gernet. *A History of Chinese Civilization*, pp. 86–87.

24 J.A.G. Roberts. *A History of China*, p. 18.

25 Hsün Tzu. *Basic Writings*, p. 158.

26 *Ibid.* p. 157.

27 *Ibid.* p. 79.

28 Jacques Gernet. *A History of Chinese Civilization*, pp. 96–97; John K. Fairbank and Edwin O. Reischauer. *China: Tradition and Transformation*, pp. 52–53; J.A.G. Roberts. *A History of China*, pp. 18–19; John A. Harrison. *The Chinese Empire*, pp. 61–64.

29 John K. Fairbank and Edwin O. Reischauer. *China: Tradition and Transformation*, pp. 53–54; J.A.G. Roberts. *A History of China*, pp. 21–22.

30 John K. Fairbank and Edwin O. Reischauer. *China: Tradition and Transformation*, pp. 55–57; J.A.G. Roberts. *A History of China*, pp. 22–23.

31 John K. Fairbank and Edwin O. Reischauer. *China: Tradition and Transformation*, pp. 55–57; J.A.G. Roberts. *A History of China*, pp. 23–24.

32 John K. Fairbank and Edwin O. Reischauer. *China: Tradition and Transformation*, pp. 57–58.

33 Peter Stearns, general editor. *The Encyclopedia of World History*, pp. 49–50.

34 John A. Harrison. *The Chinese Empire*, pp. 118–119.

35 J.A.G. Roberts. *A History of China*, pp. 30–31; John A. Harrison. *The Chinese Empire*, pp. 117–118.

36 J.A.G. Roberts. *A History of China*, pp. 30–32; John A. Harrison. *The Chinese Empire*, pp. 121–123.

37 Charles Freeman. *Egypt, Greece, and Rome*, pp. 297–313; Robin Lanefox. *The Classical World*, pp. 166–175 and 184–193.

38 Frank J. Frost. *Greek Society*, pp. 109–110; Charles Freeman. *Egypt, Greece, and Rome*, pp. 175–181; John Boardman, Jasper Griffin, and Oswyn Murray, editors. *The Oxford History of the Classical World*, pp. 237–238.

39 Nicholas Geoffrey Lemprière Hammond. *The History of Greece to 322 BCE*, pp. 443–445; Donald Kagan. *The Peloponnesian Wars*, pp. 467–491.

40 John Boardman, Jasper Griffin, and Oswyn Murray, Editors. *The Oxford History of the Classical World*, p. 240.

41 See *Plato And The Theory Of Forms*. http://www.philosophicalsociety.com/Archives/Plato%20And%20The%20Theory%20Of%20Forms.htm

42 *Plato's' Ethics and Politics in the Republic*. http://plato.stanford.edu/entries/plato-ethics-politics/.

43 Paul Cartledge. *The Spartans: The World of the Warrior Heroes of Ancient Greece, from Utopia to Crisis and Collapse*, pp. 209–227.

44 John Boardman, Jasper Griffin, and Oswyn Murray, editors. *The Oxford History of the Classical World*, p. 241.

45 *Ibid.* pp. 248–249.

46 Aristotle. *Ethics*, p. 104.

47 Aristotle. *Ethics*. Book I (Happiness and the Soul), Books II and III (Virtuous Actions), Books IV–VI and VIII–IX (Moral and Intellectual Virtue) Books VII–X (Pleasure and Virtue) and Book X (the Nature of Happiness and its link to Virtue); *Aristotle's Ethics*. http://plato.stanford.edu/entries/aristotle-ethics/

48 F.E. Peters. *The Harvest of Hellenism*, p. 119.

49 John Boardman, Jasper Griffin, and Oswyn Murray, editors. *The Oxford History of the Classical World*, pp. 152–154.

50 Thomas Holland. *Rubicon: the Last Years of the Roman Republic*, pp. 4–7.

51 Robin Lane Fox. *The Classical World: An Epic History from Homer to Hadrian*, pp. 277–287; M. Ristovtzeff. *Rome*, p. 32.

52 John Boardman, Jasper Griffin, and Oswyn Murray, editors. *The Oxford History of the Roman World*, pp. 27–32.

53 Robert B. Kebric. *The Roman People*, pp. 70–103; Michael Rostovtzeff. *Rome*, pp. 95–183; Charles Freeman. *Egypt, Greece, and Rome: Civilization of the Ancient Mediterranean*, pp. 403–444 and 450–464; John Boardman, Jasper Griffin, and Oswyn Murray, editors. *The Oxford History of the Roman World*, pp. 41–47, 51–72, 90–119 and 146–167.

54 F.E. Peters. *The Harvest of Hellenism*, p. 119.

55 *Ibid.* pp. 148–149.

56 The Kosmopolite emerged from Stoicism and Neoplatonism Cosmopolite. See John Boardman, Jasper Griffin, and Oswyn Murray, editors. *The Oxford History of the Classical World*, pp. 350–352, 467–468, 352–358, and 468–469; F.E. Peters. *The Harvest of Hellenism*, pp. 446–480. See Platonism http://www.iep.utm.edu/pla-thei/

57 Luke 10: 25–37.

58 Matthew 21: 12.

59 Mark 12: 17.

60 Luke 20: 27–38.

61 Luke 21: 5–6.

62 William K. Klingaman. *The First Century: Emperors, Gods, and Every Man*, pp. 197–202.

63 Martin Goodman. *Rome and Jerusalem: The Clash of Ancient Cultures*, pp. 315 and 556; Francis Edward Peters. *The Harvest of Hellenism: A History of the Near East from Alexander the Great to the Triumph of Christianity*, p. 480.

64 John 1: 1.

65 Psalm 33: 6.

66 Psalm 147: 15.

67 Jeremiah 23: 29.

68 Saint Justyn the Martyr. *The British Concise Encyclopedia*.

69 John Van Leuven. *Tatian, His Works, and His Theology*. A paper submitted to the Pittsburg Presbytery of the Reformed Presbyterian Church of North America, November 7–8, 2008.

70 Francis Edward Peters. *The Harvest of Hellenism: A History of the Near East from Alexander the Great to the Triumph of Christianity*, pp. 493–496.

71 Mark 12: 17.

3

The Nomads

Two Incompatible Lifestyles: Nomads versus Farmers

The oldest, longest, and most complex of wars in world history were those fought between pastoral nomads and sedentary farmers. Herders and farmers clashed over who commanded the land. These struggles took place because of the major differences that existed between the way herders and farmers used the land. Conflict always erupted wherever nomads ventured onto farmers' fields.

Herders and farmers lived off forms of agriculture that diverged so widely that vastly different lifestyles were created, which apparently could not exist alongside each other.* The artificial symbiosis between omega animals and pastoral nomads, called "extensive agriculture," required its practitioners to move continuously from place to place seeking fresh sources of grass to feed their herds. The artificial symbiosis between omega plants and sedentary farmers, called "intensive agriculture," required its practitioners to settle in one place to grow crops to feed their populations. In short, pastoral nomads had to travel to survive, and sedentary farmers had to remain in one place to do so. Thus these agriculturalists could not live in the same place at the same time and carry out their respective lifestyles.

---

*The relationship between pastoral nomads and sedentary farmers initially took the form of conflict, but also included trade. Conflict occurred whenever the nomads felt strong enough to raid sedentary cultures and take what they wanted without paying. Trade occurred whenever nomads found sedentary farmers too strong to invade without suffering significant casualties. Thus the typical interaction between nomads and farmers was one of either raid or trade.

China and the West to 1600: Empire, Philosophy, and the Paradox of Culture,
First Edition. Steven Wallech.

"Extensive agriculture" gets its name from the way pastoral nomads use the land. Here, the term "agriculture" refers to how herding nomads rely on the food generated by their omega animals that they have domesticated. The term "extensive" refers to the way these nomads use the land; they must move from place to place to feed their herds because of the amount of grass each animal needs in order to survive.† Such an "extensive" range of travel exploits the natural fecundity of the soil, while demanding little labor from its practitioners beyond protection of the herds. Also, such a lifestyle creates a form of land use that denies the existence of borders and often leads to encounters with other groups of humans, triggering violence to determine who controls the pastures.

"Intensive agriculture" similarly gets its name from the way sedentary farmers use the land. In this instance "agriculture" refers to how sedentary farmers work the soil to plant their crops, tend their fields, and harvest their food. The term "intensive" refers to the way farmers use the land; they must concentrate their labor in a limited amount of space to raise their omega plants. Such an "intense" effort generates the food surpluses that sustain sedentary cultivators from harvest to harvest. Furthermore, such a lifestyle creates a form of land use that requires the creation of borders, because farmers must fence off their fields to protect their crops and secure food sources year after year. Finally, some degree of violence must follow anytime any organism—whether human, rodent, insect, worm, mollusk, mold, or bacterium—threatens farmers' crops if they are to protect their food supply.

Since both nomads and sedentary farmers practice agriculture, and thereby create an artificial symbiosis between humans, plants, and animals, both generate increasing population pressures that eventually force encounters with other groups of people. Such encounters invariably lead to tensions that require some form of military action to relieve the stress of contact. Over the centuries, these military episodes outlined a rich history of violence whenever nomads felt strong enough to challenge sedentary farmers. In contrast, when farmers had the military advantage, nomads chose to engage in trade to acquire goods that only the sedentary civilization could produce. Therefore, both warfare and commerce punctuated a long human history of contact between two incompatible human lifestyles. Finally, the place where this repeated cycle of raid or trade took

†These animals have to eat so much grass because of its low nutrient value and high fiber content. Such poor silage requires multiple stomach chambers to slow the passage of the grass through the digestive tract, and explains why there were a limited number of nomads as compared to sedentary farmers.

on its most violent form was on the Eurasian continent. There the sedentary cultures of Europe and Asia developed numerous names for the many groups of nomads who threatened the farmer's survival. These names identified the raiding parties, the invading armies, and the "barbarians" that sometimes toppled civilizations.

Charioteers, such as the Hittites, Kassites, Mitanni, Hyksos, Aryans, and Mycenaeans, participated in one of the earliest nomadic invasions of the civilizations of Europe, the Ancient Near East, Egypt, and India. Cavalry marauders such as the Scythians, Persians, Medes, Xiongnu, Turks, Tartars, and Mongols punctuated a later era when nomads swept throughout Eurasia again. The Huns, Ostrogoths, Visigoths, Franks, Vandals, Alemanni, Burgundians, Angles, Saxons, Danes, and Jutes were among the first wave of herders to attack Rome. Later, the Avars, Bulgars, and Lombards participated in a second wave that attacked Europe. Later still, the Vikings and Magyars made up a third wave of onslaught. Finally, Tibetans, Jurchen, Turks, Manchus, and Mongols frequently assaulted China during its long, yet remarkably stable, history. These are just a few of the invaders; a far greater number of tribes have plagued the sedentary farmers of Eurasia since the dawn of civilization *c.*4000 BCE.

The geography of the area set the stage for the rate of interaction—including violent episodes—between sedentary and nomadic peoples. Eurasia, the continent comprised of Europe and Asia, had the longest history of nomadic and sedentary interaction, ranging from 3000 BCE to CE 1700. These 47 centuries witnessed almost continuous violence because Eurasia happens to lie on an east-to-west land axis that features vast, broad plains, or steppes filled with grass-rich pastures. This type of topography not only encouraged the free and easy movement of nomads but also featured the kind of consistent climate and habitat that sustained sedentary agriculture. Indeed, the Eurasian landscape seemed to have spawned the first human civilizations as well as the first nomadic raiders. The Americas, on the other hand, have a north-to-south land axis that largely discourages cultural interaction between different human communities. The American continents' wide variations in climate and habitat isolated numerous human practices and confined them to specific locations. Finally, Africa, as is wide as it is long, in a sense defied the historical patterns set up by a dominant land axis. At its widest part of the African continent lies the Sahara Desert. This vast area of sand largely restricted human interaction, its huge arid plains effectively separating life north of the desert from south of it. In short, many scholars believe that, due to its land axis, Eurasia was the continent that hosted not only the most human movement, but also the oldest civilizations.

The course of this extra-long Eurasian history was peppered with episodes of extreme violence as pastoral nomads and sedentary farmers attempted to work out their differences. One such episode, the focus of this chapter, brought to an end the ancient era of Eurasian history (4000 BCE–CE 476) and launched the Middle Ages (CE 476–1500). This clash between herders and farmers pitted vast numbers of nomadic tribes that populated the Eastern European, Russian, and Central Asian steppe against the civilizations of Rome and Han China. The end result was that the nomads destroyed the two greatest sedentary empires of the ancient world, closing out, in a sense, the first major chapter of world history, ending the ancient pattern of life in Eurasia and forcing both China and Western civilization to redefine their internal organizations.

Such destruction poses several interesting questions. What was it about the Eurasian nomads that saw them play such a destructive role in the history of two such rich and powerful civilizations at the end of the ancient era? And why did the destruction these herders wrought against Rome cause the fragmentation of the Western world into several new regimes, while China managed to recover its internal order after the fall of the Han Dynasty and go on to create an even greater and stronger imperial age? The answers to these questions depend entirely on the local histories of both great ancient empires. To begin, let us consider the role that the nomads played in ancient Chinese history.‡

The Persistent Nomadic Threat, Cannon, and China's Three Main Issues

A great many different nomadic tribes plagued Chinese history for 4700 years, from the third millennium BCE all the way up to the eighteenth century CE. The ever-present threat of a nomadic invasion along China's long northern frontier caused the Chinese to engage in elaborate defensive measures. These included: building the Great Wall of China and colonizing vast stretches of the Asian Steppe, in the process gaining control of key

‡The destruction of Rome and Han China reveals one of the many paradoxes of culture. The central paradox comes from the successes of agriculture, be it intensive or extensive. Agriculture is an artificial symbiotic relationship between humans, omega plants, and omega animals. This means that agriculture causes all three to increase in number, changing the natural environment into an artificial one. The end result is that agricultural success often leads to cultural failure. In the case of Rome and Han China, population pressures among nomads set them in motion, while internal weaknesses and human numbers in the aging Roman and Chinese Empires made both vulnerable to invasion.

oases cities across the northern deserts of this massive belt of plains. Nothing the Chinese did, however, succeeded in removing the possibility of a nomadic invasion. Only the development of modern cannons in Europe, the Middle East, Russia, and China provided sedentary cultures with the means to stop nomadic invasions.[§]

In Chinese history, the introduction of cannons as late as to the Qing Dynasty (CE 1644–191) finally allowed the Chinese to achieve a level of security across their vast, northern frontier. Massed in long lines and fired in volley, cannons permitted sufficient concentrations of power to neutralize a horde of charging cavalry. Since nomads were master horsemen, the appearance of cannons throughout Europe and Asia at roughly the same time provided all Eurasian sedentary cultures with the means to stop sudden raids from the steppe. Prior to the modern era, however, the nomads were a persistent presence that could not be ignored.

Without cannon, wave after wave of various herding nomadic tribes in the north forced the Chinese to centralize their political and military resources in order to try to protect their country. Painting Chinese history with very broad-brush strokes identifies the three major problems that faced each ruling dynasty: 1) constant nomadic pressure from the north; 2) perpetual dredging of the Yellow River; and 3) population pressures caused by successes in Chinese agriculture that sustained a very high birth rate.

Considering the growth in human numbers in this case, population pressures in China eventually consumed and exhausted every increase in surplus food production that each Chinese agricultural innovation managed to achieve. In addition, growing human numbers gradually overwhelmed and undid the traditional Chinese occupational structure, which could not hope to absorb so many competent employees. Maintaining this occupational structure, plus fighting off nomads, and constantly scooping out the abundant silt in the Yellow River's irrigation system pressed a ruling family's resources to its limits. Eventually every ruling family, every dynasty, failed, giving rise to a new one in the centuries-long Chinese dynastic cycle, a historical pattern that allowed Chinese civilization to regenerate itself again and again with spectacular success.

[§]The invention of cannon was yet another of the paradoxes of culture. The most successful of nomadic invaders, the Mongols, first led by Genghis Khan, conquered nearly all of Eurasia. This eliminated raid as a nomadic option and replaced it with trade. Trade then allowed Chinese gunpowder to travel the Silk Road under Mongol control. The movement of gunpowder next inspired warlike sedentary cultures in Europe, the Middle East, and Russia to developed cannon. Finally cannon became the chief weapon used by Eurasian farming cultures to defend themselves from and even defeat the nomads. Hence, the Mongols made their own destruction possible by their vast conquests.

Geographic Features of the Steppe and China

To understand the scope of the nomadic threat in Chinese history, one must have at least a loose grasp of the geography of Far East Asia. The birthplace of Chinese civilization along the Yellow River stretches from the Tibetan Plateau in the west to the forests of Siberia in the north and the Manchurian Plains in the east. To the south are the Jingling Mountains in central China. From this vast region, Chinese civilization spread out along the Yellow River, then moved across the Jingling Mountains into southern China, eventually reaching all the way to the South China Sea. Next the Chinese spread farther west to the north-eastern Burmese frontier and east along the South China Sea coast. Throughout north and south China flowed the two great rivers, the Yellow and the Yangzi, their floodplains producing China's food. As mentioned in chapter one, Chinese civilization began in the northern half of this complex geographic zone, the same place where the topography "invited" the first nomadic invasions.

The westernmost boundary of modern China begins at the junction of Afghanistan, Pakistan, and India. In the north-west lie the Tian Shan Mountains, whose 1000-mile length divides Chinese territory into two arid basins: the northern Dzungaria and southern Tarim. The Dzungaria received more rainfall than the Tarim Basin and therefore traditionally supported a significant pastoral population from the start of Chinese history. In contrast, the Tarim Basin was extremely dry and contained the Taklamakan Desert, a desolate wasteland. Within the Tarim Basin, however, were a series of oases that supported the famous overland trade route known as the Silk Road. East of these two great, arid basins lies the Mongolian Plateau: a flat zone rising 3000–6000 feet above sea level. Comprising the Gobi, the Ordos, and the Ningxia Deserts, the Mongolian Plateau opens onto a broad steppe on its southern fringe as well as into the farmlands of northern China. The Mongolian Plateau, and its easy access to the Eurasian steppe, exposed northern China to extensive, flat grasslands that stretched some 5000 miles from Hungary in the west through the Ukraine and Central Asia to Manchuria in the east; it supported countless nomadic tribes that could easily invade China.[1] It was the tribal peoples of this steppe, therefore, that caused the traditional Chinese civilization so much trouble. In order to try to keep the nomads of the Mongolian Plateau and the Eurasian steppe out of their territory, the Chinese constructed massive walls during several of their dynasties, hoping these enormous structures along their northern border would forestall any large-scale nomadic invasions. In addition, the Chinese and nomads fought a seemingly endless series of battles for control of the wells and springs in northern and western China.

South of this Eurasian steppe lay Chinese civilization. The Chinese cultivated the highly fertile loess plateau and silt-blown deserts that border the Yellow River and its tributaries and cut through this heartland. Annual rainfall is low in this area, in which steppe conditions prevail. The Yellow River and its tributaries, however, offer rich floodwaters and fresh silt for fertile farmlands. Unfortunately, the grasslands flow directly into the farmlands, with no natural barriers that farmers might have used to create any sort of defensive fortification against nomadic invaders. Therefore, nomads had direct access to this wide-open landscape, an easy entry point from which to attack the sedentary communities that laid the foundation for Chinese civilization. The Yellow River continues to flow east and merges with the North China plain. The Yellow, Wei, and Ku Rivers run through this flatland, their floodplains also providing rich soils for cultivation. This was the seat of China's first empire, but it was also an open invitation to the pastoral peoples on its frontiers for invasion.[2]

Nomads, Trade, and Migrations

The word "nomad" comes from *nomas* (Greek for wandering shepherd), and is an apt descriptive term for the people living north of the Yellow River basin. Powerful Tibetan, Turkish, Jurchen, Mongolian, and Manchurian tribal confederations occupied the oases in the deserts and the vast grasslands of the north. There, natural pastures fed the herds of omega animals that provided food for the pastoral peoples. These domesticated animals served both as nourishment and transportation, the latter vital to a lifestyle based on mobility. In addition to meat and milk, from which the nomads made cheese, yogurt, and liquid refreshments, sheep provided them with wool that they used to make felt tents or line the hides they fashioned into clothing. In addition, sheep droppings made an excellent fuel. Furthermore, the nomads kept a number of oxen that they used as draft animals to pull carts laden with possessions. They also used Bactrian camels; these animals were highly useful for traversing the deserts of Central Asia and therefore were particularly valuable.[3] Finally, the horse was central to the nomad's existence. It was their primary means of transportation, used as well in hunting, herding, and warfare. The type of horse upon which the nomads relied lived on the Mongolian Plateau; it was a small and hardy animal, one that managed to thrive even in the harsh climate of Central Asia. If necessary, these horses could survive only on grass, a nutrient-poor diet.

The horse played yet another role in nomadic history by becoming a key commodity of trade. In the first half of the Han Dynasty, from 202 BCE to CE 6, an era during which the Chinese were strong, they imported horses from nomads for use in helping to protect China's sedentary farms. The Chinese turned to importing large numbers of these animals because they could not afford to turn land already dedicated to plant cultivation into pastures on which to breed and raise horses. Chinese records report the exchange of silk for horses along the famous Silk Road and reveal a long history of commerce between Chinese farmers and the nomads of the northern steppe. These commercial exchanges, however, occurred only during those times when a particular Chinese dynasty proved strong enough to defend its northern frontiers. During these eras of relative peace, this commerce involved thousands of animals exchanged for millions of bolts of silk. Historians estimate the going rate of exchange at the time of the Han Dynasty to be 1 horse for 25–38 bolts of silk. The regularity of this exchange became a major portion of both the Chinese and nomadic economies, which added a commercial layer of interdependency between the peoples (erstwhile adversaries) who lived along this wide, open frontier. Once established, this exchange lasted from the Han through the Qing Dynasty, and it allowed for significant cultural interaction along the Silk Road.[4]

Added to the exchange of horses for silk was the complex interaction of oasis agriculture with nomadic tribes and the commercial centers of the Silk Road. A local economy existed that tied non-Chinese, local oasis farmers to both the commercial urban centers of the Silk Road and local nomadic tribes. These local farmers exchanged food for urban goods as well as for animals from the nomadic tribes. This trade took place independently from China. Similar to the commerce that occurred in China between Chinese cities and the countryside (i.e. urban goods for food), the nomads, the oasis farmers, and the commercial centers of the Silk Road, however, did not speak the same language. Each of the three groups formed distinct ethnic groups whose economic activities depended on its proximity to the Silk Road. Each developed a form of mutual dependency that allowed all three groups to get along peacefully. Each also developed hostility toward the Chinese whenever they tried to take command of the Silk Road, by capturing and garrisoning its commercial urban outposts.

The nomadic tribes of the Eurasian steppe belonged to the most distant and unstable element of the Silk Road. Their reliance on herding as the core of their livelihood freed them from a commitment to a sedentary way of life or a single location. They traveled across an open landscape seeking fresh pastures for their animals. Still, one feature of their lifestyle did, however, at least "tie" them to the sedentary civilization: as long as the commercial cities of the Silk Road remained independent of Chinese control, the nomads chose trade instead of raids to acquire the urban goods they needed. Yet, whenever the Chinese had control over long sections of the Silk Road, the nomads abandoned trade in favor of raids, and violent conflict inevitably ensued.[5]

In total, the ongoing series of conflicts between the nomads of the Eurasian Steppe and China constitute the longest-standing struggle in world history. The men of the Mongolian Plateau originally lived in the mountains of Siberia. When they domesticated the horse around 3000 BCE, they moved south onto the grasslands, where they acquired sheep from sedentary settlements, through both raids and trade. Their symbiotic relationships with their newly acquired omega animals prompted them to take command of as much grassland as possible. This led to constant fighting within rival shepherd bands, as all nomadic peoples of the vast plain had to move seasonally, from one pasture to another. They were simply following the dictates of summer's warmth and winter's cold.[6]

The regions that these nomadic tribes occupied included two main divisions of land. In the west lay the plains of the Ukraine, the northern Caucasus Mountains, and the Kirghiz and Kazakh steppes. In the east were the high plains of Mongolia and Manchuria. The separation of these two regions by topography, however, meant little to the nomads who lived there, as they moved easily back and forth from east and west, with seasonal circumstances and variations in climate dictating their migrations. Wherever these groups went, they fought to make sure their animals had plenty to eat. From this constant need to fight emerged the most common image of the nomad: a mounted archer covered with as much armor as his horse could carry and still move swiftly. Tibetan, Turkish, Jurchen, Mongolian, and Manchurian tribal confederations made up some of the most feared of the kinship groups that lived in this complex region.[7]

Nomadic Tactics

Firing from atop the backs of the squat, sturdy horses native to Central Asia, Tibetan, Turkish, Jurchen, Mongolian, and Manchurian soldiers became legendary accurate archers. Each mounted warrior wielded a light and highly powerful double-curved composite bow. Unstrung, these bows stood about three feet tall. Unlike most bows of the time, which were built from hardwood and curved toward the strung side, the nomad's composite bow was almost opposite in design. Its handle curved toward the archer, while the arms of the bow arched away. It was composed of a combination of materials: strips of deer and cattle horns, bone, sinew, and glues made from boiling down animal tendons and fish bones. The bow-master built the bow around a wooden core, to which he glued on layers of horn. The tensile strength of the nomad's bow was enormous and required years of practice, during which the archer had to build up his upper body muscles in order to pull, aim, and fire. Nomad boys began practicing with their bows at a very early age, and they continued to do so until they could pull their bows with ease, even while riding a horse at full gallop. As adults, fully trained as mounted archers, nomadic warriors could fire an arrow almost 500 yards; their deadly projectiles traveling at speeds of 180 miles per hour were capable of penetrating armor.[8]

Other weapons and tactics used by the nomadic warriors of the Eurasian steppe included heavy cavalry carrying lances, as well as double-edged swords. Innovations in riding gear that these nomads created or modified include the bit, reins, and stirrups, all of which helped them use the horse as a highly mobile platform for warfare. Tactics included systematically avoiding direct contact with the enemy, while harassing his ranks to deplete his resources. Only after the enemy was sufficiently weakened did the nomads engage in a full-frontal assault.

Nomadic armies typically aligned their troops into small units of ten horsemen to create their basic cavalry squadron. Then these smallest military groups combined into the hundreds, or ten groups of ten multiplied several times. Finally, they numbered in the thousands, or ten groups of a hundred, again multiplied several times. The full potential of a nomadic military force linked clans to tribes and tribes to massive kinship confederations. The largest of these armies, however, depended on the inventiveness and charisma of specific, individual tribal leaders. Tribal confederations elected these unique military commanders who wrought havoc upon sedentary cultures as long as they lived.[9]

The Charismatic Leader

When a particularly charismatic ruler took command of a nomadic army, his men suddenly became a major threat to the nearest sedentary civilization. Such a leader could successfully impose discipline on a vast and otherwise unruly body of warriors. Once a nomadic chief commanded the loyalty of his men, he could hone their fighting skills, and perfect his method of combat. Such leaders were the first to develop heavy cavalry, which could defeat the infantry formations of farmer-soldiers.

Using both heavy and light cavalry, the charismatic leader usually followed a common scenario to conquer a sedentary civilization. The leader targeted small, sedentary cities for his initial attacks. Once he captured these cities, he acquired engineers who then built siege weapons. With these towering weapons, the nomads overran major cities. Each new conquest enhanced the prestige of the charismatic leader and added new captives with urban skills to those under his control. The nomadic commander then used these skills and knowledge to wreak havoc on all fortified cities that tried to resist his assaults. The high degree of nomadic mobility, unparalleled equestrian skills, and the ability to conduct lightening raids made large nomadic forces nearly impossible to catch or defeat. Under the command of a truly effective military leader, the nomads ultimately built massive empires. In short, then, it was the charismatic leaders among the nomads who posed the greatest risks to Han China specifically, but to all Chinese dynasties generally. This threat existed, not merely in the sense of harassment along the Han Dynasty's borders, but in the sense of the potential destruction of a ruling dynasty.[10]

During the first two generations of the Han Dynasty, from 202 to 170 BCE, a particularly dangerous nomadic leader appeared among a powerful confederation composed of Turkish-Mongol warriors. Called the Xiongnu, this confederation accepted the authority of a warlord named Modun (reigned 209–174 BCE). Modun was an outstanding cavalry commander whose highly trained warriors responded without hesitation to his every order. One such command saw his warriors fire their bows at whatever target Modun indicated by hitting it with an arrow of his own. When he fired an arrow at his father in 209 BCE, his troop of 10,000 men responded immediately, so that the one fatal arrow out of 10,000 could not be detected. Acquiring the title *Shanyu* (the equivalent of the Mongol's Great Khan) in this manner, Modun set out to become the most powerful nomad in Central Asia.[11]

From 209 to 174 BCE Modun rampaged in the Ordo region along the great northern bend of the Yellow River. Han efforts to deal with Modun's cavalry proved futile, so the Chinese chose to respond with a policy of appeasement. A treaty signed in 198 BCE granted the Han emperor peace in exchange for a princess bride and regular deliveries of silk, grain, and alcohol. The Han recognized the *Shanyu* as an equal to the emperor, which violated the Han premise that the Chinese ruler was the universal sovereign of all domains under Heaven. Meanwhile, Modun achieved his goal of establishing hegemony among the steppe nomads by driving the Xiongnu's chief rivals, the Yuezhi, west toward the Amu Darya River, near the Hindu Kush Range of modern Pakistan. When Modun died in 174 BCE, his elected heir continued to harass and extract tribute from the Han

Dynasty. A pattern of raids, followed by generous treaties that granted wealth to the Xiongnu only temporarily halted the violent attacks. This pattern of raid-treaty-peace-raid again became known as the "peace and kinship" policy (*heqin*) and lasted until the reign of the Chinese Emperor Han Wudi (reigned 141–87 BCE).[12]

Han Wudi–China's Warrior Emperor

Under Han Wudi, the Chinese chose an aggressive approach to the nomads. Rather than mount a defense against invasion, as did Qin Shi Huangdi (reigned 221–210 BCE) with the first Great Wall, Han Wudi went on the offensive. Han Wudi launched a series of wars against the Xiongnu that began in his eighth year as emperor. In 133 BCE, he sent a force deep into Xiongnu territory, but the nomads that Han Wudi's army pursued simply melted away into the vast open spaces of the steppe. In 129 BCE, Han Wudi changed strategies. During the next ten years (129–119 BCE), he sent seven major armies north to occupy lands abandoned by a steadily retreating enemy. He succeeded because he began to plant Chinese colonies throughout the region to create a bulwark against the Xiongnu's return. The first two expeditions of 129 and 128 BCE prepared the way for conquest. The third, in 127 BCE, was a massive invasion into the Ordos Plateau to capture the entire great northern bend of the Yellow River. Here, Han Wudi planted 100,000 colonists. Three years later, in 124 BCE, he added another 100,000. Then he sent his armies north and west to capture the region that covered the vulnerable flank of Gansu region (the western Yellow River Basin). From there his armies crossed the Gobi Desert and pushed west as far as Lake Baikal, in Russian territory. The primary object of this drive was to capture the Tarim Basin north of Tibet so as to open a trade route to the West that would reach the fabled kingdom of Rome.[13]

When Han Wudi planned this grand strategy, he sent an agent into nomadic territory to prepare the way. The mission of this agent, Zhang Qian (died 114 BCE), generated one of the greatest adventures of the ancient world. Zhang Qian's quest entailed finding the Yuezhi (mentioned above). As already discussed, by 130 BCE, the Yuezhi had settled around the Amu Darya River, by the Hindu Kush Range near modern Pakistan. This was one of the provinces that Alexander the Great had added to his empire on his trek east against the Persian Empire (336–323 BCE). By 127 BCE, the Yuezhi had moved into Bactria, the eastern-most province of the now defunct Persian Empire. The Chinese knew the Yuezhi, and had dealt successfully with them before. Han Wudi hoped to forge a new alliance with the Yuezhi that would corner the Xiongnu by cutting off their retreat to the west.[14]

In 138 BCE, Zhang set out on his fabled trek west without really knowing his destination. The Xiongnu, however, captured him and held him prisoner for ten years. He escaped from his captors in 128 BCE, finding the Yuezhi and forging an agreement with them. He then set out for his return trip to China. En route, the Xiongnu captured him again, but he managed to escape a second time. He finally arrived in the Han capital, Chang'an, in 126 BCE. He reported on his expedition, and in so doing revealed a vast knowledge of western Asia; he was, after all, the only Chinese explorer to have seen the kingdoms of Balkh (in northern Afghanistan), Samarkand (in Uzbekistan), and Bokhara (also in Uzbekistan). Included in his report was some sketchy information about Egypt, Parthia, Media, and Babylonia, and he had carried back with him cuttings of grapes and alfalfa. Finally, he reported on a new breed of warhorses that he had found in the Fergana Valley, to the south-east of Sinkiang. These were the animals, he contended, that the Han needed to deal more effectively with the Xiongnu.[15]

To obtain these magnificent horses, Wudi waged a 25-year campaign to capture the Tarim Basin. Taking this massive region opened the trade routes west, collectively called the Silk Road. Once opened, this land-based conduit allowed the Chinese and Romans to participate in an elaborate system of trade that brought silk westwards, all the way to the gates of Rome. Because of its aridity, the Tarim Basin was also largely free of nomads. Strategically located oases, however, already supported a well-established caravan traffic that carried goods both east and west. Over time Wudi succeeded in his campaign to take control of this basin, and the whole region fell to the Chinese by 102 BCE.

Once established, the Silk Road connected China to India and Rome. The opening of this grand trade route secured for the Chinese sufficient numbers of the sought-after warhorses from the Fergana Valley to allow them to breed some of these animals successfully back in China. These valuable horses later enabled Wudi's grandson, Emperor Han Xuan (reigned 73–49 BCE), finally to complete China's war against the Xiongnu. Those Xiongnu not brought under Han control then migrated west over the next several centuries. Referring to these migrating Xiongnu, some scholars argue that this remnant band of nomads eventually arrived in Europe, where they became known as the Hun. Whatever their precise origin, the Hun would go on to visit Rome with waves of destructive raids that matched the levels of devastation suffered by China earlier (see below).[16]

The Silk Road: Revelation of a Deadly Paradox of Culture

The Silk Road now went on to play a major if unexpected role in Eurasian history. This preeminent trade route became the leading avenue of cultural diffusion across Eurasia after Han Xuan's defeat of the Xiongnu. As mentioned, cultural diffusion is one of the key factors in world history that accelerated the development of civilizations in Eurasia when compared to the isolation experienced in the Americas and Sub-Saharan Africa. Cultural diffusion allowed for the exchange of goods, plants, animals, tools and ideas that enabled Eurasian civilizations to learn valuable lessons from one another. But cultural diffusion also allowed for the movement of infection.

Rome and Han China probably would not have fallen to nomads were it not for the germs that traveled along the Silk Road to these two civilizations. Once new strains of germs, to which a particular group of people has not yet built any natural immunity, infect a sedentary culture, the microbes breed quickly among the members. The result of such epidemic waves of disease is the death of millions, meaning that, in a sense, germs played a key role in shaping the population dynamics of sedentary societies. Stated paradoxically, agriculture both increased the number of people it fed and created the very conditions that killed great numbers of these same people through epidemic diseases. Placed in the context of this chapter, agriculture granted a caloric advantage to Roman and Chinese farmers when compared to the herders of the steppe. But, sooner or later, disease neutralized this advantage and, leaving the sedentary society weakened, prepared the way for devastating nomadic invasions.

The Calorie Advantage and Diseases of Plant Cultivators

Plant cultivation supported far more people than did herding, due to the higher calorie count produced by intensive, compared to extensive, agriculture. Any animal within a herd that consumed plant vegetation converted the biomass of its diet from 100,000 calories of plant-food to 10,000 calories of meat or milk. This means that people living off plants had available 90,000 more calories than did herding cultures, and the extra calories sustained a much larger sedentary population. In addition, the quality of the two sets of calories is quite different. Plants specialists had a very high carbohydrate diet, while nomads live mostly on proteins and fat. Nomads, therefore, had more stamina than farmers, but farmers, because of the wider availability of food, outnumbered herders by ten to one.[17]

However, growing plants carried with it certain hidden dangers. A dependency on crops required farmers to stay in one place, whereas herding animals involved continuous movement. Farmers who domesticated a collection of omega plants may have enjoyed the benefits of abundance, but their numbers quickly filled the landscape. Management of the land, the seasons, water, soil, and food surpluses gradually led to urbanization, from which civilization derives its name. But civilization soon created a series of dangerous conditions. First, a large human population confined to one location soon sees its waste accumulate. Second, the narrowing of a culture's diet to 70 percent or more of carbohydrates lowered human resistance to germs, and sedentary farming prompted very close contact between farmers and their domesticated animals; such close contact opened pathways for the exchange of pathogens. And third, the confinement of farmers and their omega plants and animals to one location concentrated a large host population that soon attracted parasites. Taken all together, these conditions combined to breed diseases. Suddenly, the practice of intensive agriculture, which increased human numbers, invited diseases that decreased these same numbers. Hence, the agricultural successes of cultivation could set up its failure.

This biological paradox punished farmers much more than nomads. While farming cultures unexpectedly attracted the parasites that caused epidemic diseases due to the sedentary conditions stated above, nomads tended to avoid these same problems due to their mobility. Diseases took the lives of a great many farmers, while nomads simply migrated away from civilization's biological pitfalls. But these same cycles of epidemics also saw the farmers who survived each eruption of disease develop (and pass on to their offspring) natural immunities. These immunities, in turn, produced an arsenal of antibodies that saw future generations defeat many types of germs. In other words, different civilizations that attracted different pathogens within their borders also developed immunities to those same parasites. In time, many such diseases only infected the very young, and became known as childhood diseases. In the long run, each sedentary culture developed a collection of omega plants and animals, as well as specific endemic diseases, to create a highly complex biological environment in which they could thrive. At this point in the cycle, these same environments might be very deadly to strangers—including, of course, raiding or invading nomads.[18]

Trade and travel saw merchants unknowingly transmit dangerous pathogens from one civilization to another. This meant that trade routes carried not only goods, but also extremely deadly, silent passengers. These lethal passengers were of course germs that brought new diseases to vulnerable populations. Soon thereafter, sudden eruptions of epidemic diseases in susceptible civilizations caused a steep decline in population. The victims of these epidemics included a great many young adults capable of farming and fighting. Death among such a valuable portion of the human population severely weakened a sedentary civilization's defenses, opening that culture up to potential nomadic conquest. Just such a demographic crisis prepared the way for the falls of the Roman Empire and the Han Dynasty. Deadly disease exchanges occurred in the Roman Empire and Han China between the years CE 1–300.

Roman and Han China Suffer a Major Demographic Crisis

The Great Silk Road that emerged in the wake of Han Wudi's offensive against the Xiongnu created a commercial pathway. Goods, ideas, and germs flowed both west and east between India, China, and Rome, all along this trade route and its tributaries. In short, deadly diseases from these three civilizations traveled with the merchants who made the trip. Three major parasitic invasions surfaced in Rome and Han China as a result of trade with India. Smallpox, measles, and bubonic plague, all of which were endemic to India, erupted in the Roman Empire, while smallpox and measles erupted in China. In addition, trade between Rome and Sub-Saharan Africa through Egypt saw malaria enter the Roman Empire. Each epidemic, which erupted at various times in both the Roman Empire and the Han Dynasty, is known to us today thanks to contemporary reports. We know for certain that these epidemics killed vast numbers of people and weakened the defenses of both great empires, inviting (and exposing them to collapse from) nomadic invasions.

The first such plague to strike Rome introduced malaria to the Italian Peninsula, killing vast numbers of people during the first century CE. In CE 125, an unknown infection erupted called the Orosius plague, which followed on the heels of a famine induced by the wholesale destruction of local crops by locusts in North Africa. This event naturally reduced human resistance to infection in the area. From North Africa the Orosius plague spread to Italy. The first major, empire-wide infection was the Antonine Plague that spanned CE 165–189 and killed an estimated one-third of the total population. Believed by scientists today to have been smallpox, this plague killed vast numbers of people living throughout the Roman Empire, thereby inviting invasions of "barbaric" or nomadic groups who pushed west from their bases in the north European (German) forests. These groups of nomads, however, happened to have timed their attack poorly, for they, too, ended up catching the plague and died. The next major epidemic was the Cyprian plague, which proved every bit as deadly as the Antonine plague and lasted from CE 251 to 268. Again, nearly one-third of Rome's population perished, deeply reducing its labor pool and tax base. This second demographic crisis also led to numerous nomadic invasions, and even sparked several internal, civil wars. What followed in Roman history is known as "the crisis of the mid-third century." During this time the weakened empire suffered attacks on two frontiers: the north European Germans in the west, and Sassanian Persians in the east. From CE 234 to 284, 23 emperors ruled and died while trying in vain to solve Rome's problems. The depleted population, nomadic raids, and growing demands for taxes inspired the Diocletian reforms (CE 285–305). These reforms split the Roman Empire into eastern and western halves in the hope that each might manage to finance and defend its own borders. This split did not put an end to the mounting nomadic pressures on the frontier, although it did postpone the fall of Rome until the fifth century CE.[19]

While Rome was doing its best to address the relentless nomadic pressures with the Diocletian Reforms in the third century CE, the Han Dynasty found itself without a similarly talented leader when the plagues that hit Western civilization also visited China. The Chinese reported disease events that most historians believe to be smallpox and measles in CE 161–162, 173, 179, and 182. Striking mostly in the north, where the Chinese population was most vulnerable, the estimated death rate reached somewhere between 33 and 40 percent of the total population. These epidemics, coupled with droughts in CE 176, 177, 182, and 183 and floods in 175, killed even more people. Perceiving that the emperor had lost the Mandate of Heaven—a divine signal that the time for change had arrived—the peasantry of the late Han Dynasty rose in rebellion. The Han Dynasty did not, however, produce a ruler like Diocletian, who might have postponed the fall of their empire. Instead, a great many cliques of powerful rivals at the Han court struggled to exert their influence over imperial decisions. In effect, the rival groups divided the Han court so thoroughly that it suffered a form of political paralysis. Without an effective ruler, the great Han Dynasty failed. Such internal weakness would also expose future Chinese dynasties to nomadic invasion.[20]

Loyalty, the State, and Paradise Lost

Another subtle but powerful agency was at play that also increased the nomad's chances of destroying Rome and Han China. In both empires a powerful psychological change had set in. Among those talented people who could produce the creative energy needed to support a great empire, the impulse to work for the good of Rome and Han China waned. A general disenchantment with secular life permeated the Roman and Chinese will to support both empires. While epidemics, civil war, uninspiring leadership, and nomadic invasions swept through the Roman Empire, plagues, droughts, floods, and paralysis at court stifled any effective political response in Han China. Added to these similar sets of problems in both empires was a new concern about life after death, something that captivated people in both the Far East and Western civilization. Christianity, Buddhism, and Daoism gained adherence and distracted the Romans and their Chinese counterparts from investing in the state. Each new faith, or philosophy, drew the attention of the people away from the concerns connected to this world. In time, the will to prop up the state gave way, with a new level of indifference to secular life.[21] Since this text has already covered Christianity in chapter two, we will now focus on Daoism and Buddhism in China.

Daoism

In the late Han era, Daoism underwent a transformation, one that saw it evolve from a philosophical construct (of the *Dao*) to a religion. In intellectual circles, Chinese scholars and officials began to question the state's authorized synthesis of Confucianism-Legalism-Daoism. They revisited the ancient Daoist teachings found in Laozi's *Daodijing* and Zhuangzi' *The Book of Zhuangzi*. They argued that the emperors of the late Han Dynasty practiced the rituals of the state's ideology but did not believe in them.

Among the peasantry, Daoism took on a mystical quality that saw it begin to serve as an anti-state ideology. Peasants began to follow faith healers who promised a golden age of wealth and peace based on the *Dao* for those who united in opposition to the state. Massive peasant rebellions mobilized under this new form of Daoism transformed into the basis of a widespread populist revolution. Two prominent rebel groups, the Yellow Turbans and the Celestial Masters, launched powerful attempts to overthrow the Han Dynasty, but only managed to cause the Han Empire to splinter into warlord provinces.[22]

Faced with trying to ward off huge peasant armies, the paralyzed Han court turned to regional generals to raise local resistance. These generals defeated the peasants, or drove them so far into retreat that they were no longer a threat, but after each such victory the generals refused to lay down their arms. China split into three kingdoms, one whose warlords killed the last Han emperor in CE 220. Now three powerful families hoped to declare a new era of centralized rule, but instead they launched a new age of incessant warfare. It was in this opening era of post-Han rule and bloody chaos that Buddhism arrived in China.[23]

Buddhism

In this dangerous age, the conversion of Daoism into a religion laid an excellent foundation for the emergence of Buddhism. The underlying emphasis of Daoism was: reject imperial society and return to village life and faith in the mystical powers of the *Dao*. This emphasis pulled Chinese scholars and peasants into a state of social retreat. Withdrawal from government service and a new interest in a unitary, ineffable, and mysterious force embedded in nature were concepts quite suggestive of Buddhism. Buddhism itself had traveled along the Silk Road into Central Asia and had already taken up residence in the Tarim Basin during the age of the Kushan Empire of northern India and Central Asia (50 BCE–CE 225). The emergence of the Kushan Empire was a by-product of the Yuezhi's retreat from the Xiongnu under Modun's command (mentioned above). The Yuezhi had been driven west in the second century BCE. The Yuezhi then created the Kushan Empire, which served as a major trading center along the Silk Road, where diplomatic contacts between Rome, Sassanian Persia, India, and Han China took place. The Kushan people, devout Buddhists, began introducing this new faith into China.[24]

Moving along the chain of oasis cities spanning the Tarim Basin, Buddhism and Sanskrit (the mother tongue of all Indo-European languages) worked their way into China, taking up residence in one commercial urban center after another. By the second century CE, a regular stream of scholars and missionaries traveled back and forth from India to China seeking to spread a better understanding of the new faith.

The brand of Buddhism that entered China appealed to the disenchanted locals by speaking not only of the times at hand (i.e. human misery) but also to native Chinese ideals. Buddhism offered interesting insights into nature and the human condition, without speaking of miracles, supernatural gods, or an all-powerful creator. Buddhism defined suffering as an inescapable part of human life, but offered the individual a way out through the fostering of a well-organized self-discipline. Buddhism claimed that all human beings were actually isolated, transcendental souls separated from a singular, eternal, and divine existence to which everyone belonged. This concept of a universal, ineffable whole (i.e. a monism) was very much like the *Dao*, only more explicitly defined. The key difference is that Buddhism introduced China to a new idea, that of the transcendental, a concept missing from the *Dao*.

Buddhism told of cycles of death and rebirth shaped by a person's actions in past lives, which determined the conditions of his or her present existence. Buddhism defined these cycles of death and rebirth as a by-product of a life dictated by desire (for food, money, power, sex, etc.). Desire fooled individuals into believing that their experiences in their lives were real. Buddhism claimed, however, that only the universal, ineffable, and transcendental unity underlying everything was real. Buddhism offered an escape from the illusion of a person's individual existence by offering a meditative discipline that might lead to an awakening, known as "enlightenment." The achievement of enlightenment would see the individual's soul reunited with the universal, ineffable, and transcendental unity, awakening the person to reality.[25] The prospect of enlightenment filled the individual with rapture (i.e. a euphoric, transcendent state) through reunion with the monistic whole. Just as raindrops reunited with the oceans from which they originated, a person's enlightenment was the awareness that they had returned to their true, heavenly existence. Once the individual attained enlightenment, the struggle with the illusions of their separate lives came to an end. At that moment, an individual's relentless suffering was over. Also, at that moment, individuality ceased to exist and the soul entered paradise.[26]

While much in Buddhism struck Han Chinese as similar to the native Daoism, the new faith also infused them with a number of completely alien concepts and practices. While the *Dao* was a monistic, ineffable whole similar to Buddhism's monistic, universal whole, the *Dao* was not understood to be a transcendental unity. The idea of an existence outside time and space (i.e. the transcendental) was completely alien to the Chinese. Also, while the *Dao* suggested a retreat from civilized life similar to the Buddhist's retreat into a personal discipline, the *Dao* did not identify "the individual" or the "soul." Daoism, like the official Han ideology of Confucianism-Legalism-Daoism, had always centered Chinese life on the family. In Buddhism, however, the "individual soul," existed apart from any others, family included, and was another transcendental concept with which the Chinese now grappled. Indeed, the Chinese still believed that for every human action there was a natural reaction, and that for every event in nature there was a human response. Daoism reflected this belief, which meant a person was real if separated from the monistic, ineffable *Dao*. Buddhism, however, held that all individual acts were illusions and of no consequence to the transcendental reality. Such an idea was very hard for the Chinese to understand. The Chinese, therefore, had to select those concepts from Buddhism that they found useful and put them into a new, Chinese context.

Through this process of assimilation, Buddhism infused the Chinese worldview with certain new, abstract, and metaphysical concepts that drew the individual's attention away from the family and the travails of this world. And as mentioned, Buddhism traveled in tandem with a literature written in Sanskrit, a language completely alien to the Chinese. Finally, Buddhism's call for a retreat from this world stood in stark contrast to the traditional focus of a Confucian life, which held that human conduct was both real and formed the basis of Heaven's responses.

Despite its breaks with tradition, Buddhism had a powerful appeal to a people living in an era of increasing chaos and suffering. Famine, plague, and warfare confronted each member of a Chinese family with the prospect of a sudden death. Executions carried out on the whim of quixotic rulers seemed to mark each passing day. Buddhism offered solace and an escape from such a highly unpredictable life. Thus, in the last throes of Han China, Buddhism, much like Christianity in the collapsing Roman world, eroded the individual's loyalty to the state. In this case, the new faith helped the Chinese abandon a failed Han Dynasty, in a sense permitting them to wait patiently for the next true emperor, as long as it took Heaven to "select" him. In short, the appealing new faith not only introduced new concepts into the Chinese imagination, but it also diverted the attention of its converts away from both the state and the horrors that surrounded them in their daily lives.[27]

An Era of Chaos

While the Chinese were assimilating a new faith, China itself spiraled into chaos. First, the warlords dismembered what was left of the old Han Empire. Then the nomads crossed the frontiers, adding their special brand of destruction to the Chinese experience. Neither the pastoral invaders nor the local Chinese generals could impose their will across the land and achieve reunification. Instead, China entered a 375-year-long era of political rivalry, warfare, and instability. The entire period belied the cultural unity that was the hallmark of China's civilization.

The collapse of the Han created three large provincial kingdoms commanded by local warlords. These rival generals included Cao Cao (CE 155–220), Liu Bei (CE 161–223), and Sun Quan (CE 182–252), each of whom established short-lived dynasties. Cao Cao founded the Wei Dynasty; Liu Bei built a kingdom in Sichuan called the Shu Han Dynasty; and Sun Quan established his realm, known as the Wu Dynasty, in the lower Yangzi River valley. Thereafter each warlord struggled to make himself emperor; soon chaos began to reign in China.[28]

The Wei, Shu Han, and Wu kingdoms ultimately failed in their quests to reunite China. What they did accomplish, however, was the destruction of the old Han order. In CE 263, the Wei defeated the Shu Han, but two years later fell to a rebel general who proclaimed the Jin Dynasty (CE 265–420). In CE 280, the Jin defeated the Wu state in the Yangzi River valley. The Jin, however, soon faced a reawakened nomadic threat from the north, as a branch of the Xiongnu invaded China in CE 311. Mounted and sporting a new technology, the stirrup, this Turkish-Mongol group made good use of a much more stable seat on their horses. They drove the Jin to the south, where the fleeing Chinese rulers created a much-weakened southern state. With their defeat by the Xiongnu, the Jin split into two parts: the Western Jin (265–316) and the Eastern Jin (317–420). At the same time, northern China became a cauldron of conflict, with constant warfare among competing groups. Many of the combatants were non-Chinese nomads who filtered into the Yellow River Basin, transforming China ethnically.[29]

During this era of invasion and civil war, northern China blended together numerous combinations of nomadic and Han Chinese peoples, infusing China with new family mixtures. The influx of new peoples into China caused an assimilation process where Chinese culture prevailed, merging the victors with the vanquished. Dress, diet, language, values, and expectations all became traditional Chinese ones. (The one alien element that managed to take firm root in China during this era was Buddhism.) The definition of "Chinese" expanded, so that whoever lived in the north self-consciously denied "barbarian" traits. While this mixture of people occurred in the north, an estimated two million refugees fled from the north into southern China, following the collapse of the Han in CE 220.

The attempts of those who fled south to create a centralized state bore as little fruit as those of their counterparts in the north. But what these refugees did accomplish was the transformation of the south into a truly Chinese cultural zone. The societies of the north and the south began to look very similar. Both developed a highly stratified system of landowner-ship, private armies to defend large estates, and a teeming population of impoverished peasants bound to the land and the local lord or strongman.

During the centuries of the Han Dynasty, only ten percent of the south-ern population had been Chinese. After the fall of the Han, continued large-scale migration from north to south changed the Yangzi River basin into a region worked by millions of Chinese peasants. They emptied swamps of excess water, built rice paddies, and developed a system of flooding and draining to prepare and maintain their fields. They emptied swamps of excess water, built rice paddies, and developed a system of flooding and draining to prepare and maintain their fields. They grew accustomed to a new, gentler climate in which they cultivated new crops, thereby heavily infusing the Chinese diet with rice. They also imported silk worms, grew mulberry trees to feed the worms, and started silk-weaving enterprises to compensate for the loss of their property in the north. Finally, long-distance trade to and from all of China continued despite the collapse of a centralized regime. The southern Chinese exported silk, bronze, and lacquer ware through Guangzhou to markets in Persia and South-east Asia, in exchange for textiles, pearls, ivory, incense, and coral.[30]

The Fall of Rome

While China was experiencing its great era of dislocation from 220 to 581 BCE, the Roman Empire also endured a period of nomadic pressures that would transform Western civilization. In a manner similar to the Chinese, the Romans were about to enter a highly complex period where they attempted a policy of ethnic assimilation with their potential enemies. As Germanic tribes moved into Roman territory, Rome sought alliances with some of these groups of warlike peoples to fill vacancies in their military caused by disease and civil war. Indeed, Roman military recruiters embraced Germanic tribes, using them as auxiliary units within the larger Roman army, while incorporating alien forms of military equipment and tactics. Meanwhile, Rome's original forces continued to employ older, well-established methods and weaponry. This made warfare a far more complicated enterprise in what was emerging as a new cultural zone that would be called Europe. Perhaps the most complex feature of this era was the frequency with which nomadic troops changed sides, shifting back and forth between friend and foe of Rome. This new feature of unreliable allies became common even during the life of a generation's commanders. The instability of this military era partially underlines the fragile defenses that Rome mounted in its waning centuries. And once this weakness had set in, serious trouble would erupt in the empire in the third century CE.

The Danube

All along the Danube River, the years CE 200–300 witnessed Gothic (German) tribes increase pressure on Roman defenses as these nomadic peoples migrated west into Europe from the Eurasian Steppe. The first Gothic incursion started in CE 238, when Germanic tribes sacked Istria near the mouth of the Danube River (i.e. Rome's European south-eastern frontier).[31] Within a decade, Emperor Decius (reigned CE 249–251) lost his life as his army tried to force the Goths back across the Danube. This proved to be the opening episode in the long period of chaos during the third century, mentioned above.[32]

As the Goths moved south, they displaced other peoples along the Roman frontier, and formed new confederations of tribes to try to keep the lands they had taken. Along the upper Danube, several confederations, the Vandals, the Quadi, and the Marcommani, forged new tribal unities and chose to invade the Roman Empire together, rather than fight among themselves and other rival nomadic enemies. For the next 50 years, emperor after emperor tried to stabilize the western half of the Roman Empire without success until the Diocletian reforms mentioned above. Still, pressures exerted on Rome by the Goths continued to swell, and by the fourth century CE spilled back into the Roman territory.

The Rhine

Returning to the years between CE 200 and 300, the Rhine Valley presented a different military picture to that along the Danube. While the Danube attracted more Germans than the Romans could manage, the Rhine Valley offered a measure of protection. Fewer Germans along the Rhine allowed the Romans a chance to patrol this river with flotillas of soldiers and thereby fortify certain crossing points. Still, various German tribes made their way into the Roman Empire, requiring a military response. On the upper Rhine, the Alamanni unified and prepared an invasion of the Italian Peninsula in the CE 260s. At the same time, another Germanic group, known as the Franks, built a confederation of their own and threatened Gaul. Then, yet another Germanic group, the Saxons, began a series of raids in towns and villages along the North Sea. Stability throughout the vast northerly lands of the Roman Empire was only partially restored before the reign of Julian (reigned CE 361–363). He confronted the Alamanni on the right bank of the Rhine near Argentoratum (Strasbourg) and defeated them in CE 357, thanks to the high degree of discipline within his army. This weakened the Gothic threat along the Rhine for quite some time, to the end of the reign of Emperor Theodosius I (reigned CE 379–395). He continued to inflict casualties among these marauding Germans. More trouble resurfaced, however, during the regency of Flavius Stilicho (*c.* CE 359–408), when the Goths took advantage of an empire freshly weakened due a hostile split between its eastern and western halves. This time the Visigoths acquired a new leader in Alaric (*c.* CE 370–410), as discussed below.

The Xiongnu, the Huns, and the Germans

Remember that Han Xuan had driven the Xiongnu west, back in the first century BCE; the vanquished Xiongnu then migrated across the Eurasian steppe as a Turkish-Mongol confederation, pushing numerous Germanic tribes out of their path and towards the Roman Empire. The first of the German tribes that these Turkish-Mongol migrants (now known as the Huns) encountered (and ultimately displaced), were the Alans, who lived along the Don River in present-day Russia. The Huns attacked the Alans, driving some of them west, which caused a shockwave in Europe that the Germans called *Völkerwandering* (the wandering of tribes). Over the course of the fourth and fifth centuries CE, numerous groups of Germanic tribes began to flee farther west in response to the mounting pressures exerted by the Huns. The *Völkerwandering* eventually caused the "steppe" and the "forest" Germanic groups to renew their invasions of the Roman Empire, from the third through to the fifth centuries CE. The end result was a tangle of Germanic peoples entering the Roman Empire, creating a complex era of invasion.[33]

What followed was a shock wave of attacks on a once mighty empire. While the Western Roman world tried to deal with each individual tribe that entered its territory, the Romans ultimately failed. The German invaders then sacked Rome twice: once in 410 when a tribe called the Visigoths under Alaric took the city, and a second time when another tribe called the Vandals succeeded in capturing this once mighty capital. After this there was a tortuous series of invasions by many different tribes, and Rome's failure to halt these nomadic assaults led to the disintegration of the Latin-speaking half the once mighty empire, ending the ancient era of Western civilization. Now Rome joined Han China as a victim of the nomads.

Chinese Potential for Reunification versus Western Fragmentation

While the Western Roman Empire now lay in fragments, the Chinese planned to restore centralized rule, even an empire. For the following centuries, Western civilization would be divided along three main lines: the surviving Eastern Roman Empire, the emergence of a Medieval Europe, and the rise of Islam in the Middle East. This division would completely shatter the unity, or centralized authority, of what was once Rome. In contrast, in the wake of the Han Dynasty, China would manage to foster the re-emergence of a new dynasty and even a new dynastic cycle.

The assimilation of nomadic tribesmen into Chinese culture, or sinicization, was far more successful than any Western attempts to absorb and acculturate German nomads who had invaded Roman society. Chinese assimilation was so complete that the former nomads of the steppe came to give up their own names, languages, and systems of beliefs in favor of all things Chinese.

Nothing of this nature occurred in the now highly Germanic Europe. Roman legal practices, concepts of property, the partial assimilation of Latin into Romance languages, and the practice of the inheritance of land and titles would find their way into German kingdoms established in the old Roman provinces of England, Gaul (France), Iberia (Portugal and Spain), and Italy. In contrast, areas unoccupied by Rome prior to its fall, such as Germany and Eastern Europe, would have far more difficulty assimilating valuable lessons from Rome. The non-Roman regions would remain distinctly German until Slavic tribes came to occupy Poland, Bohemia, and much of the Balkans, or the Magyars took over Hungary. Romania, however, did maintain a distinct Roman flavor even though it had been a Roman province only briefly. More powerful than secular institutions, the Christian religion would ultimately convert the European Germans and Slavic tribes to a single faith, whether they had occupied ex-Roman provinces or not. But it was Germanic ways that became the dominant cultural voice in Europe from CE 500 to 1000, meaning that, now, any similarities between Chinese and Western civilization all but ceased.

Some scholars state that the division of the Islamic, Catholic, and Greek Orthodox worlds was enough to preclude a reunification of Western civilization. But a closer look at the new Germanic traditions, as they blended with Greco-Roman and Catholic ideas in Europe, points to as pronounced an internal barrier to reunification as the rise of the Middle East and the survival of Eastern Roman Empire. What China achieved reflects the survival of the Confucian ideal as a workable state ideology that blended Confucianism with Legalism and Daoism, and animated Chinese politics after the fall of the Han. Hence, the Chinese systematically implemented a political philosophy specifically designed to enforce political traditions that attracted and held the full support of the Chinese people. In contrast, Europe was left with the Christian faith as a unifying belief system during the Middle Ages (CE 500–1500). But the medieval church worked diligently to establish its command of the spiritual world as superior to, and independent from, the state as master of the secular world. The church claimed that the transcendental spirit of God infused its institutions with divine power, which operated on a plain above that of the state. The state merely ruled the temporal world, which was the world of the flesh.

These distinctions claimed by the medieval church were consistent with the ancient Greco-Roman philosophical worldview that subordinated all matter to transcendental form as found in the Socratic worldview. And then, after the demise of the citizen, the *kosmopolite* shifted attention away from politics towards the universe. This was also the message embedded in Jesus' ministry when he declared: "Render unto Caesar what is Caesar's and unto God what is God's." Hence, medieval Europe placed political action and concerns of the spirit into two different institutional realms. And it was this division that joined Islam and Greek Orthodoxy to deny Catholic Europe the same potential for unity as found in China.

Furthermore, after the fall of Rome, Catholic Europe was left with a far less centralized agricultural base than China. Ex-Roman provinces could supply their own food requirements without the aid of a centralized state as required by China. Remembering that the Roman Empire relied on a highly diversified economy in which every one of its provinces could manage to feed itself if needed, the economic necessity for reunification was simply missing. Then, the invasion of Germanic tribes that splintered the Western Roman Empire added jealousy and warfare as barriers to reunifications, as each new medieval kingdom fought another to try to secure its new domains. Such political fragmentation imposed the requirement of developing local agriculture to fuel the armies needed to defend the emerging medieval kingdoms. Therefore, both politically and economically, the foundation for a reunification of one "Western civilization" in Europe no longer existed.

In contrast, China relied heavily on its traditional family-based system of agricultural labor to organize and perform the massive amount of labor needed to manage their powerful and dangerous rivers. Long ago in Chinese history, the people had learned that if they worked together, they reduced their chances of suffering disaster and increased their chances of generating abundant food surpluses. Well-established traditions and rituals still worked to remind the Chinese people of their mutual obligations to serve one another as they toiled away on very narrow patches of arable land in the land's two great river valleys. Family obligations, filial piety, a system of well-defined occupational names, and a formalized state ideology all reinforced common practices and time and again drew the Chinese back to a common set of political habits. Nothing like this intense integration of ideological beliefs and political actions existed in medieval Europe. Therefore, after the fall of Rome what was left of Western civilization in Europe had neither the agricultural base nor the set of political and religious institutions needed to draw Europeans back together and reunite them in a manner similar to China.

Now a new era of history began. For China, a golden age would emerge once the Chinese achieved reunification. Explored in the second half of this text, this new age for China would include major agricultural innovations along a set of population dynamics that would plague Chinese history. Continued philosophical speculations among Chinese scholars further synthesized political ideology with political action. And increasing nomadic pressures continued to pull the Chinese together. In other words, China would live up to its ancient ideals for much of the Middle Ages.

In contrast, Europe would fragment into rival political domains, the luster that once was Rome forever lost. Slowly, the Middle Ages (500–1500) would unfold. An eclectic mix of Germanic, Catholic, and Greco-Roman cultural features would fuse into a new culture that proved more dysfunctional than functional. During the Early Middle Ages (500–1000), Germanic customs found among the invading Gothic tribes would dominate the cultural landscape. During the High Middle Ages (1000–1300), medieval Europe would see the German tribes slowly give way to an emerging Christendom where the Roman Catholic Church would become dominant. Finally, during the Late Middle Ages (1300–1500), a Greco-Roman revival known as the Renaissance would mark the end of the medieval era. Post-Roman Europe would, therefore, seem to be the opposite of Medieval China: Europe, a shadow of its ancient past, and China, a superior expression of its ancient heritage. The history of this new age belongs to the second half of this text.

Notes

1   See The Steppe. *Encyclopedia Britannica*. http://www.britannica.com/EBchecked/topic/565551/the-Steppe
2   Dun J. Li. *The Ageless Chinese: A History*, pp. 3–4; Jacques Gernet. *A History of Chinese Civilization*, pp. 3–4; John K. Fairbank and Edwin O. Reischauer. *China: Tradition and Transformation*, pp. 3–4.
3   Gerard Chaliand. *Nomadic Empires from Mongolia to the Danube*, p. 7.
4   Christopher Beckwith. *Empires of the Silk Road: A History of Central Asia from the Bronze Age to the Present*, p. 22.
5   *Ibid.* pp. 26–27.
6   Gerard Chaliand. *Nomadic Empires from Mongolia to the Danube*, pp. 8–10.
7   Christopher Beckwith. *Empires of the Silk Road*, pp. 58–70.
8   Thomas J. Craughwell. *The Rise and Fall of the Second Largest Empire in History: How Genghis Khan's Mongols Almost Conquered the World*, p. 22.
9   Gerard Chaliand. *Nomadic Empires from Mongolia to the Danube*, pp. 10–11.
10 *Ibid.* p. 11.

11   This biographical account comes from Si-ma Jian's *Records of the Historian Si-ma Jian* as quoted in Gerard Chaliand. *Nomadic Empires from Mongolia to the Danube*, p. 22.

12   Paul S. Ropp. *China in World History*, pp. 25–27; J.A.G. Roberts. *A History of China*, pp. 29–30; Gerard Chaliand. *Nomadic Empires from Mongolia to the Danube*, pp. 23–24; Christopher Beckwith. *Empires of the Silk Road*, pp. 5–6 and 70–73.

13   John A. Harrison. *The Chinese Empire*, pp. 126–130; Paul S. Ropp. *China in World History*, pp. 27–28.

14   Gerard Chaliand. *Nomadic Empires from Mongolia to the Danube*, pp. 24–25; John A. Harrison. *The Chinese Empire*, pp. 127–128.

15   Gerard Chaliand. *Nomadic Empires from Mongolia to the Danube*, pp. 24–25; John A. Harrison. *The Chinese Empire*, pp. 127–128.

16   Paul S. Ropp. *China in World History*, p. 28; Gerard Chaliand. *Nomadic Empires from Mongolia to the Danube*, pp. 26–27; Étienne de la Vaissière. "Huns et Xiongnu," *Central Asian Journal*. Volume 49, Number 1. pp. 3–26. See Christopher Beckwith. *Empires of the Silk Road* for counter arguments, pp.72–73, and endnotes 51 and 52 on pp. 404 and 405.

17   Jared Diamond. *Guns, Germs, and Steel*, p. 169.

18   William. H. McNeill. *Plagues and People*, pp. 36–43; Jared Diamond. *Guns, Germs, and Steel*, pp. 202–214.

19   William. H. McNeill. *Plagues and People*, pp. 103–114; Frederick F. Cartwright. *Disease and History*, pp. 11–15; and Charles Freeman. *Egypt, Greece, and Rome: Civilization of the Mediterranean*, pp. 550–555.

20   William. H. McNeill. *Plagues and People*, pp. 117–120; John A. Harrison. *The Chinese Empire*. p. 180; Paul S. Ropp. *China in World History*, pp. 35–36.

21   Michael Rostovtzeff. *Rome*, p. 318; Charles Freeman. *Egypt, Greece, and Rome: Civilization of the Ancient Mediterranean*, pp. 592–604; John A. Harrison. *The Chinese Empire*, pp. 169–170, 180, and 210–211; Paul S. Ropp. *China in World History*, pp. 35–36.

22   John A. Harrison. *The Chinese Empire*, pp. 180–181; Paul S. Ropp. *China in World History*, pp. 40–41.

23   John A. Harrison. *The Chinese Empire*, pp. 181–184, Paul S. Ropp. *China in World History*. p. 37; Christopher I. Beckwith. *Empires of the Silk Road*, p. 85; Gerard Chaliand. *Nomad Empires from Mongolia to the Danube*, p. 27.

24   John A. Harrison. *The Chinese Empire*, pp. 169–170; Paul S. Ropp. *China in World History*, pp 41–44, The Kushan Empire, http://depts.washington.edu/silkroad/exhibit/kushans/essay.html, and Kushan Empire (*c.* 2nd century BC to 3rd century AD) http://www.metmuseum.org/toah/hd/kush/hd_kush.htm

25   John A. Harrison. *The Chinese Empire*, pp. 169–170; Paul S. Ropp. *China in World History*, pp 41–44; J.A.G. Roberts. *A History of China*, pp. 44–46.

26   John A. Harrison. *The Chinese Empire*, pp. 169–170; Paul S. Ropp. *China in World History*, pp. 41–44; J.A.G. Roberts. *A History of China*, pp. 44–46.

27 John A. Harrison. *The Chinese Empire*, pp. 169–170; Paul S. Ropp. *China in World History*, pp. 41–44; J.A.G. Roberts. *A History of China*, pp. 44–46.

28 John A. Harrison. *The Chinese Empire*, pp. 182–184; Paul S. Ropp. *China in World History*, pp. 41–44; J.A.G. Roberts. *A History of China*, pp. 44–46.

29 Paul S. Ropp. *China in World History*, pp. 41–44; Susan Wise Bauer. *The History of the Medieval World: From the Conversion of Constantine to the First Crusade*, pp. 13–20.

30 Paul S. Ropp. *China in World History*, pp. 37–39.

31 Emperor Trajan (reigned CE 98–117) conquered Romania (CE 101–102) in an effort to stabilize the Danube frontier, but the Emperor Hadrian (reigned CE 77–138) realized that Rome could not hold this new province and soon retreated back to the Danube.

32 Jane Penrose. *Rome and Her Enemies: An Empire Created and Destroyed by War*, p. 236; Charles Freeman. *Egypt, Greece and Rome*, p. 551.

33 Gerard Chaliand. *Nomadic Empires from Mongolia to the Danube*, p. 53.

4

Contrasting Medieval China and Europe

Unexpected Consequences

The fall of Han China and the Western Roman Empire left the institutions of both great civilizations in ruins. The Chinese, however, managed to retain a strong cultural heritage and a functional political ideology that drew them toward a common goal: the restoration of imperial rule. In short, the great civilization of the ancient era might have fallen, but the Chinese still firmly believed in their ancient imperial practices: they viewed their long history as a natural process of integration of the correct philosophical beliefs and cultural traditions. For the Chinese, these were beliefs that created the right balance between political, moral, and divinely sanctioned conduct. In addition, the eventual reunification of China seemed natural to the vast majority of Chinese people, who dedicated themselves to achieving this goal. Furthermore, by this time the thoroughly sinicized nomads who had conquered the northern half of the Han Empire shared these same goals and a common vision: China had properly decoded Heaven's secrets and had created the appropriate rituals needed to maintain order within their civilization.

But like every aspect of civilized life, the success of China at recovering its past led to unintended consequences. Tradition is behavior repeated time and again without question. A culture observes its traditions, and repeats its behavior, because it views such conduct as sacred. This being said, the success of the Chinese in recovering their ancient heritage also trapped them in that heritage. Although the hallmark of Chinese history is the dynastic cycle, the fact that this cycle renewed itself illustrates the

China and the West to 1600: Empire, Philosophy, and the Paradox of Culture,
First Edition. Steven Wallech.
© 2016 John Wiley & Sons, Inc. Published 2016 by John Wiley & Sons, Inc.

pitfalls of repeated behavior, without question. This is not to say that the
Chinese did not strive to improve on their traditions with each successive
dynasty, because this simply is not the case. But the Chinese were trapped
within the boundaries of these traditions, which they could not falsify.

In contrast, Western civilization lacked any such clear traditional bonds
between a generally held political ideology and a past imperial rule.
Although many medieval kings tried to create such a bond, no such resurrected empire materialized. Part of the reason for this failure was due to
the economic diversity of the old Roman Empire (see chapter one). Unlike
China, which required a unified political effort to feed its entire people,
each medieval European kingdom discovered it could produce the food it
needed locally to support itself. Another reason for this failure at reunification was the disintegration of Western civilization into an Islamic, a Greek
Orthodox, and a Roman Catholic cultural zone, each one of which viewed
the others with mistrust and hostility. Still another reason for the failure at
reunification was that the newly installed Germanic kings of the Middle
Ages fought one another as rivals for the premier political title of ultimate
ruler. This military contest produced so many combatants that it created
too many combinations of alliances for any one of them to prevail.
Finally, the failure to reunite was undone by the emergence of three
legitimate, feudal estates in Europe: those who fight (kings), those who
pray (priests, monks and nuns), and those who work (peasants). The three
estates separated the primary cultural functions of each kingdom into
different, and often, competing institutions.

One of the principal institutions of Medieval Europe was the Roman
Catholic Church. During the High Middle Ages (1000–1300), it worked
diligently to establish its role (shepherd of the spiritual world) as superior
and independent from that of the state (protector of the secular world).
The church made its claims to this superiority based on the assertion that
it served the transcendental spirit of God, and the state merely served the
temporal world of the flesh. Therefore, the clergy increasingly solidified its
stance concerning the separation of the church from the state. This divide
had, as mentioned, found coherent philosophical expression prior to the
fall of Rome in Augustine of Hippo's *City of God*: the church was the City
of God (eternal) and Rome was the city of man (temporary). This allowed
the former to take precedence over the latter and survive Rome's fall.
Augustine's theology then became a fundamental source to justify the role
of the medieval church during the Middle Ages.

But once again, like every aspect of civilized life, the failure of Europe to
recover its ancient imperial past led to unintended consequences. In this
case, the failure of medieval Europe to thoroughly recover its ancient past

also freed Europeans to engage in cultural innovations beyond what their ancestors had imagined. While the hallmark of Chinese history is the dynastic cycle, which speaks to the renewal and improvement of an ancient heritage, Europeans were now free to, and in some cases had no choice but to, break new cultural grounds. This is why historians divide the Middle Ages into three distinctive eras: the Early Middle Ages (500–1000) in which Germanic tribes dominated the historical record; the High Middle Ages (1000–1300), when the Roman Catholic Church captured the European imagination; and the Late Middle Ages (1300–1500), when Western European kings consolidated their power in the midst of a demographic crisis, even as the papacy failed to provide assurance of salvation. These institutional shifts in authority between the German tribes, the pope, and the king unleashed the Renaissance (1300–1600), which, in turn, saw Western civilization recover much of its ancient learning and ushered in critically important features of the modern era. In effect, the failure of Europeans in resurrecting their ancient, highly centralized form of civilization did not trap Europeans within the limits of their traditions. But it actually allowed them to falsify certain aspects of their heritage and emphasize new practices that completely reshaped their culture.

Revisiting the Paradox of Agriculture

Agriculture produced the food surpluses that fed civilization and allowed humans to reproduce in increasing numbers. The steady increase in number then created population pressures that every civilization had to resolve. Any such resolution, however, only sufficed until the next technological advance in agriculture, which always led to a growth in population and renewed population pressures. A civilization's need to feed could eventually place too much of a strain on a culture's institutions, or the resources of the local ecology, and cause that civilization simply to collapse. Or, the innovative powers of the human imagination might once again save a culture's means to feed its people and allow that civilization to thrive. Ultimately, there seemed to be a lurking concern that in the distant future agriculture might not produce sufficient food to feed everyone. Still, this is a problem that all civilizations have always had to address.

Agriculture creates a set of conditions that greatly influence all civilizations. These circumstances create "the conditions of possibility" for every human community. These conditions set the limits on what a civilization can do, based on the people the civilization feeds. This does not mean that agriculture causes a civilization to act in a certain way; rather, it nudges a culture in certain directions. The productivity of traditional Chinese agriculture supported the creativity that developed in China during the medieval era. This creativity made China the wealthiest civilization of the Middle Ages. Agriculture did not spawn Chinese creativity, it only made its creation possible, and Chinese culture itself generated the golden age described below.

Just as in China, medieval European agriculture created the conditions of possibility for Europe. These institutions then struggled with one another to define the boundaries of their legitimate authority. Agriculture did not cause the specific events that made up the history of this struggle; it merely fed the people tangled up in their disagreements. Agriculture fed the peasants who produced the food, as well as the artisan and merchant who ate the food surpluses and produced urban goods. Agriculture did not define peasant labor as legitimate and urban labor as illegitimate; rather, medieval men who commanded political and religious authority made these decisions. It was they who forced artisans and merchants to defend themselves and declared their activities as legitimate by creating laws and a legal system that changed the institutions of medieval Europe.

Herein lies the paradox of culture as embedded in agriculture. It creates the food that people eat. This food gives them energy. They use this energy to make their claims to political power and religious authority, or declare their philosophical insights, make their scientific discoveries, seek their social changes, or struggle to achieve economic success. Agriculture does not cause the people of a civilization to act in a certain way; it merely feeds the people. If food production stops, the people die, the civilization collapses, and that particular story ends. The paradox of culture is that agriculture creates the conditions for human success in food production that causes an increase in population, but then that civilization no longer has enough food. In other words, agriculture's successes might lead to civilization's failures.

With an understanding of the paradox of agriculture, one can move on to consider how the various farming communities adjusted to the demands of their different civilizations. These agricultural patterns have already been well established for both ancient China and Western civilization. Now one must wonder, what were the specific circumstances in medieval China and Europe that saw one civilization resurrect its ancient practices and the other fall into disunity? The answer lies in the creativity of both civilizations. The rulers of China opened the Grand Canal, a great transportation conduit that linked northern and southern China into one economy, and redefined land tenure through the implementation of the "equal-field system," launching an era of extraordinary prosperity. Europe acquired a new type of plow that made accessible land that the Romans could not cultivate and happened to enjoy the benefits of an era of excellent climate that helped to feed a revived civilization. The end result was a transformation in food production as well as the relocation of agriculture's center of gravity in both civilizations.

Taking the Chinese example first, the surviving Han people combined with completely sinicized nomads under just the right circumstances to overcome the barriers to reunification. This thorough assimilation of pastoral peoples into sedentary life found no equal anywhere else in world history. The result was a resilient culture that revealed a level of vitality that exceeded the accomplishments of the Han. This resilience fed off the productivity of southern China: the new agricultural source that supported Chinese civilization. The first signs of this resilience, and economic success, emerged in the rise of the Sui Dynasty in CE 581.

The Sui Dynasty (581–618)

During the 375 years of chaos that followed the fall of the Han Dynasty, the Chinese living in both northern and southern China expected a full recovery of imperial unity. A major cultural hurdle, however, stood in the way. The powerful aristocratic families in the south, who saw themselves as the guardians of traditional Chinese culture, denied union with the nomads of the north. These southern Chinese aristocrats looked upon the peoples of the assimilated nomadic tribes who ruled the north as lacking the necessary refinements of Confucian etiquette, ritual, and social norms. Meanwhile the people of the nomadic regimes of the north sought legitimacy by acquiring Chinese manners, names, and language. They possessed advanced military skills that the south lacked, and they tended to view the people of the south as decadent, weak, and pompous. The two groups' assessment of one another pitted the north against the south in a contest of domination that postponed the desired reunification. It seemed that only a great show of brute force could affect the common goal of restoring a unified China to imperial rule.[1]

By the middle of the sixth century,* China remained divided into four main political units. The Northern Zhou ruled the northwest, and the Northern Qi ruled the northeast. To the south, the small state of Liang ruled the middle Yangzi River valley, and the Chen Empire ruled the lands to the south of the Yangzi. The Northern Zhou and Northern Qi vied for

---

* Hereafter the absence of BCE or CE indicates that the date is in the CE.

control of the Yellow River, but the continuous threat of nomadic invasion from the northern steppe limited their ability to attack one another.

The principal threat of invasion along the northern border came from the Tujue people. They were Turks who occupied the Manchurian Plain. As long as the Tujue remained united under a charismatic leader named Tuobo (died 581), they continued to molest the Zhou and Qi. With the death of Tuobo, however, the Turks split into two realms and temporarily ceased their incursions, thus freeing the northern kingdoms of China to challenge one another for control.

Shortly before this pivotal development, the Northern Zhou had turned a blind eye to the risk of nomadic invasion and launched an attack on the Northern Qi. In 577, the Northern Zhou defeated and assimilated the Northern Qi. Then, four years later with the death of Tuobo, a freed and united north under the Northern Zhou turned its eyes toward southern China. By 589 the armies of the Northern Zhou had overrun the Liang Kingdom on the Yangzi and captured the Chen Empire, making them the rulers of all of China.

In the years during which the Northern Zhou were completing their conquest of the south, a small group of non-Chinese aristocratic families sat on the throne. One was the Yuwen clan, who held the throne in 580. Another was the Xianbei, which produced the next emperor of China, Yang Jian (lived 541–604; reigned 581–604).

Born and raised in a Buddhist temple, Yang Jian married a Buddhist woman from a prominent Xiongnu family and rose to power early in life. He won a military reputation in the Northern Zhou's campaign against the Northern Qi, and he arranged for his daughter to marry the heir to the Yuwen monarchy. When his son-in-law's father died, however, the son-in-law began to exhibit dangerously unstable behavior. This led Yang Jian to plot a palace coup and take power. Yang Jian's successful coup then sparked a civil war, but his selection of skillful generals and bureaucratic subordinates gave him the upper hand. With his victory over the Yuwen forces, Yang Jian decided to kill off all the members of this clan, eliminating 59 princes and their families. By 589, his conquest of China was complete, and the Xianbei clan now ruled a unified culture. Some eight years earlier (581), he proclaimed himself the emperor and began the new Sui Dynasty (581–618). As emperor, he took the imperial name Sui Wendi.[?]

Sui Wendi displayed considerable military talent in adopting the effective cavalry tactics of the nomads, and he quickly rebuilt the Chinese empire. He also proved to be a competent administrator by reconstituting a centralized imperial bureaucracy. Although he had scant regard for scholars, he reinstituted the imperial examination system. The exams occurred three times per year and awarded three levels of degrees. Successful candidates received appointments in the bureaucracy, which added to the ranks of the men Sui Wendi had already appointed. He then started construction of the Grand Canal (see below), which would revolutionize Chinese agriculture, and he established the "equal-field" system (also see below), which increased the total acreage under cultivation. Finally, he developed a household registry system to increase the government's access to accurate census information, and he used the data to develop efficient tax collection.[3]

Sui Wendi was skillful enough to rule uninterrupted until his death in 604, but his son, Sui Yangdi (reigned 604–618), was not such a talented leader. Consumed with a desire for imperial power and glory, Emperor Sui Yangdi sought to surpass his father in every way. Immediately upon taking the throne, Sui Yangdi undertook the construction of a new capital at Loyang; this despite the fact that his father had just finished building a capital at Chang'an. Sui Yangdi also rebuilt sections of the Great Wall of China, completed the construction of the Grand Canal (a major feat), and expanded China's frontiers. He also launched a disastrous war against Korea that consumed the men and resources of three major expeditions without success. His excessive commitment to construction and warfare thoroughly drained the government's coffers and the court's vitality. Like the Qin, he literally exhausted China, both financially and in terms of the expenditure of human life.[4]

Sui Yangdi's most important contribution to Chinese agriculture was the completion of the Grand Canal, the construction of which his father had, as mentioned, started. The Sui Dynasty focused its political and military resources in northern China to defend against nomadic invasion, even as Chinese agriculture was rapidly shifting into southern China. This move occurred because the south had been thoroughly colonized during the era of chaos that had immediately followed the fall of the Han. Sui Yangdi dedicated five years to the completion of the Grand Canal (605–610), in the process of which he conscripted somewhere between two and six million peasants. These workers dug new channels and connected them to the main canal that produced the longest inland waterway in world history. Once completed, the Grand Canal was over 1600 miles long and linked the tax-and-grain hungry garrisons and governmental offices in the north with the rich rice-producing fields of the south. In the process of completing the Grand Canal, however, Sui Yangdi had killed an estimated three million peasants over the course of five years.[5]

The completion of the Grand Canal only added to the enormity of overseeing issues of water management, something that only a strong central government could handle. And like the Great Wall, construction of the canal (in only half a decade) came at a staggering cost. The canal project alone might have financially exhausted China, but to couple it with the building of a new capital, the rebuilding of sections of the Great Wall, and the implementation of extensive military campaigns proved too much. Finally, by rounding up millions of men for forced labor and military services, Sui Yangdi threw the Chinese population into unbearable misery.

Within his lifetime, Sui Yangdi destroyed the accomplishments of his father. The last straw came with yet another of his military schemes: a simultaneous war against the Turks and the Koreans. Once again the powerful Tujue threatened China from the north, which required the full attention of the government from 581 to 615. Achieving victory would demand a combination of diplomacy, intrigue, and military prowess. But Yangdi's multiple projects left him unable to focus properly on the new and very real military threat. In 615, the Tujue reunited and cut off an army under Yangdi's command in the Ordos region, along the great northern bend of the Yellow River. It was only the actions of a young general named Li Shi-min, who proved to be an exceptionally talented officer that saved the life of the Sui emperor. But when Sui Yangdi returned to the capital, he faced a fresh rebellion in the south near Nanjing, an event that would mark the beginning of the end of his reign.[6]

The Tang Dynasty (618–906) and the Rejuvenation of China

In 617, the same young general who had saved Sui Yangdi on the Ordos plateau, Li Shi-min, launched a revolt in the north. Li was the son of Li Yuan who, in turn, was the governor of the large province of Shaanxi in north-central China. Li Shi-min was also the grandnephew of Sui Wendi and another member of the Xianbei clan. Li Shi-min managed to orchestrate the assassination of Sui Yangdi and claimed the throne for his father, Li Yuan. Li Yuan became the first emperor of the Tang Dynasty in 618. In that year, however, the Tang controlled only Shaanxi province. To capture the rest of China required a grand military leader. Establishing Tang rule throughout China therefore fell to the son, Li Shi-min, given that he was a highly talented general. From 618 to 621, Li Shi-min waged a bitter struggle to consolidate the Tang's hold on northern China. Once accomplished, Li Shi-min took the fight south, and from 621 to 624 struggled to add the south to the Tang's imperial realm. Thus, even though the Tang Dynasty officially began in 618, the reunification of China under the Tang's reign was not complete until 624, or 404 years after the fall of the Han.[7]

Although Li Yuan officially became the Tang's first emperor, the real genius behind the rebellion and reunification of China was his son, Li Shi-min. To this day, however, Li Shi-min's role in the actual rise of the Tang remains shrouded in controversy. Clearly, Li Shi-min's claim to power involved assassination and rebellion, and he went on to become the Tang's second emperor though murder and imprisonment.

Only two years after consolidating the Tang's hold on southern China in 624, Li Shi-min ambushed his older brother, Li Jiancheng, the crown prince, and Li Yuan-ji, a younger brother, at the Xuanwu Palace Gate, killing them both. Li Shi-min then forced his father, Li Yuan, into house arrest, where he remained until his death in 635. To justify these disloyal acts, Li Shi-min claimed that Li Jiancheng and Li Yuan-ji had been plotting to murder him, leaving him with no choice but to take drastic actions in self-defense. When one remembers, however, that it was Li Shi-min who had convinced his father to lead the rebellion against the Sui that established the Tang Dynasty in the first place, his murderous actions seem suspicious.

Nevertheless, the official histories of the Tang Dynasty record that Li Yuan was a vacillating father who lacked the capacity to lead decisively. These same records state that Li Jiancheng was a timid lad who also would not have had the capacity to rule capably, and that Li Yuan-ji was simply a debauched fool. These records also depict Li Jiancheng as jealous of Li Shi-min's military victories and bent on deposing the successful young general. They also state that even though he had concerns, Li Shi-min refused to act until 626, at which point he became finally convinced that in order to survive he would have to remove both Li Jiancheng and Li Yuan-ji. With his two brothers dead and his father removed from power, Li Shi-min went on to become Tang Taizong (reigned 635–649), one of China's most successful monarchs.[8]

As the first unquestionably competent Tang ruler, Emperor Tang Taizong, long since nicknamed the "green-eyed lad," had already established himself as a charismatic leader, an outstanding commander, and a brilliant administrator. Since nearly all Han people are noted for their black irises, clearly a green-eyed lad had come from non-Han stock. This reveals the degree of assimilation that had already taken place during the years of chaos (220–581) when China absorbed an ethnically heterogeneous population of (conquering) nomads into the existing Han population. A green-eyed emperor of a reunified imperial China also underlined the degree of cultural assimilation that must have taken place to raise a man of

Han-Turkish extraction to the seat of power. Like Sui Wendi before him, Tang Taizong represented the consequences of the post-Han "melting pot" era during which Han and non-Han peoples had intermarried for centuries. This period blurred the genetic and ethnic lines to create a new Chinese people of multi-ethnic origin.[9]

When he came to power, the immediate problem facing Tang Taizong was, in a sense, an old one: the Tujue Turks. The Tujue Turks were the nomads who dominated Tang foreign policy for 41 years after Tang Taizong's death. While it took him eight years to capture China, he was to spend the rest of his life fighting these Turks. His victories against them, however, ultimately were so thorough that his heirs brought China within sight of becoming the greatest empire in Eurasian history (see chapter six). The Tang Dynasty commanded a vast amount of territory, ranging from Korea and southern Manchuria in the north-east to Northern Vietnam in the south, and as far west as present-day Afghanistan. But as the Tang grew, its leaders realized that no amount of land acquisition offered sufficient barriers to threats posed by the people living on the northern steppe. No matter what actions a competent ruler took, China would always have to face confrontation with the nomads to the north.

The Tang Economy

The greatest single economic factor in support of the Tang Dynasty was the role of the Grand Canal in connecting the rich, rice-producing lands of the south with the war-torn provinces in the north. With the Grand Canal in place, southern China became the primary source of grain in Tang history; the south yielded the vast majority of all the food consumed by a reunited China. Now the Tang employed the Grand Canal to bring grain to its restored capital at Chang'an.

Chang'an was the political center of the Tang for several reasons, some of which seemed to be at odds with one another. The most practical reason for the selection of Chang'an as the seat of government was that it proved to be the best military site in the north, one from which a standing army could continuously face the nomads. The selection of a defensible location made sense in military terms, if not in economic ones. If one considers the cost of bringing food up to the capital from the south, then the Chinese might have wanted to move their political center from the Yellow River down to the Yangzi River. Such a move would have eliminated the expense of transporting grain over 1600 miles, which indeed became a major drain on the economy. But removing

money/(transport)
vs
protecting
the North

the capital farther south would, of course, have reopened the north to nomadic invasion.[10]

Given the fact that Chang'an grew into the largest city of the medieval era, with an estimated population of a million people living within its walls, and another million living in its suburbs, the expense of feeding its residents was enormous. If the Tang emperors had chosen to relocate their capital, say to Nanjing or Hangchow, the cost of supporting the government would have fallen significantly. But then, of course, the armies of China would have been in the north fighting the nomads, while the emperor was in the south administering the land. The loyalty of China's commanding generals might have been called into question, which would have undermined the power of any sitting emperor. This proved to be a conundrum that none of China's dynasties would be able to solve.[11]

Another practical reason for keeping the capital in the north was easy access to the Silk Road, the premier trade route of Eurasia. The great Silk Road started in Chang'an and cut northwest through the Tarim Basin. This meant that Eurasian commerce, and access to essential warhorses, required a defense of the strategic oases located within the basin. Also, since the residents of Chang'an lived on imported southern rice, the state had to ensure that a regular supply of grain reached the capital from the Yangzi to keep this trade route open. One key concern of Tang Taizong, therefore, was land reform.[12]

The entire financial system of Tang Taizong's state, as well as that of his early successors, depended on how the Tang's subjects used the land. In theory, the state owned all the land. This meant that the Tang could define land tenure. Thus, one of the immediate goals of Tang Taizong's regime was to bring all of China's arable land back under cultivation; the state made every effort to transform all of the acres that had fallen into disuse due to warfare back into productive fields. Also, the state provided financial support to all the peasants currently working their land and producing food. For example, the state made low-interest loans to poor farmers to prevent them from falling into debt to moneylenders charging excessive fees.[13]

The Tang also modified the land use pattern first implemented by Emperor Sui Wendi's "equal field system." The equal-field system that Sui Wendi oversaw had not, as already mentioned, originated with him. It had begun during the Wei Dynasty (386–534) as part of the ex-nomads' transition from herding to plant cultivation. As a land tenure scheme, the equal-field system bestowed 80 *mu* of state-owned land on every adult male; ownership of the land reverted back to the government after the death of the adult male. A Sui *mu*, however, differed from a Zhou *mu*

(1046–256 BCE). The Sui *mu* was 0.15 European acres, while a Zhou *mu* had been 0.00056 acres.†

In other words the Sui *mu* secured a small farm of twelve acres for every adult male in a family, which led to the creation of large farms, whereas the land holdings of an entire Zhou family came only to 15 acres. Most significant, the Sui's equal field system gave each male an additional 20 *mu* of *personal* land that could be *inherited* by the adult male's heirs. Old and sick adults in Sui peasant families received 40 *mu* of state land, widows 30 *mu*, and, as landowners, both received 20 personal *mu*. Buddhist priests and monks received 20 state *mu*, craftsmen 10 *mu*, and merchants 10 *mu*. Additionally, every three individuals, or five slaves, in a household received 1 *mu* of orchard land. The amount of land lent to Chinese families increased substantially if they held aristocratic rank, but none of the state *mu* could ever be sold. Inheritors, however, could sell personal *mu*, but only after the death of the original recipient. Buddhist monasteries became economic powerhouses under this system of land distribution because they sheltered thousands of eligible monks. Ultimately, the distribution of all this state land achieved its goal: the conversion of thousands of nomads from a dependence on herding to plant cultivation. Sui Wendi had simply continued this system, but he also expanded it and managed it in such a way as to secure a reliable tax base.

The Tang increased the land grants started by Sui Wendi. They allotted 100 *mu*, at 0.15 acres per *mu*, to each peasant male between the ages of 21 and 59. This was an increase of 20 extra *mu*. The family of this peasant could inherit one-fifth of this estate, while four-fifths reverted to the state upon the death of the peasant. Given the Chinese practice of raising sons who remained within an extended family, this practice led to large farms compared to ancient Zhou standards. Each peasant family paid an annual tax on their land holdings in the form of grain, cloth, or labor. The amount paid by the head of each household depended on: the fertility of his fields, the size of his family, and the location of the estate. The inherited one-fifth of the estate could not be sold because the state did not want huge farms to grow out of any failed smaller ones. The method of allocating the one hundred *mu* was complex: fertile fields had to be balanced with pastures and woodlands. Besides the land used by peasants, the government owned acreage that could be rented out to those who wished to use it to make extra income and for the pasturage of large herds. Military outposts on the

---

†The change in the size of the *mu* from the Zhou to the Sui Dynasty reflects the impact of the iron plow. The introduction of this tool increased the efficiency of a peasant's labor, seeing much more land come under cultivation in less time.

northern frontier also received land on which the garrisoned soldiers were expected to produce their own food supply.

So long as the Tang Dynasty's rulers remained vigilant and the population remained small enough (this in light of a high death rate thanks to waves of epidemic disease, famine, and warfare), the system worked well. Its economic rationale was to increase food production, keep estates in the hands of peasants, and allow these peasants to cultivate their holdings for their own benefit. A separate, partly political, partly economic objective was for the state to retain control of the land. Yet, as the size of China's population grew due to the stability created by Tang Taizong's regime, internal flaws in the system began to bubble to the surface. As prosperity increased, so, too, did the number of peasants and their family members. And as their numbers increased, so, too, did the demand for the allotted 100 *mu* of land. Eventually there was not enough land to go around, especially when each successive generation of peasant families retained 20 percent of a Tang farm. Slowly the long-forbidden practice of the sale of land eroded, and huge estates began to reappear. With the increasing size of these estates, more land was taken out of the recycling pattern, further undermining the functionality of the equal field system. And in light of all the additional land that the Tang continued to bestow on the old, the sick, widows, women and children, monks and nuns, and artisans and merchants (as had the Sui), the amount of available acreage declined even further and the recycling process broke down.[14]

The other drawback to Tang Taizong's land-tenure system was the additional allotment of land granted to state officials. These men received large estates, ranging from a few *qing* to 100 *qing* (one *qing* equaled 100 *mu* or fifteen acres). These privately owned acreages became inheritable estates. And since there was a steady increase in the number of state officials over time, an ever-increasing number of acres became unavailable for peasant use. In addition, service to the state meant that the official did not have to pay his full share of taxes. But to take the land owned by such a person off the tax rolls was to reduce the income of government by the very people that supposedly served the state. At the same time, the cost of administering China grew in proportion to the size of the population, even as available land for allotments in the equal field system continued to decline.[15] Making matters worse, all of the land that the large monastic orders had accumulated under the equal field system ceased to be taxed.

This situation shifted a disproportionate amount of the revenue burden on those peasants still using their state-owned plots. Hard pressed in the first place, these peasants began to work on the lands of state officials to make ends meet, or they sold the one-fifth of their estate illegally. As the tax burden increased on peasants, they fled to the protection of land magnates with official connections in the hope of escaping from their onerous revenue obligations. This process eventually destroyed the equal field system and allowed for the reappearance of wealthy landowners controlling vast tracts of land in a kingdom with limited arable acres.[16]

Whenever large estates began to reappear in China, the wealth accumulated by the growing number of landed magnates became linked to the imperial examination system that prepared candidates for imperial appointments. Large estates provided the means to support the sons of wealthy landowners to study and take the exams. Since Tang Taizong had maintained this system of recruiting state bureaucrats, Tang officials, imperial exams, and landed estates became thoroughly intertwined. Once a scholar-candidate acquired a post in the bureaucracy, he could use his influence to reward his father or patron for supporting his studies. This meant that, gradually, the foundation of Tang agriculture, the privately operated peasant farm, disappeared. This also meant that the vested interests of the imperial regime, the bureaucrat himself, who was supposed to safeguard against such land ownership erosion, actually participated in it. Slowly the wealth of China's agriculture slipped from the state's fingers into the hands of wealthy landlords.

The steady erosion of the tax base due to the gradual failure of the equal-field system reduced state revenues, while external nomadic pressures continued to increase. The loss of royal income and the burdens of command gradually undermined the will of Tang leadership. It was easier to enjoy the pleasures of the imperial harem than face the troubles of the state. Eighty-six years after Tang Taizong took power, the internal flaws within the equal-field system combined with mounting nomadic pressures to overwhelm a Tang emperor. Emperor Xuanzong (reigned 712–756) began his reign well, but the burdens of state, and the beauty of one woman, Yang Guifei (one of China's "four great beauties"), undermined his ability to rule. He became enamored with Yang Guifei's charms and showered her with favors. He elevated members of her family to positions of power despite their incompetence. Then, defeat on the battlefield against new Islamic forces expanding east overwhelmed Xuanzong's administration, and the Tang began its long downward spiral.

The combined incompetence of members of Yang Guifei's family and the rising new Islamic powers in the Middle East, caused chaos near the end of Xuanzong's reign. In 750 the spread of Islam in the Middle East[‡] created

---

[‡] The Islamic forces that defeated the Tang at the Talas River grew out of an expansion generated by the Umayyad and the Abbasid Dynasties. These two Arabic tribes produced the caliphs, or the successors to Muhammad, that built the Middle East.

a military barrier to Chinese armies expanding their western frontier. This led to a major confrontation in 751 near Samarkand, an oasis city just north of modern Afghanistan. The local Tang army and the Muslims met on the Talas River, where the Islamic forces annihilated their opponents. This military setback broke the Tang's hold over its outposts in Central Asia. They withdrew their forces east, leaving behind only scattered garrisons to protect their western holdings. This new state of affairs gave Central Asian nomads the initiative in warfare (see chapter six). Finally, rebellion in 755 forced Xuanzong to flee Chang'an, but not before his bodyguard insisted that he execute Yang Guifei, since it was she whom the people held responsible for China's woes.[17] Yet the downward spiral of the Tang, once started, could not be stopped.

blame
ti women

The Song (960–1279): The Golden Age Continues

The complete collapse of the Tang Dynasty did not occur until 906, which indicates the ability of China's vast network of local governments to function even as the empire fragmented into pieces. The Song Dynasty (960–1279) was the next to assume central authority, replacing the Tang some two centuries after the disastrous events of the 750s. The Song Dynasty, however, did not officially begin until 54 years after the fall of the Tang. The very short gap of a half-century between the fall of the Tang and the rise of the Song indicates the hold that the traditional mechanisms of power had gained on the Chinese imagination after 906. When the Han Dynasty collapsed in 220, it took the Chinese 375 years to reestablish their imperial forms of government, but the Song replaced the Tang in 54 years. While the Song did manage to restore imperial rule, it was a substantially smaller empire then that of the Tang. Nonetheless, the Song's economy proved to be more than equal in productivity to the larger Tang.

To deal with the constant nomadic threat along China's northern frontier, the Song chose to use a professional army. This was a military development of the late Tang era that came into use to replace drafted peasants. Raising the funds needed to pay for a standing army of professional soldiers, however, required an expansion of the Song's agriculture, a move that turned out to be one of the major hallmarks of the Song Dynasty. Between 700 and 1100, the Chinese economy developed along the Yangzi River and raised levels of production that matched those of England at the beginning of the eighteenth century. This extraordinary economic development sustained a dynamic system of production and trade that raises questions as to why the Chinese did not undergo an industrial revolution. To answer this question, one must consider what the Song economy achieved, and then look at Chinese culture to see just how predisposed it was to spontaneous industrial change.

The Song Economy

The Song economy excelled in five major categories. The first was agricultural productivity. This the Song achieved through a program of internal colonization all along the course of the Yangzi, where rice cultivation had started. Internal colonization was a distinct Chinese process of bringing farmers into a region and preparing unused farmland for cultivation. During the first two centuries of the Song, migration south accelerated. More and more peasants moved to the Yangzi to engage in rice cultivation. This migration into southern China caused an expansion of rice paddies upriver, while Chinese peasants improved their techniques of wet farming. They developed the capacity to plant and harvest two crops instead of one during a single growing season. To ensure soil fertility, the Song also engaged in a form of agroecology, the method of rendering human waste safe for use as a fertilizer for food crops. The Song converted human feces into fertilizer through a process whereby they dug pits, filled them with human dung, and allowed the heat that accumulated within the pits to kill the pathogens in the dung and neutralize its odor. They discovered that if the temperature in these pits reached 150°F, then within 24 hours the human feces was safe to use.[18] The Song peasant next spread the rendered human waste on their fields to ensure bountiful harvests twice a year. This development created what scholars called a "Green Revolution (i.e. a radical increase in food production)."[19]

The early Song began this green revolution with policies designed to help peasant farmers. The first two Song emperors, Song Taizu (reigned 960–972) and Song Taizong (reigned 976–997), distributed food relief and seeds, published manuals on cultivation, attempted land reform, and added tax exemptions to aid peasant farmers. By the time of the third and fourth Song emperors, Song Zhenzong (reigned 997–1022) and Song Renzong (reigned 1022–1063), conditions for peasants had improved substantially. But the momentum of agricultural change had begun to level out, and huge farms slowly started to absorb smaller ones during Song Renzong's reign. The Song had begun to slip into the Tang's pattern of land magnates and tax-exempt estates.[20]

The second economic development entailed advances in waterborne transportation. The Song developed an integrated system of canals and waterways that laced together regional productive specialties and generated many pockets of lively local trade. At the same time, the Song improved on shipbuilding by developing vessels with watertight chambers. They also added navigational devices such as the compass, and they connected river commerce with oceanic voyages that brought a substantial supply of foreign goods into China.[21]

The third area of economic development centered on the establishment of currency and credit. During the Tang, the state continually ran short of copper to coin new strings of cash. The Song solved this problem by turning to a paper currency backed by an expanded mining of copper (see below). The supplies of copper during the Song were 20 times greater than during the Tang. Added to the new paper currency system were promissory notes and instruments of credit that facilitated transactions and did not require an immediate metal money supply to back their value.[22]

The fourth economic change introduced by the Song was the sheer volume of trade itself. The Song had managed to link their rural output with urban manufacturing so that primary goods such as food, raw materials, and fuel joined manufacturing and the luxury trade to create a fully articulated system of exchanges. Unlike any other dynasty up to the Song, commerce developed as a branch of exchanges that did not become a target for punitive taxation. Back in the sixth century BCE, Kong Fuzi (Confucius) had stated in the *Analects*, "The gentleman understands what is moral, the petty man understands what is profitable."[23] This Confucian quote indicated a major distrust of trade: the gentleman was a selfless, noble scholar, and the petty man, a selfish immoral merchant. The Han and the Tang Dynasties had interpreted this passage to mean that they should control merchants with punitive taxation. They developed taxes similar to the "sin" tax used in Europe. This practice tended to drive wealthy merchants out of commerce and into investing in land, which was held in higher regard. The Song Dynasty did not impose such punitive taxes on trade. They saw the benefit of a lively commerce as part of a fully integrated economy. One consequence of this change in taxation was an expansion of Chinese urbanization. A peculiar side effect, however, was that the Song maintained the same ratio of people living in cities to those working the land common to all Chinese history, 1 to 9. Now, however, commerce and food production grew hand in hand.[24]

The fifth and final important development in the Chinese economy took place over the course of both the Tang and the Song: an emphasis on technological innovation. During this golden age, all manufacturing expanded rapidly, with technical improvements taking place throughout China. Print block moveable type and rag paper facilitated the making of paper currency. The invention of gunpowder produced a high explosive that redefined mining and increased the supply of copper. Watertight locks made the development of canals a common practice. And the development of a fine porcelain assigned China's name to high quality table settings called "china." How these innovations fitted into the developing Song economy can be seen in iron production as a specific example. Coal replaced charcoal as a fuel to work iron. Hydraulic machinery replaced manual bellows to blow air through the new fuel. And the use of gunpowder permitted the expansion of new tunnels in mines to allow greater access to ores. Taken together these innovations allowed iron production to generate 114,000 tons of metal compared to 68,000 in England in 1788, nearly 800 years later.[25]

The extraordinary successes of the Song in integrating rural food production with urban manufacturing and trade raises an interesting question: why did the Song fail to have an industrial revolution? The five major economic areas of expansion undertaken during the Song certainly suggest the possibility of such a revolution. The answer to why such an event never occurred during the Song Dynasty requires some historical speculation.

First of all, the Chinese were deeply enmeshed in a traditional mindset that emphasized repeating expected behaviors without question. This outlook spurred the great increases in the food supply and manufactured goods during the Han, Tang, and Song Dynasties without the interjection of any modern ideas. It also produced a system of labor based on an exceptionally strict work ethic within well-established occupations. The yields of the traditional Chinese division of labor in the Middle Ages matched England's productive yields on the cusp of the Industrial Revolution in the eighteenth century, and this without having to abandon any well-established practices. China's advantage, however, was its use of a far larger population in a much larger realm.

Second, during the formative years of the Han Dynasty, the Chinese had integrated a Confucian, Daoist, and Legalist synthesis of beliefs into a cohesive ideology that dictated the limits to traditional state action. In other words, the Chinese did not venture outside their own worldview, or its sources, save for the import of Buddhism, to adjust their traditional outlook.

Third, the Song, like the Tang and the Han, had a highly integrated political state that participated directly in the Chinese economy as a producer, licenser, and consumer. Song rulers had the power to legalize the production of any item they chose. They licensed all enterprises, and they bought whatever they wished so as to move a product from one market to another within China. In effect, the state defined the boundaries in which the individual producer could act. These rules set limits on innovation and restricted the possibility of spontaneous change.

Fourth, the Song economy followed a traditional pattern of the distribution of wealth. Over time, the limited supply of arable land in China, and the natural tendency of the peasantry to produce as many children as they could feed, pressed food production to it limits. Then, as a growing population drove the peasantry into a perpetual state of poverty, money-lenders and rich landlords snatched up smallholders' farms in order to build vastly expanded estates. These new land magnates then used their massive holdings to finance more loans and to educate their sons and protégés for the imperial exams. With sons and protégés in the state bureaucracy, tax-exemptions to large estates reduced state revenues and the Song repeated the same errors of the Tang.

And, lastly, once established as the legitimate dynasty, the Song restricted individual freedom in a manner similar to the Han and the Tang. Everyone in China understood Chinese philosophy to the degree that they all understood that correct behavior relied on well-established traditional relationships. In China, a person derived his or her identity from their name. The family name defined occupation and place in society. The personal name placed the individual within the family by gender, birth order, and the rank of the mother in her relationship to her husband. For an individual to change his occupation through industrial innovation would require abandoning the filial relationships assigned to him by name.

Taken all together, the reasons for the continuity of tradition sited above explain why the Chinese produced such spectacular productivity but did not have to or want to extend their technical and economic innovations into an industrial revolution. Both the Tang and the Song are examples of vast successes achieved by a traditional society. The rise and fall of each dynasty marks a common pattern of failure within Chinese tradition, but does so without invalidating any of its successes. This is why the Chinese had come to expect the recovery of unification after the fall of each dynasty, as well as why the nomads on the frontier chose to accept this tradition and assume a Chinese identity through the process called sinicization. No culture could match China's productivity during the medieval era. This wealth both fed and maintained China's reunification.

The wealth generated by the Tang and the Song provided the economic foundations of a golden age. The completion of the Grand Canal and the use of the equal field system supported the early Tang and defended the frontier. The major increases in agricultural output combined with a massive expansion of trade during the Song to create a fully integrated Chinese economy. So long as the economies of both dynasties functioned as intended using imperial rule, the surplus wealth needed to maintain order in China flourished. Problems arose only when internal contradictions within each economic system surfaced. For example, when the Tang Dynasty watched its equal-field system erode and land magnates reappear, then the burden of the state could no longer match the external pressures ever present on the steppe. In the case of the Song, the rigidity of traditional practices limited the possibility of spontaneous change and visited upon China the same erosion of the tax base that plagued the Tang. Hence, the golden age of both dynasties ended for common cultural reasons that boiled down to tradition: repeated behavior without sufficient questioning of conduct ultimately undermines a regime.

A Nomadic Interlude

In the twelfth century, a nomadic tribe similar to the Turks, called the Mongols, lived across the Central Asian Steppe in scattered encampments. To think of the Mongols as a separate ethnic lineage apart from the Turks, however, is inaccurate because of several shared practices. Large steppe tribes such as the Mongols and the Turks systematically kidnapped women from one another for rape then marriage. They also exchanged male and female slaves, fostered shared alliance, and coerced military recruitments. Highly mobile populations such as these two nomadic communities knew no boundaries and intermixed among one another.

Like the Turks, the Mongols spoke a similar Altaic language, comprised a large population of about 700,000 people in the 1100s, but did not produce towns, fortresses, or sedentary farms. Divided by clans that together formed tribes, the Mongols, just like the Turks, were a family of people without any system of government. Leadership came from charismatic rulers who inspired sufficient loyalty to win elections as the great khans. Without such a leader, however, these scattered encampments remained divided, often suffering from internal blood feuds caused by kidnapped slaves, raped wives, and forced recruitments. Yet, it was the Mongols who, under the inspired leadership of several charismatic rulers, ultimately produced China's next dynasty: the Yuan.[26]

The Yuan Dynasty (1279–1368) captured power in China in stages that spanned three generations of rulers. As each generation came to power, ever-greater portions of China fell under its control. The Mongols eventually took command of the Han people, however, without having experienced a high degree of sinicization. This absence of acculturation to Chinese ways made the Mongols an anomalous population to lead such a major sedentary civilization. In other words, they had not yet adjusted sufficiently to a sedentary existence, or completely grasped Chinese culture, to successfully run such a civilization for any length of time. This explains why the Yuan Dynasty produced the shortest era of imperial rule: a mere 89 years. These nomads tried to rule the Chinese people, but ultimately did so with only marginal success.

The Mongol conquest of China began with the reign of a particularly charismatic leader known as Genghis Khan (1162–1227). He, however, did not establish the Yuan Dynasty. In 1211–1227, he conquered most of northern China but did not fully understand the people he was about to rule. He did, however, display good judgment. He placed a sinicized Qidan nomad named Yelü Chu Cai (1189–1243) in charge of his new domain. Then Genghis Khan turned his attention to conquering all of Central Asia's steppe lands (see chapter six for the details).

Yelü Chu Cai worked for the great khan as a secretary and advisor. Yelü Chu Cai immediately had to block efforts by Genghis Khan's relatives to convert Chinese farmland into pasturage. He succeeded in doing so, but not before poor nomadic leadership had already led to a level of economic chaos. The temporary replacement of grain production with livestock by Mongol local rulers caused an immediate loss of food surpluses that resulted in famine. The problem of the general famine they had caused did not seem to bother these nomads, for, as they saw it, the purpose of conquest was to displace defeated people, acquire wealth, and use the newly gained land as they pleased. In addition, in their rampage across Eurasia the Mongols developed a reputation for "glorious slaughter,"[27] something that makes an estimate of all the people they killed extremely difficult, because they viewed death by conquest and occupation as a natural part of the human condition. Fortunately, Yelü Chu Cai was able to reverse these poorly thought out actions, but only after the conquered northern Chinese had suffered considerable pain.[28]

When Genghis Khan died, Ögödei (1186–1241) became the second great khan. This new generation of Mongols left southern China largely unmolested, while completing the conquest of the north by 1234. Ögödei would not go on to establish the Yuan Dynasty, either. He, too, focused his appetite for conquest on lands adjacent to the northern steppe. He did so by sending one of Genghis Khan's grandsons farther west. This Mongol general was Batu, who extended Genghis Khan's empire deep into present-day Russia and Eastern Europe. Meanwhile, Yelü Chu Cai persuaded Ögödei to use northern China as a rich tax resource, by exploiting its productivity in grain cultivation rather than in the raising of livestock. Under Ögödei's rule, Yelü Chu Cai was initially given a free hand to use rational agrarian principles for both governing and taxation. The result was the emergence of a very strong sinicized state centered in Dadu, today known as Beijing. Dadu gave the Mongols easy access to the steppe on China's northern frontier for purposes of defense. The style of rule Yelü Chu Cai imposed was military in nature, since the Mongols did not distinguish between civil and military branches of power. He also converted northern China into a system of feudal estates ruled by prominent members of Ögödei's family.

As the Mongol expansion into northern China continued, the rich city of Kaifeng along the central Yellow River fell in 1233 (again, see chapter six for the details). This victory allowed the Mongols to capture a large number of Chinese civil servants to run the newly acquired territory. Ögödei took advantage of these Chinese scholar-bureaucrats to re-establish the Confucian competitive examination system on the advice of Yelü Chu Cai. Slowly, a Chinese bureaucracy started to become a counterweight to Mongol misrule. In time, however, a powerful anti-Chinese faction at Dadu tried to overrule Yelü Chu Cai's efforts at sinicizing the Mongol regime in China. One of their tactics focused on taxation. This anti-Chinese group opposed Yelü Chu Cai's rational tax program based on yearly food surpluses in favor of "tax farming." Tax farming was a method of raising taxes whereby the state sold the right to collect revenues from a province to a "tax-farmer." After this agent paid a lump sum to the state, the "tax-farmer" was then free to take as much wealth from the province as he wanted. This disastrous system lasted until 1251, when Kublai (1215–1294) became the third-generation ruler of northern China. Kublai restored Yelü Chu Cai's original tax program.[29]

Under his administration of northern China, Kublai maintained a true Chinese system of agriculture in which northern China recovered its productivity and became the chief source of wheat and millet production for Karakorum, the Mongol capital on the Mongolian steppe. In other words, from Dadu, Kublai fed Karakorum, which had grown so large that food from northern China was necessary to feed the new capital of the Mongol empire. A dispute in 1260, however, broke out between Kublai and his younger brother, Arik Böge, as to which one of them would be the next great khan of the entire Mongol empire. Arik Böge won the election held to decide the matter, but strife between the two brothers intensified into open warfare that threatened to disrupt the Mongol domain. Then, in 1262, a drought struck the steppe north of China and destroyed the grass supply needed to feed the Mongols' essential animals. As Mongol herds and their horses began to die, the role of Chinese wheat and millets increased in importance. This catastrophe placed intense pressure on Arik Böge to surrender the title of great khan because northern China did not suffer a similar shortage of food. Without Kublai's grain, the Mongols of Karakorum would have starved, which gave Kublai a strategic advantage. Left with no choice, Arik Böge capitulated to Kublai in 1263, and the Mongols called a *quriltai*, the assembly of leaders that elected their great khans.[30]

Circumstances had elevated Kublai to the post of great khan. One of Kublai Khan's first acts was to exile his younger brother from Karakorum: Arik Böge left the Mongol capital, retreated onto the steppe, grew ill, and died in 1266. Kublai Khan's poor treatment of Arik Böge, however, ultimately shattered the unity of Genghis Khan's empire. Hülügü, another of Genghis Khan's grandsons, had conquered much of the Middle East; he broke away from Kublai Khan's rule to take over Mongol control of Afghanistan to the border of modern-day Turkey. Möngke Khan, Batu's son, took command of Russia. And Kublai Khan found himself left with Siberia and northern China. He therefore turned his attention to the conquest of southern China. From 1266 to 1279, Kublai Khan engineered the capture of the Southern Song (1127–1279). Then, in 1279, Kublai Khan claimed the Mandate of Heaven (for all the details of this conquest, see chapter six). It was Kublai Khan, therefore, who established the Mongol, or Yuan Dynasty of China. However, Kublai Khan's new regime retained a great flaw: its fiscal policy.[31]

Kublai Khan instituted a dual tax system. In northern China, the Mongols levied either a head tax based on the number of taxable adults, or a land tax based on the number of acres under cultivation. The tax they imposed depended on which one would yield the greatest revenues. In southern China, the Mongols kept in place the Tang system of taxation: a twice-yearly levy on rice. On top of these taxes, Kublai's empire used a paper currency that he instituted during his initial rule in the north. As long as Kublai Khan reigned, this use of paper money worked, for he employed Muslim financial ministers who carefully restricted the amount of paper money in circulation to match the supply of goods. After Kublai Khan died, however, such fiscal restraint disappeared and the value of Mongol money collapsed.[32]

Before he died, Kublai Khan decided to impose a system of inheritance to transfer power from one Mongol ruler in China to another (see chapter six). The use of the *quriltai* had proven too disruptive in Mongol imperial history to maintain a stable Chinese dynasty. Each time a great khan died, the Mongols assembled their notables in a *quriltai* to elect a new leader. The political rivalries that played out during these elections tended to disrupt military campaigns, resulting in considerable bloodletting. Kublai Khan therefore preferred the Chinese method of succession, inheritance, so he chose an heir apparent to the throne, Temür Khan, before Kublai died. Temür Khan was Kublai Khan's grandson (reigned 1294–1307), and he followed in his grandfather's footsteps. He ruled wisely, but he did not have any sons to whom he could transfer power according to the tradition Kublai Khan had tried to establish. What followed was a succession of eight different emperors in twenty-six years and sheer chaos (see chapter six).[33]

The Mongols never fully understood what it took to run a sedentary civilization. Out of all the Yuan emperors, Kublai Khan and Temür Khan alone exhibited the skills to manage a complex agricultural society. Together their two reigns amounted to only 28 years of effective rule (1279–1307). This means that the Mongols created an unparalleled episode in Chinese history that one can only describe as a nomadic interlude. Their incompetence as Chinese emperors was evident to the Chinese people when the Yuan failed to dredge the Yellow River. The river flooded disastrously in 1300, changed course, and drove millions of Chinese farmers from their homes. Decades of agricultural disruption followed this disastrous flood because the Yuan's efforts at controlling the Yellow River with dams and dykes failed. By 1352, Mongol abuses in printing paper currency (they printed more than could be backed by metal or goods) denied the Yuan Dynasty the resources to bring the Yellow River under control. Peasant rebellions then followed, as it was perceived that the Yuan had clearly lost the Mandate of Heaven.[34]

The Mongols ruled for an insufficient amount of time to have truly become a Chinese dynasty, and part of their legacy was the development of an intense hostility among the Chinese toward "barbarians." This hostility translated into a new xenophobia in which the Ming Dynasty (1368–1644) imposed a version of China's political ideology and traditions with a new level of rigidity. This rigidity further trapped the Chinese within the bounds of their established traditional practices and undercut the high level of creativity displayed during the Tang and Song Dynasties. The paradox of Chinese culture now had a firm grip on the Chinese imagination: repeated behavior without question exacerbated the internal contradictions in the Chinese lifestyle.

Evolution of Feudalism during the Fall of Rome

Ancient Western agriculture reached its apex during the imperial half of Roman history (30 BCE–CE 476). Yet prior to this era, agriculture underwent a gradual if thorough change. In the years preceding the civil war that destroyed the Roman Republic (133–31 BCE), the rise of latifundia infused the agrarian system with numerous slaves. So many were held in bondage that the number of slaves within the Roman economy came to make up a significant part of the empire's population. Although estimating the total number of slaves living within the empire is a very difficult thing to do, the most common figure at which scholars arrive is approximately one-third of the city of Rome's population and somewhere between two to ten percent throughout the provinces. Since Rome housed approximately a million people, the slaves within the city made up an estimated 300,000–350,000 people. In the provinces, 2 percent of 60 to 70 million people is 1.2 million at the low end, and 10 percent is 7 million at the high end. These figures, however, refer to the period during which the empire had reached its maximum size, prior to the cycle of plagues that devastated the population on several occasions.

Yet, once the empire stopped expanding, the number of slaves began to decline. Most scholars observed that Roman slaves did not reproduce their own numbers because their masters often segregated them by sex in separate barracks. Also, for many slaves, their will to live proved less powerful than their opportunities to reproduce. This means, for example, that when the Antonine and Cyprian plagues hit (between 164 to 189 and 251 to 268 respectively), more slaves died than free people, who had a stronger will to survive. As a result, and the addition of new provinces, remained the only way Rome could maintain its huge pool of slave labor.

By 117, Rome had added the last of its new provinces. These included Britain, and the temporarily controlled Dacia (modern Romania). Roman farming after 117 continued to use slaves on latifundia in Italy, North Africa, and Egypt. Away from these areas peasants worked small and medium-sized farms. This made Roman cultivation consistent with its ancient roots, even if viable citizenship had already ceased to exist. Roman manuals on cultivation argued that slave labor worked best on those farms large enough to allow the production of commercially valuable crops such as grapes and olives. Peasants, then, were the ones who grew the staple food crops.[35]

The latifundia continued to function, but when slave numbers declined, replacements became necessary. Since the empire had reached its maximum size by180, the slave population began to erode shortly thereafter. Increasingly, Roman agricultural texts began to refer to farm labor on these large plantations as *coloni*. Originally, the term meant tenant farmers or renters who held a lease. Over time, the *colonus* status became an inherited position in the Roman economy. But during the fourth and fifth centuries, under Emperors Diocletian (reigned 285–305) and Constantine (reigned 313–337), the *coloni* became trapped on the land. Both emperors issued edicts that fixed occupations and compelled everyone to register his location for tax purposes. By 390, the *coloni* had become serfs (i.e. peasant labor bought and sold with the land). This meant that when owners sold their land, their *coloni* went along with it as part of the same sale. After 390, *coloni* could not sue their landlords, could not serve on Roman juries, and could not serve in the army. Also, they could not take holy orders to become a priest.

Although serfdom appears to be very similar to slavery, unlike slaves, serfs were free to marry, raise a family, and transfer any privileges they had to their offspring though inheritance. Despite the fact that a serf's life was far worse than free peasant labor, serfs had far more to live for than did slaves. Serfs survived in greater numbers than slaves due to the ability to form families, which was something slaves could not do. Also, serfs did reproduce their numbers as a matter of choice, a power slaves lacked. And, lastly, serfs proved to be a viable replacement for the slave population that Rome had lost.

These late imperial edicts, and the serfdom they created, reveal that Rome required *coloni* to remain in their villages (see below). The goal was to assign these newly minted serfs to landlords to secure their labor, while also stabilizing the tax base. By the end of the fourth and beginning of the fifth centuries, the Roman Empire had developed both secular and church estates that operated on this form of trapped farm labor. Called *villa*, these new proto-feudal plantations became increasingly common throughout the empire; in addition to fixing the labor force and tax base, they also came to function as strongholds for protection against increased nomadic raids. Small and medium-sized farms joined one another to form villages of agrarian labor that served a common *villa* by providing food in exchange for protection. Such estates also became self-sufficient sources of subsistence as trade eroded due to the breakdown of Rome's defenses. From 300 to 500, the empire began to fragment, and local populations were left to fend for themselves. Peasants living at the subsistence level felt that little had changed since they had long suffered poverty as part of their daily lives. As conditions grew worse, however, more and more farmers bound themselves over as *coloni* on *villas*, and barter replaced currency.[36]

As mentioned in chapter three, the breakdown of the Roman Empire due to nomadic pressures and internal decay had compelled the Emperor Diocletian to divide the state into two halves in the fourth century. The Western half developed its own tax base, had its own emperor (an augustus) and its own heir apparent (a caesar). The Eastern half also had the same set of rulers. Although Emperor Constantine briefly reunited the realm during his reign, the East/West division became permanent after 337. Now, each half of Rome's divided regime faced its own military threats. The German tribes that followed the Visigoths into Rome after 378 occupied a significant portion of the Western half of the Empire. The Eastern half survived as the Byzantine Empire, but first faced a Persian threat and later an Islamic one. The fragments of what was once a massive, 2.2 million-square-mile Roman regime splintered into three cultural zones: Greek Orthodox, Islamic, and Roman Catholic. The Western Roman Empire broke apart, and numerous new political units emerged during the Middle Ages. Each of these new political units fashioned a new military, social, and economic agreement called "feudalism" in the European (and Roman Catholic) portion of what had been the Roman world (see below).[37]

Medieval Agriculture: The Rise of Feudalism

The confinement of Western civilization into northern, central, and western Europe saw its farmers have to make major adjustments to, what for many of them were, new climatic and soil conditions. Europe north of the Alps was unlike the Mediterranean world that had fed the ancient peoples of Western civilization. The prevailing winds of northern Europe carried moisture from the Atlantic to all lands north of the Loire River in France and the area north of Istanbul in Turkey. Every few days, in these northern climes, powerful storms drenched the soil, a pattern of precipitation that differed significantly from the mild, rainy season of the Mediterranean world. This year-round, heavier precipitation soaked a heavily forested landscape and presented waterlogged mud to the Romans. They could not grow wheat or barley in this landscape because both plants tended to drown in the wetter conditions. Colder winters also inhibited moving agriculture, as the Romans had practiced it, into these northerly regions. The beginning of a warm period that lasted from 800 to 1300 created better circumstances for a positive change in the state of cultivation in what was left of Western civilization. These new conditions, however, meant nothing until the introduction of a new type of plow and the rise of a new a system, feudalism, took hold. Only then did agriculture in northern Europe begin to flourish. The new type of plow was known as the moldboard, while the new political/agricultural system of feudalism also provided a new kind of military protection from nomadic incursions for those who worked that land and their rulers. [38]

The Moldboard Plow

Long in use in China, the moldboard plow made its way into Europe via
the nomadic migration of the Franks and Anglo-Saxons who had used it
to cultivate the thick soils of Germany east of the Rhine River. As mentioned in chapter one, the plowshare of a moldboard cuts, lifts, and turns
the soil. Pulling this type of plow through the soil made small mounds of
earth in the damp fields of northern Europe. These small mounds provided elevated soil above the waterlogged mud, and prevented the wheat
and barley seeds planted in the mounds from being swamped in the
drenched landscape before they had a chance to sprout. In contrast, the
Roman plow, the ard, merely scratched the surface of the soil. Use of
the ard had worked well in the thin soils and semi-arid landscape around
the Mediterranean Sea, where wheat and barley could grow during the
mild winters, when most of the annual rainfall caused these plants to
germinate. Wheat and barley then grew until the dry season began in
spring, the summers being so hot the hard-baked soils were unfit for
planting. So while the ard was of little use to the northern farmers, the
moldboard plow functioned well by elevating wheat and barley just
enough to create the dry conditions both plants needed. This allowed
the Franks and the Anglo-Saxons to transport Roman crops onto soil that
the Roman plow could not have turned.[39]

Dragging a moldboard plow through the heavy soils of northern Europe,
however, required a great deal of force in order to overcome the friction
generated in the process. Therefore the use of the moldboard plow required
the combined strength of several draft animals assembled into a team, which
necessitated that peasants pool their resources. In addition to this new technique of using the moldboard plow, medieval Europe saw the development
of a new village based agricultural system where peasants could assemble
their tools and animals for a form of cultivation that benefited everyone.

The Horse Collar and Horse Shoes

In addition to the moldboard plow the other technological innovations
included the horse collar and horseshoes. Use of the horse collar and
horseshoes converted the horse into an effective draft animal, largely
replacing the ox. A team of horses proved faster and more efficient than
oxen in plowing fields, giving these new draft animals a greater capacity to
increase the land under cultivation each year.

Prior to the advent of the horse collar, oxen dragged the moldboard
plow through farmlands using the two-field system. The two-field system

had farmers cultivating one field and leaving the other one fallow. The fallow field rested, the weeds that inevitably grew becoming fertilizer when plowed under during the next growing season. The following year, farmers alternated fields: cultivating last year's fallow field, and resting the cultivated one. This meant that the use of oxen caused farmers to waste 50 percent of arable land.

With the introduction of the horse collar, however, Europeans developed the three-field system. Now the farmer could cultivate two fields simultaneously while leaving the third fallow each growing season. This system only left 33.3 percent of the estate fallow (and out of production) at any given time. It is important to note that these changes did not begin to take place until the tenth century, when they finally opened up land left previously unused by the Romans. This fact has much to do with the great violence experienced by the people of medieval Europe in the period after the fall of Rome and up to year 900. So, even though it is indisputable that the use of the moldboard plow, horse collar, and horseshoes greatly changed European history, once begun, it took several hundred years for this style of cultivation to come into common use.[40]

Feudalism

Local protection from nomads came from the newly developed military system that modern historians called "feudalism" (also see chapter five). Using the new bits, reins, and stirrups developed by Turkish and Mongol nomads mentioned in chapter three, the Germans developed a new form of heavy cavalry we call "knights." These soldiers could withstand the assaults of nomadic marauders and provide protection to local farmers, but such armed guards were expensive. Also, since money had fallen out of use with the collapse of the Western Roman Empire, payment for these soldiers came in the form of landed estates. Each estate included a fortified stronghold, the peasants and animals needed to pull a moldboard plow through the fields, and the food surpluses required to feed all the people involved. Such a system took four centuries to develop, from 500 to 900. Once in place, the peasants that used the moldboard plow felt secure enough to pool their draft animals and work as teams to cultivate the land.[41]

As fortune would have it, medieval European agriculture and feudalism began to spread into northern Europe just when a change in the climate seemed to welcome the new civilization. Indeed, the fall of Rome and onset of the Early Middle Ages (500–1000) happened to coincide with a major shift in the European climate: a cold era ended in the year 800, with a warm one lasting from 800 to 1300. This saw Rome's omega plants cross the Alps into northern Europe and a new growing environment at just the right time. Still, climate, the land, and the bounty of the sea set the limits on the newly emerging medieval European economy. Even with the change in climate, agriculture north of the Alps remained a tenuous affair, as the success of the venture depended heavily on the vagaries of the climate. Droughts, severe winters, and unseasonably wet summers could destroy entire harvests; several bad growing seasons in a row could, and at times did, spell disaster. In addition, the annual harvest defined the fortunes of people high and low: kings, popes, lords, vassals, priests, monks, nuns, artisans, and peasants. Nevertheless, the new and increasingly more stable weather conditions Europe experienced from 800 to 1300 served as an unqualified blessing for the medieval European farmer.[42]

Summer after summer produced warm weather in June, just at the time when growing wheat and barley ripened, and then continued into July and early August. Hectic days of cutting and gathering grain followed, and rich food surpluses began to fill Europe's storage silos. With surpluses of carbohydrates collected, the northern European poor who lived off the land now had time to supplement their diet with proteins they acquired from engaging in large-scale fishing, hunting, and livestock raising. Meanwhile the wealthy found time to participate in their political and military adventures as they tried to shape the medieval state. In hindsight one can see that the complex contractual conditions that matured into the system known as feudalism received the food surpluses it had needed to develop at just the right time.

By the ninth century, life in medieval Europe reached a refined state in which the serfs now had a fairly clear picture of their role in society. Administration of the land arose from royal or papal grants that bestowed estates on noblemen and the clergy. The king commanded the secular world, and the pope shepherded the soul. These grants of land created feudal proprietorship by splitting the *title* of the land from the *possession* of an estate: the grantor retained the title, but the grantee gained possession. This laid the foundation of the lord-vassal relationship among the kings and nobles. Barons (from *baros* meaning men), knights, bishops, and abbots took possession of the land and leased out their holdings to *villeins* (serfs). Villeins worked the soil on scattered holdings that the moldboard plow defined.

The European moldboard plow required a team of 4–8 draft animals to pull it through the thick, heavy soils of northern Europe. This plow would not be owned by one serf family. As mentioned, teams of peasants had to pool their resources. Thus, one day's labor only prepared "the long acre," a strip of land 16 yards wide and 220 yards long, for cultivation. Each serf within a team using the moldboard plow would receive his long acre by turn at the end of each day. If a team comprised ten serfs, each serf's strips of long acres had nine other long acres in between. These scattered holdings within one of the fields of the three-field system produced food that belonged to more than one lord. By the eleventh century, the average European serf was a member of a complex community that provided food for several powerful men in the new feudal network. Labor services constituted the rent paid by the serfs for the protection they received from each lord. The rigidity of this agricultural system tolerated few additions to the population, since this pattern of land use had come into existence at a time when human numbers were declining. Hence, feudalism was very sensitive to the population pressures caused by the warm period from 800 to 1300.[43]

The Impact of Climate and Medieval Agriculture on Feudalism

Because the warming trend in medieval Europe proved so beneficial for agriculture, the population soon exceeded what the system of feudalism could absorb. To understand how agricultural prosperity impacted feudalism, one must see the latter as a legal, social, political, and land-tenure system. The legal aspect of feudalism used binding, lawful contracts between lords and vassals to define possession of the land in exchange for military service. The social portion centered on the "status" assigned by an "estate," granting a person his rank and defining a military, ecclesiastical, and occupational position in society. The political feature linked a political "state" to the same "estate" that made one the legal synonym for the other. The land-tenure issue granted an individual command over the land as a source of agricultural production to sustain a local estate/state/ status within society. Each aspect of feudalism fitted into the economic, political, social, religion, and/or military make-up of a kingdom.[§]

Such a system could only tolerate one heir per estate in order to define a clear system of religious authority, political power, military duties, and economic viability. Too many surviving offspring would require dividing estates beyond their capacity to function. Therefore, the feudal system adopted by medieval Europe could not absorb a growing population.

As a result, the high numbers of surviving offspring in feudal society during the warm era from 800 to 1300 saw feudalism break down and grow dysfunctional. This eventually led Europe to a transition from the

---

[§] In feudal law, an estate was a state and a status. Hence the possession of an estate made its owner a state with a specific status.

Early Middle Ages (500–1000) to the High Middle Ages (1000–1300). The curious feature of the failure of feudalism was that it required families to expel excess sons into a world of expanding estates and new occupations in order to survive. This led to a flowering of culture.

During this new, bountiful era, a revival of Western culture began that eventually lifted Europe out of the collapse of antiquity, through feudalism, and into a vibrant new civilization (see chapter five). Growing populations saw Europe expand to find new estates on which to perpetuate the necessary agricultural growth. This era of expansion, however, proved to be one that witnessed great violence. The survival of too many sons and daughters produced by powerful nobles and poor serfs alike, needed an outlet to absorb the extra numbers that feudalism could not absorb. The sons of knights soon exited Europe in a cycle of wars known as the Crusades, which saw the Islamic world begin a retreat south out of Europe. Muslim-controlled lands shrank permanently in Spain, Portugal, Italy, and Sicily and temporarily in the Levant (the Holy Lands). In addition, the movement of surplus peasants onto new farms saw the opening up of ever more fields for cultivation, which of course also increased the population in Europe. Now, portions of this booming population moved into towns and cities, seeking new opportunities. The revival of the urban settings of Western civilization stimulated medieval commerce, so that a whole new realm of occupations that existed completely outside the feudal hierarchy emerged. These were occupations based on the recovery of money as an economic tool. Money, however, still existed outside the legitimate realm of feudalism (also see chapter five).[44]

Internally, a power struggle began between the pope and the Holy Roman Emperor during this new era of prosperity. Prior to this rejuvenation of culture, from 500 to 1000, the role of the king/chief as warlord and defender of his tribe was critical: he provided protection from continuous nomadic incursions. The most powerful of all the kings of Europe, the Holy Roman Emperor, ruled a set of estates that formed the bulwark of defenses against nomads invading Central Europe from the Eurasian steppe. Part of his royal power was the right to appoint the bishops of Central Europe, including the pope. During the High Middle Ages (1000–1300), however, the nomadic threat diminished. Now the church rose to a pre-eminent place in society, as the keeper of souls. The papacy successfully argued that the soul was transcendental, the body only temporal; therefore, the authority of the pope should exceed that of the king. Reinforced by the developments in theology that occurred with the appearance of colleges and universities, the pope prevailed in his struggle for power over kings (see chapter five). His greatest victory came against the Holy Roman Emperor.

To understand the magnitude of this struggle, one must understand the arena of the contest: the Holy Roman Empire was a massive collection of estates that ranged from the Netherlands through Germany, into Italy, Austria, and Hungary. This struggle between the pope and the Holy Roman Empire divided the territories of central Europe into two camps. At first it was a contest between the pope and the emperor, but soon it evolved into a struggle between two armed factions: the Guelphs versus the Ghibellines. The Guelphs comprised the pope, his allies in Bologna, Florence, Genoa, Milan, and Naples, and the Dukes of Saxony and Bavaria. The Ghibellines comprised the Hohenstaufen family, heirs to the Holy Roman imperial throne, their loyal German vassals, and the island of Sicily. The struggle began in the eleventh century and lasted into the fifteenth century, concluding with a papal victory. What triggered the struggle in the first place was, as mentioned, the decline of the nomadic threat from Eurasia, and the struggle of the rival parties as each side insisted that its authority was supreme.[45]

The Emergence of a New Medieval Economy

As the pope fought the emperor for power, new villages and towns sprang up all over Europe. Villeins cut back forests at the request of their lords. Some landlords freed their serfs as an incentive to move them to new estates, and competing lords sought new farm laborers to work their freshly opened fields. Warmer summers and milder winters allowed small communities to cultivate even marginal acreage and work fields at higher altitudes. Lands in England, Scotland, Germany, and Scandinavia that previously had been considered unusable came under the axe. Felled forests and damp moors began receiving the efforts needed to bring former "wasteland" under cultivation. Primary goods (i.e. food, fuel, and raw materials) from the land not only fed local populations but also provided a new class of artisans with the resources they needed to produce urban goods and put them into commercial circulation. Money to make purchases reappeared, while guilds (licensed workers' associations) sprang up to supply both necessities and luxuries. Service rents (rural labor for military protection) gave way to monetary fees, so that lords, bishops, and abbots acquired the money they needed to make the purchases they sought to run their estates. Emerging colleges and universities joined the growing urban communities as new establishments designed to serve a rejuvenated population seeking the answers to life's basic questions. In short, a general renaissance took place before the Renaissance that marked the beginning of the modern age.[46]

The Late Middle Ages (1300–1500)

The fragility of medieval agriculture struck home, however, when seven weeks after Easter in 1315, sheets of rain transformed the fields of Europe into giant quagmires. The late spring deluge continued through mid-summer and into the fall. Entire stands of wheat and barley drowned where they stood, leaving the would-be harvest rotting. In the wake of this catastrophic event, food shortages swept Europe, leaving thousands starving, though not dead. As it turned out, this horrible year signaled a change in the climate that continued into 1316 and lasted to 1321. During this short period more than a million and a half people perished from starvation, while all across Europe those who survived did so in a weakened state, susceptible to disease. This was the beginning of the mini-ice age that marked the second era of medieval agriculture (1300–1500). Famine set in motion a period of death, one that the spread of the bubonic plague would shortly accelerate. Rats carrying the fleas infected with the strain of bacteria responsible for the plague spread what soon came to be called the Black Death, from China to Europe via the Silk Road from 1300 to 1347. After 1347, and continuing until 1352, the Black Death continued its rampage throughout Europe, killing an estimated one-third of the total population and causing a major demographic crisis.[47]

Demographic crises have the potential to undermine a culture's internal organization, setting it up for collapse, the fall of Rome and Han China being cases in point. But such a crisis might also spur a major social, political, and technological realignment within a civilization's institutions. Such was the case in Europe during the Late Middle Ages (1300–1500). During these two centuries, the most significant political development among many was the aforementioned shift in the relative power of the church as compared to that of the state. This shift in power resulted in part from medieval Europeans looking to the pope for guidance during what were especially bad and frightening times. Ultimately, however, when it appeared to the people that the pope failed to deliver what was needed, power began to shift back toward the kings.

During the Late Middle Ages, the demographic crisis that linked famine to the bubonic plague signaled to many people that God was angry with Christendom. Naturally, this directed their attention to the papacy for answers. The papacy, however, had just suffered a major series of setbacks that undermined the authority of the pope. These setbacks included the Babylonian Captivity and the Western Schism, which nearly destroyed the pope's credibility and redirected the people's attention from the papacy to kings.

The Babylonian Captivity of the Papacy and Western Schism

The Babylonian Captivity** lasted from 1309 to 1378 and removed the papacy from Rome, relocating it in Avignon, France. This kept the pope safely away from volatile Roman politics that plagued the election of popes, but also created a French bias in papal policies. This French bias became critically important as France went to war with England and each country fought the other from 1337 to 1453 (i.e. the Hundred Years' War). This brutal and lengthy conflict caused the English and their allies to condemn the papacy as an ally of France.

During the 69 years of the Babylonian Captivity, famine, plague, and warfare worsened. The people of medieval Europe began to interpret these three causes of death as the coming of the Apocalypse, the triumph of good over evil, and the end of the world. The four horsemen of the Apocalypse, famine, pestilence, warfare, and death, were supposed to signal the end of the current age, as long promised in the last portion of the New Testament, called Revelations. Late medieval Europe (1300–1500) saw God's rage at Christendom as having grown to the point when the beginning of the end was at hand. Soon, a spiritual crisis developed and hardened.

This spiritual crisis troubled Europeans, who wondered if the pope should return to Rome to free himself of his French bias. The return of the papacy to Rome finally took place in 1377, but it led to an even greater papal catastrophe, known as the Western Schism. The returning pope, Gregory XI (reigned 1370–1378), arrived in Rome in 1377, and then died one year later. His death caused the papacy to face a sudden, unfortunate vacancy in the volatile Roman environment. The cardinals, most of whom were now French, thanks to the papacy's lengthy stay in Avignon, concluded that for their own safety they should elect an Italian pope, and chose Urban VI (reigned 1378–1389).

As it turned out, however, Urban VI disliked the French composition of the College of Cardinals. Once he took up his office in Rome, he purged the College in order to select priests of his own liking. The dismissed French cardinals retreated to safety in Avignon, declared Urban VI's election null and void, and promptly selected a second pope, Clement VII (reigned 1378–1394). Clement VII took up residence in Avignon, and now two popes reigned in Europe. Each newly elected pope declared his papacy as the only legitimate one, which of course eroded the authority of both. The rest of Europe did not know which pope was the truly ordained Vicar of Christ.

** The "Babylonian Captivity of the Papacy" is the name used by some historians to describe the Avignon Papacy.

As the Hundred Years' War raged between France and England, the French monarchy naturally aligned itself with the Avignon papacy. The English king clearly preferred the Roman pope. Meanwhile, the rest of Europe picked sides. Scotland, Castile and Aragon joined France, and the Holy Roman Empire, Italy, Austria, Hungary, Poland, and Scandinavia joined England. Two major reform movements began that anticipated the Reformation (1517–1648) by rejecting papal authority: the Lollards of England, and the Hussites of Bohemia. Both would be suppressed by the papacy after the Western Schism was resolved in 1418 during the Council of Constance. At this council, the great churchmen and kings of Europe assembled in an attempt to reform the Catholic Church. They would restore the papacy to one pope, but fail to change the major flaws within the church.[48]

The Rise of Royal Power in Western Europe

While the Hundred Years' War continued, the kings of England and France proceeded to consolidate their holds on their realms. The institutional developments in France and England that facilitated the prosecution of the war produced significant political changes. Among these changes was the creation of a stable coinage to pay for mercenary soldiers, the development of regular taxation to keep the war chests funded, and the establishment of a standing army to enhance the centralized power of both monarchs. The assembly of the great notables of both realms in their respective *parlements*,[49] the Estates General of France, and the Parliament of England, helped to create a proto-national identity. And the inclusion of the bishops and great lords in both *parlements* brought church and state politics in line with the king's will, as the papacy remained divided. The resolution of the war in France's favor, with the French king driving the king of England off his French estates, clarified territorial policies in both countries. Now, the English focused on what served their island realm best, while eliminating their king's determination to dominate French politics. Also, removing the interest of the English crown from its vast holdings in France allowed the French king to rest easier in clear command of his domain.

Parallel to the developments in England and France were similar military actions undertaken on the Iberian Peninsula. There, protracted warfare in Catholic Spain and Portugal against the Muslims (known also as the Moors) produced similar institutional changes. Both Spain and Portugal also developed a *parlement* to fund a standing army, standardize coinage, and impose regular taxation in both countries. This modernization also created a similar sense of territorial sovereignty, as the papacy suffered through the Babylonian Captivity and the Western Schism. Portugal, Spain, England, and France then underwent a common, Western European process of political consolidation, one that enhanced royal authority over the church.[50]

Social Changes

Every walk of life in European society responded, in its own way, to the demographic crisis of the Late Middle Ages. The largest burden fell on the peasantry, which made up nearly 90 percent of the population and produced the food that fed those of all other ranks and occupations. The high death rate from famine and plague cut deeply into the peasantry, but the demand for their labor remained as strong as ever. Some lords expected their surviving peasants to continue to produce at the same levels achieved prior to the demographic crisis. Others, however, used the loss of so many of their peasants as an excuse to clear their land completely and make room for livestock. Kings and princes of large and small states alike imposed higher taxes on their peasants. They hoped that the higher tax revenues would cover the costs of their inflated political ambitions as they struggled to consolidate their holds on their realms. Soon peasant rebellions erupted throughout Europe, the beleaguered poor rising up in protest against the injustices imposed by their rulers.[51]

Meanwhile, the journeymen artisans living in the cities of Europe were not fairing much better than the peasants. The artisans did, however, have the advantage that the demand for their labor continued despite the thinning of their ranks, but the guild masters who controlled the journeymen laborers got used to windfall profits as survivors flocked into towns and cities to purchase goods in celebration that they had survived. These guild masters refused to share their new wealth with their workers, and hostility soon arose among journeymen, with spontaneous episodes of violence erupting in the cities.[52]

This widespread discontent among the peasants and journeymen artisans led to a new level of warfare triggered by social injustices. In 1323–1328, the peasants revolted in Flanders against excessive taxes imposed by the ruling count. In 1358, the peasants of France rebelled for several months against the taxes levied to pay for the Hundred Years' War. In 1378, the textile workers in Florence revolted against the government of the town, in which guild masters had imposed regulations on wages. In 1381, English peasants rebelled against the nobility and crown for the excessive taxes of the Hundred Years' War. In all cases, those in power put down the rebellions. The poor lost in their attempted rebellions because they lacked the skills of effective organization, planning, and capable leadership. The peasants and journeymen were also unwilling to attempt to take the highly radical measures needed to change society. They simply wanted to restore the lives they had known and enjoyed before the demographic crisis.[53]

The nobility also changed substantially in the wake of the demographic crisis. As their rents declined sharply with the death of so many of their peasants, they felt their social and economic standing eroding. In addition, invasion from the east began to threaten Europe, as the Mongols created the second largest empire in world history during the thirteenth century (see chapter six). Finally, the church had failed to provide adequate spiritual guidance during the demographic crisis, due to the Babylonian Captivity and the Western Schism.

But even in the face of all this change and instability, the nobility still had access to power and chose to use their political clout to force their peasants to compensate for the lost rents. Legal action taken in *parlements* fixed rents on surviving villeins that compelled them to work harder than ever. Also, when sheep began to replace crops on land cleared in the wake of the plague, *parlements* sanctioned such actions. Furthermore, these same *parlements* fixed wages that artificially reduced the cost of production and kept prices on luxury items low. Besides *parlementary* actions, organized and armed campaigns against peasant and artisan rebellions reinforced the will of the rich to have their way in maintaining their standing in society.

Finally, the *bourgeoisie* (urban artisans and merchants that came to form a new, middle class) acquired new social and economic standing. By the fifteenth century, the death rate from the plague slackened and things began to improve. Towns had, in a sense, benefited from the changes wrought by the crisis. Surviving townspeople typically fared better than those living in the countryside, even in troubled times. This was because those living in towns made money in occupations that could respond quickly to new circumstances when compared to the rigidity of feudal, rural life. Merchants from the northern port cities of Germany formed a trade alliance known as the Hanseatic League and gained control over trade in the Baltic and North seas. In addition, well-established commercial network cities linked Flanders to northern Italy via the Rhine River, seeing the merchants living in northern Italian cities maintain an iron grip on the Mediterranean trade. Increased wealth in the medieval towns of Western Europe created an emerging class of people who gained political clout by forming corporations. They petitioned kings and princes for royal charters that legalized the existence of their corporations. Members of these newly minted legal bodies began to link their prosperity to the taxes they paid, which their rulers acknowledged as highly valuable. New business practices, especially in banking and finance, facilitated royal ambitions, thereby linking the prosperity of towns and cities with the royal consolidation of power. Improved record keeping facilitated transactions that allowed for full compensation in commercial actions for those towns and cities engaged in trade. The rising income of those whose wealth existed outside the legitimacy of land, compelled the king, the church, and the nobility to reconsider the role of money in a newly prosperous realm (see chapter five).

Contrasting Systems: A Unified China versus a Fragmented Europe

As this chapter shows, the system of food production in medieval China proved far less fragile than that of medieval Europe. As a result, the Chinese had the material means to return to imperial rule and a pragmatic political ideology that served them very well. They also created a centralized administrative and military system that waxed and waned throughout the course of each successive dynasty. This oscillating system produced a spectacular level of wealth unmatched by any other culture in Eurasia during the Middle Ages. New dynasties gained absolute control over food production only to lose it eventually, when population pressures and a growing number of large, landed estates began to enjoy too many tax exemptions and grow wealthy and strong, as the government grew poorer and weaker. Nonetheless, no other system of political control and food production in the medieval world could match the wealth that China managed to achieve.

Ironically, the spectacular successes of Tang and Song China would end up trapping the Chinese in their traditional practices. Then, the dysfunctional nomadic interlude known as the Yuan Dynasty reinforced China's commitment to its ancient heritage. Finally, the resurrection of that ancient heritage during the Ming Dynasty (1368–1644) carried with it a new level of rigidity and xenophobia (see chapter six). This mindset would cause China to abandon the innovative spirit of the Tang and the Song Dynasties in favor of repeated behavior, as is common in tradition. The loss of China's creative flexibility enjoyed during the Tang and the Song would reduce China's prospects of maintaining its place as the wealthiest culture of Eurasia after the fall of the Ming, after which a largely isolated China would slip behind Western civilization as the latter, freed from tradition due the failure of its institutions, began to modernize.

Over the course of the same era, Western civilization retreated north across the Alps into medieval Europe, surrendering the wealth of its eastern and southern provinces to the Byzantine Empire and the Islamic world. This relocation of Western civilization into Europe, with its different soils and growing conditions, necessitated the development of a new system of food production, one using new types of technology and draft animals. In time, the integration of Germanic practices with the surviving trappings of Greco-Roman and Roman Catholic culture created a system of agriculture that rested on feudal contracts rather than imperial rule. Coupled with the separation of church and state into two legitimate estates, feudalism produced parallel systems of land tenure, one vested in kings, princes, lords, and vassals, and the other dedicated to popes, bishops, abbots, priests, and monks; the division ensuring a thoroughly divided political landscape. From this setting a series of changes began spontaneously within medieval European culture.

These spontaneous changes reflected a combination of circumstances and dysfunctional medieval institutions that resulted in modernization. Climate, timing, and an overlapping system of rival estates produced just the right social, economic, political, and religious conditions for medieval Europe's traditional culture to erode. Climate aligned a warm era from 800 to 1300, with abundant crops and growing population pressures to produce a series of institutional adjustments that left the traditional boundaries of feudalism behind. Then a cold snap followed from 1300 to 1500 and caught medieval Europe with a maximum number of people just when crop failures, plague, and a dysfunctional papacy compelled Europeans to realign their loyalties towards kings. Finally, proto-national consolidation patterns in Western Europe led to the rise of a new political structure of power in France, England, Spain, and Portugal that laid a foundation for the beginning of the modern era. Now, only a parallel adjustment had to be made within the balance between the Greco-Roman, Roman Catholic, and Germanic elements found in medieval European culture to unleash a theological and philosophical re-evaluation of Western civilization. This parallel intellectual development is the subject of the next chapter.

Notes

1   Paul S. Ropp. *China in World History*, p. 50; J.A.G. Roberts. *A History of China*, p. 46.
2   Paul S. Ropp. *China in World History*, p. 50; J.A.G. Roberts. *A History of China*, p. 46.
3   *The Sui Dynasty (581–618)*; Paul S. Ropp. *China in World History*, pp. 51–52; J.A.G. Roberts. *A History of China*, pp. 48–49.

4   Paul S. Ropp. *China in World History*, pp. 51–52; J.A.G. Roberts. *A History of China*, pp. 48–49.

5   Paul S. Ropp. *China in World History*, p. 51.

6   J.A.G. Roberts. *A History of China*, p. 50; Paul S. Ropp. *China in World History*, p. 52–53.

7   John A. Harrison. *The Chinese Empire*, p. 215; J.A.G. Roberts. *A History of China*, p. 52; Paul S. Ropp. *China in World History*, p. 53.

8   John A. Harrison. *The Chinese Empire*, p. 216; J.A.G. Roberts. *A History of China*, p. 52; Paul S. Ropp. *China in World History*, p. 53.

9   J.A.G. Roberts. *A History of China*, p. 53.

10   For the best explanation of this problem, see John A. Harrison. *The Chinese Empire*, pp. 225–227 and 317–318.

11   John A. Harrison. *The Chinese Empire*, pp. 225–227 and 317–318.

12   The Silk Road. http://ess.uci.edu/~oliver/silk.html

13   Mark B. Tauger. *Agriculture in World History*, pp. 48–49; *The Equal Field System-Tang Dynasty (618–907)*. http://www.chinaknowledge.de/History/Tang/tang-econ.html

14   John A. Harrison. *The Chinese Empire*, pp. 226–227.

15   *Ibid.* p. 227.

16   *Ibid.* p. 227.

17   Paul S. Ropp. *China in World History*, 59–60; J.A.G. Roberts. *A History of China*, pp. 64–69; John A. Harrison. *The Chinese Empire*, pp. 238–242.

18   See *Feedback on Night Soil: Composting Human Waste.* http://www.motherearthnews.com/nature-and-environment/composting-human-waste-zmaz73sozraw.aspx

19   Mark A. Tauger. *Agriculture in World History*, p. 49; Paul S. Ropp. *China in World History*, p. 78; J.A.G. Roberts. *A History of China*, p. 99.

20   *Ibid.*

21   Mark A. Tauger. *Agriculture in World History*, p. 49; Paul S. Ropp. *China in World History*, p. 78; John A. Harrison. *The Chinese Empire*, p. 265.

22   Mark A. Tauger. *Agriculture in World History*, p. 49; Paul S. Ropp. *China in World History*, p. 78; John A. Harrison. *The Chinese Empire*, p. 265.

23   Confucius. *The Analects*, p. 74.

24   Paul S. Ropp. *China in World History*, p. 78; John A. Harrison. *The Chinese Empire*, p. 265.

25   Paul S. Ropp. *China in World History*, p. 78; J.A.G. Roberts. *A History of China*, p. 99; John A. Harrison. *The Chinese Empire*, p. 265.

26   Thomas J. Craughwell, *The Rise and Fall of the Second Largest Empire in History*, p. 9.

27   George Lane. *Genghis Khan and Mongol Rule*, p. xxxv.

28   Frank McLynn. *Genghis Khan: His Conquest, His Empire, His Legacy*, pp. 416–425; Thomas J. Craughwell. *The Rise and Fall of the Second Largest Empire in History*, pp. 10–11; J.A.G. Roberts. *A History of China.* p. 103; John A Harrison. *The Chinese Empire*, p. 296.

29 Frank McLynn. *Genghis Khan: His Conquest, His Empire, His Legacy*, pp. 416–425; Gerard Chaliand. *Nomadic Empires from Mongolia to the Danube*, pp. 72–73; John A. Harrison. *The Chinese Empire*, pp. 294–297.

30 Gerard Chaliand. *Nomadic Empires from Mongolia to the Danube*, pp. 72–73; Thomas J. Craughwell. *The Rise and Fall of the Second Largest Empire in History*, pp. 230–231 and pp. 231–232.

31 Thomas J. Craughwell. *The Rise of the Second Largest Empire in History*, pp. 233–234; John A. Harrison. *The Chinese Empire*, pp. 297–303.

32 Thomas J. Craughwell. *The Rise and Fall of the Second Largest Empire in History*, p. 251.

33 John A. Harrison. *The Chinese Empire*, p. 299; Paul S. Ropp. *China in World History*, p. 85; J.A.G. Roberts. *A History of China*, pp. 112–114.

34 Mark B. Tauger. *Agriculture in World History*, pp. 24 and 26.

35 John Morris Roberts. *The New Penguin History of the World*, p. 178; Mark B. Tauger. *Agriculture in World History*, p. 27.

36 John Boardman, Jasper Griffin, and Oswyn Murray, editors. *Late Antiquity: A Guide to the Post-Classical World*, pp. 130–164; Michael Rostovtzeff. *Rome*, pp. 309–324; Charles Freeman. *Egypt, Greece, and Rome: Civilization of the Ancient Mediterranean*, pp. 555–563 and 587–605.

37 John Morris Roberts. *The New Penguin History of the World*, pp. 417–418; Mark B. Tauger. *Agriculture in World History*, p. 37; William H. McNeill. *A History of the Human Community: Prehistory to the Present*, pp. 266–269.

38 John Morris Roberts. *The New Penguin History of the World*, pp. 417–418; Mark B. Tauger. *Agriculture in World History*, p. 37; William H. McNeill. *A History of the Human Community: Prehistory to the Present*, pp. 266–269.

39 John Morris Roberts. *The New Penguin History of the World*, pp. 417–418; Mark B. Tauger. *Agriculture in World History*, p. 37.

40 Norman F. Cantor. *The Civilization of the Middle Ages*, pp. 195–204.

41 Brian Fagan. *The Little Ice Age*, pp. 25–26; Mark B. Tauger. *Agriculture in World History*, p. 36.

42 George Gordon Coulton. *The Medieval Village*, pp. 70–71; Peter Linehan and Janet Laughland Nelson, editors. *The Medieval World*, p. 64; John B. Morrall. *The Founding of the Western Tradition: the Medieval Imprint*, pp. 99–100, 102–105, and 107.

43 Maurice Keen. *The Pelican History of Medieval Europe*, pp. 73–135; Roy C. Cave and Herbert Henry Coulson. *A Source Book of Medieval Economic*, pp. 325–327; John Rogers Commons. *The Legal Foundations of Capitalism*, p. 240.

44 Norman F. Cantor. *The Civilization of the Middle Ages*, pp. 405, 407, 421–22, 522–523, and 525.

45 Brian Fagan. *The Little Ice Age*, pp. 17–18; Maurice Keen. *The Pelican History of Medieval Europe*, pp. 73–135.

46 Brian Fagan. *The Long Summer: How Climate Changed Civilizations*, p. 248, Black Death.

47   Norman F. Cantor. *Civilization of the Middle Ages*, pp. 496–498.

48   *Parlement* is a generic term for assembly halls, where powerful men met with their kings to consider what policy to follow.

49   See The Spanish and Portuguese Reconquest, 1095–1492. http://libro.uca. edu/bishko/spr1.htm

50   See *Social capital and politics. Guilds and urban rebellion in Ghent and Bruges (14th–15th centuries)*. http://www2.iisg.nl; Jan Dumolyn and Jelle Haemers. *Patterns of urban rebellion in medieval Flanders*. http://www.sciencedirect. com/science/article/pii/S0304441810500321

51   Jelle Haemers (Universiteit Gent). *Social capital and politics. Guilds and urban rebellion in Ghent and Bruges (14th–15th centuries)*. http://www2. iisg.nl; Jan Dumolyn and Jelle Haemers. *Patterns of urban rebellion in medieval Flanders*. http://www.sciencedirect.com/science/article/pii/ S0304441810500321

52   Jelle Haemers (Universiteit Gent). *Social capital and politics. Guilds and urban rebellion in Ghent and Bruges (14th–15th centuries)*. http://www2. iisg.nl; Jan Dumolyn and Jelle Haemers. *Patterns of urban rebellion in medieval Flanders*. http://www.sciencedirect.com/science/article/pii/ S0304441810500321

53   Jelle Haemers (Universiteit Gent). *Social capital and politics. Guilds and urban rebellion in Ghent and Bruges (14th–15th centuries)*. PDF Document. http:// www2.iisg.nl, and Jan Dumolyn and Jelle Haemers. *Patterns of urban rebellion in medieval Flanders*. http://www.sciencedirect.com/science/article/pii/ S0304441810500321

5

China and Medieval Europe: Cultural Orthodoxy and Creativity

The agricultural and commercial innovations developed by Song China (906–1279), plus the bounty of food production and urban development in medieval Europe during the High Middle Ages (1000–1300), reached full maturity at nearly the same time. The food surpluses generated by both civilizations from 600 to 1300 fed the people that created the geographic internal coherence in each area. Each culture integrated its economic, political, social, philosophical, theological, and religious institutions. China achieved its primary objective, restoration of imperial rule; medieval Europe struggled with a dysfunctional mixture of competing political and religious claims to authority. These diverging cultural developments found full expression in the flowering of each culture's worldview.

While the Early and High Middle Ages (500–1300) was a time of adherence to tradition for both China and Europe, a fundamental difference between the two cultures endured. In the wake of the fall of its ancient civilization, Chinese society operated under a revised but functional political ideology: one that incorporated a political, traditional, and divinely sanctioned belief system that justified the imperial office of each ruling dynasty. This belief system created a revived ideology called "neo-Confucianism" that reinforced the ideals of royal power as had been established during the Han Dynasty. It did so by adding the transcendental influences of Buddhism to the Han's traditional Confucianism, Daoism, and Legalism. In China's case, therefore, the "state" and "church" worked in synergy, one solidifying and justifying the other.

China and the West to 1600: Empire, Philosophy, and the Paradox of Culture,
First Edition. Steven Wallech.
© 2016 John Wiley & Sons, Inc. Published 2016 by John Wiley & Sons, Inc.

This flowering of the traditional imagination in China reached full bloom during the Song Dynasty (960–1279). This dynasty produced the greatest amount of wealth that China had seen to date, due to the vibrant commercial economy it fostered (see chapter four). Such prosperity fed a rich, urban society that felt fully justified in China's traditional philosophical worldview. In the midst of this prosperity, a subtle hostility toward Buddhism surfaced, because this foreign (Indian) faith had challenged Confucianism during the Tang Dynasty (618–906). This measure of hostility inspired Confucian scholars to reinvent their belief system. They felt that the best way to do so was to import transcendental concepts so important to Buddhism into Confucianism. They hoped that their neo-Confucianism would fill the intellectual space occupied by Buddhism even as the new Confucian ideology undermined Buddhism's role in China. They succeeded so well, in fact, that they created an orthodoxy that would dominate the Chinese imagination from then until the modern age (up to 1905). The only pitfall to their success was the degree to which they had trapped China in a traditional worldview. This saw the Chinese repeat their behavior without question, even as the circumstances in Eurasia were undergoing change. These changes occurred most dramatically in Europe.

During the High Middle Ages (1000–1300), medieval Europe underwent its first renaissance, a minor revival of Greco-Roman knowledge when compared to the famous Renaissance of 1300–1600. Fed by the agricultural practices that had been successfully moved north of the Alps (see chapter four), this minor renaissance revived the theological imagination of medieval Europe after the era of nomadic invasions ended (500–1000). The new agricultural era, and accompanying renaissance, enjoyed the support of a vibrant new urban society that encouraged the urban skills, those that had largely been lost to Western civilization since antiquity: literacy, computation, and critical thinking. Using these revived skills, a revitalized theology emerged in medieval Europe that differed sharply from the Chinese pattern of beliefs. This revived theology reinforced the separation of the church from the state because the soul of the individual (served by the church) was more important than the body (protected by the state). This rekindled theology drew inspiration from the Aristotelian philosophy that Western civilization had lost with the fall of Rome. The recovery of this philosophy began when the growing population in medieval Europe between 1000 and 1300 sought to recapture the lands lost to the Muslims during the rise of Islam (632–1000, see chapter four). Contact with the Arab world through the Crusades led medieval Europeans to acquire Arabic commentaries on Aristotle. These commentaries filled the medieval imagination with a worldview lost to Roman Catholic Europe after 500.

Inspired by this recovery of ancient knowledge, medieval Europeans began to rethink their theological worldview (see below).

The revival of theology that followed then fuelled a dispute between the papacy and the kings of Europe over who held the ultimate authority to command the loyalty of the people. During the Early Middle Ages (500–1000) kings commanded Europe. They did so because they provided the protection needed to prevent nomads from destroying civilization. They used the church as a prop to their power by appointing bishops who did their bidding. But when their defenses matured under feudalism, their successes against the nomads reduced the urgency invested in their power. Churchmen began to rethink their role in society. Did they not serve God and make available salvation to all humanity? Was not this service far more important than protection from death? Was the church able to perform this service if kings appointed churchmen to positions of authority within the church? To help purify the church from any secular contamination common during the Early Middle Ages, churchmen used the revived theology of the High Middle Ages to redefine their role in society.

Feudalism helped these churchmen in this endeavor because it recognized the legitimacy of land as the singular device to identify an estate, a state, and status. This pattern of integrating the economic identity of land with its political and social configuration made each estate a political entity. Since feudalism linked a temporal, military system with the transcendental services offered by the church, medieval Europe divided itself into three legitimate estates: 1) those who pray; 2) those who fight; and 3) those who work. Each estate then took on the characteristics of a state.* This became increasingly evident in the contests over ultimate authority within a medieval kingdom.

In this struggle, the pope had the advantage of a universal church established in every kingdom in Europe. In contrast, kings only commanded their local domains. The pope also conveyed a transcendental message that justified his authority over the temporal power of the many kings. But the pope also suffered a major disadvantage: Jesus' ministry had placed his voice outside the Roman, as well as all subject, states. This allowed Jesus to speak with a pure, sacred, and unsullied spiritual voice. He riled against the impurities of a life committed to any established, secular, and worldly institutions. But as one of the medieval estates, the church itself was a legitimate part of the established order, something Jesus' vision of sin

*This link between estate and state is most evident in the French Estates General: the first estate was the church, the second was the nobility, and the third became the common laboring classes. Each had a single vote during periods when called upon to support the king.

condemned. This placed the medieval church in a difficult position: to maintain power and challenge Europe's kings, the popes also tended to act like these very same kings. This paradox went unresolved throughout the Middle Ages (500–1500).

Meanwhile, between the years 900–1300 both China and Europe refined their orthodoxies and achieved remarkable sophistication in their revitalized beliefs. Both civilizations renewed the vision of justified behavior that reflected the significant social and political changes that had occurred after the fall of their respective ancient civilizations. The nature of these changes, however, sharply differentiated Chinese civilization from medieval Europe. The Chinese would find themselves both enriched and ensnared in the brilliance of their traditions. The aspect that ensnared them also held them in place in terms of their beliefs and actions. In contrast, the Europeans would discover that the dysfunctional nature of their traditions would compel them to modify their institutions in ways that ended up pushing them toward modernization. These two very different stories will unfold in the remainder of this text.

The Economy, Administration, and Formation of a Chinese Orthodoxy

During the Song Dynasty (960–1279) China came closer to the Confucian ideal than at any other time in its history. A supremely productive economy fed a small but wealthy civilization that generated a higher level of prosperity than had the proceeding Tang Dynasty. During the Song's reign, the Chinese had completely colonized the entire length of the Yangzi River. They also integrated the river's productive potential with the older, established practices of the north. Rice replaced millets as the principal grain in the Chinese diet. The raising of two crops a year instead of one doubled the calories available to feed a refreshed Chinese creativity. A vibrant commercial system reduced the Confucian prejudice against merchants. A paper currency system backed by an increased supply of valuable metals, thanks to innovation in copper mining, generated sorely needed capital. Monies produced in this vibrant economy sustained a high volume of exchanges between the countryside and the city. The thorough integration of supply and demand created a form of geographic internal coherence unprecedented in medieval world history.

Of all the sectors of the Song's integrated economy, none generated more income than commerce. But those who engaged in commerce drew the envy of the "scholar-gentry," the new class of state officials that had replaced China's old aristocracy (see below). Confucian tradition, however, excluded state officials from participating in trade, due to Kong Fuzi's view of the "petty man" (i.e. the immoral merchant mentioned in chapter four). The scholar-gentry's economic arena rested solely on agriculture, which was another of Kong Fuzi's standards of conduct: only land produced new wealth and therefore benefited society. Many members of the scholar-gentry class, however, by-passed this prohibition on trade by placing a younger son who had failed the imperial exams in commerce. These young men forged contacts with merchants, in this way facilitating the acquisition of illicit wealth for the families of the scholar-gentry. Simultaneously, merchants started to place their more-learned sons, those who did pass the exams, on the path of scholarly endeavors. Soon the sons of merchants began entering the state bureaucracy though successful completion of the Song imperial exams, and they used their contacts with scholar-gentry families for promotion. Nonetheless, there remained social barriers between the established scholar-gentry families and those of merchant upstart bureaucrats. But the ranks of talented men engaged in philosophical speculation suddenly mushroomed.

During the Song Dynasty, recruiting these talented men for service in the imperial bureaucracy became a fundamental goal of the ruling emperors. To achieve the perfect selection of the best men, three objectives surfaced as essential to the state's success: 1) refine the examination system; 2) improve the educational facilities; and 3) develop a method of sponsorship whereby seasoned officials nominated worthy candidates for rapid promotion. Achieving these three goals became the target of the first three Song emperors' attention.

Fulfilling the first goal, Emperor Song Taizu (reigned 960–972) re-established the Tang Dynasty's annual examination of promising candidates. During his first years in power, Song Taizu rejuvenated a system that produced a very small but qualified number of successful graduates. Under Emperor Song Taizong (reigned 976–997) the number of students earning the highest degree, the *jinshi*, reached 140 per year. During Emperor Song Zhenzong's reign (997–1022), so many candidates attempted to take the exam for the *jinshi* at the capital, Kaifeng, that a major reform followed. The Song rulers soon developed a process whereby annual exams occurred at the sub-prefecture or district level, triennial exams took place at the prefecture level, and triennial exams began at the capital. The sub-prefecture exams awarded the lowest degrees, the prefectures granted the middle degrees, and the capital identified the highest degree recipients. These various levels allowed those seeking entry into the imperial bureaucracy access to the tests that measured their merit.

To ensure objective evaluation of a candidate's performance, the Song then created a system of blind readings that ensured the grader did not know the candidate he evaluated.[1]

The second objective, to improve China's educational facilities, also drew attention from the Song's first three emperors. They built an officially sponsored series of schools located both in the capital and the prefectures. This was another extension of the old Tang Dynasty's policy of widely educating potential scholars. The Song economy, however, allowed for far more of these educational services. Also, new schools with local libraries housing the Confucian *classics* sprang up throughout the Song domain and ensured the availability of knowledge to many promising young men. At Kaifeng, an imperial university opened that served all candidates that qualified to attend. This non-preferential access to the highest levels of education differed from the older, restrictive practice of limiting access to the children of state officials.[2]

The third Song goal, develop a system of sponsorship to promote talented Song officials, seemed to contradict the objective qualities of the examination process, but this practice allowed experienced bureaucrats to find gifted men in unexpected places. This method of promotion used the Confucian principle that men of good judgment possessed the ability to find virtue among their subordinates and nurture these talents until young officials were ready to take on more responsibly. The exams identified clever men. Promotion based on the judgment of seasoned ministers, however, identified men of courage, character, and initiative. This third objective allowed the Song to advance the best and the brightest in their culture. Now the Song had the intellectuals required to initiate philosophical and administrative innovations that could match the dynasty's economic achievements.[3]

Song Administrative Innovations

The Song Dynasty also perfected their administrative institutions. The Song developed a centralized bureaucracy based on merit, while the emperor drew heavily on the advice of his civilian ministers. Once again the Song's officials ensured that China was deeply committed to the *classics*. One of the key recommendations of the *classics* was that when it came to everyone below the emperor, merit not heredity should be rewarded. The Song emperors complied by abandoning the imperial habit of the Han and the Tang to play favorites among their aristocrats, eunuchs, wives, and concubines. The Song also raised their scholar-officials to new heights of power, placing them above military commanders within the bureaucracy. Finally, the Song elevated their state officials to the pinnacles of status, in time wholly replacing the hereditary aristocracy with educated gentlemen. As a result, the Song experienced a cultural renewal that enhanced their system of political power and social prestige.[4]

Under the Song, the Chinese elite achieved their entry in political society solely by passing the imperial exams. Those families that wished to maintain their position within Chinese society had to educate their sons in the *classics* in order that they, too, could pass the exams. The exams themselves became much more intense, requiring years of preparation, so that only a small group of highly qualified scholars had access to imperial posts. Thus, the new social group known as the scholar-gentry became the new aristocracy, living up to the literal meaning of the Greek term *aristocracy* (rule by the best).[5]

In the early years of the Song, the imperial administration was still relatively small. But in time, just as had happened during the Tang, the number of graduates from the imperial exams eventually outstripped the number of jobs available. Nonetheless, the Song's administrative system continued to recruit only the best of available candidates. Once hired, the performance of these officials underwent intense professional scrutiny, the state keeping a complete dossier on the bureaucrat's employment history. To further improve performance, Song officials were prohibited from serving in the prefectures of their birth, and they could not remain in a single prefecture for any significant length of time. The idea here was to ensure that a state official focused solely on the needs of the state and not on the requirements of his immediate or extended family's prosperity.[6]

From this pool of very talented men, as well as the schools that educated them, a renewed investigation into the official state ideology began. The wealth that the Song had generated fed a brilliant population who fully accepted the principles that they believed created their prosperity. They wanted to ensure that this affluence remained a common experience among those willing to work hard to achieve it. They turned their attention to consider how China had reached these heights. Their review of Chinese philosophy spurred the development of a new orthodoxy that remained in place until 1905—the year that marked the moment when modernization from Europe would grant Europeans enough power to force the Chinese to abandon their traditional worldview.

The Renewed Confucian Orthodoxy

All of these social and educational factors created a class of gentlemen who laid the foundation for a new era of intellectual refinement in China. It is from this hyper-erudition that neo-Confucianism emerged. "Neo-Confucianism" is a historical term used to describe the modifications made to Confucian philosophy in the twelfth century. These changes, which the Song espoused as corrections, reinterpreted the Zhou *classics* and blended them with elements of Buddhism and Daoism. The goal of the new ideology was to produce rational answers to age-old questions about the origins and natural processes of the universe. Neo-Confucian scholars formulated responses to these questions by weaving the accepted Confucian principles of knowledge, ethics, and personal conduct with the transcendental principles of Buddhism and Daoism. In this manner, they hoped to create a complete understanding of the Way, one that would finalize China's knowledge of the universe. This effort reflected the same impulses that had led to several major social, economic, and political reforms attempted in the eleventh century by men such as Fan Zhongyan (989–1052), Ouyang Xiu (1007–1072), and Wang Anshi (1021–1086). All three had hoped to create the ideal society in China by refining the design of the state and the policy of land use to sidestep past errors that had resulted in chaos. All three men had failed.

By the twelfth century, Chinese officials had abandoned major political and land use reform efforts in favor of concentrating on a way to revise Chinese philosophy. These Song scholars looked to the teaching of a Tang official named Han Yu (768–824), who led them on a new philosophical quest. Han Yu had reconsidered the value of Confucianism as a rival of Buddhism and demonstrated the usefulness of Mengzi's (372–289 BCE) philosophy as the ideological foundation for imperial rule (see chapter two). Han Yu's goal was simple but difficult to achieve: find the laws of nature that should govern all social relationships.[7]

Song scholars refined Han Yu's strategy (after the fall of the Tang), when they tried to eliminate Buddhism as a potential rival to neo-Confucianism; they did so by absorbing Buddhist concepts into their renewed Confucian philosophy. In other words, the early neo-Confucian scholars imported transcendental concepts from Buddhism into their own works, infusing Kong Fuzi's and Mengzi's explanation of human relationships with these completely foreign ideas. Given the new availability of printed texts, the result of the Song's inventions of moveable type and rag paper, the work of the neo-Confucian scholars reached a very wide audience. This expanded reading community then sustained a growing consensus that the revisions to Confucianism were indeed the correct approach to a better understanding of the Way. Ultimately, the achievements of the neo-Confucians were both original and stifling. They were original in the sense that neo-Confucianism created a new synthesis of transcendental principles with an older, well-established philosophical ideology. They were stifling in the sense that, having convinced so many people that their new belief system was the ultimate explanation of the Way, no other type of revisions were attempted for centuries after these major changes. In other words, this was the final revision.

Neo-Confucianism emerged from the work of several scholars over the course of many years. Each of these scholars added something new to the emerging ideology. All of them taken together produced new layers of ideas that integrated into a revitalized Confucian worldview that the final scholar converted into the new orthodoxy. Taken all together, each previous scholar therefore laid a foundation for the last one, Zhu Xi (1129–1200), who generated the system of beliefs that completely entranced the Chinese.

The first scholar, Zhou Dunyi (1017–1073), opened the way to neo-Confucianism by laying down a foundation of ideas that launched the new ideology. Zhou Dunyi created a cosmology that infused Confucianism with a transcendental explanation of all things found in nature; the idea of the transcendental was completely absent from Confucianism prior to his work. All his creative energy therefore went into explaining how the transcendental agency found in the universe fitted into accepted Chinese traditional practices. Zhang Zai (1020–1077) was the second scholar; he added to Zhou Dunyi's achievements by linking the transcendental agency established by Zhou Dunyi to Confucian ethics. Zhang Zai explained how hidden within the transcendental forces of nature were ethical principles that regenerated the physical order found in the universe. These ethical principles comprised a universal substance that permeated nature, made itself known to China's ancient Sage kings, and found its way into the *classics* as the venerable principles identified by Kong Fuzi. Cheng Yi (1033–1107) added further to Zhou Dunyi and Zhang Zai's work by developing an overriding, immutable, and eternal law within the transcendental order of things that directed all the forces of nature. This perpetual, everlasting law guided the ethical forces found in nature to make available to humans the signs and omens that they needed to align their conduct with the practices outlined in the *classics*. Cheng Yi's brother Cheng Hao (1032–1082) went one step further; Cheng Hao linked the universe and humanity to a common understanding of where good and evil came from within nature. According to Cheng Hao, evil came from our physical make-up and good came from our capacity to reason. Humanity purified itself from evil by focusing the mind on the correct study of things found in the *classics* as the wellspring of Confucianism. Reason infused nature with a common ethical agency that linked human conduct with the transcendental substance found in nature. Taken all together, the work of Zhou Dunyi, Zhang Zai, Cheng Yi, and Cheng Hao laid a foundation for Zhu Xi to complete the development of neo-Confucianism.[8]

Neo-Confucianism took its final step, and complete form, with the work of Zhu Xi (1129–1200). He systematized the new philosophy. Zhu Xi argued that the rational principle found in all things in nature is transcendental, incorporeal, one, eternal, unchanging, and always good. This rational principle is the metaphysical agency that directs order in nature. It was accessible to humans through the power of reason. In contrast, are the physical, many, transitory, and changeable, in other words, all things found in the world that surrounds us. These many things are both good and evil. Together, the rational principle (i.e. the transcendental agency) and the many physical things found in the world combine to make up the universe; they are ever present but separate entities. Zhu Xi identified human nature, as part of the rational, transcendental agency, while feelings and emotions were part of the physical world. He added mind and heart as physical, but in its most subtle form. When a mother gives birth to a child, the rational and the physical arrange themselves in varying degrees of power within the newborn in a manner consistent with human nature, feelings and emotions, and mind and heart. This marriage of rational and physical, however, occurs at different levels within each individual. The problem confronting humanity is seeking the rational within individuals, so that collectively humankind might learn to command the physical.[9]

The way this alignment of the rational is achieved is to cultivate knowledge within the individual. According to Zhu Xi, such knowledge can be acquired in a variety of ways: travel; personal associations; observations of nature; and, above all, study of the *classics*. Knowledge reveals a hidden truth in every subject, and the understanding of this truth links the mind with other truths in other forms of study to combine into a universal truth. This universal truth was that the rational embedded in all things as the agency that had to take precedence over the physical so that ethics could govern the universe. Humanity discovered the rational by studying the *classics*. The *classics* revealed the rational as it existed in nature. And education aligned human consciousness (personal reason) with natural law (universal reason) so that human conduct could obey the Way.[10]

As a person acquires knowledge, an accumulative effect of the rational increases through all the sources the scholar uses.[†] Conscious and diligent effort increases the force of reason buried everywhere in the inquiry until it achieves a critical mass. At that moment, the constituent parts of the

---

[†]During the Song Dynasty, liberties enjoyed by women came under attack as practices common to the nomads. The freedom women experienced during the Tang disappeared because Song scholars assigned these practices to the habits of nomads. A process of subordination then followed as a sign of the new "civilized" way to conduct oneself. Song scholars concluded that women should stay at home and give birth to children.

rational buried in all things suddenly reveals itself to the student in a manner similar to the Enlightenment that sends rapture through the Buddhist. The Confucian scholar had now gained the innermost secrets of nature available to humanity, and for the first time he could say he understood the meaning of life. Such a person is not only wise, but also free to act morally without fear of evil.[11]

The way to moral perfection, however, raises many questions. How does any one person, with such a short lifespan, gain insight into nature quickly enough to acquire wisdom before death? What is the relationship between true knowledge and the moment of sudden Enlightenment? And how does one follow the most direct path toward completing this journey? If knowledge comes from a variety of sources, and every individual differs from one another, then how did one know if the path chosen was the best one? To respond to these many questions, Zhu Xi reminded all those who questioned his philosophy that all knowledge already had a home—in the classics. He specifically referred to the *Analects* of Kong Fuzi, the *Book of Meng Zi*, the *Great Learning*, and the Doctrine of the Mean taken from the *Book of Rites* as the four primary sources. He argued that the power of reason permeated these four works, the standard texts that pointed the way to an awakening of wisdom. In other words, the Chinese had, in effect, reclaimed and re-embraced the teaching of their ancient civilization.

Zhu Xi then pointed out that Enlightenment can come to any person, but only the sage can achieve a full awakening. Lesser persons can take solace in discovering their duty to society by acquiring enough reason for self-regulation and becoming law-abiding subjects of the emperor, the holder of the Mandate of Heaven. Understanding enough to emulate a sage is the first step toward becoming a gentleman and conforming to the universal principles of morality embedded in nature. Such obedience to the rational, the power of reason, the social order, and morality was consistent with the transcendental order of things in the universe. Hence, the universe, the law, social relationships, morality, and proper conduct all aligned themselves around the metaphysical nature of reason as it governed reality.[12]

Zhu Xi's world system made sense to the Chinese. His version of neo-Confucianism opened the way to self-cultivation as a practical activity open to anyone who wished to follow it. Aimed at personal perfectibility, Zhu Xi's worldview made virtue attainable. Zhu Xi's neo-Confucianism trumped Buddhism and Daoism by making both intelligible to everyone through his ideology, and by linking them to everyday life. The actions of a good government were the same as those of personal conduct, as both relied on the rational as the universal principle. The importance of Zhu

Xi's new synthesis was that the universe, state, and individual aligned with the same metaphysics that the rational mind could comprehend. In time Zhu Xi's work prevailed over all other worldviews found in China and became a strict orthodoxy. His version of neo-Confucianism would define once and for all, and thereby limit, the boundaries of inquiry into human conduct in China.[13]

This formulation of the Song's powerful and functional new philosophy represented the highest achievement of China's golden age. When the Jurchen invaded northern China and forced the Song Dynasty to flee south, neo-Confucianism continued to serve as the theoretical basis to distinguish the True Way (its title) from human error. Neo-Confucianism created an intellectual barrier between the nomads in power in the north and what it truly meant to be "Chinese" in the south. This helped the Southern Song (1115–1279) survive the loss of the north to the Jurchen, who captured half of China between 1115 and 1127. The Southern Song continued to prosper even within its sharply reduced domain. And even after the Mongols finally completed their conquest of China and established the Yuan Dynasty in 1279, neo-Confucianism continued to help the Chinese preserve their own strong identity. Indeed, the ultimate effect of the Mongol era was to accentuate the habits of the Chinese, which caused them to turn in on themselves and even caused the Mongols to emulate and then adopt some of China's culture. This introspective turn of events led the Chinese to nurture even more diligently those beliefs and practices that distinguished them from everyone else in the world. And these habits reinforced the sense of superiority that the Chinese felt whenever they compared the brilliance of their civilization to that of any of their neighbors—and later the agents of far-flung European nations. This new level of inwardness infused the Chinese with a conservative level of conduct that further calcified their vision of nature and humanity's role within it. What emerged was an even more intense commitment to imperial rule based on the True Way as the orthodox political ideology.[14]

Foundations of a Medieval European Orthodoxy

Unlike China, medieval Europe created an economy that did not integrate its rural and urban components. Feudalism recognized the legitimacy of land (i.e. real estate) but not the wealth of cities, their marketplaces, or their money and goods (i.e. incorporeal property). In the scheme of feudalism, "real" stood for actual or legitimate, and "estate," as we have seen, represented state and status. Feudalism also used "incorporeal" to mean "without body," or illegitimate, and "property" to identify something owned that is of value. "Incorporeal property," therefore, became an oxymoron: it meant something of value (an existing thing) that, in the legal sense, did not exist. Hence, land was an actual, legitimate thing, but money and goods were not.[15] This meant that feudalism built a system of military and religious institutions based on land, but did so without recognizing the role of cities.

As a result, the German chiefs who occupied the lands lost by the Western Roman Empire did not understand how to run a complex urban civilization. Cities required literacy, computation, and critical thinking skills to maintain a market economy. But all of the conquering German chiefs were illiterate. To run their new realms, these chiefs relied on clerics whom they called "clerks" to administer their domains. Happily, the surviving Roman Catholic Church had the skills needed to administer an emerging kingdom. Coincidently, the clergy lacked the will or the means to kill nomads in self-defense. The clerics, therefore, required the protection offered by a newly minted German king from any further nomadic invasions. As a result, German kingdoms formed alliances with the Roman Catholic Church.

Waves of nomadic invasions from 500 to 950 nearly destroyed medieval Europe's urban life. Cities shrank because the nomads entering Europe saw cities as easy targets. Urban centers held the wealth of Rome, offered opportunities for pillage, and provided a rich reward for any chief seeking the spoils of war. While cities housing the wealth of civilization suffered destruction, farms remained valuable because they fed the people. Feudalism, therefore, grew up as a system of defense in the countryside to protect food production, and largely let cities fall into disuse. Only monasteries and cathedral towns served as the most prominent surviving urban centers during the Early Middle Ages because those were the places in which the clerics lived. Meanwhile, feudalism reached full maturity by the year 950, just when the nomadic invasions came to an end.

Kingship During the Early Middle Ages (500–1000)

The first step in establishing feudalism was the creation of "kingship." The term "king" actually derived from an old Germanic word for chief: "Koenig." The German tribe most responsible for converting a "Koenig" into a "king" was the Franks. The Franks were a tribe that first occupied Gaul (France) in 485 and then expanded into Germany and Italy by 800. Their success in creating this new, massive realm belonged largely to the efforts of one noble family called the Carolingians. The Carolingians served as the rulers of the Franks, but not as their kings; instead, the Carolingians served as the mayors of the royal Merovingian household. From this office, the Carolingians spread Frankish power across what eventually became the Holy Roman Empire.

During the third generation of Carolingian leadership, Charles Martel (reigned 714–741) saved Christian Europe from being overrun by Islamic forces. He defeated the Muslims after they had conquered North Africa and Iberia, halting their spread farther north into Europe. His success, in effect, kept the Muslims south of the Pyrenees Mountains on France's southern border. Those Muslims on the Iberian Peninsula, also known as the Moors, had been determined to conquer the rest of Europe, but Charles Martel stopped them at the Battle of Poitiers in 732, his success incumbent on his introduction of the use of heavy cavalry reinforced by a highly disciplined infantry.[16]

Charles Martel's heir, Pepin the Short (reigned 741–768), built on his father's victories, and it was he who transformed Carolingian authority from the office of mayors into that of kings. Pepin did so when he came to the aid of the papacy against the Lombards. The Lombards were yet another Germanic tribe that had invaded the crumbling Roman world and conquered part of Italy. They then threatened the survival of the papal office because they followed a form of Christianity that Roman Catholics saw as a heresy. This heresy emerged prior to the fall of Rome, when Father Arius, an Eastern Roman priest, claimed that Jesus was similar to but not the same as God. The danger of this point of view had led to the Council of Nicaea in 325 where the Bishop of Alexandria, Father Athansius, established the concept of "consubstantiation:" Jesus and God comprised the same divine substance (see chapter two). To save the pope, three centuries later, Pepin struck an agreement with Pope Zacharias (reigned 741–752): in exchange for Carolingian protection against the Lombards, the pope would crown Pepin as king of the Franks. Both parties fulfilled their parts of the pact, and the Carolingians became the new kings of the Franks.

Pepin's heir, Charlemagne (reigned 768–814) was the next great Carolingian king. He was a powerful ruler who completed the conquest of the Lombards, thereby adding Italy to the Frankish holding. He also defeated the Saxons, rounding out Germany as part of his realm. In 800, Pope Leo III (reigned 795–816) crowned Charlemagne the Holy Roman Emperor, who now ruled all the lands from the northern tip of Spain to France and into Germany and Italy. In this year, a clear image of a Christian king was firmly planted in medieval Europe. At the same time, the king's duty to protect the papacy and Christendom took root. Finally, the symbolic gesture of the pope crowning the king suggested to later generations that the authority of the king came from God and God alone. This hinted at the superior authority of the Vicar of Christ, the pope, over that of the king.

Charlemagne's death brought a weak king to power, Louis the Pious (reigned 814–840). His incompetent rule saw the splintering of Charlemagne's vast political realm into fragments, as Louis' sons fought over portions of the empire. It was this fragmentation of the Carolingian Empire that created the circumstances that led to the rise of feudalism. As Charlemagne's grandsons proceeded to divide his realm, a third and, as it turned out, final wave of nomads invaded Western Europe. This round of invasions by Norsemen (Vikings) and Magyars (Mongols) forced local nobles to find new ways to defend their lands by themselves. They did so because the weak Carolingian kings could no longer mobilize a general defense. The system these local kings and noblemen created became feudalism.

Feudalism

Modern scholars know feudalism as a system of land ownership, land use, and military service, with several defining characteristics. The first is pragmatic. Feudalism is a group of political and legal institutions that create a system of decentralized government; this form of government placed public power in private hands by dividing the kingdom into a number of privately held estates. The second is contractual. Feudalism is based on a legal and contractual relationship between grantor (the lord) and grantee (the vassal). The grantor owns an *allodium*, that is, land given by God to a lord that is free of any obligations: his title deed. The grantor gives a portion of his *allodium* to the grantee as a *benefice*, the right to occupy and use the land during his lifetime. Upon the grantee or vassal's death, the estate and all rights to it return to the lord. In a second contract, the grantor gives the land as a *fief* to a vassal. In a fiefdom, the vassal has the right to possess and use the land during his lifetime, but also the right to transfer his possession to an heir upon the grantee's death. In return for receiving the *benefice* or *fief*, the vassal must, in addition to working the land productively, provide military service when called on to defend the lord's domain. The third defining characteristic of feudalism is a compound institutional feature. One can look at feudalism as an integration of the social, economic, and political elements of society. The "estate" is the food-producing portion of a kingdom, or the economic component. The "estate" creates a "state," the political component. And the "state" assigns to the grantee a social rank or "status," the social component. All three defining characteristics, the pragmatic, the legal, and the compound, are central to one's understanding of feudalism.[17]

Feudalism produced a relatively stable communal arrangement that allowed medieval agriculture, which happened to coincide with a climatically warm era, to work its productive wonders (see chapter four). From 900 to 1300, feudalism spread and effectively repulsed any further nomadic invasions. The heavy cavalry supported by feudal estates fed both warhorses and knights whose military prowess more than matched marauding nomads. Quick responses by mobilized knights made nomadic raids too costly for steppe tribes to continue after 950. A new age of relative peace ensued, and Europe entered an era of bounty that generated the food surpluses necessary to feed and sustain a growing population (also see chapter four). But, as always, a large population density seemed to evoke the paradox of culture. In other words, eventually cultural, environmental, and/or biological pressures created by the dramatic increase in human numbers caused the rigid and unbending feudal institutions to crack and then fail. The result was a change in the legitimate conditions of medieval life in the West.

The Illegitimate Circumstances of Cities

Feudalism recognized the legitimacy of only three "estates": those who pray (clerics), those who fight (knights), and those who work to produce food (villeins). All of these occupations were rural. Feudalism, therefore, excluded any urban profession. This meant that those who lived in towns, people such as merchants and artisans, fell outside the three estates and were technically illegitimate; legally, they simply did not exist.

Part of the reason why feudalism assigned an illegitimate status to towns and those whose occupations were tied to them was that the conquering German tribes did not understand city life. Life in a town simply fell outside the nomad's experiences. Nomads could understand a rural existence because a rustic life seemed to produce cycles of time that repeated regularly. The year followed a calendar's cycle of seasons; the day used the orbit of the Sun as it circled the Earth (nomads believed they lived in a geocentric, or Earth-centered, universe). These patterns of time produced predictable routines confirmed by agriculture: planting, weeding, harvesting, and allowing the land to rest. These cycles of time also repeated with a reliability that required no unusual skills to understand. Illiterate Germans felt comfortable in this stable setting.

In contrast, life in the city was cluttered with an ambiguity that nomads could not easily handle. No two days were the same. Time shifted from moment to moment in the marketplace, making profit and loss unpredictable. New skills were essential: literacy, computation, and critical thinking.

These skills multiplied within a city, making the population unpredictable within the eyes of the powerful men who commanded the great estates of feudalism. It reassured them, therefore, to declare the urban setting an illegitimate environment.

Kings and nobles, the powerful secular lords of "estate," looked with suspicion upon those who lived in cities.‡ Clerics also had difficulties with city people because the latter typically came from humble origins and worked in occupations practiced only by the outcasts of medieval Europe: the Jews and Arabs. Land bestowed "estate, state, and status" on kings, dukes, knights, bishops, abbots, priest, and monks. These men despised the *burghers* (city dwellers) as social inferiors. Kings, dukes, knights, bishops, abbots, priests, and monks refused to recognize burghers as legitimate people who possessed any rights to freedom of action as defined by the term "estate." Therefore the men of "estate" used their "freedom," or power, to harass, extort, tax, and humiliate the burghers during the era when urban and commercial recovery had begun (the tenth and eleventh centuries). The men of "estate" drove the burghers to form corporations for their own self-defense. A corporation was either a legal franchise sanctioned by royal charter, or a commune of burghers assembled in a stronghold to conduct business. Wherever royal charters formed corporations, the kings that "legalized" cities received a tax in the form of money. Money, however, was an income that existed outside the legitimate boundaries of feudalism, so kings' use of money led them into non-traditional forms of behavior. Wherever a commune of burghers assembled for mutual defense, this illegitimate gathering of merchants and artisans formed their own city-states. They used their money to hire soldiers to defend their cities, yet these city-states clearly existed outside the boundaries of feudalism, or medieval tradition.[18]

The economic growth that Europe experienced between 950 and 1100 saw a rejuvenation of urban life. This rise of cities occurred after the Early Middle Ages (500–1000) when waves of nomadic tribes destroyed the rich city system created by Rome. Every new medieval city that emerged during the High Middle Ages (1000–1300), however, was an illegitimate assembly that either had to pay to defend itself or seek the protection of a great lord. As these cities became part of the medieval social and economic make-up, their influence on European culture and society grew and became prominent. All of them brought a sudden increase in literacy, mathematical skills, and critical thinking to medieval Europe's worldview.

---

‡The use of quotes in this paragraph emphasizes the feudal definitions of estate, state, status, and freedom.

Since these skills determined how well one survived in an urban setting, emerging cities tended to favor intellectual endeavors over military adventures. In the long run, this was a major boon to the papacy as Christendom began to rethink the role of the church in medieval society. The papacy and the church thrived on the intellectual enterprise of theological inquiry, while the king lived in a world immersed in combat. The inhabitants of cities, therefore, initially favored the pope over kings.

Indeed, one of the major changes the rising influence of cities supported was the declaration by the papacy of its independence from all kings. This declaration launched a struggle that would last for more than three centuries (1000–1300). The conflict started with what became known as the Gregorian Revolution, which pitted two remarkable men against one another: Pope Gregory VII (reigned 1073–1085) and Emperor Henry IV (reigned 1053–1105). The quest for the liberation of the Catholic Church from the state, launched by Pope Gregory VII, inspired a wave of mini revolutions that took place in colleges and universities throughout Europe. These were among the new corporations that developed with the re-emergence of cities. These centers of learning supported the development of a legal profession as well as the refinement of medieval philosophy and theology, all of which originally supported the papacy. The end result was an "awakening" of the Western imagination.

The Gregorian Revolution

In 1053, The German Electors chose Henry IV as their new king.§ These electors were the great nobles of the Holy Roman Empire that Otto I (reigned 936–973) had re-established after the breakup of the Carolingian system. Otto acquired the imperial crown after he defeated the last invasion of steppe nomads at the Battle of Lechfeld, near modern Augsburg, in 955. There he broke the power of the Magyars and in so doing liberated Europe from any further nomadic threats from the east for the next two centuries. Otto's victory also created a new dynasty that ruled both Germany and Italy and placed the new emperor in a position of power that allowed him to appoint the bishops of his realm. One of these bishops was

§The way kings gained their crowns varied in medieval Europe. In Western Europe, where the old Roman provinces made up the new medieval kingdoms, the practice of inheritance became common. In Central Europe, where new lands conquered by Germanic tribes joined Western civilization, no Roman precedent of inheritance existed. This meant that the rulers of Central Europe, the Holy Roman Emperors, followed the nomadic practice of transferring power through an election of one of a chief's sons. The German nomads that conquered the Western Roman Empire, therefore, relied on the fighting men of the tribes to name the new king.

the pope, which made the church subordinate to the monarchy until the Gregorian Revolution. Seven generations after Otto's rise to power, Henry IV came to the throne as a child when his father, Henry III (reigned 1039–1053), died unexpectedly. As a child, Henry IV held no real power because he was a minor, and his subordinates, the bishops and the electors, saw his youth as an opportunity to win their independence from royal authority. The bishops, including the papacy, grew accustomed to ignoring the king of Germany and emperor of the Holy Roman Empire. They wanted their freedom to continue to operate in this manner when Gregory VII became pope in 1073.[19]

Pope Gregory VII decreed the abolition of imperial authority over all bishops in 1075. In the papal edict entitled *Dictatus Papae*, Gregory declared that since God alone created the Roman Church, the papal office answered only to the divine being. In addition, since only the papal office was universal in Christendom, no other territorial or temporal authority took precedence over the pope. And since the pope was the supreme authority in Christendom, papal power went beyond the judgment of any other human being. In effect, Gregory had declared a new institutional reality: papal authority alone was universal and plenary. All other powers in the world, kings, nobles, bishops, and abbots, were particular and dependent on the pope. Hence, the church was not only independent from the emperor, but also superior in power to any other ruler in Europe.[20]

To Henry IV, Gregory's decree posed a highly dangerous blow to royal power, as the church controlled more than one-third of the lands within his territory. In addition, the policy established by Henry's great, great, great, great, great grandfather, Otto I, had used churchmen as governors of his domain because they were the empire's only literate and loyal vassals.**
If Gregory's decree succeeded, the Holy Roman Emperor would lose control of his political, financial, and administrative structure. Furthermore, both Otto and Henry had seen control of the church as the only means to control their electors and secure the central authority of the monarchy against Germany's great lords. And yet, for Henry to act against Gregory now was to risk excommunication, which would release all of Henry's subjects from his power. Excommunication excluded a baptized Christian from the church's sacraments (the means to achieve salvation) because the church declared that the person excommunicated was so offensive to God morally that he no longer belonged to the Christian community. An excommunicated king lost the command he held over all his estates,

---

**Bishops held *benefices* and had no heirs. Their estates reverted to the crown, and their loyalty went to the man who appointed them.

which released his nobles and clerics to act as they pleased. Such an act by the pope would destroy a king's authority. Immediately, a contest of wills began between Gregory and Henry that pitted the moral might of the papacy against the military might of the emperor.[21]

In the long course of this contest, both men managed to achieve major successes. Gregory excommunicated Henry in 1076, forcing him to submit to the authority of the pope in order to prevent a rebellion of his entire realm. This compelled Henry to beg forgiveness from Gregory in 1077 to achieve reinstatement. After being reinstated in the church, Henry then rebelled in 1080 and appointed an antipope (i.e. a second pope to undermine Gregory's power). Henry also invaded Italy to enforce his will. The invasion forced Gregory to flee Rome and seek the protection of Robert Guiscard, the Norman ruler of southern Italy. Gregory died in 1085 while in exile, but Henry then had to face a rebellion of his great nobles, who now sided with Gregory's successors. This led to a civil war that raged for the remainder of Henry's life. Henry died without resolution to the issue of papal versus royal authority in 1105, some 20 years after Gregory's death. A compromise of sorts finally took place in 1122 at the Concordat of Worms. There the new Holy Roman Emperor surrendered his right to invest the bishops of his empire in office, but he retained the right to point out who would succeed. This was a compromise of form that did not settle the dispute. It did, however, raise a good question: in the entire course of the Gregorian Revolution, which side had won?[22]

Modern scholars continue to debate the answer. During the conflict both parties gained major advantages. Gregory's ability to force Henry to submit to papal authority after being excommunicated symbolically proved that the pope had the greater divine power. But Henry's ability to drive Gregory into exile, where he died, demonstrated the king's capacity to control papal politics and, as it were, matters of this world. What followed was an ongoing confrontation, in effect a medieval cold war between church and state that prompted each generation of popes and emperors that followed to constantly measure their capacity to control one another. Given the fragmented system of power available to both popes and kings within feudalism, each party could find allies during their various reigns to keep the question of papal independence an open one. The end result, however, was that the Holy Roman Empire began to break apart. In Germany, those who elected emperors won enough independence in their realms to elevate their status from dukes to princes, or rulers of small *allodia*. In Italy, the corporate communes banded together to form urban leagues that could raise armies and successfully face imperial armies and begin to operate as independent city-states.

A Revival of Learning: The Medieval Orthodoxy

As this ongoing struggle between emperors and popes continued to unfold, an awakening of the medieval mind occurred. The revival of cities and trade sparked a general desire for learning. This new quest for knowledge stimulated an institutional commitment to the recovery of the ancient (classic) Greco-Roman texts that had simply been lost to the people of Europe until the advent of the feudal era. These rediscovered texts led to a hunger for Greco-Roman philosophy, Roman law, Greek medicine, and Greek astronomy and physics. This new craving for learning coincided with new claims of power by the papacy, which elevated the role that Latin played as the universal language of medieval Europe. As the keepers, in a sense, of the Latin tongue, the church rose to new pinnacles of power. Now, along with the safekeeping of the soul came a new command over speech and literacy; the command of Latin gave the church a growing monopoly on belief, something that reinforced its own claims as an independent estate. To understand how the church gained control over belief, one has to remember that during the Early Middle Ages (500–1000) the only literate people of Europe comprised mostly clerics.

During the Early Middle Ages, a small number of clergymen, mostly monks, had struggled to protect what was left of the ancient Greco-Christian worldview from the nomadic invaders. Among the treasures of the past that these men had saved were the writings of Porphyry (232–304), Augustine of Hippo's *Confessions* and *The City of God*, and the writing of Ancius Manlius Severius Boethius (480–525). Porphyry was a Neoplatonist philosopher of the third century who wrote about every aspect of Greek philosophy and science as they applied to both life and pagan religions. As mentioned in chapter two, Augustine of Hippo was the great theologian who explained the fall of Rome to the Roman people, as well as the role of the church in the future of humanity. And Ancius Manlius Severius Boethius was a minister of Theoderic, the Ostrogoth, who captured Italy in the fifth century. Boethius found himself condemned to death for disloyalty in 525, but prior to his execution, he spent most of his life in the pursuit of learning, as well as his vast project of translating and commenting on philosophical texts. All three authors provided the primary sources of Christian theology, neo-Platonism, and Aristotelian logic that had survived the destruction of the Early Middle Ages (500–1000). These sources excited the beginnings of curiosity during the High Middle Ages.

Unfortunately, prior to the revival of commerce and cities, the continued destruction of Roman culture by wave after wave of nomadic invasion caused the loss of much of Europe's Greco-Roman heritage. Included in the casualties was the ability to read, write, and speak Greek. Thus, Latin alone had survived as the language of the church and of universal knowledge. As a result, Latin helped to define the "estates" within European Christendom and separate the church from the realms ruled by kings. In medieval Europe, the newly arrived Germanic tribes spoke what became known as the "vulgar" languages. "Vulgar" defined a language spoken within a feudal "state" ruled by a king or nobleman who commanded a population of uneducated people. In medieval Europe, the languages of the invading nomads blended with Latin in the old Roman provinces to create the Romance languages of Italian, French, Spanish, Portuguese, and Romanian. In Central Europe, the Germanic tribes kept a pure German tongue because they settled on lands outside the old Roman Empire. Two new linguistic anomalies developed during the High Middle Ages. When the Duke of Normandy conquered England, Norman French blended with Saxon German to create English. And, when Otto I defeated the Magyars, they retreated to Hungary, where the Hungarian language developed.

After five centuries of chaos during the Early Middle Ages, a process of change began during the eleventh century that coincided with the end of the nomadic invasions and the liberation of the papacy. This change occurred as a parallel event to the recovery of commerce and the re-emergence of towns. This change also reflected a new inquisitiveness about the order of things in the universe, a new inquiry that went well beyond the certainties offered by biblical revelation, the authority of the church, and the fragments of Aristotle and Neoplatonism that had survived the fall of Rome. The hallmark of this new movement of thought was the shift in the relative importance of monasteries as compared to cathedrals.

The Survival and Resurrection of Learning

During the Early Middle Ages (500–1000), monasteries served as the key institutions that preserved and advanced classical thought. During the High Middle Ages (1000–1300), cathedrals replaced monasteries as the centers of thought that ushered in a new age of intellectual inquiry. The reason behind this shift is that monasteries were ideal for preserving Greco-Roman thought because of the rigorous discipline they imposed on the monks they housed. This discipline, physical, behavioral, and intellectual, functioned well in protecting the works of the past in the face of nomadic destruction. During the High Middle Ages, however, this monastic discipline proved too rigid. Instead, the cathedrals, which were constructed in or near the new urban centers, brought learning from the cloistered monasteries in the countryside to an urban populace. These new cities offered a more flexible intellectual environment, one in which clerical and secular scholars could respond to the new curiosity inspired by the illegitimate conditions of urban life.

Like a city at the time, a cathedral was a corporation. This institutional design gave cathedrals legal standing, just as charters defined enfranchised cities. As a legal entity, a cathedral had the authority to perform certain "secular" religious services that, in a sense, brought the church into the world of laypeople. In other words, the priests who served in those parishes administered by a cathedral and its bishop belonged to the "secular clergy," that is, they worked with the general population and provided the services that secured salvation. All of the clergymen who served in the cathedral itself, however, were not necessarily priests. Some of these men were "canons," lawyers who developed the laws that governed the cathedral as the center of the city. Since all members of the clergy had to be literate, monks, priests, and canons all had the ability to read, write, add, subtract, and keep records. A canon, however, did not have to follow the rigorous discipline of a monk, and was not distracted by having to perform the daily services of a parish priest. Instead, canons spent their lives in scholarly endeavors, working to discover the means to make the church in general more effective and independent. The questions they answered gave the cathedral schools the opportunity to develop more freely and to follow their own lines of reasoning.[23]

This general trend, however, does not mean that all the great intellectuals of the High Middle Ages worked solely in cathedrals. Two great medieval thinkers, Lanfranc (*c.*1000–1089) and Anselm of Canterbury (1033–1109), are good examples of transitional figures because both men worked in cathedrals as well as served as monks (see below). Each developed a career as a great intellectual at the beginning of the High Middle Ages, served as a monk, and ended up at the cathedral at Canterbury. There they took on the role of the secular clergy, in which they redefined the intellectual life of England as the archbishop. Lanfranc took this office as the first Norman Archbishop; Anselm was the second one.[24]

The greater freedom enjoyed by cathedrals (as compared to monasteries) led to the development of universities. Universities were corporations that emerged out of the cathedral schools of the eleventh century, and continued to appear across Europe in the twelfth and thirteenth centuries. And like the cathedrals, in time universities took on a legal identity of their own; in their case, the universities needed to be a corporation to function as independent sources of knowledge. By the twelfth and thirteenth centuries universities began to change with the conservation, dissemination, and advancement of knowledge. New universities continued to appear because of the growing demand for instruction in law, medicine, and theology, a demand driven by the rise of church power during the pope's long struggle with the Holy Roman Emperor. The new universities also launched a *renaissance* inspired by the urbanization that followed in the wake of the commercial revival.

The rising authority of the papacy and the intellectual function of the cathedrals led the canons throughout Europe to develop canon law. This legal system comprised the regulations of the church that governed dogma (the established practices of the clergy) and explained the mysteries bound up in the sacraments. Canon law made the church the best-governed institution during the High Middle Ages, and it inspired an interest in the law itself. In contrast to this development of law, the mysteries embedded in the sacraments motivated a separate inquiry into theology. This second inquiry set theology apart from the law as a unique discipline. Because those who studied theology assumed that they could explain the nature of God with their newly attained knowledge, this discipline became the "queen of the sciences," meaning, as it turned out, that theology set the stage for all other fields of study.

While the church sought independence from kings, the formation of universities, urbanization, and the rejuvenation of commerce inspired a secular interest in the law as a means to protect incorporeal property (i.e. the illegitimate wealth of commerce, money and goods mentioned above). Without legal protection, incorporeal property, as opposed to "real estate," could suffer the assaults of the men of "estates." Also, students trained in Roman law while attending the universities became the natural allies of kings, who sought to reform the structure of power within their realms. This alliance allowed medieval European kings to keep abreast of the new powers acquired by the pope with his development of canon law.[25]

To meet the demand for the study of law, students who attended the new universities acquired degrees that licensed them to provide the services specified in their diplomas. At first, the term "university" meant that each student was part of a corporate existence, a member of a legitimate community of scholars. And at the time, the university drew its students from all walks of life and subjected them to the same sort of licensed instruction. Later, the value of the education one could attain at a university changed, when popes and kings recognized that students educated there could enhance clerical and royal power if brought into the service of the church or the state. With the support of such powerful men, the term "university" described something more than merely a corporation; this term defined "universal" knowledge.

During the High Middle Ages, universities formed in Salerno, Naples, Rome, Florence, Bologna, Padua, Grenoble, Basel, Heidelberg, Cologne, Vienna, Prague, and Leipzig to represent the intellectual life of Central Europe. At the same time, universities formed in Seville, Salamanca, Toulouse, Avignon, Montpellier, Bordeaux, Poitiers, Bourges, Orleans, Paris, Oxford, Cambridge, Glasgow, and St Andrews to constitute the scholarship of Western Europe. Both sets of chartered schools attracted talented individuals to acquire the new knowledge. As a result, each university tried to entice the best teachers in the arts, sciences, theology, law, and medicine to join with their students to develop the best institutions of higher learning as part of the new fabric of society.[26]

The universal acceptance of a college degree derived from the new interest that kings and the papacy placed in these recent schools as they spread throughout Europe. Yet, since the church was still in the process of developing a universal worldview for Christendom, anyone receiving a degree from a university had to swear loyalty to dogma. Thus, all graduates from the new educational institutions had in effect become agents of the church through these new schools. The way these schools formed, however, varied geographically. Those found in southern Europe attracted rich and powerful men to take the initiative to create the first universities and become their first students. Those found in northern Europe began later when their professors banded together to seek corporate status.

Theology and the Emergence of Scholasticism

These universities produced a series of exceptional clerics who stepped forward to help the church revive theology and philosophy during the High Middle Ages. These exceptional men stressed God's all-powerful nature, and they believed that their use of reason and language made God's will accessible. They based this opinion on the ancient Greek concept of *logos* (see chapter two). These scholars revived *logos* as the idea behind Plato's forms, and Aristotle's final cause. For them, *logos* permeated nature as the will of God, who was both the creator and the soul of the universe. They argued that since *logos* meant word, speech, and logic, and facilitated an understanding of universal knowledge, it could also help humanity rediscover an understanding of God's plan.

Emerging in the eleventh century, men like Lanfranc and Anselm (mentioned above) set the standard for learning. Lanfranc was an Italian churchman and one of the first to launch the new wave of education prior to the rise of universities. Educated in Italy, initially, he crossed the Alps into France and turned to theology in order to study with the leading theologians at the cathedral school in Tours. Later, he taught at the cathedral school at Avranches, and later still he founded the Abbey at Bec in northern France. There he taught, among others, Anselm of Canterbury and Anselm of Badagio (who later became Pope Alexander II). Lanfranc became entangled in theological disputes with his teachers after establishing himself at Bec, but he managed to extract himself from trouble at the church councils of Vercelli (1050), Tours (1054), and Rome (1059). Twenty years after the council at Rome, he composed a medieval classic entitled *De Corpore et Sanguine Domine* (the Body and Blood of the Lord) that defined the doctrine of transubstantiation and became dogma for the remainder of the Middle Ages. Finally, Lanfranc ended his career as the Archbishop of Canterbury, because he was the chief religious advisor to the Duke of Normandy, William the Conqueror. William conquered England in 1066 and brought his nobility and clergy with him across the English Channel.

Anselm of Canterbury had the same type of transitional career as Lanfranc and, as mentioned, also ended up as the Archbishop of Canterbury. Anselm's fame, however, comes from a much broader role in the development of medieval philosophy than simply the refinement of dogma. He is best known for his distinctive method of argument: *fide quaerens intellectum* (faith seeking understanding). Anselm was a Christian Platonist who drew much of his approach from both Augustine of Hippo and Boethius (mentioned above). Anselm is most famous for his proof of the existence of God, using what became known as the "Ontological Arguments."[27]

The first ontological argument came from his treatise called the *Monologion*, which begins with the existence of good in our world. If good exists, then an immediate source for good must also exist. If such an immediate source exists, then it must derive from a supreme good. If a supreme good exists, it must come from a being responsible for such a condition. Such a being can only be God. His second ontological argument comes from the treatise *Proslogion* and argues along a similar line of reasoning. He begins in the *Proslogion* by postulating the conceptual existence of a being greater than any other that can be imagined. He argues that anyone who has an imagination and the capacity to reason would come to conceive of such a being. Then he argues that a being greater than any other that can be imagined cannot be the greatest being unless it also exists in actuality. He contends that existence is that state of being which gives this Supreme Being its ultimate, conceivable supremacy. He concludes, therefore, that God exists. And because God exists, Anselm adds, everything else exists.[28]

The work of Lanfranc and Anselm of Canterbury revealed a new level of sophistication in Europe's cultural landscape. These two transitional figures demonstrated the new dimensions of the medieval imagination as well as the quest for a clearer link between human understanding, God, and the new role of the church in medieval life. The work they started picked up momentum with the establishment of universities. The greatest figures of these universities appeared during the twelfth century, in such men as Peter Abelard (1079–1144),[tt] Bernard of Clairvaux (*c*.1090–1153), and Peter Lombard (*c*.1095–1160). These three men set the tone for a contest between logic and faith that formulated a medieval style of thought called scholasticism. Scholasticism did not pit logic against revelation in the same sense that knowledge separated from faith at the hands of William of Ockham (1285–1347) during the Late Middle Ages (see below). Nor did scholasticism represent the way science challenged religion after the scientific revolution (see chapter seven).

Unlike the separation of faith from knowledge during the Late Middle Ages (1300–1500), "scholasticism" defined a set of scholarly and instructional techniques developed during the High Middle Ages. "Scholasticism" obtained its meaning from the Latin *scholasticus*, which identified a "master of a school." Instead of the dispute between faith and knowledge mentioned above, scholasticism created a style of instruction that began in Bologna (founded in 1088). This style used questions and answers, dialogue, and disputation to discover the truth. From Bologna scholasticism then moved throughout Europe to become the method of instruction for three centuries. The term "scholasticism," however, did not mean a uniform method of inquiry; instead, it varied from place to place depending on "the master of the school." What scholasticism produced in common among all the schools was the universal curriculum that defined the focus of the university itself.[29]

One of the premier scholastic masters of the High Middle Ages, Peter Abelard, defined medieval logic. According to Abelard's theory of logic, propositions are sentences that are either true or false. What a proposition says is what it represents as an assembly of words. Words are universal but imprecise concepts that signify the meaning of the things that they name. Words take various forms: nouns, adjectives, verbs, and adverbs. Words are objective, they form a system of classification for things found in nature, but they are not universal manifestations of the things themselves, as Plato had claimed (see chapter two). Rather they are thoughts that carry con-

---

[tt]Abelard poses an interesting question concerning the role of a cathedral versus monastery education. He was the product of a cathedral education at Notre Dame, opened his own school outside Paris after breaking with his teachers, and is reputed to have helped found the University of Paris. He had a disastrous romance with Heloise (died *c*.1164), impregnated her, and suffered castration at the hands of her uncle, the canon of Notre Dame. He then ended his career as a monk.

ceptual uncertainties about things that only propositions can resolve. Words can be assembled into propositions, and propositions can be assembled into arguments that have the coherence of logic. Logic resolves the imprecision of words, and propositions, organized in logical sequences of sentences, achieve the coherence of truth.[30]

Using this theory, the body of Abelard's work demonstrated the lack of logic in the accumulated texts of the church. These documents provide sentences that failed to provide a rigorous and coherent understanding of Christianity. Collectively they state things that violate the law of contradiction, the intent of the church fathers, and the Holy Writ. The words used by the church did not have the logical precision that Abelard's theory required. Abelard's rival *scholasticus*, Bernard of Clairvaux, objected to this approach. Bernard's reaction to Abelard's writings condemned his text for placing logic before faith. Bernard reversed the priority of logic and faith and used faith to cement together the apparent incoherence of the church texts. Bernard challenged Abelard on the basis of faith and succeeded in getting Abelard's work condemned at the Council of Sens in 1141. This destroyed Abelard's reputation because the Council of Sens' condemnation was Abelard's second one. The first had occurred at the Council of Soisson in 1121.[31]

Peter Lombard achieved what Abelard set out to do but had done so imperfectly in his masterwork, *Sic et Non* (Yes and No). In Lombard's masterpiece, *Liber Sententiarium* (the *Book of Sentences*) he achieved the synthesis that Abelard's prologue to *Sic et Non* had proposed but not attained. Indeed, Lombard's *Book of Sentences* became the key work used by medieval scholars to teach logic during the High Middle Ages. The *Book of Sentences* used a strategy that started with a brief summary of the issues at hand. It then went on to cite several quotations from Scripture and the church fathers to support the presentation. Next Lombard addressed apparent contradictions as represented in the words and propositions of these cited texts to seek a resolution in the meaning behind the words. In effect, he tied the prologue of Abelard's *Sic et Non* to the body of his text and achieved the resolution that Abelard had posited. This approach defused the power of logic as represented in *Sic et Non* and realigned it with revelation.[32]

The Recovery of Aristotle, A Contrast with China, and a new European Orthodoxy

During the twelfth century, the Crusades (mentioned in chapter four) had opened new avenues of communication between Europe and the Muslim world that ended up restoring the entire corpus of Aristotle to medieval Europe. Regular contact with the Islamic regions of the ancient

Roman Empire, especially through Spain, Sicily, and the Levant, had introduced Europe to Arabic commentaries on Aristotle. These commentaries provided the Aristotelian explanations of the universe based on observations. The brilliance of Aristotle's explanations not only stunned the medieval imagination, but posed a powerful question for scholars of the High Middle Ages. How could someone who had lived long before Christ have created such a vast and compelling explanation of nature without the aid of divine revelation?

The profound impact of this question caused medieval European scholars to reconsider the relationship between a philosophical inquiry and the revealed truths of Scripture and the church fathers. Aristotle became the unquestioned medieval authority concerning the secular world. In a sense, he had the same level of influence on European scholarship that Buddhism had on Confucian philosophy. Both Buddhism and Aristotle caused the Chinese and medieval Europeans, respectively, to reconsider their basic beliefs about the universe and to generate new and workable syntheses. Both produced powerful syncretism that became so compelling within their respective cultures that they came to dominate philosophy and science for the remainder of their different traditional eras. Yet two major differences distinguished the syncretism that occurred in China and medieval Europe. The first was that Buddhism was completely alien to the Chinese experience before its arrival during the fall of the Han, while Aristotle was already part of the Western medieval consciousness. The thoughts of Aristotle existed as fragments in the works of Boethius and Porphyry that the Early Middle Ages preserved for medieval Europe. The shock of the High Middle Ages, however, was the revelation of the overwhelming power of the entire body of this Greek philosopher's insights into nearly every discipline of human inquiry.

The second major difference was that the Chinese syncretism occurred within a functional political ideology thoroughly integrated with the political institutions of the Tang and Song Dynasties. The European syncretism saw no such union because medieval Europe placed the church and the state in separate "estates." Medieval Europe was a collection of conflicting feudal "estates, states, and statuses" as well as the emerging new "corporations" that rivaled one another for legitimacy. During the High Middle Ages, two major areas of conflict arose, as mentioned. The first was the rise of the papacy at the expense of imperial power in Central Europe. And the second was the illegitimacy of cities and incorporeal property within feudalism. The new syncretism between Aristotle and Catholic dogma now added a third major pattern of dispute within the medieval tradition, a conflict that emerged during the Late Middle

Ages and continued to unfold during the early modern era (see below). The overwhelming authority of Aristotle during the High Middle Ages joined his worldview with medieval theology in an uneasy marriage of ideas that led to endless disputes. In addition, the welding of his sciences to Catholic dogma would require the church to defend ancient Greek physics and astronomy against developments that occurred during the Copernican Revolution of the early modern era (see chapter seven).

Thomas Aquinas, Master Theologian

The medieval syncretism between Aristotle and Christian theology was the brainchild of Thomas Aquinas (1225–1274). The key elements of Aquinas' synthesis began with his treatment of the multiple paths that led to an understanding of God. As Aquinas saw it, theology functioned as an intellectual tool to address the role of God directly; philosophy was a more indirect route that required a marriage between Aristotle's politics and Augustine of Hippo's Neoplatonic interpretation of original sin. A third path was a union between the divine creation and the Aristotelian sciences, as the two blended into one system of understanding nature.

Aquinas clearly distinguished between a philosophical inquiry into nature and a theological investigation into the majesty of God. For him, philosophy revealed the truth through the light of reason, and theology presupposed faith in divine revelation. Both served as sources to understand sacred doctrines. Yet, while reason could demonstrate the processes of nature as governed by causation, philosophy could not unveil those things that only God has chosen to reveal to humanity. The revelation of these divine things required faith as the initial point of departure to open the mind to the secrets buried in Scripture. Despite the fact of there being two different paths to solving the mysteries of the world, the two had to unite as one route to God. Aquinas argued that since God had created both paths, they had to have a common purpose: to enlighten humanity. The synthesis between philosophy and theology became the ultimate path to God.

Aquinas' union of theology with philosophy viewed God as both the divine creator of all things (theology) and the cause behind all events in nature (philosophy). God not only made the universe and gave it purpose, but was also the active agency behind all natural processes. Accordingly, God linked the Christian concept of creation with an Aristotelian model of causation. All physical events in the universe produced a series of immediate causes and local effects (Aristotle's physics). But events required an ultimate cause to set the series in motion (Christian theology). Aristotle had proposed an unmoved Prime Mover as this ultimate cause. Aquinas declared the Prime Mover to be God. Aquinas then linked all natural processes to divine purposes to close the loop between theology and philosophy. His success in this endeavor created such a powerful synthesis that scholasticism had no new ground to break after Aquinas. He had completed the journey from Aristotle to God that became the *Summa Theologiae* of the Roman Catholic Church.[33]

The union of Aristotelian philosophy with Christian theology in Aquinas' masterful synthesis linked the legitimacy of Greek scientific speculation with Catholic dogma in a manner that satisfied the needs of the thirteenth century. The study of Aristotelian philosophy as a co-equal partner to Christian theology, however, legitimized scientific inquiry for its own sake. Indeed, Aquinas' faith that the two forms of scholarly study, theology and philosophy, would lead to the same conclusions was based on his faith in the creator. God is a being who gave humanity all the tools that people needed to understand his universe. But the expectation that scientific inquiry and theology would arrive at the same mental destination was a risky assumption to make. Over time, the methods that Aristotle's scientific inquiry infused into the Catholic worldview broke apart the union Aquinas set out to create. This breakdown of beliefs occurred with the crises the church faced in the Late Middle Ages (1300–1500).

The Late Middle Ages and a Split in Medieval Europe's Imagination

The crises of the Late Middle Ages comprised the famine, plague, and warfare mentioned in chapter four. This collective disaster devastated the population, but did not distract Europe from the intellectual ferment started during the High Middle Ages. Even in the midst of a frighteningly high death rate that was interpreted to forecast the events of the Apocalypse, medieval Europe demonstrated a continued passion for learning. What emerged from 1270 to 1500, however, appears to have been an intellectual split in the medieval imagination. One approach was an intellectual revolution that led to the Renaissance (1300–1600). The other approach speaks to the waning of the Middle Ages (1300–1500).

Intellectual developments in Europe during the Late Middle Ages witnessed these two distinct cultural attitudes, even as they contradicted each other. Italy was breaking out of the medieval mold. Italian intellectuals started a reawakening of Greco-Roman values that liberated the medieval individual from tradition and ushered in the modern era. In contrast, the rest of Europe was bringing to a conclusion the ideas and sensibilities inspired by the philosophical developments of the twelfth and thirteenth centuries. These intellectuals perpetuated a belief in the orthodoxy of Aquinas, but found themselves confronted with an enraged God who visited famine, plague, and warfare upon a sinful Christendom. Some interaction occurred between the two intellectual trends, but each in its own way drew Europe toward two distinct events in the modern age: the continuation of the Renaissance (1500–1600) and the Reformation (1517–1648 (see chapter seven)).[34]

The Renaissance blossomed in Italy and ultimately replaced the medieval concept of legitimate "estates" with individualism. The new emphasis on each and every human being as a singular person inspired Italian intellectuals to define the capabilities of the individual as an actor with a free will that had the potential to leave a mark on posterity. Simultaneously, elements of the Italian Renaissance inspired northern European scholars to lay the foundation for the Reformation. The Renaissance scholars of northern Europe picked up the banner raised by Italy and focused on Christianity by elevating the voice of the individual in protest against the established Roman Catholic Church. Yet, once this protest took on an organized form after 1517, it sought goals very different from those of the Renaissance. The Protestant sects that challenged Roman Catholicism sought to subordinate the free will of the individual to God's majestic and predestined plan. Together, the Renaissance and the Reformation pulled Europe in opposing directions that tore the social fabric of medieval Europe to shreds. What eventually emerged were the elements of the modern era (see chapter seven).

What the Renaissance and Reformation represent is this split in the European imagination. This split began at the close of the High Middle Ages in 1300 and focused on issues raised by assimilating Aristotle into medieval theology. These issues dwelled on an old question from ancient Greece: which is more real, transcendental ideas or the objects found in nature? This question resurfaced at the end of the High Middle Ages and launched a new era of inquiry during the Late Middle Ages (1300–1500).

The philosophers addressing this ancient Greek question divided along two main lines: the Franciscans that rejected Aquinas, and the Dominicans that supported him.[‡‡] While the Dominicans found that their champion, Aquinas, clearly focused on transcendental ideas as central to their theology, the Franciscans found two champions that centered their inquiry on individual objects. One was John Duns Scotus (1266–1308), and the other was William of Ockham (1287–1347). Both championed the observation of objects over universals (i.e. Aristotle's final cause), so that the world of

---

[‡‡]One should note that Aquinas was a Dominican monk, the order that supported his orthodoxy, and his opponents came from the Franciscans, a rival order.

ideas for Scotus and Ockham depended entirely on the evidence offered by natural bodies. Duns Scotus was timid in developing this position, but William of Ockham was forthright.

Duns Scotus differed sharply from Aquinas in several key ways. Aquinas had accepted Aristotle's contention that transcendental forms existed in nature as final cause (i.e. the purpose behind every natural process). Aquinas then added God as the creator of these transcendental forms, and declared that both coexisted in final cause. Transcendental form was sensible to humanity as a part of cause and effect and could be understood through the use of reason. In the same sense, God was sensible through studying the world by using Aristotelian physics. Despite our ability to sense and understand form and God, however, Aquinas argued that it is not possible to experience either as separate from nature. Thus, to understand God, one needed both philosophy and theology.[35]

Duns Scotus rejected Aquinas' contention that philosophy could lead to an understanding of God. Duns Scotus proposed instead that philosophy led solely to a full understanding of nature. He argued that forms exist only in the human mind as ideas, and not as transcendental components of nature. Forms, however, were not simply figments of the imagination; rather, they were grounded in reality. The human mind recognized forms as universal classes of individual things. Humans could grasp the link between forms and things through the sensory observations of objects, and then, by using reason construct ideas in the human intellect. This approach, however, could not be used to understand God's will as in Aquinas' use of final cause. God and forms were not the same. Therefore, human knowledge of the natural world was not the same as our knowledge of the divine. Duns Scotus died, however, at the height of his intellectual power, without completing his work. That task fell to William of Ockham.[36]

William of Ockham completed what Duns Scotus had begun by 1320. In doing so, Ockham caused a revolution in medieval scholasticism. His revolution separated knowledge generated by observation and logic (i.e. truth based on ideas that correspond to what we see, hear, smell, touch, and taste) from faith (i.e. the existence of beings such as God, the soul, and Heaven independent of our experiences). This separation had been suggested by Duns Scotus, but it was Ockham who made the distinction absolute.

Ockham argued that knowledge did not coincide with "being" (i.e. transcendental forms) as Parmenides, Plato, Augustine of Hippo, and Aquinas had claimed. Instead, knowledge rested on logical propositions comprised of ideas divested of any metaphysical content. Ockham stated that the idea of things exists only as concepts in the human mind.

He claimed that the basis of ideas are the characteristics that individual objects share with one another. For example, "pencils" shared common characteristics, such as graphite columns surrounded by tubes of wood that could be sharpened at one end and used for writing or drawing. Observation of these shared characteristics generates concepts that are merely forms of thought (i.e. the idea of "pencil"). These forms of thought are then captured by words: the articulation of the noun "pencil." Conceptual forms joined as words in logical constructions called propositions, which contain truth only when these sentences correspond with objects in nature based on observation.[37]

Ockham held that since words such as "God," the "soul," and "heaven" do not appear to us as observable objects, they cannot be known logically. They form a realm of concepts belonging to faith alone. Only revelation and intuition can provide an understanding of these concepts. God, the soul, and heaven exist beyond the powers of reason, observation, and human knowledge. Hence, Ockham separated knowledge from faith and sent both down separate paths.

In the realm of science, Ockham's emphasis on things as observable objects over supposed transcendental forms laid a foundation for modern data collection. Medieval scholars such as Robert Grosseteste (1168–1253) and Roger Bacon (1214–1294) had already anticipated Ockham's style of observation as the basis for their inquiries. Both stressed the need for careful examination of objects and the use of experimentation in their scientific exploration of Aristotle's teachings of the physical universe. The work of Grosseteste and Bacon therefore supported Ockham's conclusions.[38]

Ockham's separation of faith and knowledge liberated science from theology. Science dealt only with observation and logic, theology only with revelation and intuition. Ockham's focus on individual objects, their similarities, and their differences allowed those who followed him to create the possibility of accurate data collection. The use of this newly collected data then allowed fifteenth and sixteenth-century observers to experiment with, and even test, Aristotle's physics. The result of these tests caused the Copernican Revolution in 1543.

At the same time, however, the liberation of faith from knowledge also launched a search for primitive, original Christianity as expressed in a quest to rediscover the pure voice of Jesus. This quest created a hunger for a church free of medieval politics that gained momentum during the course of the sixteenth century. Ultimately, Ockham became a major contributor to a movement that opened the door to the remainder of the Renaissance, modern science, and the Reformation simultaneously. All three were to forge a path into the modern era (see chapter seven).

Conclusions

Aquinas' orthodoxy disintegrated under the pressures that Ockham's logic generated. At the same time, the impulses that the Italian and the North European Christian Renaissances liberated now led to a rupture between faith and knowledge during the Early Modern Era. This rupture became known as the Scientific Revolution and the Reformation (see chapter seven). Furthermore, this rupture sent faith and knowledge down two completely different historical paths.

Meanwhile, the numerous corporations that fueled the intellectual reawakening of Europe during the High Middle Ages also encouraged this split between faith and knowledge. So many different institutional outlets for the historical development of law, philosophy, and theology permitted a dynamic debate between rival medieval sources of knowledge. These differences in avenues to discovery of the truth found in knowledge also fueled the struggle between the church and the state. The separation of church and state, and the contest between the pope and kings, saw each side sponsor its own ideological support systems. Sustained by a scholasticism that emphasized questions and answers, dialogue, and disputation, this style of inquiry fueled an intellectual ferment that traveled beyond the bound of an official orthodoxy. Furthermore, the existence of illegitimate property (i.e. money and goods) in centers of trade (cities) provided resources for new institutions of higher learning (universities) that allowed for the contradictions produced by faith and knowledge to find expression. The result was a liberation of the European imagination from tradition, without limit as to where the inquiry might or should lead. The changes this launched, in turn, placed a value on change itself and laid a foundation for modernization.

In contrast, during the same era in China, the union between belief (an accepted philosophical ideology) and action (imperial rule) reached full maturity. The scholar-gentry of the Song era (960–1279) established an orthodoxy that endured well into the modern era. This orthodoxy consolidated the power of the emperor, built an efficient administration of scholar-bureaucrats, and facilitated centralized authority in China that lasted until 1905. While Europe struggled without success to integrate philosophical and religious beliefs into a coherent ideology to provide an unquestioned consensus concerning political action, the Chinese managed to create exactly this integration. In fact the Chinese even achieved a new level of internal coherence that exceeded the accomplishments of the Han Dynasty (202 BCE–CE 220). Unfortunately for the Chinese, their success in this endeavor also ultimately limited future creativity in their political, social,

and economic imagination. Ironically, as Europe's traditions failed, this cha[
state of affairs unleashed the forces of modernization. Meanwhile, as Chir
tradition achieved full maturity, its success denied any possibility of m
ernization. This, perhaps, was the best example of the paradox of culture.

The end result was that Europe faced continual changes in its fundame
beliefs and political practices. In contrast, China settled into a new leve.
comfort with its ancient institutions. These diverging paths would ultimate
set both cultures on a collision course after 1500.

Notes

1   J.A.G. Roberts. *A History of China*, p. 83; Paul S. Ropp. *China in World History*, pp. 67–68; John A. Harrison. *The Chinese Empire*, p. 269; *Song Taizu (AD 927–976)* http://www.chinadetail.com/History/HistoricFiguresSong Taizu.php

2   J.A.G. Roberts. *A History of China*, p. 83; Paul S. Ropp. *China in World History*, pp. 67–68; John A. Harrison. *The Chinese Empire*, p 269; *The Renaissance of Neo-Confucianism.* http://www.chinaknowledge.de/Literature/Classics/ neoconfucianism.html

3   J.A.G. Roberts. *A History of China*, p. 83; Paul S. Ropp. *China in World History*, pp. 67–68; John A. Harrison. *The Chinese Empire*, p. 269.

4   Paul R. Ropp. *China in World History*, pp. 67–68 and 73–74; J.A.G. Roberts. *A History of China*, pp. 81–85.

5   Paul R. Ropp. *China in World History*, p. 73; John A. Harrison. *The Chinese Empire*, pp. 269–273.

6   J.A.G. Roberts. *A History of China*, pp. 82–84; *Song Taizu (AD 927–976)*. http://www.chinadetail.com/History/HistoricFiguresSongTaizu.php; John A. Harrison. *The Chinese Empire*, pp. 269–273.

7   John A. Harrison. *The Chinese Empire*, pp. 251–253; *Han Yu (768–824)*. http://web.whittier.edu/academic/english/Chinese/Hanyu.htm

8   John A. Harrison. *The Chinese Empire*, pp. 282–283; Robert Audi. *Chou Tun-yi*, pp. 120–121; Joseph A. Adler. *Zhou Dunyi: The Metaphysics and Practice of Sagehood*; John A. Harrison. *The Chinese Empire*, pp. 283–284; Robert Audi. "Ch'eng Yi." *The Cambridge Dictionary of Philosophy*, p. 115.

9   John A. Harrison. *The Chinese Empire*, pp. 286–287; Robert Audi. *The Cambridge Dictionary of Philosophy*, p. 121; *Zhu Xi's Views on Human Nature, On Zhu Xi's Theory of Mind and Methods of Self-Cultivation.* http://www2. kenyon.edu/Depts/Religion/Fac/Adler/Reln471/Chu-mind-self-cult.htm

10   John A. Harrison. *The Chinese Empire*, pp. 286–287; *Zhu Xi's Views on Human Nature.* http://www.iun.edu/~hisdcl/h425/zhuxi.htm; *On Zhu Xi's Theory of Mind and Methods of Self-Cultivation.* http://www.iun.edu/~hisdcl/h425/ zhuxi.htm; http://www2.kenyon.edu/Depts/Religion/Fac/Adler/Reln471/ Chu-mind-self-cult.htm

11 John A. Harrison. *The Chinese Empire*, pp. 286–287.
12 John A. Harrison. *The Chinese Empire*, pp. 286–287; *Zhu Xi's Views on Human Nature.* http://www.iun.edu/~hisdcl/h425/zhuxi.htm; *The Neo- Confucian, Zhu Xi.* http://www.fsmitha.com/h3/phil-asia02.htm; *On Zhu Xi's Theory of Mind and Methods of Self-Cultivation.* http://www2.kenyon.edu/Depts/Religion/Fac/Adler/Reln471/Chu-mind-self-cult.htm
13 J.A.G. Roberts. *A History of China*, p. 97.
14 *Ibid.*
15 See *Feudal System Legal Definition: A Social and Land Use in Europe during the Middle Age.* http://www.duhaime.org/LegalDictionary/F/FeudalSystem.aspx; *Incorporeal Property Law and Legal Definition.* http://definitions.uslegal.com/i/incorporeal-property/
16 Victor Davis Hanson. *Carnage and Culture: Landmark Battles in the Rise of Western Power*, pp. 135–170.
17 Norman F. Cantor. *The Civilization of the Middle Ages*, pp. 195–196; George Holmes. *The Oxford History of the Middle Ages*, pp. 116 and 180.
18 Norman F. Cantor. *The Civilization of the Middle Ages*, pp. 231–232; Robert Hessen. *Do Business and Economic Historians Understand Corporations?* pp. 6–7; *Burghers.* http://www.encyclopediaofukraine.com/pages%5CB%5CU%5CBurghers.htm
19 Norman F. Cantor. *Civilization of the Middle Ages*, pp. 265–271; George Holmes. *The Oxford History of Medieval Europe*, pp. 131–134; Maurice Keen. *The Pelican History of the Medieval Europe*, pp. 77–80; Morris Bishop. *The Middle Ages*, pp. 48–51.
20 Norman F. Cantor. *Civilization of the Middle Ages*, p. 258.
21 Norman F. Cantor. *Civilization of the Middle Age,* pp. 265–271; George Holmes. *The Oxford History of Medieval Europe*, pp. 131–134; Maurice Keen. *The Pelican History of the Medieval Europe*, pp. 77–80; Morris Bishop. *The Middle Ages*, pp. 48–51.
22 Norman F. Cantor. *Civilization of the Middle Age,* pp. 265–271; George Holmes. *The Oxford History of Medieval Europe*, pp. 131–134; Maurice Keen. *The Pelican History of the Medieval Europe*, pp. 77–80; Morris Bishop. *The Middle Ages*, pp. 48–51.
23 See *Medieval Philosophy.* http://plato.stanford.edu/entries/medieval-philosophy/
24 Robert Audi. *The Cambridge Dictionary of Philosophy*, pp. 26–28; *Anselm* (*c.*1033–1109). http://people.bu.edu/wwildman/WeirdWildWeb/courses/wphil/lectures/wphil_theme07.htm
25 Norman F. Cantor. *Civilization of the Middle Ages*, pp. 306–318; *Medieval Law.*
26 For images and a timeline see *The Origins of Universities.* http://www.cwrl.utexas.edu/~bump/OriginUniversities.html.
27 "Anselm." *The Cambridge Dictionary of Philosophy*, pp. 26–28; Anselm (*c.*1033–1109).
28 *Anselm on God's Existence.* http://www.fordham.edu/halsall/source/anselm.asp

29 Robert Audi. *The Cambridge Dictionary of Philosophy*, pp. 716–717.
30 Norman F. Cantor. *Civilization of the Middle Age*, pp. 330–343; *Peter Abelard. The Cambridge Dictionary of Philosophy*, pp. 1–2; Maurice Keen. *The Pelican History of Medieval Europe*, pp. 97–99.
31 Norman F. Cantor. *Civilization of the Middle Ages*, pp. 330–343; "Peter Abelard." *The Cambridge Dictionary of Philosophy*, pp. 1–2.
32 "Peter Lombard." *The Cambridge Dictionary of Philosophy*, pp. 575–576.
33 Norman J. Cantor. *Civilization of the Middle Ages*, pp. 443–448; "Thomas Aquinas." *The Cambridge Dictionary of Philosophy*, pp. 31–34.
34 Norman J. Cantor. *Civilization of the Middle Ages*, pp. 529–530.
35 *See John Duns Scotus.* http://plato.stanford.edu/entries/duns-scotus/; *William of Ockham.* http://plato.stanford.edu/entries/ockham/
36 Norman F. Cantor. *Civilization of the Middle Ages*, p. 532; "Duns Scotus." *Cambridge Dictionary of Philosophy*, pp. 212–213.
37 Norman F. Cantor. *Civilization of the Middle Age*, pp. 532–533; *William of Ockham.* http://plato.stanford.edu/entries/ockham/
38 Norman F. Cantor. *Civilization of the Middle Ages*, p. 534; *Robert Grosseteste.* http://plato.stanford.edu/entries/grosseteste/; *Roger Bacon.* http://plato.stanford.edu/entries/roger-bacon/

6

The Nomad Apogee of Power

The Paradox of Culture Springs a Trap

The unintended consequences embedded in the paradox of culture set a trap for the nomadic tribes of Central Asia that changed Eurasian history. In explaining how this happened this chapter deviates from the previous ones, all of which provided a comparison of China and Western civilization. This chapter focuses primarily on China. This shift in focus is due to the unique circumstances confronting the Chinese: their ability to resurrect an ancient heritage, and the fact that they perpetually lay in the path of nomadic invaders. Because of China's long vulnerability to the threat of attacks from herders, this sixth chapter focuses on the final episodes of nomadic conquest in Chinese history. The nomads produced two ruling dynasties: the one mentioned in chapter four, the Yuan (1279–1368), and the other the Qing (1644–1911). By answering this central question, both will be placed in a broader historical context. Who finally won the centuries-long conflict between those who herd animals and those who sow seeds? In between these two nomadic dynasties stood the Ming (1368–1644). A brief account of this dynasty is necessary to explain how China lost a key feature of Confucianism: its cultural flexibility. In contrast, Europe escaped one last major invasion by the herding warriors of Eurasia, so the nomads played no part in the political or military history of late medieval Europe.

At the beginning of the Ming Dynasty, China sent out fleets of ships to discover what lay west of the Indian Ocean. But once the discoveries were made, the Ming Dynasty chose to abandon its findings and retreat to its homeland. In contrast, Europe began its oceanic exploration half a century

China and the West to 1600: Empire, Philosophy, and the Paradox of Culture,
First Edition. Steven Wallech.
© 2016 John Wiley & Sons, Inc. Published 2016 by John Wiley & Sons, Inc.

later, mapped out two new ocean-based trade routes, and changed global commerce as part of the modern era (1492–1945). Why did Ming China abandon its discoveries, and Renaissance Europe change world history? Part of the answer is due to the damage done to the Chinese psyche due to Mongol rule. The other part of the answer is discussed in the first part of chapter seven: the emergence of modern Europe. But before we turn to this final contrast, we must come to understand how the nomads rewrote Eurasian history.

In the final episodes of nomadic invasions, China suffered conquest not just once but twice. The perennial problem of nomadic attacks reached its apogee when the Mongols conquered the Chinese in 1279. As explained in chapter four, this was a nomadic interlude because the Mongols did not stay in power long enough to sinicize completely. This meant that the Mongols never sufficiently comprehended China's heritage and culture to rule the Chinese people effectively. The end result was an era of misrule that so soured the Chinese view of their Mongol masters that the Ming Dynasty (1368–1644) imposed an intensely rigid form of neo-Confucianism on China. This robbed the Chinese of the creativity so common to the Tang and Song Dynasties. Hence, China lost a key feature of Kong Fuzi's worldview.

Kong Fuzi had said, "Learning without reflection leads to confusion, and reflection without learning leads to chaos."[1] By "learning," Kong Fuzi meant the knowledge acquired from the wisdom of the past as found in the *classics*. By "reflection," he meant that thinking in the present had to address contemporary circumstances before the wisdom of the *classics* could be properly applied. This means that one *should not* (my emphasis) repeat one's behavior without question, as tradition requires. Instead, one should adapt tradition to present circumstances through the appropriate adjustments made to past wisdom. The Tang and the Song Dynasties came very close to Kong Fuzi's recommendation: they adjusted the Han Dynasty's ideology to their circumstances before using it. But the Ming failed to make these adjustments. The Ming overreacted to Mongol rule and did not sufficiently include Kong Fuzi's emphasis on "reflecting." Hence, the Ming imposed far too rigid a form of neo-Confucianism, one that the Manchu would inherit as, the Qing Dynasty.

Prior to the Ming, the Mongols represent both the apogee of nomadic power and its downfall. The Mongols united all of Central Asia, Russia, and China into one domain. By accomplishing this feat, they took complete command of the Silk Road. This allowed them to ensure peace throughout Central Asia for a significant period of time. This peace prevented the raids that periodically reduced human numbers, through exporting population pressures by conquest of foreign lands. Instead, peace allowed the artificial symbiosis of the pastoral way of life to add more and more nomads to the landscape, people who depended on a steady supply of grass to feed their animals. At the same time, peace secured the trade carried out along the Silk Road. This economic boon to Central Asia added even more people to the local population, as commerce became an alternative to herding.

Ultimately, the luxury of sedentary civilization worked its wonders on the Mongol hordes. The hardy men who had fought for Genghis Khan declined in number due to the casualties of war. Then disease, caused by living among farmers, spread and killed even more of them. Furthermore, those nomads who belonged to non-Mongol confederations, and farmers living in sedentary communities, increased in number until they were willing and able to break away from Mongol controls. Finally, the seduction of civilization's sumptuous wealth reduced the number of Mongol warriors willing to ride endlessly day and night to fight in defense of the vast Mongol realm. In time the great khan could no longer count on the soldiers he needed, to strike at will within his immense empire, to hold it together. In addition, the harsh, highly mobile lifestyle of the steppe, which had so toughened generation after generation of warriors, the men whom the great khans had used to conquer their enormous domain, had all but passed. Ultimately, the extreme mobility and willing warriors needed for one ruler to command the land declined even as the cultural diffusion offered by Mongol-controlled trade created new conditions that ended the pastoral way of life.

Among the Chinese goods exported all the way to Europe were two key items: one was the bubonic plague, which hit China, Russia, the Middle East, and Europe, unleashing a massive demographic crisis already mentioned in chapters four and five. The second was gunpowder, transferred from China (where it was invented) to Russia, the Middle East, India, and Europe. Gunpowder inspired the Russians, the Muslims, and the European to develop cannon. This new weapon (mentioned in passing in chapter three) changed nomadic history completely. Cannon allowed sedentary Eurasian cultures to destroy the nomadic threat of invasion by neutralizing the danger of hordes of cavalry armed with their deadly composite, recurved bow. Ironically, then, it was the Mongols who transferred to farmers the means for sedentary peoples to defeat raids and sieges by nomads. And in the long run, cannon allowed sedentary armies to march unto the steppe, corner the nomads on several fronts, and destroy pastoralism as a way of life all along the Central Asian grasslands.

What followed is a set of events that cannot be fully explored here. Two items can be mentioned briefly. One is the rise of czarist Russia based on cannon. The czars used this new weapon first to break away from Mongol rule in 1460, and then, by 1700, destroy the nomads who had previously plagued Russia throughout its history. In Chinese history, soon after the czar rose to power, the Manchu also discovered the power of cannon. The Manchu's discovery, however, reveals yet another example of the paradox of culture: the Manchu were originally nomads, but their use of cannon destroyed their style of livelihood in Central Asia.

The Manchu were the last nomadic tribe to conquer China. They did so by bringing about the fall of the Ming in 1644 (see below). But unlike the Mongols, the Manchu stayed in power long enough to assimilate enough of Chinese civilization to rule effectively. Once in power, however, the Manchu wanted to close China to any further nomadic invaders. They therefore learned about cannon and used its against people like themselves. They expanded onto the steppe successfully until they ran into the Russians doing the same thing. This led to a new balance of power in Central Asia that this chapter will explore. This means that the Manchu's story is unique to Chinese history.

The Manchu represent both the last traditional dynasty to rule China as well as the nomadic people who eliminated nomadic invasions as a threat to China. By entering China as nomads, they inherited a Ming vision of neo-Confucianism that they lacked the skills to change. Given that they were cultural consumers, and not cultural creators, they could not apply the imaginative energy of the Song to adjust neo-Confucianism to their current circumstances. Therefore, they clung to the rigidity of the Ming worldview, from the dynasty they had replaced. This continued the rule of China with the most inflexible version of the political ideology that had dominated the Chinese imagination for so long. Ultimately, one aspect of the trap embedded in the paradox of culture was sprung, and China found itself locked into an unquestioning adherence to tradition that stifled the type of creativity that past dynasties such as the Song had generated. Furthermore, a second aspect of the trap snapped shut on the nomads of Eurasia: the Mongols facilitated the exchange of goods that led sedentary peoples to acquire the means to end herding as a way of life throughout Eurasia.

Mongol Conquest and Rule

The apex of nomadic power began during the life of Genghis Khan (*c.*1167–1227) and continued throughout the lives of his sons and grandsons into the fourteenth century. This violent era of nomadic conquest and consolidation saw the pastoral peoples of Central Asia not only capture their homeland but also China, Russia, and portions of Eastern Europe and the Middle East, creating the largest contiguous empire in world history. So great was their expansion across the Asian steppe that the Mongols actually brought Europe into contact with China in a common episode of Eurasian history. A common Mongol domain actually linked the frontier of Western civilization to the core of China through the powerful but unstable command of pastoral peoples.

Genghis Khan

During the thirteenth century, the Mongols created the first enduring empire to straddle parts of both the Asian and European continents. Theirs was an empire composed of, and maintained by, a confederation of nomadic tribes. The Mongols controlled more adjoining land than any other empire in world history, a massive realm of approximately 9 million square miles (some 1 million square miles larger than Czar Nicolas II's Russia on the eve of the Revolution of 1917). The imperial system that the Mongols assembled contained a population of 110 million people, or approximately 25 percent of the estimated 430 million humans living in the world in 1200. Only a century earlier, however, the Mongols were a divided people living in a number of autonomous clans engaged in fighting one another for survival. Their constant inter-clan violence entailed a low-level warfare waged over capturing women, stealing horses, and controlling fresh pastures. This recurring cycle of violence had trapped them in a lifestyle that promised nothing of the greatness they would enjoy a mere one hundred years later.[2]

Prior to their expansion into a major world power, the Mongols numbered about 700,000 people scattered across the flatlands of Central Asia. They lived and moved about in small bands, carrying with them the felt tents that served as their primary shelters. They had no villages, towns, or cities, and they did not plant crops. They lived off herds of omega animals, mostly sheep, cattle, and horses, and they camped on the open plains during the warm summers, moving into the valleys during the very cold winters. They owned very little, enjoyed few comforts, and lacked the luxuries known to urban life. They fought among themselves over the best grasslands, the control of which determined which groups prospered and which ones starved. These violent confrontations led to blood feuds that served to keep the many groups perpetually divided.[3]

All this changed with one man (already mentioned in chapter four); this charismatic leader, Temüjin, became known in world history as Genghis

Khan. Without any doubt, Genghis Khan was a highly ambitious and boundlessly courageous man with a keen intelligence and a sharp grasp of the potential of his people. He came from a minor clan that on its own could never have achieved any of the aspirations with which his imagination teemed. He began life precariously, with the death of his father by poison at the hands of a rival nomadic band. He was on his own at the age of eleven, and he managed to survive by navigating the uncertainties of youth.[4]

Born in 1162, Temüjin faced life on the steppe as a man before he experienced puberty. The death of his father led to Temüjin's clan, the Borjigids, abandoning his family because they thought defending the dead chief's son was too dangerous. Thus, the eleven-year old Temüjin, his brothers, his mother, and a stepmother and her sons were left to survive without the protection of an adult male. Temüjin soon fought with his older half-brother, killed him, and took over the leadership of the family. Within a year, Targqutai, a member of the rival Tayichiud clan, took Temüjin prisoner out of fear of this promising young boy. Temüjin, however, escaped, galloping away on a mare given to him by a friendly family. Soon after, the Tayichiud stole Temüjin's family horses, except for his new mare. He had to recover these animals on his own. He enlisted the aid of another boy his age, succeeded in recovering his horses, and returned home in triumph. By the time he reached the age of 15 he married, but members of the Merkit people, Temüjin's mother's tribe, sought revenge for her kidnapping by his father. They stole Temüjin's new wife and his mother, though Temujin himself managed to escape. He fled into the sacred forests of the Mongols (Burkhan Khaldun) located in the Khentii Province of northern Mongolia. His escape marked him as an exceptional man favored by the gods, and he raised an army based on this newly won fame. He used his new military force to fight his first battle, recover his wife, his mother, and her servants, and to steal numerous horses along the way. This pattern of survival and success set in motion a career of further battles that marked him out as a unique leader, so that by the age of 44, his people had elected him as their great khan. Using his reputation as a war chief, Genghis Khan then organized the Mongols for conquest, and discontinued their careers of petty thievery.[5] Genghis Khan changed Mongol history completely and transformed a scattered collection of clans into a vast horde of soldiers.

Genghis Khan's military greatness stemmed from his ability to mix Mongol traditions with tactical innovations, doing away with anything that threatened to hold him or his newly united people back. He retained the military skills of individual Mongol warriors and their highly effective use of cavalry and traditional weapons. Among the latter was the composite bow, which could fire an arrow farther than any other form of archery.*

He abandoned the autonomy of the Mongol clans, as well as the Mongol status structure, replacing them with a ranking system based on talent as measured by success in battle. When Genghis Khan began his career as an empire builder, the Mongols were a poor people, their territory limited to the steppe. Genghis Khan knew, however, that great wealth existed beyond their traditional boundaries, and he set his sights on taking as much land as he possibly could. The merging of his leadership skills with merit-based military promotion and traditional Mongol cavalry tactics propelled the Mongols across Central Asia and beyond.[6]

Genghis Khan's Soldiers: The Mongols

Key to Genghis Khan's success was the quality of his soldiers. The Mongols he led had lived a harsh existence on the steppe that began in obscurity and would have remained that way had not Genghis imposed his will on the people. No one knows where, exactly, the Mongols came from, and no one would ever have tried to discover their origins if it was not for the great khan. The Mongolian language is an Altaic one, has common qualities with Turkish and Manchurian, and comes from that vast northern region that borders on China's open frontier. Some scholars link the Mongols to the same ethnic group as the Xiongnu, who had occupied the northern steppe during the Han Dynasty. Perhaps the best way to understand where the Mongols came from is to recognize that their "identity" was forged in the vast community of people who Genghis Khan assembled. Prior to the formation of the great khan's hordes, the "Mongols" merely belonged to a boundless sea of nomads who shared a common tradition and language.[7]

Like other nomads such as the Turks and the Manchu, the Mongols subsisted on their flocks of sheep, and herds of horses and cattle. They lived in round, felt tents made of densely woven wool, capable of keeping out the harsh winter winds. Their culture maintained only an oral tradition, with no written script, and left little trace of their existence. Again, to call them "Mongols" prior to their existence as a cohesive community under Genghis Khan gives a false impression. People like the Mongols, the Turks, and the Manchu needed a great ruler to set them on the path to unity. Once unified, their successes in war held them together long enough

---

*In 1794 a member of the Turkish embassy to London demonstrated the power of the composite recurve bow against the famed Welsh longbow and fired an arrow 91 yards farther.

for them to find a desirable homeland, capture it, and build a sedentary realm that might endure. The longer any such realms managed to exist, the more likely that posterity would give these people a name. United from a common cultural background that pre-existed Genghis Khan, it was he who first forged all these Mongol subgroups into a major fighting force that resulted in this new, nomadic identity.[8]

The nomadic bands that Genghis Khan united into the Mongols, married through negotiated contracts (the expensive method), or by stealing and raping women (the inexpensive one).[9] Theft of horses and women granted these men prestige, which marked them as leaders. The bloodlines produced by so many stolen women intermingled Turks, Manchu, Mongols, Tartars, and any other name sedentary people might have given these nomads. The tangle of people living on the steppe shared a common, violent heritage that only a great man could unite. A powerful reputation as a successful thief led to the rise of a warlord. Then, from successful warlords arose a great khan. Until such a great khan appeared, however, the Mongols had no common identity.

Throughout the steppe lay open pastures rich in grasses capable of sustaining countless animals. There were few prominent landmarks by which to set borders, and few defensible sites to build into fortifications. The poor soils and short growing season of the region precluded plant cultivation. Adaption to this environment required herding the local, domesticated animal life (as a source of food) and figuring out how to move herds from place to place whenever these omega animals exhausted local grass supplies. Small groups of nomads lived in tents, called *gers*, and ate meat, cheese, and yogurt, and drank milk. The close blood relations between members of these small bands meant small gene pools, requiring them to marry outside their immediate families. Marriage outside a nomadic band expanded the kinship bonds between local families and helped them to form larger bloodlines, or clans.[10]

Mongol children learned to ride shortly after they learned to walk. As adults Mongols could ride for days on end without a break. Given the vast stretches of terrain in the steppe, mobility was essential for survival, so being without a horse was a death sentence. Developing the courage needed for battle, or stealing horses and women, began with the hunt. The skills acquired by tracking and killing game tested the child's talent for horsemanship as well as his use of the bow. Transferring these skills to conducting raids against enemy clans in adulthood came naturally. Stealing women and horses during a raid built up a warrior's reputation, but actually organizing such raids added to the luster of a warrior by establishing his leadership qualities. Those who grew into the strongest leaders could create alliances between clans to form tribes and between tribes to form a unified army. Genghis Khan was such a leader, perhaps the best one who ever lived.[11]

The Great Khan's Conquests

Under Genghis Khan's leadership, the Mongols became the most successful nomadic confederation in world history. Using his impeccably trained soldiers, he initiated a steady series of conquests that saw the capture of the core of Central Asia. He began in 1206 in command of a mobile force estimated at 100,000, along with a reserve of one to two million more who allied themselves with him. With these resources, he set out to conquer the world he knew. First he defeated the Tangut kingdom of north-west China, called Xi-Xia between 1209–1211, converting the region into a vassal state, before setting out to conquer northern China itself, with the help of the southern Song.[12]

Prior to Genghis Khan's invasion, northern China had fallen to another nomadic tribe called the Jurchen, who had established the Jin Dynasty (1115–1234). While fighting the Jin to take northern China in 1211–1218, Genghis Khan learned how to capture large cities, by employing the siege weapons perfected by the Chinese artisan-prisoners that he had seen the Jin use. From this point forward, when taking a town whose people put up a stubborn resistance to his forces, Genghis Kahn slaughtered them to a man. When taking other towns whose people only resisted him lightly, he sold the entire population into slavery. In each case, however, he was careful to spare the lives of the finest intellectuals and artisans, for later use in his grand design. The people of those towns that surrendered without a fight, found themselves merely incorporated into the great khan's expanding empire. Unsurprisingly, this overall strategy created a reputation for brutality that won him many victories without having to fight his opponents.[13] All the towns he captured, he taxed, and his empire grew richer as well as larger.

Genghis Khan started the war in northern China in 1211, but turned over most of the combat to his subordinates and turned west in 1218 to attack the Kara-Khirai Empire established earlier by the Khitans (a semi-nomadic hostile tribe); he completed this task by 1219.[14] Next, he turned his attention on the Turkish kingdom of Mohammed Shah II, called Khwarazm, in western Persia and Afghanistan. Within two years, Mohammed Shah's empire belonged to Genghis Khan, who had come to command all the land between northern China and Persia.[15] In 1223, Genghis Khan returned to Mongolia to punish the Tanguts of Xi-Xia for insubordination. He thoroughly defeated these rival nomads and then returned to the conquest of northern China.[16] During the winter of 1226–1227, Genghis Khan stopped to round up some wild horses, but a group of these animals bolted and his horse panicked. A wild charge followed and Genghis Khan fell from his mount, suffering severe internal injuries. At the age of 62, his immune system failed and fever set in, Genghis Khan falling mortally ill. Before he died he divided his holdings among his sons. An assembly of Mongols called a *quriltai* elected Ögödei (reigned 1229–1241), Genghis Khan's third son, as the next Great Khan.[17]

Ögödei

As the new khan, Ögödei preferred to delegate conquest rather than participate directly in combat (save for his role in the invasion of northern China between 1230–1233). His methods nonetheless ultimately extended the empire that Genghis Khan had started, and the Mongol domain grew well beyond what Ögödei's father had built.[18] Ögödei constructed a domain assembled mostly on the talents of others: he placed his sons in positions of power so that they served as local rulers. He also encouraged one of Genghis Khan's grandsons to function as his primary general. Through the efforts of all these children, Ögödei continued the conquests that Genghis Khan set in motion.

The talented grandson of Genghis Khan that Ögödei had selected to lead his armies west was Batu, who commanded the Mongol forces that invaded Russia and Eastern Europe. He went on to conquer vast stretches of land, including European Russia, Belarus, the Ukraine, Poland, Bohemia, and Hungary. In Europe, his armies crushed two forces mobilized by the Czechs of Bohemia, and the Magyars of Hungary, to capture key strategic points in Eastern Europe. He destroyed these European armies, proving Mongol tactics superior to feudalism's heavy cavalry.[19]

With the defeat of the Bohemians and the Hungarians, the Mongols were on the cusp of conquering Europe. At this critical moment, the Holy Roman Emperor and the pope were at each other's throats. Frederick II (reigned 1220–1250) ruled the Holy Roman Empire, and Pope Gregory IX (reigned 1227–1241) governed Christendom. Even as the forces of the emperor and the pope were confronting one another on the battlefield, Europe faced a very real Mongol threat from the east. Frederick and Gregory, however, could not disengage from their hatred of one another to unite in the face of this common enemy. But at this moment in time fortune smiled on the West; Ögödei died in 1241, forcing Batu to retreat. With the death of their khan, the Mongol armies had to withdraw and return east to their heartland in order to elect the new ruler in 1242. Thus, in a sense it was the traditional Mongol practice of convening all the tribes at a *quriltai* to elect their great khans that saved Europe from almost certain conquest.[20]

Ironically, Frederick II and Pope Gregory XI despised one another so much that they almost allowed the Mongols to conquer Europe. Each one of them spent virtually his entire career determined to defeat the other's claims to power. This was a continuation of the Gregorian Revolution mentioned in chapter five. These two men could not see past their hatred for one another to realize the danger that the Mongols brought to bear on medieval Europe. Just as Batu was poised to conquer Austria, the sudden death of a single man, Ögödei, allowed Europe to escape mass destruction, by pure luck.[21]

The Mongol's Fatal Weakness: Choosing the Next Khan

The death of Ögodei prompted most of the Mongol notables, save for Batu, to return to Karakorum, the seat of Mongol power. There they held their *quriltai* to elect the next khan. Meanwhile, Ögodei's talented wife, Töregene, was named regent until the election was completed. She planned to have her son, Güyük, named the next khan despite Batu's protest. Batu objected because he and Güyük had quarreled over who commanded the Mongols in Russia during their invasion west.[22]

Töregene engineered Güyük's rise to power by using the office of regent to manipulate the election. Still, she had to overcome a major obstacle: before Ögödei died, he, too, had quarreled with Güyük over his fight with Batu, and Ögödei had sent Güyük into exile. In the 1230s, Ögödei had made it known that he wanted another of his sons, Kochu, named as his heir. But Kochu's unexpected death in 1236 undid Ögödei's plans. Ögödei then named Kochu's son, Shiremun, as his favorite. This did not, however, necessarily make Shiremun the next khan. For her part, Töregene had to manage the election carefully so that her son, Güyük, could rise to the seat of power. Everything depended on the *quriltai*, where all the possible Mongol candidates would vie for power.[23]

Töregene began using the office of regent to ingratiate herself with the electorate. She offered certain people gifts, favors, and symbols of esteem. She did the same with the officers and men of the Mongol armies. The fact that she was a woman did not inhibit her powers in any way. The Mongols, like all steppe nomads, acknowledged the right of women to speak freely on any matter that might affect the fortunes of their family. This meant that the Mongols accepted Töregene's regency without hesitation and allowed her to exercise the full political power of that position. This did not mean that Mongol women were their men's equals, for females, like horses, were considered property that one could exchange or steal. Once within a family, though, a woman did, as mentioned, have a voice in family affairs.[24]

Töregene's closest ally in her plans for her son was a woman named Fatima, once the procuress of the most successful brothel in Karakorum. Because Töregene recognized Fatima as an excellent source of political information, she soon moved her to the palace and used her spies to shape the election. Fatima earned wealth and power by aiding Töregene in rewarding and punishing members of the electorate. Ultimately, Töregene and Fatima managed to place men loyal to Güyük in key positions of power. At the same time, Töregene continued to cultivate the electorate with the rewards of power that her office permitted her to bestow. In 1246, her plan bore fruit, as the *quriltai* elected Güyük as the next great khan. Shortly after her son's election, however, Töregene suddenly died (probably from poison). Upon Töregene's death, Fatima's power ended. Since Fatima had caused quite a bit of fear during her days of wielding influence with Töregene, Güyük pronounced Fatima a witch and had her executed. [25]

Güyük's reign was a short and bloody one. He wasted no time in killing his rivals, while civil war almost erupted with Batu. Güyük died from a fever within 18 months of taking the throne. Güyük's widow, Oghul, then declared herself regent in imitation of Töregene, but she met with sharp opposition. A tangled affair of maneuver and counter-maneuver frustrated her wishes, and the next *quriltai* elected Mönkle as the great khan. He was the son of Tolui, a beloved brother of Ögödei. Once in power, Mönkle immediately sought revenge against Oghul. His first act after celebrating his election was to execute Oghul, her three sons, and her female advisers. The bloodbath then spread to all prospective rivals in Güyük's family, and then crossed the empire to kill anyone of questionable loyalty. Once he felt secure in his power, Mönkle instituted a series of reforms throughout the realm based on lowering taxes on all his subjects (this is when Yelü Chu Cai's original sinicization program was restored, as already discussed in chapter four). In doing this, Mönkle had hoped to win popular support in order to begin his conquest of new lands. For his first such move he sought to invade the Southern Song Dynasty (1127–1279) as well as the Middle East.[26]

Mönkle's Quest for Conquest

Mönkle made use of his two younger brothers, Hülegü and Kublai, to carry out his miltary campaigns. Hülegü led his army against the Middle East, where he killed al-Musta'sim, his family, and put an end to the Abassid Dynasty in 1258. Hülegü also captured the remainder of Iran, Georgia, Armenia, Anatolia, and northern Mesopotamia, adding all of these provinces to the Mongol Empire. While expanding Mönkle's domain, Hülegü destroyed the famous cult of assassins, the original suicide-terrorists of the Islamic world. He also captured their impregnable fortress in the Erburz Mountains, along the southern shores of the Caspian Sea, and slaughtered all the inhabitants except for the imam. Hülegü used the imam to persuade the other assassin strongholds to surrender. Like all other Mongol generals, Hülegü employed terror to convince the enemy to surrender and avoid destruction.[27]

Mönkle chose to command the Chinese campaign himself, but he assigned Genghis Khan's third grandson, Kublai, the task of opening up a western invasion route. Mönkle's conquest of the Southern Song began in 1258 and proceeded along several fronts, of which Kublai's route in the west was only one. The campaign of 1258 mobilized four divisions. Mönkle's generals did not want to press the attack because the Southern Song occupied a climatic zone that the Mongols were afraid to enter. These men had fought in the tropics in India, where unfamiliar diseases spread quickly among them and thwarted their campaign. Mönkle insisted on the attack, however, and a curious equilibrium unfolded. As the Mongols advanced, winning victory after victory, the number of warriors who came down with dysentery also increased. Eventually it became obvious that Mönkle's generals had been right. The number of sick and dying became too much to bear, and the Mongol invasion stalled in the late spring of 1258. Once the monsoon rains typical of southern China began, disease and tropical weather eroded the military prowess of the Mongol armies. Still, Mönkle continued to press the attack. By the summer he, too, came down with dysentery. Soon his condition worsened, which has led some scholars to think he may have contracted cholera. He died in August. Once again, the Mongols had to turn around in the middle of a campaign and return to their capital to choose a new khan.[28]

His men bore Mönkle's body back to Karakorum, where they began to assemble another *quriltai*. Kublai and Hülegü were among the generals present at the gathering, at which Kublai and his younger brother, Arik Böge, were the leading candidates for the next great khan. Kublai already had a good reputation as an administrator and general, but his love of the Chinese lifestyle made some of the other Mongols uneasy. He seemed too sedentary-minded for a true nomad, while his brother and rival, Arik Böge, struck most of the Mongols as more reliable, and the *quriltai* chose Arik Böge as the great khan. Kublai decided to retreat to his realm in northern China. There he held his own *quriltai*, in which his men elected him as their khan in 1260. He then defied Arik Böge's authority.[29]

As mentioned in chapter four, Kublai's break with Arik Böge pitted the skills of both men against one another, although Kublai had an advantage. His administration in northern China had proven highly effective, the region's agriculture succeeding so well that it became the chief source of grain for Karakorum. Meanwhile, this Mongol capital had grown in step with the expansion of the empire and now required massive supplies of food. As the break between Arik Böge and Kublai intensified, a war between the two sides broke out. Kublai soon won, due to the climate.

Kublai's ultimate victory turned on a spell of bad weather in 1262–1263, which destroyed the supply of grass on which Arik Böge's Mongols relied. Those living on the steppe needed this grass to feed their horses. Without these horses, of course, all the nomads of the steppe would soon starve. This left Arik Böge with no choice but to surrender to Kublai, and the Mongols called yet another *quriltai*. Ironically, sedentary agriculture had forced the election of Kublai as the great khan.[30]

Kublai Khan's seizure of power and his triumph over Arik Böge did not sit well with all of the Mongols, and the issue eventually led to the division of the vast Mongol empire. Möngke Temür, the grandson of Batu, broke with Kublai Khan and took Russia as his domain. Hülegü also broke with his brother, and went on to rule the Middle Eastern portions of the empire from his headquarters in Afghanistan. Finally, the rest of those Mongols who distrusted Kublai Khan's Chinese ways, and preferred the mobile life of the steppe, rallied to another of Ögödei's grandsons, Khaidu, who established a realm in the Mongolian heartlands. Kublai Khan ended up with his Chinese provinces, Tibet, and parts of Manchuria. He also inherited the considerable task of completing the conquest of the Southern Song. None of the four Mongol khans had the military resources to compel the other three to submit to one great ruler, so the unity of the mighty empire that Genghis Khan had sought to create was now lost. But these four men were also realists in the sense that they agreed to cooperate with one another to the degree that their four great empires remained a common Mongolian zone. Their domestic policies, however, gradually drew their different domains further apart.[31]

One feature of the paradox of culture had led to this fracturing of the Mongol domain (as mentioned above in the introduction of this chapter). The vast size of the domain commanded by Mönkle prior to his death could only be traversed by hardy horsemen capable or riding day and night for weeks on end. Only vast armies loyal to the great khan comprised of such horsemen could enforce his will in a timely manner. In place of these horsemen, the wealth of sedentary life had worked its wonders on the survivors of the Genghis Khan, Ögodei, and Mönkle. Many of the nomads who made up Kublai's vast domain by now had grown accustomed to the luxury of their conquered lands. While they claimed they distrusted Kublai's sedentary ways, ironically these very same ways had seduced them into refusing to enforce his will. This allowed Kublai's brothers and nephews to break away and declare their own kingdoms. In the end, Kublai became known in history as Kublai Khan, ruler of China and Siberia.

The Yuan Dynasty: A Century of Uneven Rule

As mentioned in chapter four, Kublai Khan moved the Mongol capital from Karakorum to Dadu, the Mongol name for modern Beijing. He then changed the name of Dadu to Khanbalik (Mongol for "city of the khan"). There, along the northern frontier of China, he established a true Chinese style government when he launched the Yuan Dynasty (1279–1368). This was the beginning of a new dynasty that the Han people under his control had no choice but to accept. Prior to his capture of the rest China, he applied steady pressures on the Southern Song, from 1263 to 1279, with a determination that the Chinese could not resist. He completed the conquest by 1279: for the first time, all of China had fallen under the command of a nomadic ruler.[32]

Like all other emperors, however, Kublai Khan realized that to rule the Chinese people, he would have to adopt Chinese ways. Unlike many of the Mongols that Kublai Khan ruled, he understood that the Chinese would not accept a ruler who followed nomadic ways. He therefore insisted on a Chinese protocol at his court in Khanbalik. The imperial design of his empire was also Chinese. The only major difference that his rule exhibited was in its relations with the nomads to the north. His firm command of the northern frontier placed China on a more stable footing with the steppe peoples than ever before.[33]

Domestic politics under Kublai Khan were simple and of a quality that the Chinese recognized, even appreciated. Kublai Khan's 30-year reign, from 1264 to 1294, created a stable political system. He relied on a council of state that controlled military and foreign policy, a bureau of internal affairs that controlled domestic policy, and a control bureau that ran his civil service. He placed Mongols in the chief offices of state, and he used the Chinese Confucian exams to staff the lesser posts within his administration. His rule included a system of ethnic discrimination based on the length of time his subjects had lived under Mongol rule. At the top were the Mongols. Beneath them were nomads of non-Mongol ethnicity, the level of bureaucracy composed of foreign aides and allies of the Mongols.

Third came the northern Chinese, for they had experienced Mongol rule since 1217. Last came the Han people of southern China who had not come under Mongol rule until 1279. Mongols alone could carry arms, which required a general weapons search and collection from the rest of Kublai Khan's subjects. Even Chinese troops in the Yuan armies had to surrender their arms and horses when not on a military campaign. A set of Mongol laws applied only to the Mongols of his empire, while everyone else in the empire fell under the rubric of a Chinese system of rule.[34]

Before he died, Kublai Khan decided to replace the *quriltai*, with a system of inheritance to transfer power to his heir. As he well knew, the use of the *quriltai* had proven too disruptive in Mongol imperial history to maintain a stable Chinese dynasty. In addition to factionalizing the Mongol people, the *quriltai* had regularly disrupted military campaigns. Clearly, Kublai Khan recognized that the Chinese method of inheritance was superior, so he chose his heir apparent, Temür Khan, prior to his death. Temür Khan was Kublai Khan's grandson (reigned 1294–1307). He followed in his grandfather's footsteps. Although he ruled wisely, he did not have any sons to whom he could transfer power according to the tradition Kublai Khan tried to create. What followed was a series of eight different emperors in the next twenty-six years. These years of misrule soured the Chinese in their first nomadic dynasty. They concluded that only their traditional Chinese ways truly reflected the Mandate of Heaven[35]

What soon became obvious as well was a second major weakness of the Mongol system of rule: many Mongols distrusted Chinese ways. Had Temür Khan produced a healthy, competent heir, perhaps the history of the Yuan Dynasty might have unfolded differently. Instead, an era of rule by nomads poorly assimilated to the Chinese way of life produced brawling contenders for power. These nomadic rivals caused nothing but chaos among the Chinese people. What had been a system of orderly rule now descended into unregulated mayhem. Despite the rapid succession of incompetent rulers, each Mongol emperor was still the most powerful man in China. The Mandate of Heaven required such centralization of authority. In addition, the Mongol emperor's links to the khans of Russia, the Central Asian steppe, and portions of the Middle East, placed the Yuan ruler in a strategic global position of power.[36]

What followed, however, undermined Kublai and Temür Khan's combined competent reigns of 28 years (1279–1307). The Mongols in general understood very little about managing a sedentary empire. Unlike their Han subjects, they did not grasp the demands of maintaining a large-scale and complex system of irrigation at a level necessary to effectively control the Yellow River. With the tendency for this mighty river to climb out of its riverbed, "China's Sorrow" flooded with devastating effect in 1300. Following the deluge, it took decades for the disruption of food production in northern China to recover, for during this particular disaster the river had once again changed its course. To add to the problems faced by the Mongol regime, their officials failed to take notice of the silt continually mounting in the Grand Canal. In time the silt clogged the canal, cutting off the food supplies traveling north from southern China. Finally, the Mongols did not seem to understand that they had to limit the printing of paper currency in proportion to the supply of goods, their lax fiscal policies leading to rampant inflation. Mismanagement of paper currency, failure to maintain the Grand Canal, the devastating flooding of the Yellow River, the disruption of food production in northern China, and the outbreak of bubonic plague combined to cause a ruinous state of affairs. Even attempts at reform did not help. The Mongol emperor, Yuan Shundi (reigned 1333–1369), had assigned the task of reviving Mongol power to a talented young man named Toghto (held office 1349–1355). Toghto set about raising revenues to support Yuan armies, drafted peasants to bring the Yellow River under control, and assigned even more peasants to dredge the Grand Canal. The burdens imposed on the Chinese people by the implementation of his reforms, launched a rebellion. The Chinese had lost patience with the Mongols, and would not tolerate reform under their command.[37]

The Ming Dynasty (1368–1644)

Creation of the Ming

Chinese dissatisfaction with Mongol rule found expression in 1352 in a spontaneous peasant revolt in Quangdong, far to the south in China. There, peasant rebels, steeped in Chinese tradition, were responding to signs that the Mongols had lost the Mandate of Heaven. A full-fledged general rebellion against a failing dynasty followed by 1360, catching the Mongols at a time when they themselves expressed confusion over China's role within their empire. The Mongols had never fully grasped how to fit China within their vast holdings. At first, China had played a subordinate role when the Mongols united their sprawling regime. But Kublai and Temür Khan had reversed China's position within their portion of the Mongol domain; now Mongolia played the subordinate part to the Chinese regime. Thus, as China rose in rebellion in 1360 against the Yuan, even the nomadic tribes of Mongolia were fighting against their khan stationed in China.[38]

In 1360, local rebellions spread across southern China. In addition, piracy along the Chinese coast had begun as the Yuan tried to ship grain north when silt clogged the Grand Canal. At this point, the Chinese rebels found a talented leader and future emperor in a poor peasant from southern China, named Zhu Yuanzhang (reigned 1368–1398). He defeated the Mongols in the north by 1368, entered Khanbalik, and renamed it "Beiping" (northern peace). He then declared the beginning of the Ming Dynasty (1368–1644), taking the name Ming Hongwu as emperor. Several generations later, Zhu Yuanzhang's heirs changed the name of the Ming capital once more from Northern Peace (Beiping) to the Northern Capital (Beijing). Prior to this change in city names, however, Zhu Yuanzhang had to continue to fight pockets of Mongol resistance until 1382. Meanwhile, in 1368, the Mongol court fled China for Mongolia, and only a remnant of Mongol resistance remained until 1382.[39]

How the Mongols' Bitter Rule Poisoned the Chinese Imagination

While Emperor Ming Hongwu (Zhu Yuanzhang) had completely reunited the country by 1385, the Mongols left a bitter legacy in China. For more than a century, from 1215 to 1368, the descendants of Genghis Khan had ruled part or all of China with absolute authority. When Mongol rule had reached its apex under Kublai Khan, China had become part of a larger Eurasian empire that denied the Chinese their central role in domestic politics. This loss of centrality created a sense of dislocation for the Chinese. Yuan China was now part of a larger political system and not an empire fully defined by past Chinese practices. From one perspective, China had entered a political era that produced disastrous results in terms depopulation and the despoiling of Chinese culture. From another perspective, the nomadic political system implemented by the Mongols was the most efficient and centralized, at least briefly, to date in Chinese history. Also, these nomads had finally tried to integrate the sedentary portion of China with the nomadic north to create a universal peace along a frontier that for centuries had been accustomed to violence. To some degree, both points of view are correct.

Under Mongol rule, peace and order finally became a common experience in the vast lands of the Yellow River valley. Indeed, China had (involuntarily) joined a great political system that produced an era known as the Mongol peace. One could traverse Eurasia for the first time without being assaulted by nomadic bands. Furthermore, the Yuan Dynasty imposed a brief but effective and tightly organized administration on China that exposed the entire country to the will of the emperor. Yet, the efficiency of this new government crushed the Chinese with the heaviest tax burden they had ever experienced. In addition, the design of Yuan power focused on raising armies and not on civil order. Furthermore, the Mongols took command of a mature civilization accustomed to sedentary life, a foreign experience to the new rulers.

To the Mongols, indeed, China became the most important part of their empire, yet it was only a part. The Mongols cared little for Chinese culture. They had conquered China, occupied the land, and did not admire the Chinese people as natural leaders whom they needed to mimic. The Chinese expected the Mongols to accept an inferior role as a cultural consumer of the Chinese way of life. This is what every other nomadic group that had overrun part or all of China had done sooner or later. The Mongols, however, never conformed to this expectation. In fact, the Mongols expected the opposite. They regarded the Chinese as an inferior, defeated people, useful only as a source of revenue. This insult to the Chinese people and their culture was a completely alien experience to the Chinese elite. In effect, the Mongol interlude did more damage to Chinese culture than had the mere conquest of China. The Mongols had left a permanent scar on the Chinese psyche, which was to have powerful consequences.

Ming Ideological Rigidity

By the year 1400, the Chinese under the Ming fully exhibited the scars of nomadic rule, in that this dynasty produced the greatest political and cultural controls in Chinese history as a backlash to the former rule of the Mongols. No other culture in Eurasia came close to matching the internal coherence that this restored traditional Chinese dynasty effected and enforced. This internal coherence rested on an intensely rigid Ming worldview.

As a result of their distaste for the nomads, the Ming made an unyielding commitment to past Chinese practices that sharply reduced the flexibility found within China's political ideology. Returning to the Way as prescribed by the *classics*, and implemented by Confucian doctrine, the Ming linked a new level of authoritarian rule with Chinese traditions. This new state of affairs trapped China in a commitment to past practices that would stifle the creativity and experimentation found in the Tang (618–906) and Song (960–1279) dynasties. The Ming had lost the political agility that had seen the Tang and Song oversee the golden age of Chinese history. An unbending, autocratic form of rule took hold, one that tamped down Chinese ideological innovations for the Ming and the nomadic rulers that replaced them, the Qing Dynasty (see below).[40]

Part of this rigidity could be seen in the imperial exams reinstituted by the Ming Dynasty. Once in power, the Ming insisted that a candidate had to take each level of the exam so that no one applicant could skip a test. Rapid promotion by recommendation, as practiced in the past, was out of the question for the Ming. Once the first two levels were passed, the candidate then had to take the final exam at the palace of the emperor. There, the aspirant for employment in the Ming's bureaucracy ran into a form of imperial rigidity unprecedented in any testing circumstance.

After 1487, the Ming specified in detail the form that all answers to their exams must take in order to pass. The Chinese called this rigid essay form: the "Eight-Legged Essay." The first leg (*poti*), involved "breaking open the topic," introducing it. The second leg (*chengti*), entailed "receiving the topic," couching it in an appropriate setting. The third leg (*qijiang*), was "beginning the discussion," easing the reader into the main argument. The fourth (*qigu*), "initial leg," was the cause and effect portion of the essay that laid out the main issue. The fifth (*xugu*), "transitional leg," carried the reader to the heart of the essay. The sixth (*zhonggu*), "middle leg," elaborated on the first leg by extending the cause to the positive effects the main issue would have on China. The seventh (*hougu*), "later leg," clinched the argument. And the eighth (*dajie*), was the "conclusion." The Ming imposed this model on all essays because they needed a highly objective form of grading to handle all the many exams applicants turned in annually; they concluded that evaluating form was easier than worrying about the merits of content.[41]

"Based on the specific Eight-Legged grid, examiners… literally followed the number of legs and counted the number of characters in an essay based on the requirements of balanced clauses, phrases, and characters… If a candidate could not follow these strict rules of length, balance, and complementarities, then the essay was judged inferior. One misplaced character, or one character too many or too few, in building a clause in one of the legs of the essay could result in failure."[42]

The Ming's essay form clearly took precedence over an essay's content. The confining of accepted answers to this form dominated not only the examination itself but, in a sense, also Chinese intellectual life. China had retreated from the Song's free and open style of creative essays, a hallmark of the Chinese golden age. The Ming forced a form of intellectual regression on China that plagued Chinese history into the twentieth century.[43] From 1487 to 1905, Confucianism was bound and gagged by a mental straightjacket that denied a primary principle of the great philosophy:

adjust the past to the present to adapt its wisdom to contemporary needs. The Ming seemed only interested in the shadows cast by Confucianism rather than its creative content.

The Impact of the Mongols on Eurasia

At the apex of its power, the sprawling Mongol domain, Genghis Khan's legacy, marked a unique moment in Chinese history and, as it turned, out a unique moment—albeit one unrealized at the time—in the history of Western civilization/Europe as well. Genghis Khan and his successors had created a universal empire that at one point spanned all of Eurasia. Within the boundaries of this new empire, the people served one imperial ruler by the end of Ogödei's reign. In 1241, Mongol armies under Batu's command stood on the shores of the Baltic Sea in the north and controlled all the lands south to the Adriatic Sea. The contiguous nature of Mongol holdings permitted the reopening of the Silk Road so that Italians from Venice, such as Marco Polo's uncles, Niccolo and Maffeo Polo, could travel all the way from their city to Beijing unmolested, a mere 35 years later, in 1276. Throughout the center of these lands travelers used a refurbished Silk Road, which spoke well for the potential of pan-Eurasian trade.

The level of security that allowed one to move more or less safely from one end of this mighty empire to the other came thanks to the strength of the Mongol cavalry. These mounted forces used a common battle plan that nearly always brought positive results. Basically, the massive cavalry force fanned out into separate strike divisions that moved behind a far-flung forward screen of horsemen. This forward screen served as a feint to hide the true size of the advancing forces. Once in contact with the enemy, the forward screen began a skirmish that drew the opposing army forward, whence they were soon overwhelmed by the awaiting main forces. Now the forward screen divided into two wings that spread in opposite directions towards the enemy's flanks, even as the center of the Mongol army struck the unsuspecting opposition. This enveloping action broke the opposing army up into smaller and smaller pockets of resistance. At this point the success of the Mongol forces was just a matter of time.

Under Genghis Khan, the campaigns of 1219–1223 took the Mongols from northern Persia all the way west to the Dnieper River in Russia. Under Batu Khan, the great sweep of 1237–1241 moved well into Europe. By 1241, the Mongols having completely crossed Russia were wintering in Poland and on the Hungarian plains, having already taken Budapest, Breslau, and Krakow. One wing had come to rest on the Adriatic Sea opposite Venice; another was moving along the Baltic Sea.

Finally, the central force had taken up positions to capture Vienna. In four months, Batu's strike forces had captured all the land between the Vistula River, the Baltic Sea, and the Danube River, and had destroyed the armies of Kiev, Poland, Hungary, Saxony, Silesia, Brandenburg, and Bohemia. With Hülegü's invasion of the Middle East in 1256, the Mongols destroyed Baghdad, Damascus, and Aleppo. The Mongol drive was an unstoppable force that, in a sense, only the Mongols themselves could halt. This they did after the deaths of their great khans, which required them to drop what they were doing and return to their capital to hold another *quriltai.*

Had Ogödei lived one or two years longer, then Batu would have continued his drive into Europe. Since Frederick II and Pope Gregory IX (and later Innocent IV) had not resolved their differences, the advancing Mongols would have faced a divided medieval Europe. The feudal knights of Russia and Eastern Europe had already proven incapable of dealing with Mongol tactics, so it is likely that Europe, too, would have fallen to the vast new empire. Yet, death did intervene, and the Mongols never developed an effective system of transferring power from one generation to the next. This was their primary Achilles' heel. Combined with casualties from wars and the luxuries of sedentary life, selecting a new leader ultimately brought their great empire to its knees.

The fact that Europe only narrowly escaped Mongol conquest is often overlooked in Western history. After the briefest of mentions in traditional Western civilization texts, the issue is dropped. To speculate as to what might have followed is an engaging exercise, but a fruitless one, as Europe did indeed escape. Western history continued uninterrupted. The pope and the Holy Roman Emperor continued in their struggle for power, with the pope ultimately prevailing.

While medieval Europe escaped the fate of Russia, Mongol rule over the lands that stretched from China to Europe created order on the western and eastern steppes for the first time in Eurasian history. From 1223 to 1368 the Mongols stopped, at least temporarily, the disruption of sedentary civilization. During that time, trade increased and cultural diffusion followed. As mentioned above, one of the items transferred from China to Russia, the Middle East, and Europe was gunpowder. The rapid development of firearms in all three cultures then transferred the means to defeat the Mongols as well as any other nomadic tribe that tried to imitate their tactics. This change in the circumstances of life on the steppe radically altered the future of China and Russia in particular. Both acquired cannon, developed the art of manufacturing better and better firearms, and eventually developed the techniques needed to invade, trap, and destroy herders, thereby ending the pastoral way of life on the steppe. This gradual conquest of the steppe people, however, would have to wait until the seventeenth century before cannon could work its wonders. Ironically, however, the Mongols were the very nomads who planted these seeds of nomadic destruction.

Timur the Lame: A Transitional Reign of Nomadic Terror

Signs of the changing times wrought by cannon are visible in the career of the last great nomadic invader: Timur the Lame (also known as Timur, Timurlink, and Tamerline (reigned 1370–1405)). Timur the Lame was the phenomenon of his age. He came from a division of the Mongol Empire commanded by Khaidu (mentioned above) that centered on the Central Asian steppe. By 1370, Timur made himself master of this steppe portion of the old Mongol Empire. He then began a conquest pattern that signaled the end of nomadic power in an unusual way. Despite his successes, he could not build an empire that lived beyond his death.

His plan was to recover Genghis Khan's imperial legacy. Between 1380 and 1390, he conquered Iran, Mesopotamia, Armenia, and Georgia. In 1390–1398, he invaded Russia, defeated the Golden Horde (Batu's descendents), and added the Russian estates to his domain. In 1398, he invaded northern India and captured Delhi in a quest for plunder and then retreated to his homeland. In 1400–1402, he captured Syria and Turkey. His conquests echoed the achievements of the Mongols that had preceded him.[44]

His empire stretched from Iran to China, but his methods were different from those of other Mongol conquerors. His power rested more on sedentary agriculture than on nomadic herding. His armies included the famous Mongol-Turkish bowmen, but also added infantry, artillery, heavy cavalry, and even elephants. His ferocity, tactical skills, and shrewd use of tribal politics allowed him to build a Eurasian Empire, but he did not have the ability to plant his banner permanently anywhere. The Chinese, the Ottomans, the Persians, the Muslim sultans of India, and the Mamluks of Egypt and Syria were now too resilient to remain under his power. In fact, he inflicted more damage among his own nomadic tribesmen than he did on the sedentary peoples he conquered. Whoever he judged disloyal among the nomads, he killed. When he finished, at the end of his life, he had bled the Central Asia steppe "white" (had emptied the land of people). In the end, his reign marked a final, violent spasm of nomadic warfare, as the balance of power now shifted from herders to farmers fully armed with cannon.[45]

The Bubonic Plague

Perhaps the most destructive aspect of Mongol rule—and, as it turned out, another devastating part of the paradox of culture—was a massive biological disaster enabled by the sheer size and geographic unity of the Mongol Empire. This contiguity of landmass under Mongol control allowed for the transmission of an epidemic disease known as the Black Death, from China to the Middle East and medieval Europe (see chapter four). Each of these civilizations had to adapt to the demographic crisis that followed in the wake of the plague. For the Chinese people, the Black Death was one more sign that the Mongols had lost the Mandate of Heaven. For the Europeans, the Black Death joined famine and warfare to set up a cultural consolidation pattern that led to modernization (see chapters five and seven). In each case, dramatic changes transformed the internal coherence of civilization.

In an assessment of the damage caused by the Black Death throughout Eurasia and the Middle East, scholars estimate that the number killed varied widely according to the three forms the plague took. The first form of the Black Death was the bubonic form, which killed an estimated 70 percent of its victims. This is the version of the plague that first attacks the lymphatic system, which is used to filter out internal poisons. The victim's lymph nodes fill with dead white blood cells killed in fighting the infection. These dead white blood cells, called "pus," overloaded the lymph nodes that can swell to the size of a tangerine. So much accumulated pus eventually causes the lymph nodes to fail, letting the pus spread under the skin as massive, dark-colored subcutaneous sores. The sores swell and either break through the skin, or the pus spreads under the skin and threatens damage to internal organs. If the pus fills the lungs, a new version of the plague appears: the pneumonic plague. [46]

The pneumonic plague was the deadliest of the three forms. Those who developed the pneumonic plague began to cough, spraying anyone close by with infected mucus. Once inhaled, this infected mucus immediately attacks the lungs of the new victims, 100 percent of which die. There is no defense against this version of the plague because a lung-to-lung infection rapidly destroys one's capacity to breath, causing the patient to drown in his own fluids. [47]

One other version of the Black Death is the septicaemic form. As its name suggests, this version involves blood poisoning. An unusual form, this version began at the site of the fleabite that introduced (in this case) the infecting bacteria, *Yersinia pestis* (sometimes called *Pasteurella pestis*) into the human body. What followed was an acute fulminant (i.e. sudden) infection that killed the victim so quickly that no other version of the plague could appear: 50 to 90 percent of victims hit with this version of the plague perished.[48]

So many people died throughout the fourteenth century as to deeply reduce human numbers all across Eurasia and the Middle East. Some scholars argue that the plague erupted in Central Asia first, traveled to Yuan China, and then crossed Eurasia via the trade routes. Once the plague reached the Black Sea, at about the same time as the Mongol armies, the fleas that carried it jumped onto the backs of the rats that climbed aboard ships bound for Europe and the Middle East. Others scholars claim that it started in China first and then spread across Eurasia. In both cases, this pandemic infection decimated a great many sedentary peoples. Most scholars estimate that the net loss of human life for those cultures hit by the Black Death reached somewhere from 33 to 40 percent of the total population. This number includes the survivors of the disease, those who escaped infection, and the reproductive rates of the two generations infected by the plague between 1300 and 1352.[49]

The Qing: The Second Nomadic Regime to Rule China (1644–1911)

After the Black Death, Timur the Lame, and the beginning of the modern era, one more nomadic tribe conquered China: this was the Qing Dynasty, the rise of which was yet another Chinese episode of nomadic violence. These nomads, however, came from a different quarter of the northern steppe. They penetrated China's defenses from Manchuria, a northeastern region already partially sinicized. Entry from Manchuria into China, however, required command of a fortress that guarded a strategic, easily defended pass called the Ningyuan/Shanhai.

At the eastern end of the Great Wall guarding the Ningyuan/Shanhai pass stood the fortress of Shanhaiguan. The pass itself was a very narrow plain situated between sharply rising mountains and the coast, a juncture that could easily be defended against nomadic raids with a fortress. Whoever controlled this pass controlled access to either Beijing or Manchuria, depending on the direction the army of invasion sought to travel. The Ming Dynasty that ruled China from 1368 to 1644 made command of this pass one of its key priorities. The Ningyuan/Shanhai pass remained in Ming hands until decay within the ruling imperial ranks produced the usual signs of dynastic collapse. These signs included: an emperor who reigned instead of ruled; an imperial court that suffered factions that tried to dominate the throne;

and the imposition of excessive taxes. Furthermore, famine, plague, and rebellion had also occurred.

Early in 1644, the rebel leader Li Zicheng (1606–1645) from Shaanxi Province in mid-northern China, had captured Beijing, with plans to create a new dynasty. Seeking to secure his northeastern flank, he turned his attention to Shanhaiguan. He demanded that the commander of the fortress there, Wu Sangui (1612–1678), surrender the pass to his forces. Li had Wu's parents captured and used them as hostages to force his compliance. Wu agreed but later discovered that Li had also kidnapped and sexually compromised his favorite concubine, Chen Yuanyuan (1624–1681). Valuing his concubine above even his parents, Wu now chose rebellion over surrender. Viewing his chances of success as nonexistent without aid, Wu turned to the Manchu for support. He gave these nomads the fortress in return for their aid, thus giving control of the strategic pass to a rising confederation of tribal warriors who had plotted the conquest of China.[50]

Some scholars, however, have developed a less romantic version of Wu's rebellion, one that undermines this titillating account. These scholars have argued that Wu's decision to surrender the fortress and pass to Li came too late to meet with his low level of trust for Ming officials. Li therefore ordered the slaughter of Wu's family, which alarmed the general enough to turn to the Manchu for help. At that time, the Manchu had long been planning the conquest of China and accepted Wu's offer with alacrity. The combination of Wu's army plus Manchu forces tipped the scales in favor of a nomadic victory, and yet another invasion of China began, albeit this time by a people already partly sinicized. Just how the Manchu hoped to defeat the vast population of an enormous empire, however, requires some explanation.[51]

Who Were the Manchu Nomads?

The Manchu are Tungusic in origin. One of several Siberian ethnic groups, the Manchu were a branch of the Jurchen tribes that had once ruled northern China as the Jin Dynasty between 1115 and 1234 (mentioned in chapter four). The Chinese called the Manchu the Jianzhou Jurchen. The Manchu lived in the woodlands east of the Liao River and northwest of the Korean border. Their economy was largely a pastoral one, but their close proximity to China had seen the transfer of some sedentary practices onto the Manchurian plains. Conflict between the Chinese and the Tungus peoples of Manchuria began early in Chinese history, as far back as the Shang Dynasty (1766–1122 BCE). Later, after the fall of the Zhou Dynasty (1122–256 BCE), the people of the northernmost Chinese state, called the Yen, had pushed their way into Manchuria. Later still, once the Qin Dynasty (221–206 BCE) had unified China, Manchuria became part of the new political order. Finally, the Han (202 BCE–CE 220) continued the Qin's policy of colonizing Manchuria, but the region proved difficult to hold. With the fall of the Han in CE 220, the Tungus people reasserted their independence. This meant that over the course of Chinese history from the Han to the Ming Dynasty, the Tungus people, and the Jurchen, were never thoroughly sinicized. As a result, they retained their separate identity throughout Chinese history.[52]

The Ming also tried to assert Chinese dominance in Manchuria, this in light of the migration patterns. As land-hungry Chinese peasants pushed relentlessly north of the Great Wall, onto the Manchurian plains and into the forested territories, the Jurchen nomads tried to put up an organized resistance. These nomads were not, however, as economically self-sufficient as were the Chinese. Trade between the two peoples gave the Chinese an economic advantage, one that allowed them to impose sanctions on their troublesome neighbors as a secondary method of control besides outright conquest. Since the Chinese produced the urban goods that their nomadic challengers found so attractive, it was the terms of trade that kept the pastoral peoples in line. But as the power of the Ming began to decline, and corruption infiltrated the practices of Chinese officials, hostility toward China mounted among the Jurchen tribes.[53]

Manchu Mobilization

With Ming military strength in decline, the Jurchen threat grew. Maintaining the security of the Ningyuan/Shanhai pass increased in importance but also in difficulty. Supply to the pass increasingly relied on control of the shoreline near the Shanhaiguan fortress. Situated in the Gulf of Bohai between the Liaodong and Shandong peninsulas, access by sea to Shanhaiguan proved critically important.

On land, the Chinese settlements near the Liao River came under mounting nomadic pressure. The frequency of raids in this area increased once the Manchu perceived the growing weakness of the Ming. The Chinese capacity to defend Ming colonists loosened, allowing the Jianzhou Jurchen (i.e. the Manchu) to capture valuable farmland. At this point the Ming's use of economic sanctions failed, for this policy only inspired an increase in the pillaging of Chinese holdings. By the turn of the seventeenth century, the Ming found it could no longer protect the colonists and began a gradual retreat from the area south, towards the fortress. Those colonists who refused to abandon their farms found themselves forcefully evicted by the Ming and relocated to more defensible ground. The Jianzhou Jurchen then moved into the areas left behind by the retreating Chinese farmers, expanding these nomads' capacity to support a growing population of tribesmen.[54]

The Jianzhou Jurchen nomads were technically vassals of the Ming Dynasty. Before the Ming decline, they could trade with Chinese merchants under the authority of Ming officials. The Jianzhou Jurchen exported horses, lumber, and ginseng root (a Chinese herbal medicine and tea) in exchange for a wide array of urban goods that only the Ming could manufacture. As the Ming declined, the Manchu switched from trade to raid, as was common among all nomadic tribes when witnessing the increased vulnerability of a rich sedentary culture.

From Raids to Conquest: Nurhaci Mobilizes the Manchu

While initially wealth motivated these raids, the possibility of military conquest emerged with the signs of increasing Ming weakness. The shift to conquest, however, required a leader of vision; the Jianzhou Jurchen acquired such a man with the rise of Nurhaci (1559–1626). Nurhaci imposed the name "Manchu" on the Jurchen tribes of the region and started a policy of mixed marriages and intimidation to unite his people. He secretly prepared the Manchu for the conquest of China, while using his status as a vassal to mask his intentions. He continued to send tribute to the Ming court, as was required of subordinates, maintaining a steady flow of horses and ginseng.[55]

In 1589 the Ming granted Nurhaci a Chinese title, and in 1590 he personally traveled to Beijing to pay homage to the Ming emperor, as was required by Ming protocol. At the end of the decade, he reorganized his Manchu followers into a new military formation called "banners." He grouped 300 households into a company, and 50 companies into a banner. A banner was an administrative unit during peace, and a powerful cavalry force during times of war.[56] Each unit designated their identity by the flag (banner) that they flew over their portion of Nurhaci's growing military force. Starting with four banners, his military power expanded to eight Manchu banners, at which point he added eight Mongol and eight Chinese banners.

Nurhaci's growing power finally began to alarm the Ming regime, and the emperor tried to restrict Nurhaci's movement in 1603 by confining him to a specific location. At first Nurhaci accepted these limitations, but he also began to employ Chinese officials to train his people in the bureaucratic methods of running a centralized regime. Gradually, he organized the Jurchen tribes into the Manchu state and reached out to other nomads who had not yet become part of the Chinese tributary system. In 1616, he announced the formation of the "later" Jin Dynasty to commemorate his ethnic link to the original Jin rulers of 1115–1234. In 1618, he seized the trading post and garrison town of Fushun, near present-day Shenyung, on the grounds of a document he published entitled "The Seven Great Vexations." These complaints were a justification for the rebellion that he now launched with a vengeance.[57]

The Ming retaliated by sending a large army against Nurhaci's banners. Scholars estimated that the Ming force was 200,000 strong, but Nurhaci soundly defeated them with a Manchu army of approximately 180,000. Acknowledging their military weakness against the Jurchen cavalry, the Ming adopted a delaying tactic of building strongholds in strategic locations to hamper the enemy's resistance. In response, however, Nurhaci developed a strategy of capturing and controlling the local countryside needed to feed each such fortification. By 1621, he had gained control of the Liaodong Peninsula and began to appeal to Chinese settlers and officials to abandon the Ming regime and join his rebellion. During the 1620s, he ruled about a million Chinese. In 1623, however, some of these new Chinese allies made a clumsy attempt to poison the Jurchen food and water supply and, in 1625, attempted an outright revolt. This convinced Nurhaci that he could not rely on his Chinese subjects. Also, between 1623 and 1626, the Portuguese, using their new trade route around Africa opened in 1498, supplied the Ming with cannons that they placed in their fortresses beyond the Great Wall. This deferred Nurhaci's plans. In 1626, when Nurhaci pressed his rebellion against one of these newly armed fortresses, he suffered a mortal wound and died.[58]

Abahai's Continued Conquest

Nurhaci's son, Abahai (reigned 1626–1643), took command of the Manchu rebellion and proved himself as able a leader as his father. Under Abahai, the Manchu strategy did not falter. He launched a successful invasion of Korea to secure his rear flank, and within a year, Abahai completed his conquest of the Korean Peninsula, converted it into a Manchu protectorate, and developed a lively trade in grain to supply his expanding armies. After 1628, the Ming experienced increased peasant rebellions and internal collapse, which signaled to the Manchu that the time was right to take the northern frontier of China. In 1629, Abahai captured Ming lands protected by the Great Wall, advanced to the outskirts of Beijing, and disrupted any Ming attempts to put down the peasant rebellions.

It was during this raid that Abahai realized that the Chinese could not be subjugated by conquest alone, and he returned to the northern frontier and began to study the Chinese methods of governance. In 1634, the Manchu completed the conquest of Inner Mongolia, and two years later Abahai dropped the name "Jin" in favor of the name "Qing" for his new dynasty. Qing meant "pure" and "clear," which was a propaganda ploy to counter the term "Ming" which meant "bright." In 1635, Abahai assumed the title Qing Taizong. This shift to a Chinese imperial name made Abahai wary of becoming too sinicized, so he was careful to insist that his people remain loyal to their nomadic ways.[59]

Dorgon's Regency

In 1643 Abahai died unexpectedly. His sudden death launched a dispute over the succession of power. Happily for the Manchu, a quick resolution of the issue in favor of Abahai's six-year-old son undid a potential interruption of the continued conquest of China. This six-year-old boy would grow up to become Emperor Qing Shunzhi (reigned 1643–1661), but he could not rule as a minor. Command of the continued invasion of China from Manchuria, therefore, fell to his two uncles, the regents Dorgon and Jirgalang. Of these two regent uncles, it was Dorgon who wished to continue with Abahai's plans to conquer all of China, but he had to consider if he could rely on the support of the Chinese in this enterprise. It was at this moment when Li Zicheng captured Beijing, that Wu Sangui's surrender of the Ningyuan/Shanhai pass became highly significant. Dorgon calculated that he could not defeat Li without the aid of Wu's army, nor could he face a combined army of Wu and Li should they join forces. He therefore decided to accept Wu's offer and confront the Chinese peasant leader.[60]

In 1644, Dorgon invaded China, defeated Li's army, captured Beijing, and declared to the Chinese people that he had come to avenge the destruction of the Ming Dynasty by rebels and bandits. Within a year, northern China fell under Manchu rule. The remnant of the Ming escaped to the Yangzi River, where they made Nanjing their capital. Dorgon then launched an invasion of southern China, but ran into a more spirited resistance there than he had in the north. One stubborn siege at Yangzhou, where the Grand Canal joined the Yangzi River, led to a massacre of Chinese, reminiscent of the earlier Mongol slaughters of those who opposed their advance. The massacre near the Yangzi, however, did not work the way similar slaughters had for the Mongols; instead, it stiffened Chinese resistance.[61]

Meanwhile, a second episode of Chinese opposition occurred at Jiangyin near the mouth of the Yangzi River, where the Manchu first imposed their hairstyle on their Chinese subjects. The Manchu traditionally wore their hair in a long, braided plait, and partially shaved head. The local male population refused to adopt this hairstyle and rebelled. The Manchu treated the rebels with extreme hostility and crushed this example of resistance. Once again the Manchu inspired fear and reminded the Chinese of the terrors of earlier nomadic rule, which also stiffened resistance.[62]

By the summer of 1645, Dorgon captured Nanjing, and the Ming continued their flight south ahead of his forces. The Manchu extended their control over the Yangzi River valley during the next four years, and then turned their attention back to the south. In 1649, they reached Guangzhou, opposite modern-day Hong Kong, bringing effective Ming resistance to their rule to an end. The Manchu captured and executed the last Ming emperor in 1662. Controlling China, however, proved far more difficult for the Manchu than had conquering the land. Four Chinese men still held great power. The first was Wu Sangui. He had, as mentioned, allied himself to the Manchu to aid Dorgon in the latter's capture of Beijing and defeat of the rebel Li Zicheng. Wu then fought loyally to capture several western and southern provinces, where he received a feudatory estate in appreciation of his services. A second was Geng Jingzhong (died 1682), who set up a second feudatory estate in Fujian. A third was Shang Kexi (1604–1676), who ruled Guangdong. The fourth was a pirate and patriot named Zheng Chenggong (aka Koxinga, 1624–1662) who took control of Taiwan and used the island as a springboard for raids deep into the Yangzi basin. All four men ran nearly independent states that denied the Manchu complete control over all of China.[63]

Consolidation of Qing Rule

It took the efforts of two highly talented leaders to effect the consolidation of the Manchu's hold on China: Dorgon's initial invasion and conquest, and the reign of Emperor Kangxi (1662–1722). Dorgon achieved his goal of conquest by 1649, but as it turned out he only had one year to try to establish a firm hold on China before he died. Within that year, he had begun a difficult balancing act that only he seemed able to maintain. Part of the act was trying to become a ruler who utilized the Chinese system of bureaucracy, and the other part was functioning as a vibrant Manchu warlord.

Within his last year of life, Dorgon imposed a remarkable series of reforms that had a positive effect on the empire. He reduced the heavy taxes that the Ming had used to finance the defense of the collapsing regime. He provided tax exemptions to regions severely damaged by war to ease the burden of rebuilding China. He declared a new political union wherein all Chinese and Manchu peoples would be subject to the same standard of justice. He created a diarchy (two governing bodies) in which Manchu officials worked alongside their Chinese counterparts, allowing Ming bureaucrats to retain their offices. He continued the imperial examination system weighted to favor the north to balance this region against the increasing economic power of the south. He imposed the Manchu hairstyle on all men so that no visible difference could be seen between the two major ethnic groups of China. He favored Chinese banner men who had submitted to Manchu rule before the invasion of Ming China as appointees to his principal municipal posts. He began a policy of building garrisons to station his banner men in strategic locations throughout the realm. And he planted his people within China to ensure Manchu control.[64]

When Dorgon died in 1650, Emperor Qing Shunzhi (reigned 1651–1661) was only twelve years old. Upon Dorgon's death, the other uncle, Jirgalang, tried to assume power, but a strong faction at court limited his influence to a mere three years (1650–1653). Once Qing Shunzhi took the reins of power, at the age of sixteen, he began an energetic, if erratic, rule. As emperor, Qing Shunzhi encouraged the Han Chinese to participate in government activities. He even took advice from a Jesuit named Johann Adam Schall von Bell, a German scholar who had managed to make his way to the Chinese court (see chapter seven). And Qing Shunzhi employed Chinese officials to teach his children their culture. Quite suddenly at the age of twenty-three, Qing Shunzhi caught smallpox (by now endemic to China) and died. Because of his short reign, he had done little to change or weaken the regime and power passed to the second great consolidator of Manchu rule, Kangxi (reigned 1662–1722).[65]

Qing Kangxi

Most scholars attribute the longevity of the Qing Dynasty to the innovative rule of Kangxi, who presided over China during an era of rapid population growth, extensive agricultural expansion, and widening internal commerce. Kangxi exhibited talented leadership and extraordinary energy. The length of his reign, successful defense of the realm, and dedication to enhancing Manchu power, sets him apart from Dorgon, who spent most of his lifetime conquering the Ming, dying too soon to complete the consolidation of Manchu power. It was, however, the efforts of both men that made the success of the Qing Dynasty possible.[66]

Prior to Kangxi's reign, the future of the Qing Dynasty looked bleak, due to both internal and external threats. Among the many problems facing the Manchu was their nomadic way of selecting a ruler, as they still used a form of ascension similar to that used by the Mongols. The idea of dynastic succession had not yet taken root among the Manchu tribes, but it would, as it turned out, come to be essential to imperial rule. Clan politics and continuation of a Manchu version of the Mongol *quriltai*, might have destroyed the Qing Dynasty, much in the same way it had undermined the Yuan regime. Kangxi, however, began the process of developing a rational system of succession, the nomadic method of succession having fostered cyclical bouts of factional violence.[†]

The nomadic practice of a candidate for supreme power sharing captured wealth and lands among his warriors, to garner favors and secure votes in the next election of a ruler, was too unstable a system of succession for a sedentary civilization. This method of electing a nomadic ruler had worked well for finding the most competent warrior among potential candidates of a steppe people, but it did not function well in the Chinese system of government. The entire history of imperial China, from the Han Dynasty to the Qing, relied on three basic principles: filial piety, Confucian philosophy, and the Mandate of Heaven. These three principles fostered Chinese loyalty to the ruling emperor as the "son" of Heaven. Each living emperor passed power to his designated heir, who was typically a pre-selected, surviving male of a high-ranking wife or daughter of the ruling emperor. Manchu power from Dorgon's conquest to Kangxi's reign still seemed alien to most Chinese because these Jurchen nomads had not yet fully adopted the concept of dynastic succession. Perhaps it was for this reason that southern China remained unstable so long as Wu Sangui, Geng Jingzhong, and Shang Kexi still controlled semi-independent realms, and Zheng Chenggong controlled the island of Taiwan.

In addition to the Manchu's struggles over the issue of succession, and their lack of complete control over the southern half of China due to feudatory estates, there were serious external threats. As previously, the possibility of invasion by the peoples of the northern steppe posed

---

[†]The selection process of succeeding rulers plagued nomadic history throughout the long confrontation between China and the steppe peoples of the north. This selection process worked well on the steppe because it elevated to the rank of ruler those children of the great khan that inspired confidence among his warriors. It failed once the nomads had captured a sedentary culture because this method of replacing the dead ruler created gaps in time when no one was in charge. Furthermore, it disrupted whatever nomadic military campaigns were in progress at the time of the death of the ruler. Finally, the selection process itself left hard feelings that required bloodletting to settle matters of loyalty and security.

a challenge to the Chinese ruler. Such a threat still existed when Kangxi came to the throne in 1662. From Central Asia came a threat from a tribal confederation with four different names: the Olöt, the Kalmyk, the Zunhgar khanate, and the Dzingar. All of these names identify the same branch of the western Mongols, but here only the "Olöt" name will be used. The Olöt originated near the Altai Mountains of Siberia and had migrated west to Dzungaria on the northwestern frontier of China. Besides the Olöt, there was also a theocratic state that had formed under the Dalai Lama in Tibet that posed yet another nomadic threat, this one directly from the west. Finally the rising power of the czarist Russians had reached Lake Baikal during Kangxi's reign. All of these external forces combined with the issue of succession and feudatory estates to endanger the tiny Manchu minority's future in China.

Of all these internal and external threats, the most immediate danger to Kangxi's power was the feudatory estate of Wu Sangui. When Kangxi came to the throne, he was only seven years old. When he took the reins of power, he was 19. Wu gauged him to be of little concern and rebelled when Kangxi demanded that Wu disband his armies. After disdainfully rejecting the demand, Wu made a counterproposal of confining Manchu power to Manchuria and Korea. Any insubordination within China was unacceptable to the young emperor, and war broke out in 1673. Wu had aged substantially since his original alliance to the Manchu, but he had the initial support of Geng and Zheng's family and allies. The struggle continued for five years, until Wu contracted dysentery and died in 1678. Meanwhile, the scholar-gentry, as well as the prominent Chinese families in the south now sided with the Manchu, because they preferred imperial continuity over the continued warlord system. Wu, Geng, and Zheng's heirs had failed to inspire the trust of the Chinese people living within their respective estates, and Kangxi succeeded in liquidating all three realms by 1683. To deal with Zheng's family, Kangxi imposed a drastic policy of evacuating the coastal belt of southern China to deny the pirate rebels any booty until the early 1680s. This policy of abandoning the coastal belt severely curtailed foreign trade for the first twenty years of Kangxi's reign, until the Chinese managed to take Taiwan in 1682. With Zheng heirs defeated in that year, the south fell under the Qing.[67]

Even while confronting the rebels in southern China, Kangxi also had to turn his attention to a nomadic threat from the north. The Olöt ruler Galdan (c.1632–1697) began to assemble a Mongol state in the 1670s that grew to significant size. From his base in Dzungaria, just west of Mongolia, he united a combination of oases cities through conquest, giving him control over Turkistan. Just as Kangxi's troubles with southern China were coming to an end, Galdan invaded Outer Mongolia in 1688. Meanwhile, the czar's expansion east had brought the Russians to the northern edge of Mongolia, near Amuria, and just north of Manchuria. The possibility of an alliance between the Olöt and Russians alarmed Kangxi, who, having wrapped up matters in southern China, was now free to turn his attention north. Toughened by his successes in the south, and being a natural military commander who had sharpened his skills by organizing massive hunts, Kangxi was well prepared to fight in the steppe. The only potential problem he faced was that he had never encountered the Russians before, and he had no way to gauge the potential of their threat.

From the czarist perspective, Russia had been expanding ever since the founding of an independent regime in the 1460s. Their use of cannon had allowed them to destroy the Golden Horde, the remnant state of Batu Khan's heirs in Russian territory. Cannon also allowed the Russians to spread czarist control over the steppe all the way to China's frontier. Once the Russians had captured most of the Silk Road, their expansion brought them within Kangxi's sphere of power.

Having always lived on the border of Europe, the czars wanted to employ European modernization within Russia's feudal regime to capture nomadic Asia. As a result, the czars decided to turn to the east to seek their fortunes, and revealed a determination to take control over Eurasian trade by dominating the Silk Road. The Russians hoped to be the rivals of the Spanish and the Portuguese in trade and commerce, the latter having turned their new Atlantic-based trade routes into spectacular financial successes. Spain had opened the Americas to conquest and eventual trade, and Portugal had developed an uninterrupted oceanic sea route down the west coast of Africa and around the tip of that continent east to India and China (see chapter seven). Now Russia wanted its share of the rapidly globalizing world.

The Russian effort had brought their newly acquired empire to the borders of well-established Middle Eastern and Asian cultures. To the south of Russia stood the empires of the Ottoman Turks and Safavid Persians, both of which possessed cannon with which to restrict Russian expansion into their lands. A little farther east was the Indian subcontinent, also in possession of cannon. And now the czar's military had come into contact with the Chinese. From their centralized position in Eurasia, the Russians hoped to develop diplomatic and commercial relations with China, India, and the Muslim world. For his part, Kangxi was willing to forego the complex protocol that the Chinese had developed in their diplomatic relations with foreign states, but he could only do so if contact with Russia was made informally.[‡]

One thing was certain, he was not willing to allow the Russians to forge an alliance with the Olöt and establish the czar's presence firmly in East Asia. Happily for Kangxi, the Manchu had acquired cannon from their conquest of Ming China and contact with the Portuguese. This allowed Kangxi to balance out Chinese power against a potentially dangerous northern neighbor.[68]

In 1684, Kangxi warned the Olöt to cease trading with the Russians. In 1685, he sent an army to Albazin and destroyed the most advanced Russian outpost in the Amur Valley. When the Russians returned to the area, and the Olöt conquered Outer Mongolia in 1688, the two powers threatened the Manchu all along the northern frontier. Kangxi met this threat by sending an army to Nerchinsk, in southern Siberia, in 1689. This Manchu army surrounded the czar's negotiators, who had been sent to forge an alliance with the Mongols, and forced the Russians to renounce their claims to the entire northern frontier of China in the Treaty of Nerchinsk. Then, in the 1690s, Manchu armies drove the Olöt west. Finally, the Manchu used cannon fire to crush the Olöt at Urga in 1696, a defeat that drove their leader, Galdan, to commit suicide with poison in 1697. These actions allowed Kangxi to consolidate his hold over Inner Asia, which ended the constant threat of nomadic invasions from the north. The use of cannon had finally given the Chinese the means to neutralize the highly effective nomadic cavalry. This victory over the Olöt secured Manchu power throughout the Far East and closed a very long chapter of nomadic warfare between the people of China and the people of the steppe.[69]

Continued Qing Power: New "Barbarians" Arrive from the South

Two great emperors followed Kangxi's reign: Yongzheng (reigned 1723–1735) and Qianlong (reigned 1736–1795). During the eighteenth century, the Qing Empire doubled in size. Qianlong's contribution to the history of the dynasty was the addition to Chinese territory of Tibet and Xinjiang. With regards to Tibet, Qianlong quelled a civil war there, inspired by the Olöt, and placed the Dalai Lama on the throne through

---

[‡]The Chinese protocol long dictated that a foreign ambassador kowtow before an emperor, acknowledging his superior power before any foreign policy could be conducted. The kowtow was an act of deep respect shown by kneeling and bowing so low as to have one's head touching the ground for a time.

a method of election based on lot. With regards to the Olöt, Qianlong sent several armies into the western steppe and engaged in a campaign of extermination that permanently broke the power of these tribal people. In general, however, Qianlong tolerated nomads. Like his predecessors, he demonstrated a willingness to engage in a flexible foreign policy with the pastoral tribes.[70]

The early Manchu rulers had created the *Lifan Yuan*, the Ministry of Dependencies. It was this agency that took responsibility for Qing relations with Inner Asia and Russia. It provided the intelligence and diplomacy that worked hand in hand with the army to pacify the nomadic threat, while dealing successfully with the Russians. With their success against the Olöt, the Qing could then turn its attention to the tributary system. Here Qianlong followed the well-established practices of past dynasties of accepting tribute from satellite states and rewarding their embassies with rich gifts. The most frequent of those embassies sent to China came from Korea, which averaged three per year. Besides Korea, Vietnam, Burma, Tibet, Nepal, Outer Mongolia, Chinese Turkistan, and Dzungaria joined this system of tribute states. In return for the regular exchange of gifts through the state's embassies, the Qing took responsibility for ensuring stability within all of the countries that belonged to the tributary system.[71]

While the Qing were still focused on the northern frontier, where history had taught the Chinese that they had to defend against constant nomadic invasions, a new "barbarian" approached China from the south. In the sixteenth century, Ming China faced the new presence of European adventurers called the Portuguese, who had opened a new trade route by sea to the Qing's southern coastline. Later, during the early modern era, the British and the Dutch introduced joint-stock corporations, the British East India Company in 1600, and the Dutch equivalent in 1602, both of which made their way to Qing China, seeking trade. These companies were extensions of the feudal principle of private owners using public power to achieve their commercial goals. They also belonged to a new historical event known as "the commercial revolution," which redefined global trade. The commercial revolution was, in turn, part of the process of modernization that began in Europe at the end of the fifteenth century. What emerged out of the failure of feudalism was a completely different way of organizing European political, social, economic, and intellectual institutions. This redesign of Europe's principle cultural and political institutions was, then, a spontaneous response to a failed tradition. It stands in stark contrast to China's long pattern of repeated successes in reconstituting the most successful tradition in world history. This is the subject of chapter seven.

Notes

1   Kong Fuzi as quoted and explained in David L. Hall and Roger T. Ames. *Thinking Through Confucius*, pp. 43–62.
2   Frank Mclynn. *Genghis Khan: His Conquests, His Empire, His Legacy*, pp. 32 and 489; Christopher I. Beckwith. *Empires of the Silk Road*, pp. 184–189; Thomas J. Craughwell. *The Rise and Fall of the Second Largest Empire in History*, p. 9; David Morgan. *The Mongols*, pp. 61–73; George Lane. *Genghis Khan and Mongol Rule*, p. xxxiii.
3   Thomas J. Craughwell. *The Rise and Fall of the Second Largest Empire in History*, pp. 9–10.
4   Frank Mclynn. *Genghis Khan: His Conquests, His Empire, His Legacy*, pp. 38–53; Christopher I. Beckwith. *Empires of the Silk Road*, pp. 184–188.
5   Frank Mclynn. *Genghis Khan: His Conquests, His Empire, His Legacy*, pp. 33–53 and 54–91; David Morgan. *The Mongols*, pp. 51–54; Thomas J. Craughwell. *The Rise and Fall of the Second Largest Empire in History*, pp. 28–63; Gerard Chaliand. *Nomadic Empires from Mongolia to the Danube*, pp. 60–61; David Morgan. *The Mongols*, pp. 55–61; George Lane. *Genghis Khan and Mongol Rule*, pp. 13–29. For image see *Genghis Khan's Art of War.* http://www.slideshare.net/bright9977/genghis-khan-s-art-of-war; *Genghis Khan, the creator and Leader of the Mongol empire, was born around 1165 (dates vary wildly), and died in August 1227.* http://www.leader-values.com/Content/detail.asp?ContentDetailID=799
6   Frank Mclynn. *Genghis Khan: His Conquests, His Empire, His Legacy*, pp. 92–124; Christopher I. Beckwith. *Empires of the Silk Road*, pp. 184–189.
7   Frank Mclynn. *Genghis Khan: His Conquests, His Empire, His Legacy*, pp. 8–24; David Morfan. *The Mongols*, pp. 84–95; Thomas J. Craughwell. *The Rise and Fall of the Second Largest Empire in History*, pp. 16–27; Gerard Chaliand. *Nomadic Empires from Mongolia to the Danube*, pp. 59–61.
8   Frank Mclynn. *Genghis Khan: His Conquests, His Empire, His Legacy*, pp. 8–24, Thomas Allisen. *The Rise of the Mongolian Empire and Mongolian Rule in Northern China.* In Herbert Franke and Denis Twitchett, eds, *The Cambridge History of China*, pp. 331–343; Thomas J. Craughwell. *The Rise and Fall of the Second Largest Empire in History*, pp. 16–27; Gerard Chaliand. *Nomadic Empires from Mongolia to the Danube*, pp. 59–61; Bertold Spuler. *History of the Mongols Based on Eastern and Western Accounts of the Thirteenth and Fourteenth Centuries*, pp. 23–24; George Lane. *Genghis Khan and Mongol Rule*, pp. 22–29.
9   Frank Mclynn. *Genghis Khan: His Conquests, His Empire, His Legacy*, p. 32.
10 Frank Mclynn. *Genghis Khan: His Conquests, His Empire, His Legacy*, pp. 1–25; Jack Weatherford. *Genghis Khan and the Making of the Modern World*, pp. 9–11; Christopher I. Beckwith. *Empires of the Silk Road*, pp. 184–190; Thomas J. Craughwell. *The Rise and Fall of the Second Largest Empire in History*, pp. 16–27; Gerard Chaliand. *Nomadic Empires from Mongolia to the Danube*, pp. 59–61.

11   Frank Mclynn. *Genghis Khan: His Conquests, His Empire, His Legacy,* pp. 14–16; Jack Weatherford. *Genghis Khan and the Making of the Modern World,* pp. 14–17; Christopher Christopher I. Beckwith. *Empires of the Silk Road,* pp. 184–189; Thomas J. Craughwell. *The Rise and Fall of the Second Largest Empire in History,* pp. 16–27; Gerard Chaliand. *Nomadic Empires from Mongolia to the Danube,* pp. 59–61.

12   David Morgan. *The Mongols,* p. 57; Svat Soucek. *A History of Inner Asia,* pp. 104–105.

13   Frank Mclynn. *Genghis Khan: His Conquests, His Empire, His Legacy,* pp.175–245; Christopher I. Beckwith. *Empires of the Silk Road,* pp. 184–188; Thomas J. Craughwell. *The Rise and Fall of the Second Largest Empire in History,* pp. 94–110; Gerard Chaliand. *Nomadic Empires from Mongolia to the Danube,* pp. 61–62; for images, George Lane. *Genghis Khan and Mongol Rule,* 29–45; David Morgan. *The Mongol,* pp. 61–73; Bertold Spuler. *History of the Mongols,* pp. 26–29; see *Genghis Khan's Art of War.* http://www.slideshare. net/bright9977/genghis-khan-s-art-of-war, *Genghis Khan, the creator and Leader of the Mongol empire, was born around 1165 (dates vary wildly), and died in August 1227.* http://www.leader-values.com/Content/detail.asp? ContentDetailID=799

14   George Lane. *Genghis Khan and Mongol Rule,* p. 41.

15   David Morgan. *The Mongols,* pp. 60–62.

16   Svat Soucek. *A History of Inner Asia,* p. 105.

17   George Lane. *Genghis Khan and Mongol Rule,* pp. 38–42; *Svat Soucek. A History of Inner Asia,* pp. 105–108.

18   George Lane. *Genghis Khan and Mongol Rule,* pp. 38–42; Svat Soucek. *A History of Inner Asia,* pp. 105–108; Christopher I. Beckwith. Empires of the Silk Road, pp. 189–191; Thomas J. Craughwell. *The Rise and Fall of the Second Largest Empire in History,* pp. 110–163; Gerard Chaliand. *Nomadic Empires from Mongolia to the Danube,* pp. 62–69.

19   Frank Mclynn. *Genghis Khan: His Conquests, His Empire, His Legacy,* 433–488; David Morgan. *The Mongols,* p.101; Svat Soucek. *A History of Inner Asia,* pp. 108–109.

20   Frank Mclynn. *Genghis Khan: His Conquests, His Empire, His Legacy,* pp. 448–453; David Morgan. *The Mongols,* p. 123; Thomas J. Craughwell. *The Rise and Fall of the Second Largest Empire in History,* pp. 186–205; Gerard Chaliand. *Nomadic Empires from Mongolia to the Danube,* pp. 70–71, Maurice Keen. *The Pelican History of Medieval Europe,* pp. 171–173; George Holmes. *The Oxford History of Medieval Europe,* pp. 244–246; Christopher I. Beckwith. *Empires of the Silk Road,* pp. 189–195.

21   Frank Mclynn. *Genghis Khan: His Conquests, His Empire, His Legacy,* pp. 174, 431–432, 446–448, and 486–487; Thomas J. Craughwell. *The Rise and Fall of the Second Largest Empire in History,* pp. 162–204; Gerard Chaliand. *Nomadic Empires from Mongolia to the Danube,* p. 69.

22   Frank Mclynn. *Genghis Khan: His Conquests, His Empire, His Legacy,* pp. 174, 431–432, 446–448, and 486–487; David Morgan. *The Mongols,*

pp. 102–103; Christopher I. Beckwith. *Empires of the Silk Road*, pp. 189–191; Thomas J. Craughwell. *The Rise and Fall of the Second Largest Empire in History*, pp. 124–141; David Morgan. *The Mongols*, 115–116.

23   Frank Mclynn. *Genghis Khan: His Conquests, His Empire, His Legacy*, p. 174, 431–432, 446–448, and 486–487; Jack Weatherford. *Genghis Khan and the Making of the Modern World*, pp. 161–165; Thomas J. Craughwell. *The Rise and Fall of the Second Largest Empire in History*, pp. 206–216; Gerard Chaliand. *Nomadic Empires from Mongolia to the Danube*, pp. 72–75; Christopher I. Beckwith. *Empires of the Silk Road*, pp. 189–195; David Morgan. *The Mongols*, pp. 115–116.

24   Morris Rossabi. "Mongol Women," cited in William Fitzhugh, Morris Rossabi, and William Honeychurch (eds). *Genghis Khan and the Mongol Empire*, pp. 110–111; Frank Mclynn. *Genghis Khan: His Conquests, His Empire, His Legacy*, pp. 174, 431–432, 447–448, and 486–487; Jack Weatherford. *Genghis Khan and the Making of the Modern World*, pp. 161–165; Thomas J. Craughwell. *The Rise and Fall of the Second Largest Empire in History*, pp. 206–216; Gerard Chaliand. *Nomadic Empires from Mongolia to the Danube*, pp. 72–75; Christopher I. Beckwith. *Empires of the Silk Road*, pp. 189–195.

25   Frank Mclynn. *Genghis Khan: His Conquests, His Empire, His Legacy*, pp. 174, 431–432, 447–448, and 486–487; Jack Weatherford. *Genghis Khan and the Making of the Modern World*, pp. 161–165; Svat Soucek. *A History of Inner Asia*, p. 109; David Morgan. *The Mongols*, pp. 102–103; George Lane. *Genghis Khan and Mongol Rule*, pp. 48–49; Thomas J. Craughwell. *The Rise and Fall of the Second Largest Empire in History*, pp. 206–216; Gerard Chaliand. *Nomadic Empires from Mongolia to the Danube*, pp. 72–75; Christopher I. Beckwith. *Empires of the Silk Road*, pp. 189–195.

26   Frank Mclynn. *Genghis Khan: His Conquests, His Empire, His Legacy*, pp. 174, 431–432, 447–448, and 486–487; Jack Weatherford. *Genghis Khan and the Making of the Modern World*, pp. 161–165; Svat Soucek. *A History of Inner Asia*, p. 109; David Morgan. *The Mongols*, pp. 102–103; George Lane. *Genghis Khan and Mongol Rule*, pp. 48–49; Thomas J. Craughwell. *The Rise and Fall of the Second Largest Empire in History*, pp. 216–223; Gerard Chaliand. *Nomadic Empires from Mongolia to the Danube*, pp. 72–75; Christopher I. Beckwith. *Empires of the Silk Road*, pp. 189–195.

27   Frank Mclynn. *Genghis Khan: His Conquests, His Empire, His Legacy*, pp. 174, 431–432, 447–448, and 486–487; Jack Weatherford. *Genghis Khan and the Making of the Modern World*, pp. 161–165; Svat Soucek. *A History of Inner Asia*, p. 109; David Morgan. *The Mongols*, pp. 102–103; George Lane. *Genghis Khan and Mongol Rule*, pp. 48–49; Thomas Allisen. *The Rise of the Mongolian Empire and Mongolian Rule in Northern China*, pp. 404; Thomas J. Craughwell. *The Rise and Fall of the Second Largest Empire in History*, pp. 224–237; Gerard Chaliand. *Nomadic Empires from Mongolia to the Danube*, pp. 72–75; Christopher I. Beckwith. *Empires of the Silk Road*, pp. 189–195.

28   Frank Mclynn. *Genghis Khan: His Conquests, His Empire, His Legacy*, pp. 174, 431–432, 447–448, and 486–487; Jack Weatherford. *Genghis Khan and the*

Making of the Modern World, pp. 161–165; Svat Soucek. *A History of Inner Asia*, p. 109; David Morgan. *The Mongols*, pp. 102–103; George Lane. *Genghis Khan and Mongol Rule*, pp. 48–49; Thomas J. Craughwell. *The Rise and Fall of the Second Largest Empire in History*, pp. 224–237; Gerard Chaliand. *Nomadic Empires from Mongolia to the Danube*, pp. 72–75; Christopher I. Beckwith. *Empires of the Silk Road*, pp. 189–195; *The Mongols after Genghis Khan*. http://www.chinaahistoryofwarfare.com/blog/626001-the-mongols-after-genghis-khan/

29 Frank Mclynn. *Genghis Khan: His Conquests, His Empire, His Legacy*, pp. 174, 431–432, 447–448, and 486–487; Jack Weatherford. *Genghis Khan and the Making of the Modern World*, pp. 161–165; Svat Soucek. *A History of Inner Asia*, p. 109; David Morgan. *The Mongols*, pp. 102–103; George Lane. *Genghis Khan and Mongol Rule*, pp. 48–49; Thomas J. Craughwell. *The Rise and Fall of the Second Largest Empire in History*, pp. 224–237; Gerard Chaliand. *Nomadic Empires from Mongolia to the Danube*, pp. 72–75; Christopher I. Beckwith. *Empires of the Silk Road*. pp. 189–195; and *The Mongols after Genghis Khan*. http://www.chinaahistoryofwarfare.com/blog/626001-the-mongols-after-genghis-khan/

30 Frank Mclynn. *Genghis Khan: His Conquests, His Empire, His Legacy*, pp. 174, 431–432, 447–448, and 486–487; Jack Weatherford. *Genghis Khan and the Making of the Modern World*, pp. 161–165; Svat Soucek. *A History of Inner Asia*, p. 109; David Morgan. *The Mongols*, pp. 102–103; George Lane. *Genghis Khan and Mongol Rule*, pp. 48–49; Thomas J. Craughwell. *The Rise and Fall of the Second Largest Empire in History*, pp. 224–237; Gerard Chaliand. *Nomadic Empires from Mongolia to the Danube*, pp. 72–75; Christopher I. Beckwith. *Empires of the Silk Road*, pp. 189–195; *The Mongols after Genghis Khan*. http://www.chinaahistoryofwarfare.com/blog/626001-the-mongols-after-genghis-khan/

31 David Morgan. *The Mongols*, pp. 104–109; Svat Soucek. *A History of Inner Asia*, pp. 110–114; George Lane. *Genghis Khan and Mongol Rule*, pp. 50–54; Thomas J. Craughwell. *The Rise and Fall of the Second Largest Empire in History*, pp. 224–237; Gerard Chaliand. *Nomadic Empires from Mongolia to the Danube*, pp. 72–75; Christopher I. Beckwith. *Empires of the Silk Road*, pp. 189–195; Bertold Spuler. *History of the Mongols*, pp. 165–180.

32 Paul S. Ropp. *China In World History*, pp. 80–84; J.A.G. Roberts. *A History of China*, pp. 104–114; John A. Harrison. *The Chinese Empire*, pp. 297–304.

33 Paul S. Ropp. *China In World History*, pp. 80–84; J.A.G. Roberts. *A History of China*, pp. 104–114; John A. Harrison. *The Chinese Empire*, pp. 297–304.

34 Paul S. Ropp. *China In World History*, pp. 80–84; J.A.G. Roberts. *A History of China*, pp. 104–114; John A. Harrison. *The Chinese Empire*, pp. 297–304.

35 David Morgan. *The Mongols*, p. 117; Paul S. Ropp. *China In World History*, pp. 80–84; J.A.G. Roberts. *A History of China*, pp. 104–114; John A. Harrison. *The Chinese Empire*, p. 297.

36 David Morgan. *The Mongols*, p. 117; Paul S. Ropp. *China In World History*, pp. 80–84; J.A.G. Roberts. *A History of China*, pp. 104–114; John A. Harrison. *The Chinese Empire*, pp. 297–304.

37   David Morgan. *The Mongols*, pp. 117–119; Paul S. Ropp. *China In World History*, pp. 80–84; J.A.G. Roberts. *A History of China*, pp. 104–114; John A. Harrison. *The Chinese Empire*, pp. 297–304.

38   David Morgan. *The Mongols*, pp. 117–119; Paul S. Ropp. *China In World History*, pp. 80–84; J.A.G. Roberts. *A History of China*, pp. 104–114; John A. Harrison. *The Chinese Empire*, pp. 297–304.

39   J.A.G. Roberts. *A History of China*, pp. 112–120; Paul S. Ropp. *China In World History*, pp. 83–87.

40   John A. Harrison. *The Chinese Empire*, pp. 314–316; Paul S. Ropp. *China in World History*, pp. 86–87; Dun J. Li. *The Ageless China*, pp. 301–308.

41   "The Eight Legged Essay," Princeton University. https://www.google.com/search?hl=en-US&biw=&bih=&q=%22the+eigth-legged+essay%22&oq=&aqi=&aql=&gs_l

42   *Ibid.*

43   John A. Harrison. *The Chinese Empire*, pp. 320–321; "The Eight Legged Essay;" J.A.G. Roberts. *A History of China*, pp. 122–126; Paul S. Ropp. *China in World History*, pp. 90–93.

44   John Darwin. *After Tamerlane: The Global History of Empire Since 1405*, pp. 4–6.

45   *Ibid.* pp. 4–6.

46   For the best analysis of the death rate and pathology of the Black Death see R.S. Bray. *Armies of Pestilence: The Impact of Disease on History*, pp. 19–22.

47   R.S. Bray. *Armies of Pestilence: The Impact of Disease on History*, pp. 19–22; *CDC-Symptoms-Plague.* http://www.cdc.gov/plague/symptoms/; *Septicemic Plague.* http://plague.emedtv.com/septicemic-plague/septicemic-plague-p.2.html

48   R.S. Bray. *Armies of Pestilence: The Impact of Disease on History*, pp. 19–22; *CDC-Symptoms-Plague.* http://www.cdc.gov/plague/symptoms/; *Septicemic Plague.* http://plague.emedtv.com/septicemic-plague/septicemic-plague-p.2.html

49   R.S. Bray. *Armies of Pestilence: The Impact of Disease on History*, pp. 19–22; *CDC-Symptoms-Plague.* http://www.cdc.gov/plague/symptoms/, *Septicemic Plague.* http://plague.emedtv.com/septicemic-plague/septicemic-plague-p.2.html

50   Paul S. Ropp. *China in World History*, pp. 94–96; J.A.G. Roberts. *A History of China*, pp. 136–137.

51   Paul S. Ropp. *China in World History*, pp. 94–96; J.A.G. Roberts. *A History of China*, pp. 136–137.

52   Paul S. Ropp. *China in World History*, pp. 95–97; J.A.G. Roberts. *A History of China*, pp. 134–139; Aisin Gioro and Jin Shi. *Manchuria from the Fall of the Yuan to the Rise of the Manchu State (1368–1636).* http://www.ritsumei.ac.jp; The *Origins of the Manchus.* http://history.cultural-china.com/en/183History5927.html

53   Paul S. Ropp. *China in World History*, pp. 95–97; J.A.G. Roberts. *A History of China*, pp. 134–139; Aisin Gioro and Jin Shi. *Manchuria from the Fall of*

the Yuan to the Rise of the Manchu State (1368–1636). http://www.ritsumei. ac.jp; *The Origins of the Manchus.* http://history.cultural-china.com/ en/183History5927.html

54 Paul S. Ropp. *China in World History*, pp. 94–96; J.A.G. Roberts. *A History of China*, pp. 136–137; Aisin Gioro and Jin Shi. *Manchuria from the Fall of the Yuan to the Rise of the Manchu State (1368–1636).* http://www.ritsumei. ac.jp; Wu Sangui and Tina Pamintuan. *Breaching the Great Wall: How the Manchu Conquered China.* http://www.neh.gov/news/humanities/2003-03/ greatwall.html

55 Paul S. Ropp. *China in World History*, pp. 94–96; J.A.G. Roberts. *A History of China*, pp. 136–137; Aisin Gioro and Jin Shi. *Manchuria from the Fall of the Yuan to the Rise of the Manchu State (1368–1636).* http://www.ritsumei. ac.jp; Tina Pamintuan. *Breaching the Great Wall: How the Manchu Conquered China.* http://www.neh.gov/news/humanities/2003-03/greatwall.html

56 Paul S. Ropp. China in World History, pp. 94–96; J.A.G. Roberts. *A History of China*, pp. 136–137; *Nurchai.* http://www.dartmouth.edu/~qing/ WEB/NURHACI.html; *Nurchai.* http://www.newworldencyclopedia.org/ entry/Nurhaci

57 Paul S. Ropp. *China in World History*, pp. 94–96; J.A.G. Roberts. *A History of China*, pp. 136–137; *Nurchai.* http://www.dartmouth.edu/~qing/ WEB/NURHACI.html

58 Paul S. Ropp. *China in World History*, pp. 94–96; J.A.G. Roberts. *A History of China*, pp. 136–137; *Nurchai.* http://www.dartmouth.edu/~qing/ WEB/NURHACI.html

59 Paul S. Ropp. *China in World History*, pp. 94–96; J.A.G. Roberts. *A History of China*, pp. 136–137.

60 Paul S. Ropp. *China in World History*, pp. 94–96; J.A.G. Roberts. *A History of China*, pp. 136–137.

61 Paul S. Ropp. *China in World History*, pp. 94–96; J.A.G. Roberts. *A History of China*, pp. 136–137; *Dorgon (1612–1650) Prince Regent of China.*

62 Paul S. Ropp. *China in World History*, p. 97; J.A.G. Roberts. *A History of China*, p. 138.

63 Paul S. Ropp. *China in World History*, pp. 94–96; J.A.G. Roberts. *A History of China*, pp. 136–137.

64 Paul S. Ropp. *China in World History*, pp. 97–99; J.A.G. Roberts. *A History of China*, pp. 139–143; John A. Harrison. *The Chinese Empire*, pp. 329–330 and 332–333.

65 Paul S. Ropp. *China in World History*, pp. 97–99; J.A.G. Roberts. *A History of China*, pp. 141–147; John A. Harrison. *The Chinese Empire*, pp. 326–328.

66 Paul S. Ropp. *China in World History*, pp. 97–99; J.A.G. Roberts. *A History of China*, pp. 141–147; John A. Harrison. *The Chinese Empire*, pp. 326–328.

67 J.A.G. Roberts. *A History of China*, pp. 142–143.

68 JA.G. Roberts. *A History of China*, p. 144; John A. Harrison. *The Chinese Empire*, pp. 345–347; Paul S. Ropp. *China in World History*, p. 97.

69   Christopher I. Beckwith. *Empires of the Silk Road*, pp. 189–195.
70   J.A.G. Roberts. *A History of China*, pp. 151–152; John A. Harrison. *The Chinese Empire*, pp. 345–347; Paul S. Ropp. *China in World History*, pp. 100–101.
71   J.A.G. Roberts. *A History of China*, pp. 151–152; John A. Harrison. *The Chinese Empire*, pp. 345–347; Paul S. Ropp. *China in World History*, pp. 100–101.

7

Modernization

It is an unmistakable fact that we live in the post-modern era (1945 to the present). The period prior to this is known as the modern era (1492–1945). Reaching the modern era required the rejection of tradition in favor of a new set of values that fostered modernization. These values included: a high tolerance for ambiguity (i.e. living daily with uncertainty), an expectation of change (i.e. the belief that change is good), and the development of the habits associated with innovation and risk-taking (i.e. habits that create the concept of "progress"). Traditional peoples, however, have a difficult time with any of these conditions.

Underlying these modern values is a belief in the human capacity to address the problems that people, nature, or the heavens might create, then finding solutions and, finally, ensuring that humanity will survive. The acquisition of these modern expectations raises a major historical query: How did a traditional culture (in this case Western civilization) that for centuries had repeated its behavior without question, abandon that behavior in favor of modernization? The answer lies in only one possible explanation: the traditions of such a culture grew so dysfunctional that its conventional design threatened collapse, making the adoption of new behaviors necessary for survival. Indeed, from 1300 to 1500 late medieval Europeans lived in a culture whose institutions warped, buckled, and finally twisted so far out of shape that survival led to major, even radical, innovations.

Modernization began spontaneously in the Late Middle Ages (1300–1500) in a major institutional transformation that led to a simultaneous realignment of cultural practices. Three parallel institutional revolutions combined to unleash a fourth one. First, there was the commercial revolution

China and the West to 1600: Empire, Philosophy, and the Paradox of Culture,
First Edition. Steven Wallech.
© 2016 John Wiley & Sons, Inc. Published 2016 by John Wiley & Sons, Inc.

(1492–1763). It began with the Age of Discovery that saw Christopher Columbus "discover," as far as Europe was concerned, the western hemisphere. The Americas attracted Spanish conquistadors to defeat two great native American civilizations and pillage their wealth. Furthermore, a transfer of European diseases and native American omega plants, known as the Columbian Exchange, killed so many native peoples in the western hemisphere as to create a population vacuum. At the same time, corn, potatoes, cod, and tomatoes from the Americas helped to feed a population explosion in Europe. The surplus people of Europe then turned to colonization in the "New World" to the west in search of new livelihoods. Finally, European colonists in the Americas acquired access to so many of the abundant resources of the two continents as to create a financial revolution in Europe, as well as in the western hemisphere. The commercial revolution also included the opening of an Atlantic and Indian Ocean trade route from Europe to Asia that, obviously, bypassed the overland route of the old Silk Road. What followed was an era of massive cultural exchanges between Europe, North and South America, and Africa, plus the commercial realignment of global trade between the American, African, European, and Asian continents. The collective results elevated European states to the top ranks of world power (see below).

The second revolution was a redefinition of warfare. This military revolution began when France invaded Italy in 1494, so that the French king could claim the thrones of Naples and Sicily. His march into Italy led the Italians to mobilize in opposition to the French presence in southern Italy. Marching north in retreat from Naples, the French encountered and defeated the Italians at the Battle of Fornovo in 1495. This battle lasted only one hour. Pitting a French royal army against an Italian feudal force, the decisive and devastating results of this battle ushered in a new age of combat. The French killed their opponents indiscriminately, noble and commoner alike, bringing to an end the age of chivalry, and introducing a new intensity to warfare. These changes brought more pain to the city-states of Italy when Spain challenged France's claims to Naples and Sicily; the Italian peninsula became the battleground for two very powerful royal opponents. The Italians could not match these powerful rivals, but the confrontations to which they were witness prompted a redefinition of political power in Europe. From 1495 to 1648, the refinement of military tactics led not only to the raise of royal armies across Europe, but also inspired Niccolo Machiavelli's creation of political science. In his masterpiece, *The Prince*, Machiavelli begged an Italian ruler to unify Italy, create a new kingdom, and drive the "barbarians" (i.e. the French and the Spanish) out of the peninsula (see below).

The third revolution was the Reformation (1517–1648), a religious revolution that was to splinter the Catholic Church, and lead to the break-away of Protestant sects in wars of theology as well as of the flesh; it also helped fuel the military revolution that redefined modern combat. The combatants of the Reformation were the kings and princes who disagreed over the correct version of Christianity. Finally, these wars officially removed the pope from European politics and allowed the rulers of each state to determine the religions of their realms. These decisions became final in the Treaty of Westphalia in 1648 (see below). This third revolution then laid a foundation for a fourth if slightly later revolution: the liberation of science from religion.

The Scientific Revolution (1543–1687) could not have occurred had not the Reformation taken place. Due to the marriage of Aristotelian physics and astronomy to a Catholic orthodoxy (see chapter five), the papacy became hostile towards the conclusions drawn by the Scientific Revolution. The papacy actually tried and found guilty one participant, Galileo Galilei. In 1633, the Inquisition (an institution developed by the Catholic Church to ensure orthodoxy and combat Protestantism) tried Galileo in Rome and forced him to renounce his support of the Copernican Revolution. Despite the pope's opposition, Copernicus, and his supporters, Johann Kepler and Galileo, combined to provide Sir Isaac Newton with enough information about the universe to inform a new understanding of physics and astronomy. Consequently, without the commercial revolution (1492–1763), rise of the royal army (1495–1648), and the Reformation (1517–1648), science could not have redefined our understanding of the universe through Newton's mechanics. Thus, taken all together, the massive dysfunctional mix of medieval Europe's estates, states, and statuses pushed emerging modern Europe out of the Middle Ages and into the modern era.

This chapter considers how this mix of medieval institutions unleashed these modern changes and contrasts the results with what happened—or what did not happen—in China at the same time. The paradox of culture created the circumstances that made changes in medieval Europe not only necessary but possible, beginning with a dramatic increase in the death rate caused when the warm, bountiful era of the High Middle Ages ended in 1300 and a mini-ice age began that lasted until 1800. Death by famine, disease, and warfare followed and then combined with the actions of a papacy that could not resolve its internal flaws (the Babylonian Captivity and the Western Schism mentioned in chapter four). The papacy could not change its behavior as a political estate that challenged the authority of kings. What followed was a great deal of uncertainty over salvation in the midst of a horrific demographic crisis. This state of affairs led to cries for reforms that unleashed the Renaissance (1300–1600). The Renaissance, in turn, undercut the Catholic Church's control over belief. The end result was that medieval Europe slowly laid a foundation for the parallel revolutions mentioned above.

Germanic Europe during the Early Middle Ages

The nomadic customs of the German tribes that occupied Europe after the fall of the Western Roman Empire set the tone for the Early Middle Ages (500–1000). These nomadic tribes produced the most unstable element of medieval tradition. They destroyed the Western Roman Empire and planted their customs wherever they went. These customs held common elements, but took root in different regions of Europe at different times and in different ways. The Germanic traditions then continued to develop, once planted, and their maturation reflected the local circumstances of their feudal estates.

In Italy, the Germanic customs clashed with those of the debased fragments of a surviving Roman system. Among those fragments were the papacy and a set of Italian cities that had survived Rome's fall. As mentioned in chapter four, the pope, and his urban neighbors, would form alliances to win their independence from the Holy Roman Empire once the waves of nomads had ceased invading Europe after 950. In France and England, French Salic Law and English Common Law evolved from Germanic customs and matured into discrete sets of legal traditions after 980 and 1066, respectively. In Spain and Portugal, the Germanic customs mixed with Muslim and Roman legal practices, pulling and pushing at one another as they shaped the local political landscape after 1000. In what would later become Germany, pure tribal customs dominated the law and evolved without the Roman influences found in the old Roman provinces of Italy, Iberia, France, and England. Within the emerging local German estates, warriors who supported the chief used the nomadic system of elections to pick a successor. These so-called electors slowly evolved into German princes as they won their independence from the Holy Roman Emperor, with the help of the pope after 1050 (see chapter four). In short, it was during the Early Middle Ages (500–1000) that a welter of Germanic and nomadic traditions first came to dominate the land, as each invading tribe carved out and then secured its new domain.

Each Germanic tribe that built a new domain in the old Western Roman Empire after 500 comprised a distinct kinship group, but all of the tribes shared a common worldview that included violence. They embraced the nomadic tradition of excluding strangers from access to pastures that fed their precious animals. Such a violent outlook created an obligation of obedience to an elected "*Koenig*" or chief that would eventually become "the king." Victorious tribes captured land and, where the Roman Empire once existed, joined with local ex-Roman leaders to deny entry to any of the other Germanic or Asiatic invaders pushing at the gates. Those tribes that managed to consolidate power into large estates then attempted to form stable kingdoms. Over the many years that followed the fall of Rome, these ex-nomadic tribes became sedentary (or "civilized") as they learned to grow food by sowing the land.

What emerged in the ex-Western Roman Empire were tribal states that linked each Germanic chief to his personal collection of military retainers. These retainers received distinct sets of local estates that placed all men engaged in warfare into a common relationship with the land. As mentioned numerous times, this common relationship tied an estate to a privately held state and status that defined the recipient's political, economic, and social identity. Ultimately, the linkage between estate, state, and status became the basis for feudalism.

The chief led his tribe into the ex-Western Roman Empire as a military commander, high priest, lawmaker, and judge. Each chief had gained his office through an electoral process used by nomadic tribes throughout Eurasian history. The electorate comprised "free men" who chose their chief from among eligible candidates, all of them members of the royal family. The electorate was "free" in the sense that these men had earned their independence as voters by fighting alongside the chief as his companions. They had risked their lives to defend the realm their warlord had carved out, so they received estates to support their "freedom" as a reward. Upon the death of a chief, the "free" men reviewed the merits of the male royal candidates vying for the throne. These royal candidates shared the same semi-divine character of the dead chief, while the electorate sought to ensure that only the most competent among them gained the throne.

In its earliest form, the realm captured by a chief comprised lands either taken in war or granted by local Roman officials before the final fall of Rome. The transition from the Roman era to feudalism, therefore, saw each arriving German tribe seek a realm in which free men and their chiefs could mount a defense against any further nomadic invasions. The free men within each tribe were, however, only as "free" as their respective estates permitted. Each estate bestowed upon its recipient a legitimate political identity, or state, which became a status over time. The free man took the name of the estate as his own: for example, Henry of Saxony, Richard of Essex, or Charles of Anjou. The estate defined a man's political identity and defined the boundaries of legitimate action that made this man free. Each free man ruled his estate as a private realm, but all free men were subject to the chief's will. Each man, then, fitted within the chief's own estate (kingdom) as an intermediate political state that became legalized as part of the feudal hierarchy. Some men, however, gained their freedom without an estate.*

Those men who possessed freedom without possessing land did so by swearing obedience to a man of estate who served the chief as a companion and a warrior. The subordinate free men ranged from soldiers to peasants, but each one in some way gained access to a livelihood by serving a man in possession of land. Both obeyed this intermediate ruler as if he were a chief, even if both were also still expected to obey the chief. The intermediate ruler was an estate holder who recruited the landless soldier or peasant in exchange for his labor. The intermediate ruler became what we know as a lord, and, as a lord, he took responsibility for the soldier or peasant's upkeep. This upkeep included providing his subordinate free men with generous feasts and numerous gifts. This system of sworn free men (peasants, warriors, and lords alike) became the central feature of early Germanic tribal society. In this way, the loyalty and service of all such free men extended the concept of kinship beyond an immediate family, outward to society and the king, forming the basis of the early medieval Germanic community.

A Man or Woman's Value: The Wergild

The foundation of these earliest Germanic tribal societies was the newly acquired estate system. The estate took the measure of a free man's place within the social hierarchy, a means to determine his value. The measure of this value became a specific amount known as the *wergild*, or the price one paid for injuring a particular man. Among the Anglo-Saxons, the lowest ranking free man, a peasant, had a wergild or value of 100 shillings, or one hundred oxen (in today's monetary value: $6000). In contrast, a chief's companion commanded a value of twelve to sixteen times that amount. His value ranged from 1200 shillings, or 1200 oxen, to 1600 shillings, or 1600 oxen ($24,000 for a knight, $96,000 for a baron).[1]

Among the Alemanni, the Germanic tribe that occupied the German estates of the Holy Roman Empire, the basic wergild for a peasant was 200

---

*The best example of how this freedom by estate is spelled out is in the Magna Carta. The text of this document outlines the estates of England in the thirteenth century and specifies the ancient freedoms that each estate holder had. The Magna Carta itself sought to preserve these ancient freedoms and functions as an excellent example of the rigid structure of a feudal kingdom. See *The Text of the Magna Carta at* http://www.fordham.edu/halsall/source/magnacarta.asp

shillings, while the amount paid for a king's companion could double or triple this amount depending on his status. These lower prices reflected the value the chief placed on the injured man. Serfs existed as captured ex-Roman peasants, and they were of marginal value. A serf's wergild price was only 15 shillings among the Alemanni. Those people who lived in towns that had survived the fall of Rome included artisans. The German chief set the wergild of artisans at 40 or 50 shillings.[†] The wergild not only applied to the violence or injury done to a man, but also to insults, theft, and damage to property. The social hierarchy defined the amount of these lesser crimes.

Free women were not considered as valuable as free men. Because they could not fight, free women could not hold an estate of their own. They did, however, inherit the rank of their father if unmarried, and they acquired the rank of their husband if they married. The value of a woman, or the amount of money one had to pay for injuring her, depended on her rank. For example, when a man seduced a woman, he had to pay her father or her husband half her wergild. For raping her, the perpetrator paid the full wergild. However, high-status people most likely would not accept the wergild for such crimes. Their honor required blood, so combat alone could right this injury.

The Right to Assemble

According to tribal, Germanic custom, all free men had the right to participate in a general assembly where disputes were addressed. Ancestral custom bound the chief to the task of preserving all the ancient traditions of his people. In time, however, the chief himself became the source of new laws created for cases not addressed in any previous tribal tradition. And since these Germanic tribes were undergoing the shift from a nomadic, pastoral life to sedentary farming, the role of the chief as lawgiver continually increased in importance.

This shift from enforcing custom (or tradition) to creating law formed the basis for recording of the legal codes of the various Germanic chiefs. This shift from enforcer of customs (or traditions) to creator of laws encouraged chiefs to absorb surviving Roman and Christian practices into their own codes of law—as feudal society slowly emerged from a tribal setting. Also, with the introduction of Christianity, record keeping itself became not only possible but more frequent, as illiterate Germanic rulers acquired the skills and services of literate priests and monks. Clerics, also known at the time as clerks, recorded inherited tribal laws, often adapting these to surviving Roman codes. Also, these legal codes had to define the role of the church and the Christian clergy within the emerging feudal society.

[†] Not all sources agree on the wergild that had to be paid for an injured man.

Added to the creation and recording of these Christianized legal settlements were the setting of the wergilds for the members of the clerical hierarchy. Unsurprisingly, the wergilds that clerks placed on the princes of the church were on par with those placed on noble warriors. For example, the post of an archbishop became the equivalent of a king, while a bishop equaled the value of a baron. What emerged was a blending of Roman legal concepts of property and inheritance with a Germanic distribution of estates, all of which received sanction by the church.

The Christian Component Emerges

With the introduction of the Christian church to the estate structure of the Early Middle Ages (500–1000), an institution that had survived the fall of Rome now bridged the gap between the ancient and medieval world. At the same time, as mentioned in chapter two, this Roman institution, the church, carried within it an ancient belief system that separated the spiritual message of Jesus from the Roman political landscape. This separation led to the church's claim of independence from feudal lords. But when the church first joined the Germanic realms, the separation of church and state did not exist because priests, bishops, monks, and abbots required the protection of Germanic kings from nomadic invaders. This need compelled the church to allow German kings to appoint their bishops and abbots to serve in the defense of the realm.

Then, after the kings stabilized their realms by implementing feudalism, and appointed knights as vassals, the same priests, bishops, monks, and abbots joined with the pope to declare their independence from the state as required by Jesus' ministry. But these priests, bishops, monks, and abbots had already received *benefices* (estates held during one's lifetime) from kings to support the church's sacred works. And by receiving these estates, they, too, became states and joined the political landscape (see chapter four and above). In time, therefore, the church's claim of independence eventually unleashed a cultural paradox that medieval Europe could not resolve: if the church and state were indeed to remain separate institutions, by holding an estate, did not the church also become a state and join the realm of politics?

Since feudal tradition claimed that an estate was also a state, which gave legitimacy to the political action that originated with the estate holder, then the church and state were no longer truly separated. If the church was independent from the secular state of chiefs and kings, while functioning as a religious state, then the church seemingly contradicted its own mission as a spiritual leader. This contradiction surfaced when the church preached a life free of sin, even as the holders of church estates acted as political creatures whom Jesus condemned as sinners. As political creatures, they acted in ways that Jesus had denounced: like all estate holders, they became persons engaged in worldly wickedness. This meant that even as members of the church, they often ran foul of Jesus' ministry, something that their religious vocation condemned.

Jesus' ministry spoke with a voice that promised resurrection in a heavenly realm for the righteous, or people free of sin. Sin belonged to the secular world where daily life was filled with temptations. Jesus had set up a contrast between "what ought to be," or righteous behavior, and "what is," or daily life in the secular world. Jesus' ministry, therefore, contrasted a spiritual life with the corruption fostered by the temporal world. Yet, again, since to hold an estate within the temporal world was to be a part of its corruption, the reward that the spiritual message of the church promised, heaven, and the place where the material body of the church resided, the political fabric of medieval society, stood as polar opposites. In other words, the church preached what "ought to be" and condemned "what is," but at the same time it also acted as a part of the world of "what is."

This contradiction within the church became even more pronounced during the High Middle Ages (1000–1300). When the Gregorian Revolution established the papacy as an independent estate, the authority of the pope equaled, if not surpassed, that of the Holy Roman Emperor (see chapter five). As a religious ruler, the pope took on even more responsibility for the existing order of things than the king. The rise of the papacy converted the church into the most powerful medieval state, which made it responsible for most of "what is." Part of the Gregorian claim to superior power over the emperor was the universality of this spiritual institution when compared to the geographic limits to all secular realms. Another part of the Gregorian claim to superior power over all secular lords was the church's role as the shepherd of all transcendental souls when compared to the secular lord's preservation of only temporal bodies. Yet, when the church acted like a state, this drew the church's spiritual role into the realm of politics, where sin was rife. Hence, even as the church railed against all sin in this world, the church had to take partial responsibility for its contribution to these very same sins.

The High Middle Ages and the Law

During the High Middle Ages, the formal estates of feudalism supplanted the traditional practices of Germanic society. Part of the reason for this transition from German to feudal practices was the end of the migratory period of Germanic and Asiatic invasions in the tenth century.

Another reason for this shift was the recovery of the Justinian Code of Law known as the *Corpus Juris Civilis*. How the recovery of this code occurred is uncertain, but its impact on medieval Europe is clearly known because it became part of the curriculum in medieval colleges and universities. The Code of Justinian itself is a substantial collection of laws compiled under the sponsorship of Justinian I (reigned 527–565), ruler of the Byzantine Empire (i.e. the surviving Eastern Roman Empire). This code systemized Roman law, removed archaic and contradictory statutes, added Justinian's edicts, and compiled the leading opinions of legal experts during his reign. As a code of law, the Justinian Code conveyed the legal genius of Rome to a Germanic world hungry for order.[2]

The papacy, the emperor, and kings began to employ the *Corpus Juris Civilis* in varying degrees to create a legal foundation for all estates, states, and statuses. To some extent, the influence of Roman law was an indirect result of the rise of the papacy, but the creation of stable, secular monarchies also played a part. The political structure of the various emerging kingdoms and church estates simply grew too large and complex to function well without a formal, contractual system of Germanic tribal laws. Justinian's Roman legal statutes served to clarify the emerging feudal hierarchy. This need for law also launched the legal profession. These newly minted lawyers served kings and the papacy well, as administrators who imposed a standardized form of power over the welter of traditional practices that the Germanic tribes had used.

From the law came a new level of internal coherence to feudal institutions. Each estate structure took on a more rational design. This rationality in administrative potential in kingdoms and the church clarified the function of each. Clarity of function, however, sharpened the claims of power emanating from each as well. The result was an intensification of the struggle between church and state as to which was the ultimate authority within Europe's feudal realms. Perhaps, then, one could also argue that an increase in intensity in the struggle to define ultimate authority also matched an increase in the level of sin committed by its participants.

Roman Law and Trade–the Role of Property

Parallel to the rise of the papacy, and the implementation of Roman law, was the recovery of trade during the High Middle Ages (1000–1300). This recovery combined two simultaneous events mentioned in chapter four: first, the end of the migratory era of the Early Middle Ages occurred around 950 due to the establishment of the military protection offered by feudalism; and second, an especially warm, stable climate that began at nearly the same time stimulated a boost to agriculture. The death rate due to nomadic invasion dropped sharply after 950, and exceptional harvests followed that created a new bounty made possible by the long era of warm weather. The sharp increases in food surpluses fed a growing population, but the additions of so many new people, and the abundance of so much available food, collided with the rigidity of the newly established feudal estates. So the paradox of culture surfaced once again: the successes of agriculture created increasing stresses on existing cultural institutions. In the case of feudalism, these stresses broke the bonds of a newly established tradition.

Feudalism linked the supply of land with the estates that supported the knights that defended medieval Europe against nomadic raids. But the fixed supply of available land in Europe limited the total number of estates that could feed these knights. As the total number of surviving children of knights suddenly increased due to the new food surpluses and security from nomadic raids, the possibility of providing the needed fiefs (feudal domains) to each knight's heir declined. The same was true for those who worked on these feudal estates as the villeins (i.e. the serfs that worked the land). And even when the nobility and the church cleared more land to absorb the growing population, the total number of lords and peasants still exceeded what the new estates could support.

This surplus population then began to spill outside the bounds of the newly established feudal hierarchy and left Europe, seeking new lands through military expansion during the Crusades. In addition, an alternative to feudalism began to emerge as people moved to towns to fill new artisan and commercial occupations. Those young noblemen who set out from Christendom took part in wars against Muslims in Portugal, Spain, Sicily, and the Holy Land. The surplus people who entered towns accepted employment in the "illegitimate" occupations of the city that created a new, non-feudal form of wealth mentioned in chapter four: "incorporeal property" (i.e. non-existing, or illegitimate wealth).

The "incorporeal" portion of the property found in cities literally speaks to the legal ownership of any object of value that has no social or political existence. In other words, incorporeal property was something of value economically, but feudalism did not recognize money or goods as actual. This is, of course, an explicit contradiction because such "nonexistent" items "existed" as personal property. Also mentioned in chapter four, "real estate," in the European feudal tradition, always was (and still is) land, and all the things attached to it. Now, as then, to hold land is to possess "real" (legitimate) estate, state, and status. This meant that a person who owned or possessed land was real in the legal sense of holding a legitimate political and social identity. In other words, he was a "free" man. In this manner, to own real estate was to own the political power of a state and the social standing defined by that estate. But to possess incorporeal property was to have neither state nor status. Also, such a person lived outside the boundaries of feudal society.

The recovery of trade, therefore, created numerous "illegitimate" ways of making a living, and gave birth to another curious paradox. The recovery of trade, and the resurrection of urban occupations, contradicted the new legal definitions of feudalism. This contradiction required lawyers either to create a legal identity that allowed merchants to engage in commerce, and in some cases, compelled merchants to raise their own armies for military protection, or create new political institutions. As mentioned in chapter four, the legal identity that could engage in trade became known as a "corporation" (i.e. a legal body). Originally a corporation was an organization of urban occupations that received a charter from a king, lord, pope, or bishop that "legitimized" their activity in exchange for a tax. The tax received by the grantor of the charter gave him a source of illegitimate income, which drew him into activities outside the boundaries of feudalism. Towns and cities that operated without such a charter did so at their peril. These unchartered towns could not survive without sufficient wealth to arm themselves in defense of their illegitimate incomes.

The existence of both the chartered and the unchartered towns created an economic world that came to completely contradict the feudal order. As mentioned in chapter four, feudalism only recognized three estates: 1) those who prayed (the clergy); 2) those who fought (the nobility); and 3) those who worked (the villeins). No urban activity (that of artisans or merchants) fell within any one of these three legitimate, rural occupations. Hence, for towns to exist and function, they required the addition of non-traditional activities to the feudal fabric of society. These non-traditional activities, in turn, infused Europe with modern expectations: the uncertainty of the marketplace, the need for innovation to carve out a new business model, and the belief that today is good, but tomorrow might be better. These new values drove Europe toward an unknown, non-traditional future.

This embrace of an unknown, non-traditional future caused Europeans to arm themselves with new urban skills to deal with an eroding feudal economic, social, and political landscape. As mentioned above, literacy, computation, and critical thinking skills increased, but then caused still another feature of modernization to occur: the awakening of an unquenchable curiosity. This increase in curiosity coincidently synchronized with the recovery of Aristotelian philosophy mentioned in chapter four.

The recovery of Aristotle then infused medieval Europe with a revitalized Greco-Roman vision of the universe that the Early Middle Ages nearly destroyed. As it turned out, however, the reintroduction of the entire body of Aristotle's work nearly overwhelmed the medieval European imagination.

The most successful of those who attempted to integrate Aristotle with Christian theology, Thomas Aquinas, only partially achieved his goal. But his efforts added yet another unstable element to the medieval European tradition. By uniting Aristotle and Christian theology, Aquinas imposed Greek science on the Christian faith, making the church vulnerable to a defense of its erroneous system of astronomy. Aristotle's geocentricism incorrectly placed the Earth at the center of the universe, with the Sun and the other planets orbiting our home planet. Furthermore, this marriage of worldviews forced Greek knowledge and the Christian faith into a common bond of understanding that the empirical features of Greek science ultimately denied. Finally, the resurrection of the Aristotelian worldview infused medieval Europe with a hunger for other surviving Greco-Roman books that still lay dormant in numerous monastic libraries scattered across Christendom.

Another Shift in Climate: The Late Middle Ages

In addition to adding Aristotle to feudal Europe's intellectual landscape, a change in climate undermined the cultural fabric of the High Middle Ages (1000–1300). As mentioned in chapter four, a mini-ice-age began shortly after 1300 that undercut the prosperity of the High Middle Ages and launched famine. Europe quickly lost the relative demographic vitality it had enjoyed in the years between 1000 and 1300. Within a half-century after famine hit, the bubonic plague and warfare also erupted. The increased death rate that followed left a powerful impression on the Late Middle Ages (1300–1500) as a population crisis fractured the medieval fabric of feudal Europe.

In the midst of mass death caused by famine, plague, and warfare, some Europeans decided to seek as much fame in this world as possible so that they might leave a mark on posterity before they perished. They modeled themselves on their Greco-Roman heroes such as Cicero, Socrates, Plato, Thucydides, Herodotus, and Sophocles. Others, however, wanted to prepare themselves for heaven by leading pious and humble lives. They sought the rewards of a pure Christian existence, one free of contemporary political disputes, such as those continually flaring up between popes and kings. They sought a life that imitated the essential values espoused by Jesus.

Those who developed an interest in this world lived primarily in what we now know as Italy. The greatest concentration of medieval cities had developed on the Italian peninsula due to its strategic location, basically lying at the heart of the Mediterranean trade network. These cities existed essentially as independent states built on the wealth derived from commerce. They became "city-states" without the sanctions of any feudal lord, using money and commerce to arm themselves in the fight for their independence outside the feudal tradition. As such they developed their own political institutions and made alliances with one another in mutual defense. They had already shed their medieval mentality and developed a love of their ancient heritage. As a result, during the Late Middle Ages the Italian citizens of these independent city-states set out to recover their ancient past with a passion.

This new desire to study works that dealt only with this world, rather than heaven, fueled a hunger for Greco-Roman poetry, grammar, history, ethics, philosophy, and oratory. Study of these disciplines revived a longing to find and interpret more and more texts written by the ancient Greco-Roman philosophers, dramatists, and historians. This quest led the Italians to create an entire branch of human inquiry called the humanities, which inspired modern historians to dub these Italians "humanists." A humanist is a person whom historians label as one seeking the genius embedded in the ancient concepts of civic virtue, citizenship, and free will. The correct uses of civic virtue, citizenship, and free will transformed *the individual* into *a person* (my emphasis) capable of leaving a mark on posterity—a different kind of "afterlife" from the one held out by the church. Such an individual was created by his action. A person was distinguished from all others by using the knowledge acquired by studying metaphysics (i.e. reality), epistemology (the standards that define objective truth), axiology (ethics), and aesthetics (artistic judgment). He carved a place in society by understanding history and modeling his behavior on the heroes of the ancient Greco-Roman world. He implemented the wisdom he had acquired by thoroughly grasping this ancient lifestyle. In other words, he became "a man of the world," that is, a self-possessed person capable of anything he judged to be good.

The humanist was also a person who changed our understanding of time. He rejected the medieval model of time assigned by the church. The medieval church stated that the birth of Jesus had divided time by his *eschatos*: death and resurrection. Men, such as Paul of Tarsus (10–69) and Augustine of Hippo (354–430), had marked Jesus' *eschatos* as a break in time that made his birth a sacred moment. Christianity, therefore, signified this sacred moment in our calendar with "BC" and "AD." But to do so was to create confusion for the medieval imagination over when the ancient era ended and the Middle Ages began. Medieval theologians and artists alike manifested this confusion in both their thought and the way they depicted Roman and medieval events. They thought that both belonged to the same era as marked by "AD."

The humanist, however, sensed the difference between the fall of Rome and the rise of the Middle Ages. He marked time by placing the Greco-Roman world in one era and the Middle Ages in another. In effect, he created a new understanding of the Early Middle Ages (500–1000) as the "Dark Ages" because of the loss of Greco-Roman artifacts. This meant that he lived during the "Renaissance," or the time of the recovery of Greco-Roman brilliance. Such a re-evaluation of time helped his contemporaries see that they lived in a new age, one predicated on an ancient past, but also one that rejected the recent past, that is, the traditional, feudal era. This new model of time allowed European humanists to reconsider what they thought was legitimate behavior by recreating their understanding of history and its role in their lives.[3]

A star of, and some even say the founder of, the Italian Renaissance, Francisco Petrarch (1304–1374), helped to define humanism. He did so by reviving the language of Latin through his study of Cicero, perhaps the most gifted orator of ancient Rome. Petrarch was a very talented poet. He valued life as a limited resource, and he viewed the act of writing as a slow death in which the poet surrendered his life moment by moment as his pen left words on the page. This meant that each word took on special meaning as a moment that could never be recovered. Each word, therefore, had to be perfect. This vision of time focused his contemporaries' attention on what they did with their lives. Petrarch made a success of his life. He could support himself solely on his essays and poetry. This made his life a model for his friends to imitate.[4]

Petrarch had many friends, but one of his closest was another Florentine named Giovanni Boccaccio (1313–1375). Boccaccio added to Petrarch's new literary tradition with his most famous work, entitled the *Decameron*. This told a series of bawdy and satirical stories that revealed that members of the church, who held themselves out as holy, had the same licentious appetites as the laity. Boccaccio did not limit himself only to the church; he found many walks of life filled with people of high and low status that needed to reduce the hypocrisy of their lives. He used humor as a tool to suggest reforms to all of medieval society. Boccaccio then joined Petrarch in inspiring a whole list of Florentine authors to make their city-state seem like the headquarters of the Renaissance.[5]

Following Petrarch's and Boccaccio's breakthroughs in literature, more Florentine authors added to the growing Renaissance list of publications:

Coluccio Salutati (1331–1406) and Leonardo Bruni (1361–1444) addressed the problems of urban life by dwelling on the value of such urban skills as literacy, rhetoric, and critical thinking. In politics, Matteo Palmieri (1406–1475) revived the role of civic virtue in the life of the ideal citizen in his *On Civic Life*.[6] A generation later, Marsilio Ficino (1433–1499) produced a study of Plato that created a unique philosophical outlook based on Neoplatonism, Christian theology, and German mysticism, in order to create the ideal life. A contemporary of Ficino's, Pico della Mirandola (1463–1494), liberated the individual as a secular actor in his *Oration on the Dignity of Man*. Although born in Bologna, he moved throughout Italy and settled in Florence to publish his work, which served as the manifesto for the Italian Renaissance.[7] In the next generation, Niccolo Machiavelli (1469–1527) redefined politics by reviving the ancient Roman historian Livy and applying his work to contemporary citizenship and statecraft in *Discourses on the First Ten Books of Livy*. Machiavelli also spoke to contemporary politicians in *The Prince*, in which he appealed to an Italian ruler to save Italy from the Spanish and the French (mentioned above). Furthermore, in this work, Machiavelli stripped the uses of power of its ethical dimensions, speaking openly about the raw nature of contemporary politics and how one survived in this field of action. Finally, Francesco Guicciardini (1483–1540) took the lessons learned from Machiavelli's study of political power and applied them to *History of Italy*. This text revealed why the Italian princes and the papacy failed to secure their independence after 1494, when the French invaded the Italian peninsula, redefined the art of war, and unleashed a new style of combat in Europe (see below).[8]

What all these authors had in common was a new self-awareness that unleashed a modern worldview: one that placed human conduct within a secular context that focused on achievements during one's lifetime rather than the medieval quest for salvation. By the sixteenth century, such a worldview had become commonplace. In this endeavor, however, from the fourteenth to the sixteenth century, the Italians, and especially the Florentines, led Europe in explaining the relationship between historical circumstances and political action. This new sensitivity to history emerged from their ability to distinguish between the Greco-Roman era and the Middle Ages that followed. They acknowledged that their love of Greco-Roman antiquity had created both a new age (the Renaissance) and the discovery of the ancient era (Greco-Roman times). As mentioned above, through their revival of ancient works, they also redefined the period that immediately followed the fall of Rome; they dubbed it the "dark ages," and we know it as "the Middle Ages." In other words, the fathers of the

Renaissance realized that they had unleashed something new, but they just did not have a name for it. We call it "modernization."[9]

From all the highly talented Italian authors, one stands out as unique. He was Lorenzo Valla (1405–1457). Particularly sensitive to the rhetorical and philological qualities of ancient texts as depicted by the new model of humanist time, Valla noted the differences in ancient and medieval terminology. He applied this historical sensitivity to religious documents in order to evaluate the basis of the pope's claims to his estates in Italy. One such document was *The Donation of Constantine*, the alleged legal grant of these estates to the pope, by Emperor Constantine. In *On the Donation of Constantine*, Valla argued that these legal claims rested on a forgery. The language used in *The Donation of Constantine* included medieval terms; these did not exist during Constantine's lifetime. For example, the *Donation* included the word "*fief*" to describe the papal estates, which was a feudal term unknown to a Roman emperor. Therefore, the term "fief" could not have existed during the Roman era. Hence *The Donation of Constantine* was really an eighth-century creation. Such a historical revelation completely undermined the pope's claim to his domain in Italy. At the same time, Valla's revelation reinforced the paradox that to own an estate granted its owner the power of a state and made him a politician (i.e. a sinful actor). Valla revealed these facts during an era when the demand for church reforms increased dramatically. But instead of punishing Valla for the embarrassment caused by his revelations, Pope Nicholas V (1447–1455) employed the humanist as a librarian in a new collection of books located in the Vatican.[10]

More important than *The Donation of Constantine*, perhaps, was Valla's shift in focus to the Vulgate, the official Bible of the Catholic Church. In his *Annotations on the New Testament*, Valla revealed a number of errors in the Catholic version of the New Testament concerning the historical development of church dogma. Valla discovered that Jerome (347–419), the author of the Vulgate, had imposed his contemporary fourth-century version of Roman Catholic orthodoxy on the gospels as first-century documents. Such a location of fourth-century beliefs on first-century revelations would have precluded many of the debates concerning the nature of God and Jesus that occurred during Jerome's lifetime. This suggested that Jerome's Bible had an altered fourth-century bias within it that needed correcting. Desiderius Erasmus (1467?–1534) found a copy of Valla's *Annotations on the New Testament* near Louvain and published it in 1505 (see below). The release of Valla's findings in 1505 unleashed a desire to revisit the Bible, discover its Greek and Roman sources, and ensure that the book in which Christians invested their faith was an accurate version of

God's revelations. This desire took root in northern Europe, where the Renaissance spread and took up a new life during the fifteenth and sixteenth centuries.[11]

After 1550, it was no longer the Italians who produced the most dynamic works of the Renaissance era. Italy suffered severely due to the turmoil caused by almost constant warfare, as the Valois of France fought the Habsburgs of Spain, the Netherlands, Austria, and the Holy Roman Empire to determine who would rule the peninsula. Both sides wished to become the masters of Italy, and their struggle to achieve this turned the peninsula into a battlefield from 1494 to 1559. Now northern Europe took up the torch.

The Christian Renaissance

In a sense, when humanism traveled north from Italy, Europe left the Middle Ages and entered the Modern Era. The Italian humanists had emphasized a secular concern about life. This concern centered Europe's attention on the individual, his free will, and his limited resources (i.e. the time he had to live, and the mark he could leave on posterity). This emphasis on a secular worldview became the intellectual orientation towards nature common to science. Most visible in Machiavelli's *The Prince*, this vision would find expression in the creation of political science, and then later in the Scientific Revolution (1543–1687), specifically in physics and astronomy (see below). Although, Italy largely ceased producing outstanding Renaissance works after 1550, northern Europe did not lose the focus on this world that the Italians had developed.

With this shift north, however, Renaissance humanism left behind the Italian emphasis on primarily secular matters. North European humanists chose Christian issues. As Italian humanism moved north, it also brought the Renaissance's new awareness of the difference between the ancient and medieval eras: an awareness that resurrected the Greco-Roman worldview free of any medieval contaminants. What followed was a quest for a pure Christian vision of Europe's faith, based on primary Greek and Roman documents. Ironically, this quest for a pure Christianity laid an unexpected foundation for the Reformation (1517–1648). The irony in this rested on a completely different view of humanity's free will that distinguishes the Reformation from the Renaissance. The Reformation denied free will completely, but the Renaissance enshrined it (see below).

Nonetheless, the Reformation in a sense joined the Renaissance in its challenge to the sixteenth-century version of Roman Catholicism. The Reformation, however, went beyond the Renaissance's challenges to Church doctrine by presenting a new form of Christianity that demonstrated "false" Catholic practices (see below). What followed was a break up of a unified European orthodoxy that infused Europe's religious beliefs with a new level of doubt that the Roman Catholic Church could not control. Hence, the Christian humanist played an equally important role as the secular humanist in the new age.

One way the northern wing of humanism differed from the Italian version is that the former did not have an immediate classical past to resurrect, as did Italy. The issues of the citizen, civic virtue, and individuality did not take on the importance they had in Italy. Instead, the north Europeans sought to purify their faith with a recovery of the original ancient texts that defined their religion.

While they disagreed on the best solution to the pressing religious problems of the day, they all agreed on the methods of finding the answers: applying Renaissance standards of truth to reveal a Greco-Roman vision of the world. North European humanists focused on a rebirth of Greek ethics that viewed humanity as potentially good. While a medieval scholastic theologian focused on original sin, Protestant theologians would later agree more with the medieval scholastic than the North European humanists. But the Protestant theologian would view the depraved nature of human sin as so great as to deny free will completely, while the scholastic theologian permitted its existence (see below).

Meanwhile, the northern humanist scholars also shared a common optimism with the Italians that northern humanists scholars applied to their studies. They thought that the truths they might uncover would lead to reforms within the Catholic Church, needed in light of the pope's active participation in feudal politics (see chapter five). They based this optimistic belief on the human powers of reason and free will that they believed resided in all individuals. Such a strong faith in the individual set their works apart from those of the medieval era, and placed their enquiry into church reform on the cusp of modernization.

Underlying their publications was the common goal of revitalizing Christianity by means of the new, Renaissance learning imported from Italy. In addition, going back to the Greco-Roman texts that had established the church, these scholars expected to apply the wisdom of the past to heal the wounds of their contemporary world. This is why they worked so energetically to publish all their findings. Their publications ranged from new editions of the Bible to the works of the church fathers.

Since the reformers expected the changes they sought to stem from the free will and intellect of their fellow human beings, they did not see their endeavors as revolutionary. They set out to correct errors in the Catholic

Church's interpretation of its original dogma. They also hoped to expose corruption among church officials as a form of religious curative that might repair society and put theology on the correct path. Like their Italian predecessors, the northern humanist scholars had an innate hostility toward the medieval scholastic approach to religious inquiry. They also hoped that the newly regained Greco-Roman worldview would restore Christianity in its purest, most pristine form. Those who participated in these endeavors came from all parts of Europe (including Italy) and represented an explosion of creative minds.

The Christian Humanists

In Spain, even the monarchy patronized humanism. Unexpected leaders such as Francisco Ximenes de Cisneros (c.1436–1517), Queen Isabella's confessor, regional leader of the Franciscan Order, and the Grand Inquisitor, hoped to use humanism to reform the church. To advance his reform agenda he established the new learning at an institution he founded in 1500, the University of Alcalá. Influenced by Valla, he published the Greek text of the New Testament to ensure a correct reading of Revelation. He inspired Spain's greatest humanist scholars; among them was Elio Antonio de Nebrija (c.1442–1522), who worked on the revised Bible. A long list of humanists followed. Juan de Valdés (c.1500–1541) won a reputation as a literary genius who mastered Castilian prose for use as a tool in reforming the church. Juan Luis Vives (1492–1540) applied the new learning to philosophy to reform both Spanish society and education. He did so by primarily encouraging the crown to extend Christian charity to all walks of life and instituting a system of governmental services that addressed the problems of the poor. Alfonso de Valdés, Juan's brother (died 1535), developed a strong bond with the most powerful monarch of Europe at the time: Charles I of Spain (1516–1556), also called Charles V of the Holy Roman Empire (1519–1558). Taken all together, Charles I and V ruled as the king of Spain, Archduke of the Netherlands, Luxembourg, Artois, Franche-Comté, and Austria, claimant to the kingdoms of Navarre, Naples, Sicily, and Sardinia, owner of Spanish America, and Holy Roman Emperor. Alfonso used his connections with Charles I and V to implement some of de Valdés' ideas.[12]

Humanism also found fertile ground in France. Here, too, royal patronage was critical to its pursuits and Francis I (reigned 1515–1547) supported a magnificent Renaissance court. Foremost among the French humanists was Guillaume Budé (1467–1540), who, with an excellent knowledge of Latin and Greek, served as Francis I's librarian. Budé urged the king to establish what became the College of France (1530), where the new learning joined the curriculum. Besides Budé, the leading French humanist was Jacques Lefèvre d'Étaples (1455–1536), who sought to harmonize the classical world with Catholic reform. His work revised numerous segments of the Bible and focused heavily on the church fathers. Lefèvre's devotee, Guillaume Briçonnet (1470–1533), applied Christian humanism to the practical problems of his office as Bishop of Meaux. He brought several Renaissance scholars to Meaux, including Gérard Roussel (died 1550), Guillaume Fracel (1489–1565), and Lefèvre. They all shared the same reform goals. Briçonnet also influenced Margaret d'Angoulême (1492–1549), sister of Francis I. She first became the wife of Duke Charles of Alençon and later of Henry d'Albert, King of Navarre. She supported Protestant refugees, while remaining Catholic during the Reformation (1517–1648).[13]

Among the leading French humanists was François Rabelais (1494–1553). He saw little point in attempting to reform the French church, and instead produced works that followed in the Italian vein of satirical, secular literature. His most noted works include *The Inestimable Life of the Great Gargantua, Father of Pantagruel,* a series of stories similar to the *Decameron.* In this French version of social hypocrisy, Rabelais established a new standard for humor, while ridiculing and undermining the traditional practices of medieval institutions. During the Reformation, Rabelais was every bit as impatient with Catholics as he was with Protestants. He rejected Christianity's fascination with sin, and instead sought the inherent goodness in humanity. With a strong faith in the power of human reason, he supported the sciences and the study of medicine. Finally, he turned a skeptical eye toward any attempt to link the pursuit and use of knowledge with faith.[14]

In England, the Renaissance began when Henry VII (reigned 1485–1509) restored peace to the land after the devastating Wars of the Roses (1455–1485). During this long series of wars, two branches of the Plantagenet family, York, whose family crest featured a white rose, and Lancaster, whose crest featured a red rose, mired England in a 30-year-long dispute over the royal succession. Ultimately Henry, representing Lancaster, defeated Richard III (reigned 1483–1485), representing York. Henry killed Richard at the Battle of Bosworth Field and captured the crown. With the re-establishment of peace, Englishmen renewed their cultural contact with Italy and the new Renaissance scholarship.

Two Oxford graduates, William Grocyn (1446–1519) and Thomas Linacre (1460–1524), visited Italy and imported humanist ideas to their homeland. Coupled with William Caxton's (c.1415–1492) printing press, these two scholars laid a foundation for the new learning in England.

One of the beneficiaries was John Colet (*c*.1467–1519) who attended lectures offered by Grocyn and Linacre that included the works of Marsilio Ficino and Pico della Mirandola. Colet gave lectures on St Paul's epistle at Oxford and was dean of St Pauls in London, where he used the new learning to explain the Bible in his sermons. Upon his father's death, Colet founded a humanist school in London, called St Paul's, that trained its pupils in Renaissance techniques. The greatest of the Oxford humanists was Sir Thomas More (1478–1535), whose friendship with Colet and Desiderius Erasmus (*c*.1469–1536) launched a distinguished career as a humanist.[15]

More earned his fame as a Renaissance scholar with his masterpiece, *Utopia*. This work drew upon sixteenth-century observations and Platonic studies to formulate a blistering criticism of Late Medieval England (1300–1500). In *Utopia*, More applied the new learning to England's problems, to which he suggested solutions by describing a hypothetical but ideal island-state as a model society. As imaginative and far reaching as Machiavelli's *The Prince*, More's *Utopia* stands in stark contrast to Machiavelli's study of raw political power. Whereas Machiavelli sought to define the world of politics as it *is*, a place filled with amoral princes who converted the civic virtue of the ancient world into the prowess of great military leaders, More sought to define the world as it *ought to be*, based on the wisdom of Plato. While Machiavelli found exceptional ancient princes in men such as Moses (founder of Israel), Romulus (founder of Rome), Theseus (founder of Athens), and Cyrus the Great (founder of the Persian Empire), More postulated an ideal island economically self-sufficient, intellectually vital, and ethically rich in Greco-Roman values. These two authors were men of the same era who both wanted to change the political circumstances of their respective realms, but they took opposing approaches. Machiavelli accepted the worst in humanity and sought to find out how to use these factors as a means to create a new kingdom called "Italy." In contrast, More appealed to the best in people, seeking to elevate their lives to the heights of morality to revise English politics. Neither man, however, appealed to any Christian examples as models. Instead, both of them based their solutions solely on the wisdom held out by the classical texts. While Machiavelli epitomized the secular voice of the Italian Renaissance, More represented the ancient Greco-Roman assumptions of the northern Renaissance.[16]

The German half of the Holy Roman Empire also produced humanists who followed in the footsteps of the Italians. Indeed, the connections between the German half and the Italian half of the realm were very strong during the Renaissance, given the common interests of wealthy and powerful men in both regions in wishing to secure independence from their

machiavelli?
machiavelli.

emperor. The relative peace in Germany during the fifteenth century allowed the sons of German notables to travel freely to Italy, where they gained access to the new learning. German humanists would become experts in Greek and Hebrew as well as Latin, thanks to their close association with their Italian brethren. Also, medieval scholasticism, the foundation of the orthodox Catholic worldview, had not penetrated as deeply into the German university system as it had in that of France, so the new learning mustered less opposition in the different German principalities.

The early German humanists focused primarily on the Gospels. Rudolf Agricola (1442–1485) introduced the new learning to the German principalities after having received an early education in Christian mysticism from the Brethren of the Common Life in his youth. The Brethren were a semi-monastic organization of laymen who spent their lives training students. The Brethren were famous for their piety and their interest in a new German mysticism that emphasized the inner life of the spirit in each individual. In Vienna, another German humanist, Conrad Celtis (1459–1508), acquired the new learning after studying at a number of German and Italian universities, and he used his knowledge to establish the Renaissance in Austria, and later Poland. He devoted his life to winning new students to humanism and established a circle of scholars enmeshed in the new learning. Jakob Wimplheling (1450–1528), also educated by the Brethren of the Common Life, anticipated Martin Luther in seeking primitive Christianity (Christianity in its original form) through an exploration of the Bible, to develop a clearer understanding of faith. This quest for the pure form of Christianity led Wimplheling to propose reforms in the church, and he used his skills as a historian to support his arguments. His influence reached the University of Erfurt, which became one of the most important centers of German humanism and a school that helped educate the young Martin Luther.[17]

It was, perhaps, Johannes Reuchlin (1455–1522) who represented the pinnacle of German humanism. Also educated by the Brethren of the Common Life, he went on to the University of Paris, where he became fully familiar with scholasticism. He then moved on to Freiburg, Basel, and Orleans, acquiring legal training and fluency in Greek. He became a lawyer, statesman, and educator at the court of the Duke of Württemberg and then traveled to Italy to learn about Plato. Inspired by Marsilio Ficino, Pico della Mirandola, and Lorenzo Valla, Reuchlin switched to the new learning, becoming the leading Renaissance figure in Germany and producing countless works. Along the way, he also learned Hebrew and delved into the Cabala, an esoteric Jewish method of reading the Old Testament, where he applied Valla's methods in revising the Bible.[18]

In Holland, the premier Renaissance figure was Desiderius Erasmus of Rotterdam (*c.*1469–1536). Educated by the Brethren of the Common Life, Erasmus became an Augustinian monk, and later a priest, thereby escaping the stigma of his illegitimate birth and early poverty. His work became so famous that it was published in many of the vernacular languages of Europe. He used the new learning to gain an early reputation as a scholar for his *Adages*, ancient and timely quotes, which he published in 1500. By 1506, Erasmus' translations of the Greek dramatist Euripides and the Roman poet Lucian appeared in print. During that same year, Erasmus made his first effort at enlightening the religious spirit with *The Handbook of the Christian Knight*. While continuing to develop his Christian philosophy, Erasmus ran across a copy of Lorenzo Valla's *Annotations on the New Testament*. He published Valla's work in 1505. Based on Valla's insights, Erasmus then turned his attention to translating a new edition of the Bible into Latin, using original Greek and Latin sources. Erasmus completed a Greek edition of the New Testament in 1516, and a Latin version in 1519. At the same time, he published his greatest work, *The Praise of Folly*. Focused on the ills of his day, in this work he revealed that every problem facing Christendom came solely from human folly (i.e. the vanities). But he also demonstrated that without folly, society would not exist. Without folly, governments and their supporting institutions would fall. Without folly, no one would bother to produce literature and art. And without folly, the church would lose its following. Hence, Erasmus used folly to force Europeans to face a hard truth about themselves: they had developed the formal ceremonies of Christianity to appear to be Christian, but in their hearts they were truly invested in the vanities.[19]

By 1519, Erasmus had reached the apex of his career. At this point the dispute between Martin Luther and Pope Leo X had erupted, and Erasmus' greatest works had been published. Soon after, as the Reformation unfolded, both the Catholics and Protestants condemned him for not being able to choose between their two versions of Christianity, and at this point he left the historical stage.

The Renaissance and the Reformation

As mentioned above, the Renaissance ushered in the modern era by inspiring two opposing belief systems. Each grew out of the new humanist learning and utterly shattered medieval culture. The first to occur was the Reformation, and the second was the Scientific Revolution. The question now becomes: How did the accomplishments of the Renaissance give birth to such momentous events? To answer this question, let us first consider the Reformation.

As mentioned above, ironically the Reformation belonged to an entirely different intellectual movement from the Renaissance. The Renaissance emphasized the individual, his free will, and his actions in this world, while the Reformation emphasized the majesty of God, his all-powerful predestination of all events, and humanity's helplessness in earning salvation by an act of free will. The Reformation did agree with the Renaissance on two issues: both emphasized the individual and a recovery of the purity of Christianity. The Reformation's emphasis on the individual was, however, very different from that of the Renaissance. The Reformation rejected free will by claiming that most of the Catholic sacraments, as good works, were a false path to heaven. Protestants denied most of these ceremonies because they claimed that these Catholic rituals were external gestures that misdirected the Christian's attention away from God. The Protestants emphasized faith as the solution to the problem of salvation. They argued that God's infinite mercy to forgive our sins occurred only when the individual surrendered his or her will to Jesus and experienced a mystical bond with the savior called "grace." The Reformation then used the Renaissance's new learning to purify and rewrite the Bible in order to discover the true words of God.[20]

According to the Protestants, human will was carnal: contaminated by Adam and Eve when they broke God's law and ate from the tree of knowledge. As offspring of Adam and Eve, humanity inherited this carnal will and intellect. Therefore, anything that originated from humans was equally carnal. Salvation only occurred when this eternal flaw was recognized and the individual surrendered to God. A person successfully surrendered by accepting Jesus into his/her heart, and submitted, as Adam and Eve should have done, to the almighty majesty of the Lord. But by assigning the source of grace to faith and faith alone, the Protestant made each individual Christian a priest competent to seek God's forgiveness through this act of faith. Hence, Protestants rejected the notion that the members of the Catholic priesthood were unique from all other humans due to the sacrament of Holy Order (the ritual that created priests), just as the Protestants rejected most of the other sacraments.

Nonetheless, the Reformation was an unequivocal product of Renaissance thinking. Humanism had led directly to the rethinking of religious traditions that broke the long-held control of the Roman Catholic Church over belief. The most immediate link between the Renaissance and the Reformation was the recovery of the ability to speak, read, and write Greek and Hebrew, the two ancient languages of Scripture.

Coupled with this new command over ancient languages was the new model of time developed by the Renaissance, one that clearly delineated the Middle Ages from the ancient Greco-Roman era. This model of time separated ancient Christianity from its medieval Roman Catholic version, inspiring a desire to return to the original religion of Jesus. Also, the development of the Renaissance's philological techniques more accurately revealed the original sources of the Bible and other revered church documents. Finally, the addition of the printing press after 1450 widened the audience that Renaissance scholars could reach, placing the command of belief beyond the reach of the Roman Catholic Church.

Using these new tools, the Renaissance resurrected a much clearer image of ancient Christianity based on Greco-Roman primary sources, which stood in stark contrast to the preaching of sixteenth-century Roman Catholicism. Although the Roman Catholic Church continued to provide its services during the Renaissance, it still used the theology of Thomas Aquinas, having seen no reason to abandon the fruits of medieval scholasticism. After all, tradition required repeated behavior without question—especially if that behavior was sacred. And the Catholic sacraments were indeed sacred to Roman Catholicism. But the justification came from the High Middle Ages (1000–1300).

Even so, the Renaissance's new approach had undermined this very same scholasticism because the rebirth of Greco-Roman knowledge now substituted new ideas in place of the accepted medieval orthodoxy. These achievements fueled the demands for reform, urging the church to give up its secular (political) activities in favor of preaching the gospel in its pure and simple form. Finally, the Renaissance implied that the pope should return to his role as the Vicar of Christ and cease his continual attempts to dominate European politics.

The hunger for a purer and simpler Christianity paved the way for the figures of Martin Luther and John Calvin to make their very public breaks with Catholicism. As mentioned, however, both men viewed humanity very differently from the Renaissance. This difference can best be seen in a dispute between Erasmus and Luther over free will. Erasmus believed that humanity could attain the truth only by an education in the new knowledge offered by the Renaissance. In contrast, Luther taught a divine truth as found only in the Bible (indeed, one corrected by Renaissance techniques). As a result, both men had to reject one another's view of humanity.[21]

The logic used by Erasmus and Luther over their dispute concerning free will originates from each man's perspective. Erasmus contended that to deny free will is to assign evil to God:

Those who deny any freedom of the will and affirm absolute necessity, admit that God works in man not only the good works, but also evil ones. It seems to follow that inasmuch as man can never be the author of good works, he can also never be called the author of evil ones. This opinion seems obviously to attribute cruelty and injustice to God, something religious ears abhor vehemently. He would no longer be God if anything vicious and imperfect were met in him.[22]

Luther argued that one must address the problem of free will from God's point of view, His omnipotence, His omniscience, and His omnipresence:

This, therefore, is also essentially necessary and wholesome for Christians to know: *That God foreknows nothing by contingency, but that He foresees, purposes, and does all things according to His immutable, eternal, and infallible will.* "Free-will," is prostrate, and utterly dashed to pieces. Those, therefore, who would assert "Free-will," must either deny this thunderbolt, or pretend not to see it, or push it from them… God has promised certainly His grace to the humbled, that is, to the self-deploring and despairing. But a man cannot be thoroughly humbled, until he comes to know that his salvation is utterly beyond his own powers.[23]

Neither argument can be refuted from its own perspective. From the human point of view offered by Erasmus, to assign evil to God, as the predestined purpose He allowed behind worldly events, is "abhorrent to religious ears." From God's perspective as argued by Luther, an all-powerful and all-knowing God that is everywhere at once cannot be ignorant and passive in the decisions that assign salvation and damnation. Hence, the European worldview expressed by both men at nearly the same time split along opposing lines: one (Erasmus' line) that the Renaissance and science would follow; the other (Luther's) led to the Reformation.

John Calvin joined Luther in reducing humanity to a state of utter powerlessness in winning God's grace. In the place of free will and the Catholic sacraments, which the papacy contended earned salvation, Luther and Calvin asked their followers to surrender themselves completely to Jesus' grace through faith (mentioned above). This request viewed human nature as utterly corrupted by original sin, which merited nothing more than the plague, famine, and warfare that had scarred the Late Middle Ages (1300–1500).[24]

Luther and Calvin built upon an image of God that emerged from this apocalyptic fear and converted it into religious passion. Then both of them coupled this dire view of human nature with the contention that the power of faith alone could liberate the worshiper from the sacramental demands of Catholicism. In so doing, ironically, Luther and Calvin reinforced the power of the individual as an actor, a concept born of the Renaissance. But this liberation of the individual then appeared as paradoxical: every man, woman, and child could seek their own salvation through faith (seemingly an act of human will), but each person also had to utterly deny that this very same free will existed. Calvin resolved this apparent paradox by stating that God already knew who would seek His grace, and He merely permitted the gesture to occur. To us it appeared as free will, but in fact salvation was already predetermined. The Reformation (1517–1648) then shattered the unity of Christendom and set Europe free to contemplate all manner of alternative beliefs about the universe.

The Renaissance and the Scientific Revolution

One of the alternative beliefs was science. Due to the newly liberated intellectual environment created by the Reformation's breakdown of a universal Catholic orthodoxy, an intellectual space opened up for the sciences to unveil a new theory of the universe. The Scientific Revolution (1543–1687) took root in this new intellectual setting. This revolution was clearly a re-evaluation of reality inspired by the Renaissance. Led by the Italian and North European humanists, the Renaissance motivated new assertions about the capacity to reason. It also celebrated the ability of the individual to define his or her role in the world as a thinking agent with a free will. Finally, the Renaissance inspired individuals to find practical solutions to contemporary problems.[25]

During the Late Middle Ages, one set of problems emerged from the dissemination of William of Ockham's philosophy (mentioned in chapter five). Medieval philosophers addressing the sciences, as outlined in Aristotle's corpus of works, had discovered several anomalies in Greek astronomy and physics. The contemplation of these anomalies inspired a revolution in the European imagination that shattered the ancient, traditional worldview. Common sense had, for centuries, suggested that the Earth was stationary and that God had set the heavens in motion in orbit around our planet. The Bible had reinforced this vision of the universe with numerous references to the Sun and the Moon orbiting the Earth. Yet Greek astronomy, as represented by its premier theorist Claudius Ptolemy (*c.*90–168), had generated several unsolvable problems. Ptolemy's geocentric (Earth-centered) universe, for example, required such complex orbital features that he could not accurately forecast the location of the planets in relation to each other and the Sun. And no matter what medieval astronomers did to try to correct Ptolemy's model, it failed to work with any predictable precision.

Where Ptolemy failed was in the complexity of his system. He had devised an image of the universe wherein a planet's motion entailed a large orbit (the deferent), numerous smaller orbits (epicycles), and an off-center, center point (the equant) that was other than the Earth. If his model of the geocentric universe was correct, the center point of the system should have been the Earth. But the month of February had only 28 days in it, and July and August each had 31 days; this meant that winter was a shorter season than was summer. This lopsided arrangement suggested an oblong, as opposed to a perfectly round, design to the year. This in a sense undid the notion of the Earth as the center of his universe because a geocentric model mandated seasons of equal length. In his model, every planet as well as the Sun would have to orbit the equant (off center, center) in harmony with one another. But Ptolemy's geocentric model could find no such common center point that would account for the movements of the Sun, the planets, and the Moon, let alone put Earth at that center point. Although astronomer after astronomer tried to use Ptolemy's astronomical system to forecast the location of the planets in their orbits around the Earth, none could make it work. The combination of all these accumulated failings inspired Nicolas Copernicus to propose an alternative model: the heliocentric, or Sun-centered, universe.

It was Nicholas Copernicus (1473–1543) who finally developed the new model of the solar system. He grew up in Poland, studied at the University of Krakow, and traveled to Italy seeking a career in the Roman Catholic Church. He served the church as a canon (church lawyer), but during his studies developed a love of astronomy that kept him busy for the rest of his life. He developed his heliocentric model by 1530, but chose not to publish it until he could rest assured that he was absolutely correct. This desire for perfection came from his understanding that his model was revolutionary, and he could not tolerate publishing a flawed design. He waited until he fell fatally ill, published on his death bed, and dedicated his work to Pope Paul III (reigned 1534–1549) hoping to reduce its revolutionary impact with papal support. In this hope, he failed.

The Copernican model was indeed revolutionary, but it did not completely solve the problems posed by Ptolemy's geocentric system. The Copernican model did simplify and describe planetary motion with greater accuracy. Flaws, however, within the Copernican model surfaced quickly: first, the Sun is not really the center of our solar system because planetary orbits are elliptical, and ellipses have two centers; and second, the Sun certainly is not the center of the universe. But Copernicus' work, shocking and considered heretical at the time, did launch a momentous debate during the Reformation (1517–1648). As the papacy lost control of Europe's traditional beliefs concerning God and nature, this debate unleashed an inquiry into the question: is the geocentric or heliocentric model more accurate in describing planetary motion? The end result was a series of discoveries that ultimately destroyed the ancient Greek vision of the universe. In so doing, this debate also undermined the Roman Catholic orthodoxy by reminding Europe that Thomas Aquinas had allied Christian dogma with Aristotelian physics and astronomy during the High Middle Ages (1000–1300).

The Greek, and later medieval Christian, model of the universe had described a small and intimate place populated with heavenly bodies. These heavenly bodies included a series of planets, the Sun, and the Moon, all of which God had created and set in motion within a finite series of orbits. God also governed his creation with an omnipotent will and providence. In the place of this highly personal and intimate universe came a model that stunned the European imagination. Thanks to the use of the telescope, Europeans had discovered that: the universe existed in an envelope of infinite space; God's realm, heaven, was no more perfect than the Earth; the universe had more than one center, or rather, an infinite number of centers; and gravity governed as a universal and amoral force that did not distinguish between good and evil. Copernicus launched this revolution and Johannes Kepler, Galileo Galilei, and Sir Isaac Newton consolidated its conclusions in what became known as the Scientific Revolution (1543–1687). The end result was the collapse of a traditional worldview in Western civilization. At the same time, science infused Europe with doubt concerning all past practices that tradition had prescribed. Furthermore, along with the development of doubt, a new mindset ultimately forced Europeans to question their most basic beliefs about the world around them. These same questions then released the individual—whose power had been brought to the fore by the thinkers of the Renaissance—to find new answers to some of the oldest questions. The modern imagination had emerged from the consequences of the Scientific Revolution. The term for planetary motion, "revolution," became the term for modern change.[26]

Voyages of Discovery and their Consequences

While the Renaissance, Reformation, and the Scientific Revolutions shattered the medieval imagination, three other parallel events contributed to the demise of European traditions. These were: 1) the voyages of discovery (1416–1498); 2) the commercial revolution (1492–1763); and 3) the rise of the royal army (1494–1648). The voyages of discovery began when the monarchies of the Iberian Peninsula, Portugal and Spain, sought new trade routes to India and China that by-passed Muslim-controlled lands in the Middle East. The mariners of both crowns set out using the Atlantic in search of an ocean-based trade route to Asia free of the foreign interference that was always encountered along the ancient Silk Road. The Spanish sailed west, and the Portuguese sailed south. Both succeeded by using existing technology: the caravel and navigational tools. The caravel was a type of sailing ship designed to withstand most of the weather encountered on the high seas of the Atlantic: violent storms, strong winds, and powerful currents. Their navigational tools, the compass and astrolabe, allowed the ship's pilots to estimate their location north, south, east, and west from any point at which they found themselves.

The Renaissance's fascination with all things Greek and Roman reminded late medieval Europeans that the world was round, overturning the common sense belief that it was flat. In the second century BCE, Eratosthenes (*c.*275–195 BCE) had calculated the Earth's circumference by noticing that when the Sun was directly overhead in Syrene (Aswan), it cast a shadow of 7.2 degrees in Alexandria. Eratosthenes then noted that to cast a shadow in one city when the Sun cast no shadow in another was to form an arc in a circle. He then imagined this arc to be part of a circle along the spherical surface of the Earth. Next he divided 7.2 degrees into the 360 degrees of a circle, which equals 50. He then calculated the direct distance between Alexandria and Syrene to be 500 miles. Finally, he multiplied 500 times 50 to get 25,000 miles (the Earth's circumference is actually 24,901 miles). He missed the mark by 99 miles because the Greeks did not standardize the unit of measurement he used to calculate the distance, the stadia. Next, Claudius Ptolemy applied Eratosthenes' findings to geography and developed a system of longitude and latitude to locate a place on the Earth's surface. Portuguese explorers and Christopher Columbus used versions of this information to sail on their voyages of exploration.[27] The Portuguese sailed south, down the west coast of Africa, then around the southern tip of that continent, and continued on a northeasterly course to trading ports in Asia. But Columbus and his Spanish crew sailed west, and instead of arriving in Asia, landed in the Americas. The end result of both efforts was the commercial revolution (1492–1763).

The commercial revolution was a redefinition of global trade based first on the rapid conquest of two wealthy Native American empires, the Aztecs and the Inca (1519–1560). These events led to the pillaging of the Americas' vast wealth, namely the discovery of great veins of silver and gold. This great influx of precious metals into Europe triggered a price revolution in the form of inflation. Inflation, then, spurred economic changes across all of the European kingdoms because inflation itself means: "demand exceeds supply." Such relentless demand spurred production in countries that responded to the new economic opportunities, while new trade routes opened up new avenues of global exchange. At the same time, European colonization in the Americas helped exploit the wealth of the 16 million square miles of land that Europeans viewed as the "New World," what we know today as the western hemisphere. Simultaneously, the planting of new trading outposts all along the African coast and through-out Asia opened new commercial opportunities with ancient Eurasian markets free of the middlemen of the Middle East and Mongol empires. Finally, the unsettling power of economic change based on this vast new influx of incorporeal property accelerated changes that had already been set in motion by the Renaissance and the Late Middle Ages.

Concurrent with Spain and Portugal's explorations, and opening of new trade routes and markets, was a shift in the tactics of combat first started in the Late Middle Ages. It was during that time that the demographic crises of famine, plague, and nearly continual warfare unleashed an era of political and military consolidation that ultimately elevated the role of the king above that of the pope (see chapter four). Wars between France and England, and in Spain and Portugal against the Muslims, had linked representative institutions called *parlements* to their kings in order to facil-itate the financing of the long-drawn-out conflicts. England's Parliament, France's Estates General, and the Cortes of Spain and of Portugal assem-bled men of estate as well as men of corporate towns to grant their kings sums of money to fund wars. In each country these assemblies united the church with the state in support of the king, in order that they might achieve a common goal.[28]

These various assemblies foreshadowed the legislative bodies of the modern nation-state, but originally only represented "free" men of estate and merchant corporations. What emerged with these *parlements*, and the support of kings, was a new type of army, one founded on behalf of the monarchy but funded through taxation by those who possessed real estate and incorporeal property. This new military comprised professional soldiers that formed specialized units carrying an arsenal of the latest weapons. They approached war with a far more lethal intent than had the practition-ers of the decidedly more chivalrous medieval combat. Simultaneously, the act of making war received an influx of funding, thanks to the wealth gen-erated by the commercial revolution (1492–1763). This new source of affluence linked the global commercial changes centered on the new trade routes with the rise of this new type of army and warfare to create a com-mon event. Furthermore, this new style of military recruited soldiers from outside the feudal nobility: that is, professional mercenaries. In short, England, France, Spain, and Portugal had each developed a new instrument of war financed by the will of the king and supported by all his notable men of estate. Meanwhile, the principalities and city-states of central Europe lacked these new sources of power.

In 1494, one of these new-styled armies confronted the forces of the independent city-states of Italy at the Battle of Fornovo (mentioned above), in which the new, royal army shocked the Italians with the efficiency of this new instrument of warfare.[29] One of the Italians who looked on as his countrymen suffered invasion following Fornovo was none other than Niccolo Machiavelli, who wrote his famous manifesto *The Prince* (*c.*1513). Machiavelli noted that these wars, fought on the Italian peninsula, pitted the Habsburgs, rulers of Spain (supported by the Netherlands, Austria, and the Holy Roman Empire) against the Valois of France. Both dynasties turned Italy into a battlefield as they tried to determine which one would rule the peninsula. Written in the midst of these struggles, Machiavelli's *The Prince* sought to inspire an Italian political leader to unify Italy to save the peninsula from these foreign armies. But this famous Renaissance work also liberated the political and military imagination of Europe, by the author's deft demonstration of a series of important facts. First, Machiavelli stated that all princes (and by "princes" he meant rulers of European states) had one task, and only one task, before them: to make war (which entailed both fighting it and preparing for it). Second, he defined the greatest heroes of antiquity, Moses, Romulus, Theseus, and Cyrus the Great (mentioned above) as those princes who created new states rather than those who inherited old ones. Third, he labelled the pope a political anomaly: a prince without an army. And fourth, he stated that success in politics required a rational, amoral mindset that used ethics as a mask to hide a prince's real intentions.[30]

Machiavelli's model of princely conduct viewed politics in the same way that the Scientific Revolution described the universe. Both were realms one could engage and understand through the use of reason and, as such, both were places that operated free of any moral considerations. Gravity did not distinguish good men from bad when it operated as a natural force. Princes must act in a similar manner: they should use good men and bad depending on the services a ruler required. Princes had to become the natural forces that governed the state. In Machiavelli's case, such an amoral view of power regarded politics as both a means to an end (i.e. the uses of power to achieve a goal) as well as an end in itself (i.e. the purpose of power, the command of the state).

Similarly, in the philosophical response to the Scientific Revolution (1543–1687), an English ex-politician turned philosopher, Sir Francis Bacon (1561–1626), declared, "knowledge is power," that is, by using the new empirical methods of science, one gained power over nature. But this was a power that lacked moral content and could be used in ways that required a reassessment of human purposes. To achieve this power, one had to reject "the idols of the mind," that is, the conventions of the past as well as the prejudices of tradition. The first of these idols was "the idol of the tribe," or the impulse to impose on nature our desires and needs as false purposes (e.g. Aristotle's final cause, or Christianity's God). The second, "the idol of the cave," was the impulse for individuals to presume that the presuppositions of our education, our readings, or our use of our favorite authorities existed in nature (i.e. the authority of our traditional worldviews). The third, "the idol of the marketplace," was the acceptance of conventional wisdom as truth without evidence (i.e. the blind use of brilliant arguments such as those found in Christian scholasticism). And fourth, "the idol of the theater," or our use of received theories due to their ingenious construction (i.e. the true aim of acquiring knowledge must be independent of the manner of presentation).[31]

Just as Bacon viewed knowledge as power unencumbered with the prejudices of the past, so Machiavelli's view of politics was an exercise in the raw might offered by the military and unencumbered by traditional moral considerations. Kings had to appear moral, but their goal was to impose their authority without any rival challenges. Such a view required kings to gain a monopoly on coercion, which they could do only through command of a powerful, royal army. The need for such an army inspired financing the military through the representative bodies cited above, the *parlements*. Meanwhile, the commercial revolution (1492–1648) flooded Western European monarchies with ample supplies of incorporeal property (i.e. gold and silver) from the Americas and the gold coast of Africa. At the same time, the religious conflicts inspired by the Reformation, caused wars between 1556 and 1648, giving European kings ample opportunity to test and refine the art of war.

When the last of these wars finally ended in 1648, the role of the church remained paradoxical in European politics. The Treaty of Westphalia that drew the Reformation-inspired warfare to a close also produced two contradictory clauses on the topic of religion. First, the treaty removed the pope from politics, seemingly separating the church from the state. Then, the treaty granted the king, or prince, the power to determine the official religion to be practiced in his realm, which, of course, seemed to reunite the church with the state, if only on the local level. The removal of the pope from politics and granting kings the power to choose which religion their subjects would practice did, however, create a new concept: sovereignty. The treaty had, therefore, elevated the king to the role of master in both politics and religion,[32] a major step in the direction of the formation of nation-states.

The nation-state would slowly emerge from the after-effects of the Reformation. But the voyages of discovery, the commercial revolution, and the rise of the royal army each played a role in redefining the state. Each contributed to modernization because all three provided the means to resolve an ancient problem: who ultimately commanded the state, the pope or the king? The royal army, fueled by the wealth of the commercial revolution, made possible by the riches generated by the voyages of discovery, concentrated power in the hands of the king. As mentioned above, however, the state itself grew into an abstract concept, one far more complex than the medieval estate belonging to one man. The state now comprised a king, his *parlement*, his army, and the means to pay for war, which went hand in hand with the emerging concept of an economy: the resources needed to make money. An economy included both the king's subjects and his men of estate, which laid a foundation for the concept of "the public."

Modernization reached full maturity in Europe by 1750, by which time global commerce centered on Western Europe. In addition, distinct sovereign states had emerged in Western Europe, and science and warfare had ended religion's monopoly on knowledge in the European imagination. Furthermore, a new intellectual revolution was well underway: it became known as the Enlightenment (1690–1789). This was a revolution that spoke with the voice of the Renaissance but no longer relied solely on ancient learning as its guide. The Enlightenment saw European intellectuals adopt the use of the new tools of science to explore politics and to extend the uses and goals of political power beyond Machiavelli's recommendations. Indeed, the Enlightenment redefined the purposes of the state, new purposes that involved not only the well-being of the rulers but the well-being of the "public."

As it progressed, the Enlightenment created a new political weapon called "public opinion." This new weapon sought to redefine politics to improve the lives of everyone living within the economic and social setting defined by the state. The Enlightenment stated that the power of reason alone could resolve humanity's issues using science as its tool. Ultimately public opinion reunited Europe's philosophical beliefs with its political activities, which had been separated long before, in ancient times with the end of citizenship in Greek and Roman history (covered in chapter two). Modernization linked politics with economics and social organization through an intellectual inquiry into justice, as a common human experience.

Public opinion judged results and reviewed the state in which people lived, producing either a positive or negative consensus. The positive consensus justified the state and those who ruled it. The negative consensus called for, even demanded, change. The Enlightenment expected this change to be peaceful, for, like the Renaissance, the Enlightenment viewed humanity as rational. What lay ahead, however, was revolution in both British America and France. These revolutions, coupled with Britain's Industrial Revolution, created the nation-state.

Meanwhile, with the reunification of belief and action in Europe, Western civilization had finally broken completely free of its traditional past and found itself on par with the level of success that China had achieved. In China's case, the union of belief and action relied solely on its traditional worldview (see below). In Europe, the Enlightenment and public opinion finally allowed the Europeans to match and surpass what the Chinese had accomplished centuries earlier. The price of the Enlightenment, however, was the abandonment by Europeans of their failed ancient and medieval traditional practices, as well as many of their inherited customs and sacred rituals.

China does not Modernize: The Pitfalls of Tradition

The course of China's medieval history from the fall of the ancient world to the eve of modernity in Europe was nearly the polar opposite of that of Europe during the Middle Ages. China never suffered from a failure of its traditional system. Quite the contrary, it was the most successful traditional culture in Eurasian as well as world history. By 1400, China was the wealthiest civilization in the world as compared to Muslims, Indians, Europeans, Sub-Saharan Africans, Mesoamericans, and Andean Amerindians.[‡] China's great success sprang from an imperial system that repeatedly regenerated itself. The end result was a China that produced ever-better versions of its ancient institutions, the reasons for this success resting squarely on the strength of Chinese tradition.

[‡] The Muslims lived in a desert environment in which one had to keep moving in order to survive. Their traditional occupations were herding, oasis agriculture, and commerce. The Indians came from a subcontinent that failed to unify politically for any length of time. Their civilization suffered centuries of disunity and constant internal warfare. This text has already dealt with Europe's failed medieval culture. Sub-Saharan Africa suffered from geographic isolation that slowed cultural development, while climate and soil conditions denied the use of foreign tools, and disease produced a biological barrier to migration that lasted until 1850. Mesoamerican and Andean Amerindians lived in a geographic quarantine, remained technologically in the Stone Age, produced temple economies comparable to those of ancient Egypt and Mesopotamia, suffered very few diseases, struggled with over population, and periodically suffered collapse.

Chinese tradition had produced centuries of political unity and power thanks to a number of key factors that included intensive agriculture, a rich landscape of loess soil, a violent river, and a highly vulnerable northern frontier. Taken together, these factors joined with a political ideology that sustained an exceptional work ethic and family discipline in support of imperial rule. In other words, the material requirements and levels of cooperation necessary to generate surplus food production and self-defense fused with China's political ideology and work ethic to produce a strong and centralized—as well as highly traditional—government and society.

Over the course of Chinese imperial history, a continuous process of agricultural colonization spread traditional practices and beliefs all along the course of the Yellow River, and these were successfully transferred to the south, where they spread along the Yangzi River valley. The differences in climate from the wheat and millet-producing north to the rice-producing south encouraged the Chinese to assimilate every ethnic group they encountered in the course of their expansion. In doing so they managed to harness two very difficult rivers and to integrate both fertile basins (by building and maintaining the Grand Canal). Called sinicization, this process of acculturation integrated vast numbers of people into a brilliant and wealthy traditional culture. With the addition of the rice-producing south to the realm during the medieval era, China enjoyed an unmistakable golden age that no other people or country in the world could match in terms of productivity and innovation. All of this success occurred within the boundaries of Chinese tradition, which remained unscathed, despite the numerous tests leveled against it.

The one flaw within Chinese traditional practice, however, was the paradox that their spectacular successes continuously led a seemingly endless cycle of dynastic failure. This successive pattern of the rise and fall of dynasty after dynasty started anew every time a new imperial family took control of China. Each family that ruled China generated an era of stability and peace. This general condition of well-being stimulated population growth, so that the total number of Chinese people eventually outstripped the productive potential of a dynasty's arable land, as well as exceeded what the occupational structure of the regime could support. These episodes of decay reflected the most ancient of cultural paradoxes: the artificial symbiosis of agriculture generated increased the human population and placed relentless pressures on all organizations, making them vulnerable to collapse.

To try to combat this cyclical pattern, each new dynasty began its rule with policies of land reform and extensive colonization of new acreage. This is why Chinese culture spread from north to south. And in the wake of this southward expansion, the Chinese developed a system of internal commerce to meet local needs. From 900 to 1300, a lucrative commercial economy took root and grew in China. This commercial economy used the trade routes that developed in conjunction with the Tang and the Song Dynasties' expanded control of the Yellow and Yangzi River basins (906–1279). With the addition of the Grand Canal, the regional variations in Chinese agricultural and urban production enabled a thorough integration of supply and demand. The variations in food production and urban labor from one Chinese province to the next linked the products of each through trade. Such commercial prosperity, particularly that developed by the Song Dynasty, included a system of credit, the use of paper money, and an expansion of numerous business enterprises. The Song integrated the basic components of a market economy on a scale unmatched by any world culture of the Middle Ages. Despite these spectacular commercial successes, China did not, as has been mentioned repeatedly, experience an industrial revolution like that found in Europe (see below).

This lack of industrialization in China reveals another internal paradox within Chinese traditional culture. Commerce, and the merchants who lived off trade, belonged at the bottom of the Confucian social hierarchy. Confucian philosophy viewed the profit motive with suspicion and as morally bankrupt; yet, Chinese merchants were people who generated vast amounts of wealth for China (as well as the merchants themselves). In contrast, the Chinese valued agriculture above all other economic occupations, considering it as the only truly productive component of the economy; yet, Chinese peasants were the poorest people in the Chinese social structure. This topsy-turvy view of the Chinese social structure remained in place throughout Chinese history until the twentieth century.

Meanwhile, traditional Europe shared China's opinion of agriculture, viewing it in an ethical rather than economic context. Hard work and delayed gratification encouraged both Europe's God and China's Heaven to reward the diligent with nature's bounty. All other human occupations merely ran on the energy sustained by the food surpluses that those who worked the land generated. Europe would discover the principle of production based on human labor during the Enlightenment, but China remained convinced that only agriculture added to humanity's wealth. This led the official state ideology of China to continue to place commerce at the lowest level of economic status. Many of China's dynasties even imposed punitive taxes on the wealth accrued by those involved in the commercial occupations in order to limit their income. These taxes often drove rich merchants to invest in land to escape the social stigma of their enterprises.

The remarkable growth of commerce in a culture that held trade in such low esteem raises an important question: Why didn't the great successes of

Chinese commerce lead to an industrial revolution similar to the one that took place in Europe (which was at the same time in the thralls of the commercial revolution (1492–1763))? Part of the answer lies in the fact that for commerce truly to succeed, it has to have governmental support. Paradoxically, China's form of highly centralized authority could have served that need very well. China's government built and maintained the remarkable water management systems that fueled Chinese agriculture and incidentally supported a vast network of commercial exchanges. The process of maintaining such a complex waterway system required extensive bureaucratic controls, and so gave birth to a large civil service. But those who staffed the vast bureaucracy received a highly traditional education that systematically devalued commerce. At the same time, much of China's resources went into educating and staffing this bureaucracy and produced officials who carried their prejudices against commerce into their roles in government (see the Zheng He voyages below). In order to sustain the union of north and south through the water management system, extensive imperial controls were required over all the lands commanded by a dynasty. These controls ensured the productivity of the entire traditional Chinese system, but also set limits on what each Chinese individual could do with his life. These limits precluded the spontaneous integration of individual innovations of the type needed to launch new industries. Furthermore, the government imposed severe labor taxes on its people, a heavy burden that stifled the development of a free labor market, even though it managed to produce magnificent public projects such as the Great Wall of China and the Grand Canal. Finally, much of the wealth produced by Chinese agriculture and water management had to be invested in defense, for each successive dynasty faced a nomadic threat across a vast and open northern frontier. China's geographic location just south of an enormous open space occupied by violent nomadic confederations, forced emperor after emperor to dedicate his life to protecting his civilization. Any sign of weakness exhibited by a dynasty, or a reigning emperor, only encouraged the feared nomadic invasion. Taken all together: water management; a bureaucracy educated in the value of agriculture and prejudiced against commerce; extensive imperial controls over land management; a heavy labor tax dedicated to public works; no free labor market; and the financial drain of defending the empire against nomads, set limits on what any dynasty could hope to achieve. The end result was that the vast wealth of China had boundaries because of the extraordinary cultural limits imposed on the Chinese by their traditional solutions. In this powerful paradox of culture, success retarded innovation and ensured failure though a pattern of rigid adherence to tradition.

Added to these traditional restrictions was a Confucian philosophy that tried to hold the whole system together. Chinese traditional rule operated on a philosophy that integrated belief with action in a way that contrasted sharply with medieval Europe. While Europeans emphasized the need to separate church and state (but failed to do so), the Chinese took the opposite approach. Their state apparatus ran on a highly educated stratum of their society that passed a set of imperial exams designed to identify those most skilled at Confucian philosophy. This group of scholars carried a moral outlook into their imperial occupations that infused the Chinese state with an overarching belief in the natural powers of "Heaven." In the Chinese worldview, Heaven was a natural agency that inspired several sage kings in China's distant past to impose a set of critically important ethical rituals on Chinese society. These ethical rituals were those practices that defined the occupational structure of China and designated the appropriate actions of each family (and each family member) within the traditional Chinese division of labor. This traditional division of labor sustained the actions of families and supported the prosperity of China's civilization. Any deviation from these ethical practices caused Heaven to send omens of disaster as warnings to correct everyone's conduct. Set at the heart of this philosophy was the emperor, who held the Mandate of Heaven, the single most important person when it came to enforcing these ethical rituals. All persons recruited into the imperial bureaucracy had to demonstrate knowledge of these rituals as well as the ways of Heaven. They also had to display an artistry that conformed to the literary requirements of a very sophisticated examination system.

The integration of local and central power in Chinese civilization through a common ideology and recruiting technique stands in sharp contrast to Western civilization. The breakdown in belief and action in the Greco-Roman world dates back to the Peloponnesian Wars and continued throughout the rise and fall of the Roman Empire. Then it seeped through into the Middle Ages and took up residence in the complex mix of feudal estates, states, and statuses. Europe did not achieve a unity of belief and action until the modern era, which was born by the Enlightenment, when public opinion became a powerful new political weapon. China achieved integration between belief and action much earlier, during the Han Dynasty, which flourished at roughly the same time as Rome, and the Chinese maintained this integration for more than 2000 years, into the twentieth century. Europe would have to experience modernization before it could match China's far earlier level of success.

Dynasty after dynasty used this traditional system to justify its existence, and each dynasty rose and fell as if adhering to a natural cycle of birth and death. Each dynasty followed on the failure of the last, with ever-shorter periods of chaos in between each episode. In addition, each dynasty seemed to improve on what previous dynasties had left in the wake of collapse. For example, the Tang (618–907) and the Song (960–1279) generated larger (in the case of the Tang), wealthier (in the case of the Song), and more innovative regimes then the Han. The Yuan (1279–1368), however, generated an anomaly in Chinese history, a blip described as a nomadic interlude. But what followed the Yuan was the Ming Dynasty (1368–1644), which produced a return to native rule and sought to expunge any lingering feature of nomadic culture. The Ming generated a very rich civilization, one that emphasized Chinese tradition with a level of intensity unprecedented in Chinese history. As a result, the Ming was spectacularly wealthy but also extremely rigid. To illustrate this point, consider the Ming's often overlooked Age of Discovery (1405–1433).

The Chinese Version of the Voyages of Discovery

Emperor Ming Yongle (reigned 1403–1424) decided to discover which societies existed to the south and west of China. He commissioned a series of voyages that preceded the accomplishments of the Portuguese and the Spanish by 87 years. These voyages, however, generated quite different results from those of Europe. First of all, Emperor Yongle's expeditions were on a scale that literally dwarfed those undertaken by the Iberian explorers and their royal sponsors. Second, only two reigns after that of Emperor Yongle, Emperor Ming Zhengtong (reigned 1436–1464) decided to abandon the Chinese age of discovery and had the fleet grounded, and the Ming did not undergo a commercial revolution (see above) as had occurred in Europe. The obvious question, one that many scholars have asked, is: Why? To answer this question, one must view China's age of discovery from a Chinese perspective.

To initiate this era of Chinese exploration, Emperor Ming Yongle reviewed his talented servants and chose Zheng He (1371–1433) to command China's fleets. Born Ma He in Yunnan province, Zheng He's family was of a line of Muslim Persians who had settled in China with the Mongol invasion of the Yuan Dynasty. His great, great, great grandfather was Sayyad Ajjal Shams al-Din Omar, who served in the Yuan administration as governor of Yunnan. His great grandfather continued in the service of the Mongols as commander of their garrison in Yunnan. In 1381, his father died defending Yunnan from the Ming Emperor Hongwu (reign 1368–1398). Zheng He himself was only eleven years old when the

Chinese captured and castrated him, so he entered the Ming court as a eunuch. Emperor Ming Yongle was very impressed with Zheng He, making him the Grand Director of the court, and he eventually rose to the rank of Chief Envoy for the Ming Dynasty. Now the emperor made him an admiral, fitted out a fleet of ocean-going ships, and sent Zheng He on his first of what would be a total of seven voyages.[33]

The first voyage occurred between 1405 and 1407, during which the admiral and his men visited places whose names represent the vast stretches of the Indian Ocean during the Middle Ages: Champa, Java, Palembang, Malacca, Aru, Samudera, Lamdri, Ceylon, Kollam, Cochin, and Calicut. The second voyage took place between 1407 and 1409 and made many of the same stops as the first one. The third voyage, which occurred between 1409 and 1411, again repeated the same stops but added Siam, Kayal, Coimbatore, and Puttanpur. The fourth began in 1413 and lasted until 1415, repeating the same pattern, but this time adding stops in Sumatra, Pahang, Kelantan, Hormuz, the Maldives, Mogadishu, Barawa, Malindi, Aden, Muscat, and Dhofar. The fifth voyage took place between 1416 and 1419 and repeated the same stops as the fourth. The sixth voyage, the last one sponsored by Emperor Yongle, occurred between 1421 and 1422 and explored all of the Arabian Peninsula and the east coast of Africa. Near the end of Ming Emperor Xuande's reign (1426–1435), the last voyage took place between 1430 and 1433 and visited 17 different states along the shoreline of the Indian Ocean. In total, Zheng's highly successful voyages brought the Ming Dynasty in contact with East Africa, Arabia, Brunei, India, the Malay Archipelago, and Thailand. These contacts opened the possibility of a commercial revolution in China long before Christopher Columbus' trip to the western hemisphere or Vasco da Gama's voyage around the southern tip of Africa and on to India.[34]

The scale of the Zheng He's Ming-sponsored voyages, when compared to Christopher Columbus' efforts, illustrated the magnificent wealth and power of the Ming Dynasty in contrast with that of Spain. Zheng He sailed with a fleet of 62 large vessels and 225 smaller ships on his first voyage; other voyages varied in size, but fell within roughly the same range of vessels. His largest crew comprised 28,000 soldiers and sailors. The ships he used were Chinese "junks" whose name came from the Malay term *adjong* (pronounced djong). Each of the junks had a "U" shaped hull, a long drag board or leeboard to stabilize the ship, and steering rods that required the strength of three men to move. These ships also featured watertight interior compartments. The fleet included vessels dedicated to carrying fresh water or the growing of vegetables to supply the whole expedition. The largest ships in Zheng He's mighty fleet were 394 feet long, 83 feet wide, and 36 feet deep. In contrast, on Christopher Columbus' first voyage 59 years after Zheng He's last trip, he commanded a fleet of three ships and a crew of 90 men. The largest ship among these, his flagship the *Santa Maria*, was barely 72 feet in length, 26 feet across, and 6 feet in depth. Columbus' vessels did, however, have a centerboard and fixed rudder, which made them more maneuverable than ships with a leeboard and three-man steering rod. It was these European innovations that allowed Columbus to cross the Atlantic, which typically experienced more violent storms than did the Indian Ocean.

The differences in size and scale of these two different explorations raise important questions in light of the fact that after 1433, Zheng He's voyages of exploration came to a halt. Many historians chide the Ming for this decision because halting further exploration denied China an opportunity to beat Europe in capturing control of Eurasian trade and spreading Ming influence. But this historical judgment belies several important considerations. One of Columbus's main motivations was clearly to seek new trade routes to the Indies, but did the same type of goal underlie the Chinese efforts? The Spanish obviously hungered after access to great wealth, which the Chinese already seemed to possess.

Second, the scale and size of the Chinese voyages as compared to the Spanish venture illustrates the abject poverty of fifteenth-century Spain in contrast with the wealth of the Ming Dynasty. The size and majesty of Zheng He's fleet indicates that China was already the destination others cultures would seek in order to grow wealthy in trade. If seen from this perspective, then one might consider Chinese culture as one that had already achieved the pinnacle of success. In short, the relative poverty of all of China's neighbors did not seem to justify the expenses of these voyages.

Third, the Chinese voyages did not seem to be about creating commercial outposts to exploit new trading partners and commercial routes. Ming China was already the wealthiest culture in Eurasia, nearly self-sufficient in its economy, and during Emperor Yongle's reign, in no need of improving on their circumstances. Columbus' sponsors, Queen Isabella of Castile (reigned 1474–1504) and King Ferdinand of Aragon (reigned 1474–1516), however, hungered for foreign treasure. Both monarchs had already discovered the correlation between incorporeal property (money) and power (potential sovereignty) at the dawn of the modern era.

Fourth, from the Chinese point of view, commerce, as mentioned repeatedly, belonged in its "rightful" place, at the bottom of the social scale. The Confucian social hierarchy had long placed scholars at the top, peasants, second, artisans, third, and merchants last.[35] Scholars believed that they alone understood the Way and used this knowledge to define the social hierarchy. For them, this social scale was natural, and they used it to guide the emperor in the critical decisions that kept China on a path consistent with the demands of the Mandate of Heaven. They argued that only peasants produced new wealth, which they did through agriculture. Artisans, they maintained, took the precious energy created by food and converted it into durable goods that met some of the necessities but all of the luxuries of life. Finally, merchants should come last because they did not create anything. Rather, they merely moved goods around, from a place of supply to a place of need, and reaped rewards for their unremarkable efforts and travels. According to this social hierarchy, commerce clearly was the least important economic function of civilization, especially in a culture as rich as China, where everything a gentleman could want already existed.

Fifth, keep in mind that Zheng He's court title was "Chief Envoy." This means that his mission was more diplomatic than commercial in design. Instead of seeking markets, Zheng He's primary concern was to gather critical intelligence about China's potential enemies and allies who lay beyond the always-troublesome northern frontier. All Chinese emperors focused most of their attention on the region north of the Yellow River, a zone without topographical barriers to invasion, and where the military function of diplomacy was probably foremost in Emperor Ming Yongle's mind. Chinese foreign policy looked to the outside world to better understand the dangers surrounding China. After assessing all foreign lands as potential friends and foes, the most pressing strategic consideration facing the Ming Dynasty still remained the nomads of the steppe. Finally, keep in mind that from 1410 to 1424, Yongle spent nearly all his time on the northern frontier, engaged in expeditions to secure this highly unstable border, which explains why the Ming is known for building the most elaborate form of the Great Wall.

Finally, during Zheng He's sixth voyage, Emperor Ming Yongle actually considered canceling any further expeditions because of their expense. Since the Chinese did not consider these voyages commercial efforts, they did not generate profits. Rather, when viewing them as diplomatic ventures, Zheng He would have used the Chinese Tributary System as his model: give gifts of greater value to foreign dignitaries than a Chinese ruler received to gain political support for the empire. Yongle's decision to discontinue exploring the Indian Ocean, however, came too late to stop the seventh voyage, and he died before any further action could be taken. His son, Emperor Hongxi, who reigned briefly from 1424 to 1425, also planned to cancel any further voyages by Zheng He, because Hongxi wanted to move the Ming capital from Beijing to Nanjing, on the Yangzi River. Ming Hongxi hoped that by moving the capital south he would reduce the state's vulnerability to nomadic invasion, while greatly reducing the expense of transporting food from south to north along the Grand Canal. He died, however, before either decision could be implemented. His son, Emperor Xuande (reigned 1425–1435), reversed both decisions. He kept the capital in Beijing and financed the seventh and last of Zheng He's voyages. Emperor Xuande hoped to recover the military and diplomatic glory of Yongle's reign. But upon Xuande's death, Emperor Zhengtong (reigned 1435–1464) finally issued the Han Jin Decree, which permanently ended Ming exploration of the Indian Ocean and closed China's coast to trade. Emperor Zhengtong did so on the advice of his Confucian scholars, who despised eunuchs and distrusted commerce. They told Zhengtong that the renewed military pressures on the northern frontier required his full attention, that these pressures had increased state expenses to the point where the empire could no longer afford its maritime adventures. They posed the question: Why continue to explore foreign lands that could not add to the existing wealth of such a spectacular empire?

When viewed in this historical perspective, ending China's further voyages makes sense. After all, traditional China was already the wealthiest civilization in the known world in 1433 (the last year of the last voyage). The sheer size of the Chinese empire, its capacity to repeat and improve on a vibrant tradition, and its abundance of surplus food easily sustained an ancient and powerful imperial system. This imperial rule produced spectacular cities, generated an occupational structure with exceptional skills, and relied on a powerful work ethic unmatched anywhere in the world. Finally, the Chinese imperial system created art, literature, and philosophy that reflected an unprecedented political philosophy and produced such a powerful model of civilized conduct that it seemed to seduce all its neighbors.

In fact, sinicization became a general phenomenon for both sedentary and nomadic peoples that bordered on China: the cultures of Korea, Japan, Vietnam, Laos, Cambodia, Siam, and Burma all reflected Chinese influences. The nomads who invaded China and conquered portions or all of the empire found that they had to become "Chinese" in order to reap the rewards of such a vibrant and wealthy culture. But the degree to which the Chinese succeeded in seducing their neighbors and sustaining their tradition of repeated dynastic successions never allowed them to escape the limitations of their own worldview.

Conclusion

The great paradox of Chinese culture and history, then, is that China's traditions both generated a brilliant civilization and set rigid limits on its achievements. While the integration of Confucian ideology with the culture's politics, economy, and social structure granted China an une-qualed form of internal coherence, each dynasty eventually hit a ceiling of productivity that it could not breech. Dynasty after dynasty rose and fell within a cycle that the Chinese came to accept as natural. And this cycle was consistent with the most ancient of all cultural paradoxes: agriculture not only generated vast supplies of food, it also produced a growing population that soon absorbed this vast wealth. This meant that within each Chinese dynasty was a certain innate inflexibility of design that disal-lowed significant and critically important changes. What changes Chinese tradition did allow were key shifts from an old dynasty to a new one that expanded on existing practices but did not alter them. It was as if each new dynasty had to sweep aside the accumulated dross of the previous regime before it set out on its own (but always similar) reconstruction of Chinese society. And when each such reconstruction did occur, it always took place within the boundaries firmly fixed by Chinese tradition. This made the dynastic cycle both possible and inescapable. Hence, China was doomed to return to its past practices in order to refine them and elevate them to a new level of existence. Yet this new level of performance could never break the bonds of tradition. For China, the paradox of culture saw the Ming retain its traditions and turn inward, cutting itself off from potential global trade.

At the same time, Europe as it stood on the cusp of Modernization rejected tradition, and split Roman Catholic Christendom into heteroge-neous but sovereign states. Each of these sovereign states enforced its own brand of Christianity and resolved the problem of whether the king or the pope ruled. Then these sovereign states managed to acquire enough wealth and power to modernize, eventually pulling the rest of the world into the Modern Era with them.

Modernization itself infused first Europe's territorial states, such as Spain, Portugal, Holland, Sweden, England, and France, with the means to plant colonies and build commercial empires. Then, the Enlightenment unleashed public opinion and generated national consensuses that either justified or overthrew these territorial states through revolution. Ultimately public opinion created nation-states that linked citizenship with a positive, public consensus to sustain a national government, a national tax code, a national legal code, a national bureaucracy, a national army, and nationalism. At the same time, commercial capitalism, following on the Europe's Age of Discovery, laid a foundation for the Industrial Revolution. This, in turn, generated mass transportation and mass production that allowed for the geographic integrate of the nation-state's urban and rural components. Industry did so by joining together a nation's economy with its social structure through urbanization, literacy, mathematical skills, and the ability for each citizen to engage in critical thinking. These last four skills further mobilized a nation's public opinion to the degree that a positive consensus sustained the political and military will for European nation-states to take command of world empires. Finally, when Europeans ventured out into the world, they found that they had acquired enough wealth and power to change other cultures like that of China, finally forcing them to abandon their ancient practices. Thus, the paradox of culture laid a very subtle trap for China: a tradition that produced fabulous wealth also limited future achievements, which allowed the poor, feudal states of Europe eventually to surpass a mighty traditional empire.

When considering China's successful loyalty to tradition, Europe's failed feudal customs stand out in sharp contrast. Nonetheless, both traditional China and modern Europe produced original and vibrant civilizations. One created a tradition that functioned very well but trapped its practitioners within a set of limited boundaries. The other created a tradition that failed completely and forced its practitioners to adapt to the ever-changing circumstances of their evolving culture. One remained traditional for over two millennia while the other modernized. Each did so because of the internal contradictions, the paradoxes, of its culture.

Notes

1   *Wergild.*   http://www.britannica.com/EBchecked/topic/639839/wergild; *What is the Wergild?* http://csis.pace.edu/grendel/projs2003a/Nikki&Sevag/ wergild.htm; *Anglo Saxon England II.* https://faculty.history.wisc.edu/ sommerville/123/123%2051%20Anglo%20Saxons%20II.htm; *Anglo-Saxon Culture.* http://public.wsu.edu/~delahoyd/medieval/anglo-saxon.html

2   *Justinian Code: Ancient Rome/Byzantine Empire.* http://orias.berkeley.edu/ summer2004/summer2004justiniancode.htm; *Medieval Source Book: The Institute 535 CE.* http://legacy.fordham.edu/halsall/basis/535institutes.asp

3   De Lamar Jensen. *Renaissance Europe: Age of Discovery and Reconciliation*, pp.144–147; William Manchester. *A World Lit Only By Fire: The Medieval Mind and The Renaissance Portrait of an Age*, pp. 105–110.

4   J.H. Plumb. *The Italian Renaissance*; James A. Patrick (ed.) *Renaissance and Reformation*, pp. 1049–1055; De Lamar Jensen. *Renaissance Europe: Age of Discovery and Reconciliation*, pp. 123–124; William R. Estep. *Renaissance and Reformation*, pp. 24–25.

5   James A. Patrick. *Renaissance and Reformation*, pp. 111–115; De Lamar Jensen. *Renaissance Europe: Age of Discovery and Reconciliation*, pp. 124–125 and 146; William R. Estep. *Renaissance and Reformation*, pp. 25–28.

6   De Lamar Jensen. *Renaissance Europe: Age of Discovery and Reconciliation*, pp. 125–128, 131–133, and 146; J.H. Plumb. *The Italian Renaissance*, pp. 58–67.

7   De Lamar Jensen. *Renaissance Europe: Age of Discovery and Reconciliation*, pp. 134–137; Harold J. Grimm. *The Reformation Era: 1500–1650*, pp. 61–63.

8   James A. Patrick. *Renaissance and Reformation*, pp. 1073–1077; De Lamar Jensen. *Renaissance Europe: Age of Discovery and Reconciliation*, pp. 143–144 and 147–149; Marvin Perry. *An Intellectual History of Modern Europe*, pp. 49–54; Harold J. Grimm. *The Reformation Era: 1500–1650*, pp. 61–63.

9   James A. Patrick. *Renaissance and Reformation*, pp. 414–426; De Lamar Jensen. *Renaissance Europe: Age of Discovery and Reconciliation*, pp. 144–147; Harold J. Grimm. *The Reformation Era: 1500–1650*, pp. 61–63; William Manchester. *A World Lit Only By Fire: The Medieval Mind and The Renaissance Portrait of an Age*, pp. 106–110.

10   De Lamar Jensen. *Renaissance Europe: Age of Discovery and Reconciliation*, pp. 128–129 and 385; Harold J. Grimm. *The Reformation Era 1500–1650*, p. 61.

11   De Lamar Jensen. *Renaissance Europe: Age of Discovery and Reconciliation*, pp. 128–129 and 385; Harold J. Grimm. *The Reformation Era: 1500–1650*, pp. 61–61, 76, 78, 80, and 104; *Lorenzo Valla*. http://plato.stanford.edu/entries/lorenzo-valla/#LifWor; *Lorenzo Valla*. http://seop.leeds.ac.uk/e

12   De Lamar Jensen. *Renaissance Europe: Age of Discovery and Reconciliation*, pp. 370–373; Harold J. Grimm. *The Reformation Era: 1500–1650*, pp. 64–66; *Juan Luis Vives (Joannes Ludovicus Vives)*. http://plato.stanford.edu/entries/vives/

13   De Lamar Jensen. *Renaissance Europe: Age of Discovery and Reconciliation*, 367–370; Harold J. Grimm. *The Reformation Era: 1500–1650*, pp. 66–67; *Guillaume Briçonnet (1470–1533)*. http://www.britannica.com/EBchecked/topic/79228/Guillaume-Briconnet

14   James A. Patrick. *Renaissance and Reformation*, pp. 1176–1179; De Lamar Jensen. *Renaissance Europe: Age of Discovery and Reconciliation*, pp. 395–397; Harold J. Grimm. *The Reformation Era: 1500–1650*, pp. 67–68.

15   De Lamar Jensen. *Renaissance Europe: Age of Discovery and Reconciliation*, pp. 376–377; Harold J. Grimm. *The Reformation Era: 1500–1650*, pp. 68–70.

16   James A. Patrick. *Renaissance and Reformation*, pp. 924–932; De Lamar Jensen. *Renaissance Europe: Age of Discovery and Reconciliation*, pp. 378–381 and 321–322; Harold J. Grimm. *The Reformation Era: 1500–1650*, pp. 69–70.

17 De Lamar Jensen. *Renaissance Europe: Age of Discovery and Reconciliation*, pp. 236– 237; William R. Estep. *Renaissance and Reformation*, pp. 45–47, and 373–376; Harold J. Grimm. *The Reformation Era: 1500–1650*, pp. 58–59 and 70–73.

18 De Lamar Jensen. *Renaissance Europe: Age of Discovery and Reconciliation*, pp. 375–378 and 236–237; William R. Estep. *Renaissance and Reformation*, pp. 45–47; Harold J. Grimm. *The Reformation Era: 1500–1650*, pp. 58–59 and 73–75.

19 James A. Patrick. *Renaissance and Reformation*, pp. 356–363; De Lamar Jensen. *Renaissance Europe: Age of Discovery and Reconciliation*, pp. 236–237 and 382–388; William R. Estep. *Renaissance and Reformation*, pp. 45–47, and 78–93; Harold J. Grimm. *The Reformation Era: 1500–1650*, pp. 58–59 and 77–85.

20 James A. Patrick. *Renaissance and Reformation*, pp. 1188–1200; Marvin Perry. *An Intellectual History of Modern Europe*, pp. 54–58.

21 Robert C. Solomon and Kathleen M. Higgins. *A Short History of Philosophy*, pp. 155–158; De Lamar Jensen. *Renaissance Europe: Age of Discovery and Reconciliation*, pp. 387–388; William R. Estep. *Renaissance and Reformation*, pp. 114–133; Harold J. Grimm. *The Reformation Era*, pp. 83–87.

22 Desiderius Erasmus. *On Free Will*, Ch. VIII. Sec. 59.

23 Luther. *The Bondage of the Will*. http://www.covenanter.org/Luther/Bondage/bow_toc.htm

24 James A. Patrick. *Renaissance and Reformation*. Volumes 1. pp. 178–190; Robert C. Solomon and Kathleen M. Higgins. *A Short History of Philosophy*, pp. 158–160, 314–316, and 351–355; William R. Estep. *Renaissance and Reformation*, pp. 234–246.

25 James A. Patrick. *Renaissance and Reformation*, Volumes 1, pp. 265–272; De Lamar Jensen. *Renaissance Europe: Age of Discovery and Reconciliation*, pp. 195–197; Marvin Perry. *An Intellectual History of Modern Europe*, pp. 65–67.

26 For a complete history of the Copernican Revolution see Thomas Kuhn. *The Copernican Revolution: Planetary Astronomy in the Development of Western Thought*; also see James A. Patrick. *Renaissance and Reformation*, Volumes 1 and 2, pp. 265–272 and 460–468.

27 De Lamar Jensen. *Renaissance Europe: Age of Discovery and Reconciliation*, pp. 330–333; William R. Estep. *Renaissance and Reformation*, pp. 95–110.

28 De Lamar Jensen. *Renaissance Europe: Age of Discovery and Reconciliation*, pp. 261–283; William R. Estep. *Renaissance and Reformation*, pp. 95–110.

29 *The Battle of Fornovo (1495), according to Alessandro Beneditti*, and *The Battle of Fornovo 1495*. http://motor1.physics.wayne.edu/~cinabro/other/fornovo.html

30 Niccolò Machiavelli. *The Prince*, pp. 49–76.

31 Niccolò Machiavelli. *The Prince*, pp. 49–76; Robert Audi. *The Cambridge Dictionary of Philosophy*, pp. 60–61.

32   James A. Patrick. *Renaissance and Reformation*, Volumes 5, pp. 1330–1339; *Peace Treaty between the Holy Roman Emperor and the King of France and their Peace Treaty between the Holy Roman Emperor and the King of France and their respective Allies.* http://avalon.law.yale.edu/17th_century/westphal.asp
33   J.A.G. Roberts. *A History of China*, pp. 122–123; Paul S. Ropp. *China in World History*, pp. 87–88; John A. Harrison. *The Chinese Empire*, p. 316.
34   J.A.G. Roberts. *A History of China*, pp. 122–123; Paul S. Ropp. *China in World History*, pp. 87–88; John A. Harrison. *The Chinese Empire*, p. 316.
35   Also see: *Confucius.* http://plato.stanford.edu/entries/confucius/

Select Bibliography

Allisen, Thomas. "The Rise of the Mongolian Empire and Mongolian Rule in Northern China." In Herbert Franke and Denis Twitchett, eds, *The Cambridge History of China*. Volume 6 (Cambridge: Cambridge University Press, 1994).

Ancient Greek Colonization and Trade and their Influence on Greek Art. http://www.metmuseum.org/toah/hd/angk/hd_angk.htm

Anglo Saxon England II. https://faculty.history.wisc.edu/sommerville/123/123%2051%20Anglo%20Saxons%20II.htm

Anglo-Saxon Culture. http://public.wsu.edu/~delahoyd/medieval/anglo-saxon.html

Anselm (c.1033–1109). http://people.bu.edu/wwildman/WeirdWildWeb/courses/wphil/lectures/wphil_theme07.htm

Anselm on God's Existence. http://www.fordham.edu/halsall/source/anselm.asp

"Anselm." *The Cambridge Dictionary of Philosophy*, pp. 26–28.

Aristotle. *Ethics.* Translated by J.A.K. Thomson (New York: Penguin Classics, 1986).

Aristotle's Ethics. http://plato.stanford.edu/entries/aristotle-ethics/

Aristotle's Forms of Government. http://politicsandgovernance.blogspot.com/2010/06/aristotles-forms-of-government.html

Audi, Robert, Editor. *The Cambridge Dictionary of Philosophy* (New York: Cambridge University Press, 1995), pp. 120–121.

Bard, Mitchell. *Pharisees, Sadducees, and Essenes.* http://www.jewishvirtuallibrary.org/jsource/History/sadducees_pharisees_essenes.html

Bauer, Susan Wise. *The History of the Medieval World: From the Conversion of Constantine to the First Crusade* (New York: W.W. Norton, 2010).

Beckwith, Christopher. *Empires of the Silk Road: A History of Central Asia from the Bronze Age to the Present* (Princeton: Princeton University Press, 2009).

China and the West to 1600: Empire, Philosophy, and the Paradox of Culture,
First Edition. Steven Wallech.
© 2016 John Wiley & Sons, Inc. Published 2016 by John Wiley & Sons, Inc.

Biot Report. *The Secret of China's Vast Loess Plateau.* #357, May 7, 2006. http://www.semp.us/publications/biot_reader.php?BiotID=357 and http://news.stanford.edu/news/2011/june/china-reap-part3-061511

Bishop, Morris. *The Middle Ages* (New York: Houghton Mifflin Company, 2001).

Blazquez, J.M. "The Latest Work on the Export of Baetican Olive Oil in Rome and the Army." *Greece and Rome.* Volume 39, Number 2, 1992.

Boardman, John, Griffin, Jasper, and Murray, Oswyn, Editors. *Late Antiquity: A Guide to the Post-Classical World* (Cambridge, Massachusetts: The Belknap Press of Harvard University, 1999).

Boardman, John, Griffin, Jasper, and Murray, Oswyn, editors. *The Oxford History of the Classical World* (Oxford: Oxford University Press, 1986).

Boardman, John, Griffin, Jasper, and Murray, Oswyn, Editors. *The Oxford History of the Roman World* (Oxford: Oxford University Press, 1991).

Bray, R.S. *Armies of Pestilence: The Impact of Disease on History* (New York: Barnes and Nobles as arranged by James Clarke & Co., Ltd, 1996).

Burghers. http://www.encyclopediaofukraine.com/pages%5CB%5CU%5CBurghers.htm

Cantor, Norman F. *The Civilization of the Middle Ages* (New York: Harper Perennial, 1994).

Cartwright, Frederick F. *Disease and History* (New York: Dorset Press, 1972).

Casson, Lionel. "Trade in the Ancient World." *Scientific American.* Volume 191, 1954.

Cave, Roy C. and Coulson, Herbert Henry. *A Source Book of Medieval Economic* (New York: The Bruce Publishing Company, 1965).

CDC–Symptoms-Plague. http://www.cdc.gov/plague/symptoms/SepticemicPlague. http://plague.emedtv.com/septicemic-plague/septicemic-plague-p.2.html

Chaliand, Gerard. *Nomadic Empires from Mongolia to the Danube.* Translated from French by A.M. Berrett (New Brunswick: Transaction Publishers, 2008).

Chew, Sing C. *World Ecological Degradation: Accumulation, Urbanization, and Deforestation 3000 BC–AD 2000* (New York: Alta Mira, a division of Rowman & Littlefield Publishers, Inc. 2001).

Chinese History—Zhou Dynasty 周 *(11th. cent.–221 BC): government and administration.* http://www.chinaknowledge.de/History/Zhou/zhou-admin.html

Clement of Alexandria (c.150–211). http://www.religionfacts.com/christianity/people/clement_alexandria.htm

Clement of Alexandria. http://www.newadvent.org/cathen/04045a.htm

Commons, John Rogers. *The Legal Foundations of Capitalism* (Clark, New Jersey: The Law Book Exchange Limited, 2006).

Confucius. http://plato.stanford.edu/entries/confucius/

Confucius. *The Analects* (London: Penguin Classics, 1979).

Cosmopolite. http://www.etymonline.com/index.php?term=cosmopolite

Coulton, George Gordon. *The Medieval Village* (Cambridge, Massachusetts: Cambridge University Press, 2010).

Craughwell, Thomas J. *The Rise and Fall of the Second Largest Empire in History: How Genghis Khan's Mongols Almost Conquered the World* (Beverly Massachusetts: Fair Winds Press, 2010).

Darwin, John. *After Tamerlane: The Global History of Empire Since 1405* (New York: Bloomsbury Press, 2008).

Diamond, Jared. *Guns, Germs, and Steel: The Fate of Human Societies* (New York: W. W. Norton & Company, 1999), pp. 186–187.

Dumolyn, Jan and Haemers, Jelle. *Patterns of urban rebellion in medieval Flanders.* http://www.sciencedirect.com/science/article/pii/S0304418105000321

Erasmus, Desiderius. *On Free Will.* Translated and edited by Ernst F. Winters. *From Erasmus to Luther: Discourse on Free Will* (New York: Frederick Unger, 1961), Chapter VIII. Sec. 59.

Estep, William R. *Renaissance and Reformation* (Grand Rapids, Michigan: William B. Eerdmans Publishing Company, 1986).

Everitt, Anthony. *The Rise of Rome: The Making of the World's Greatest Empire* (New York: Random House, 2012).

Fagan, Brian. *The Little Ice Age* (New York: Basic Books, 2000).

Fagan, Brian. *The Long Summer: How Climate Changed Civilizations* (New York: Basic Books, 2004).

Fairbank, John K. and Edwin O. Reischauer. *China: Tradition and Transformation* (Boston: Houghton Mifflin Company, 1989).

Feedback on Night Soil: Composting Human Waste. http://www.motherearthnews.com/nature-and-environment/composting-human-waste-zmaz73sozraw.aspx

Feudal System Legal Definition: A Social and Land Use in Europe during the Middle Age. http://www.duhaime.org/LegalDictionary/F/FeudalSystem.aspx

Fitzhugh, William, Rossabi, Morris, and Honeychurch, William (eds). *Genghis Khan and the Mongol Empire* (New York: W.W. Norton & Company, 2013).

Freeman, Charles. *Egypt, Greece, and Rome: Civilization of the Ancient Mediterranean.* Second edition (London: Oxford University Press), pp. 400–401.

Frost, Frank J. *Greek Society.* Fourth edition (Lexington, Massachusetts: D.C. Heath and Company, 1992).

Fulford, Michael. "Territorial Expansion in the Roman Empire." *World Archaeology.* Volume 23, Number 3, 1992.

Genghis Khan, the creator and Leader of the Mongol empire, was born around 1165 (dates vary wildly), and died in August 1227. http://www.leader-values.com/Content/detail.asp?ContentDetailID=799

Genghis Khan's Art of War. http://www.slideshare.net/bright9977/genghis-khan-s-art-of-war

Gernet, Jacques. *A History of Chinese Civilization.* Second edition. Translated by J.R. Foster and Charles Hartman (Cambridge Massachusetts: Cambridge University Press, 1999).

Goodman, Martin. *Rome and Jerusalem: The Clash of Ancient Cultures* (New York: Random House, Inc., 2007).

Greek Tectonics and Seismicity. http://geophysics.geol.uca.gr

Grimm, Harold J. *The Reformation Era: 1500–1650* (New York: The Macmillan Company, 1966).

Guillaume Briçonnet (1470–1533). http://www.britannica.com/EBchecked/topic/79228/Guillaume-Briconnet

Haemers, Jelle (Universiteit Gent). *Social capital and politics. Guilds and urban rebellion in Ghent and Bruges (14th–15th centuries).* http://www2.iisg.nl

Hammond, Nicholas Geoffrey Lemprière. *The History of Greece to 322 BCE* (Oxford: Clarendon Press, 1967).

Han Yu (768–824). http://web.whittier.edu/academic/english/Chinese/Hanyu.htm

Hanson, Victor Davis. *Carnage and Culture: Landmark Battles in the Rise of Western Power* (New York: Doubleday, 2001).

Harrison, John A. *The Chinese Empire: A Short History of China from Neolithic Times to the End of the Eighteenth Century* (New York: Harcourt Brace Jovanovich, Inc).

Hessen, Robert. *Do Business and Economic Historians Understand Corporations?* (The Hoover Institution: Stanford University, May 1989).

Holland, Thomas. *Rubicon: the Last Years of the Roman Republic* (New York: Anchor Books, 2003).

Holmes, George, Editor. *The Oxford History of the Middle Ages* (Oxford: Oxford University Press, 1988).

Hopkins, Keith. "Economic Growth and Towns in Classical Antiquity." *Towns in Societies.* Edited by Peter Abrams and E. Wrigley (Cambridge: Cambridge University Press, 1978).

Hopkins, Keith. "Roman Trade, Industry, and Labor." *Civilizations of the Ancient Mediterranean: Greece and Rome.* Edited by Michael Grant and R. Kitzinger (New York: Charles Scriber and Sons, 1988).

Hopkins, Keith. "Taxes and Trade in the Roman Empire 200 BC–AD 400." *Journal of Roman Studies.* Volume 70, 1980.

Horst, Pieter van der. *The Origins of Christian Anti-Semitism.* http://jepa.org/article/the-origins-of-christian-anti-semitism

Hurd, Lindsey. *St Augustine's The City of God.* http://www.fortifyingthefamily.com/cityofgod.htm

Incorporeal Property Law and Legal Definition. http://definitions.uslegal.com/i/incorporeal-property/

James H. Breasted: the University of Chicago Faculty, A Centennial View. http://www.lib.uchicago.edu/e/spcl/centcat/fac/facch10_01.html

Jensen, De Lamar. *Renaissance Europe: Age of Discovery and Reconciliation.* Second edition (Lexington, Massachusetts: D.C. Health and Company, 1992).

Jianping, Ye, Zhengfeng, Zhang, and Zhenghong,Wu. *Current use of Arable Land in China, Problems and Perspectives.* http://www.agter.asso.fr

John Duns Scotus. http://plato.stanford.edu/entries/duns-scotus/

Juan Luis Vives (Joannes Ludovicus Vives). http://plato.stanford.edu/entries/vives/

Justinian Code: Ancient Rome/Byzantine Empire. http://orias.berkeley.edu/summer2004/summer2004justiniancode.htm

Kagan, Donald. *The Peloponnesian Wars* (New York: Penguin Books, 2003).

Kebric, Robert B. *The Roman People* (Mountain View, California: Mayfield Publishing Company, 1993).

Keen, Maurice. *The Pelican History of Medieval Europe* (Harmondsworth, Middlesex: Pelican Books, 1967).

Klingaman, William K. *The First Century: Emperors, Gods, and Everyman* (New York: HarperCollins Publishers, 1990).

Kuhn, Thomas. *The Copernican Revolution: Planetary Astronomy in the Development of Western Thought* (Cambridge Massachusetts: Harvard University Press, 1992).

Kushan Empire (c. 2nd century BC–3rd century AD). http://www.metmuseum. org/toah/hd/kush/hd_kush.htm

Lane Fox, Robin. *The Classical World: An Epic History from Homer to Hadrian* (New York: Basic Books, 2003).

Lane, George. *Genghis Khan and Mongol Rule* (Greenwood Guides to Historic Events of the Medieval World). Edited by Jane Chance (Westport Connecticut: Greenwood Press, 2004), p. xxxiii.

Lee, Dorothy A. *Matthew's Gospel and Judaism*. http://www.jcrelation.net/ Matthew%27s+Gospel+and+Judaism.2201.0.html?L=3

Legge, James. *The Works of Mencius: the Chinese Classics*. Second edition, revised (Oxford: Clarendon Press, 1893).

Li, Dun J. *The Ageless China: A History*. Second edition (New York: Charles Scribner's Sons, 1971).

Linehan, Peter and Nelson, Janet Laughland, Editors. *The Medieval World* (London: Routledge, 2001).

Lorenzo Valla. http://plato.stanford.edu/entries/lorenzo-valla/#LifWor

Lorenzo Valla. http://seop.leeds.ac.uk/e

Lugenbehl, Dale. *The Golden Mean*. https://teach.lanecc.edu/lugenbehld/201/ handouts/Golden%20Mean.htm

Luther. *The Bondage of the Will*. Translated by Henry Cole. http://www. covenanter.org/Luther/Bondage/bow_toc.htm

Machiavelli, Niccolò. *The Prince*. Translated with Introduction by George Bull. (Hammondsworth Middlesex, England: Penguin Books, 1979).

Manchester, William. *A World Lit Only By Fire: The Medieval Mind and The Renaissance Portrait of an Age* (New York: Little Brown and Company, 1993).

Mclynn, Frank. *Genghis Khan: His Conquests, His Empire, His Legacy* (Boston: Da Capo Press, Member of the Perseus Book Group, 2015).

McNeill, William H. *A History of the Human Community: Prehistory to the Present*. (Englewood Cliffs, New Jersey: Prentice Hall, 1993).

McNeill, William. H. *Plagues and People* (New York: Anchor Books, 1976).

Medieval Philosophy. http://plato.stanford.edu/entries/medieval-philosophy/

Medieval Source Book: The Institute CE 535. http://legacy.fordham.edu/halsall/ basis/535institutes.asp

Mithen, Steven. *After the Ice: A Global Human History 20,000–5000 BC* (Cambridge, Massachusetts: Harvard University Press, 2003).

Morgan, David. *The Mongols* (Oxford: Basil Blackwell, 1986), pp. 61–73.

Morrall, John B. *The Founding of the Western Tradition: the Medieval Imprint* (Harmondsworth, Middlesex: Pelican Books, 1967).

Nash, Daphne. "Imperial Expansion under the Roman Republic." *Centre and Periphery in the Ancient World*. Edited by Michael Rowlands, Mogens Larsen, and Kristian Kristiansen (New York: Cambridge University Press, 1987).

Needham, Joseph (1986) *Science and Civilization in China: Volume 4, Physics and Physical Technology, Part 3, Civil Engineering and Nautics* (Taipei: Caves Books Ltd.), p. 271.

Neolithic Tomb at Dawenkou. http://depts.washington.edu/chinaciv/archae/2dwkmain.htm

Nurchai. http://www.dartmouth.edu/~qing/WEB/NURHACI.html

Nurchai. http://www.newworldencyclopedia.org/entry/Nurhaci

On Zhu Xi's Theory of Mind and Methods of Self-Cultivation. http://www2.kenyon.edu/Depts/Religion/Fac/Adler/Reln471/Chu-mind-self-cult.htm

Patrick, James A. (ed.) *Renaissance and Reformation.* Volumes 1–6 (New York: Marshall Cavendish Reference, 2007).

Paul Cartledge. *The Spartans: The World of the Warrior Heroes of Ancient Greece, from Utopia to Crisis and Collapse* (New York: The Overlook Press, 2003).

Peace Treaty between the Holy Roman Emperor and the King of France and their respective Allies. http://avalon.law.yale.edu/17th_century/westphal.asp

Penrose, Jane. *Rome and Her Enemies: An Empire Created and Destroyed by War.* Introduction by Tom Holland (Oxford: Osprey Publishing Ltd, 2008).

Perry, Marvin. *An Intellectual History of Modern Europe* (Boston: Houghton Mifflin Company, 1993).

Peters, F.E. *The Harvest of Hellenism: A History of the Near East from Alexander the Great to the Triumph of Christianity* (New York: Barnes and Nobles Books, 1970).

Plato And The Theory Of Forms. http://www.philosophicalsociety.com/Archives/Plato%20And%20The%20Theory%20Of%20Forms.htm

Plato's Ethics and Politics in the Republic. http://plato.stanford.edu/entries/plato-ethics-politics/

Platonism. http://www.iep.utm.edu/pla-thei/

Plumb, J.H. *The Italian Renaissance* (New York: First Mariner Books Edition, 2001).

Randsborg, Klavs. *The First Millennium AD in Europe and the Mediterranean* (Cambridge: Cambridge University Press. 1991).

Robert Grosseteste. http://plato.stanford.edu/entries/grosseteste/

Roberts, J.A.G. *A History of China.* Second edition (New York: Palgrave Macmillan, 2006).

Roberts, John Morris. *The New Penguin History of the World.* Fifth edition (London: Penguin Books, 2002).

Roger Bacon. http://plato.stanford.edu/entries/roger-bacon/

Ronald Knapp consultant *Chinese Geography and Maps*. http://afe.easia.columbia. edu/china/geog/maps.htm

Ropp, Paul S. *China in World History* (New York: Oxford University Press, 2010).

Rostovtzeff, Michael. *Rome* (London: Oxford University Press, 1960).

Sangui, Wu and Pamintuan, Tina. *Breaching the Great Wall: How the Manchu Conquered China*. http://www.neh.gov/news/humanities/2003-03/ greatwall.html

Shaoting, Yin. *The Source, Types and Distribution of Chinese Plows*. Sessions III. The Folk Implements and Folk Techniques. pp. 103–104. http://www.himoji.jp

Solomon, Robert C. and Higgins, Kathleen M. *A Short History of Philosophy* (New York: Oxford University Press, 1996).

Song Taizu (AD 927–976). http://www.chinadetail.com/History/Historic FiguresSongTaizu.php

Soucek, Svat. *A History of Inner Asia* (Cambridge: Cambridge University Press, 2005).

Spuler, Bertold. *History of the Mongols Based on Eastern and Western Accounts of the Thirteenth and Fourteenth Centuries* (New York: Barnes and Nobles Booksby, Arrangement with the University of California Press, 1996).

Stearns, Peter, General editor. *The Encyclopedia of World History*. Sixth edition (New York: Houghton Mifflin Company, 2001).

Stoicism. http://thephilosophersmail.com/perspective/the-great-philosophers-2-the-stoics/ http://dictionary.reference.com/browse/cosmopolite

Tatian (AD 110–180). http://www.earlychurch.org.uk/tatian.php

Tauger, Mark B. *Agriculture in World History* (New York: Routledge, 2011).

The Apologists. http://www.christianchronicler.com/history1/apologst.html

The Battle of Fornovo (1495), according to Alessandro Benedittii, and The Battle of Fornovo 1495. http://motor1.physics.wayne.edu/~cinabro/other/fornovo. html

The Biography of Jesus. http://www.biography.com/people/jesus-christ-9354382

The Bronze Age. http://mygeologypage.ucdavis.edu/cowen/~gel115/115ch4. html

The Duke of Zhou. http://www.iub.edu

The Early Historical Documents on Jesus Christ and the Chronology of Jesus' Life. http://www.newadvent.org/cathen/08377a.htm

The Eight Legged Essay, Princeton University. https://www.google.com/ search?hl=en-US&biw=&bih=&q=%22the+eigth-legged+essay%22&oq=&a qi=&aql=&gs_l

The Equal Field System-Tang Dynasty (618–907). http://www.chinaknowledge. de/History/Tang/tang-econ.html

The First Council of Nicaea: AD 325. http://www.papalencyclicals.net/Councils/ ecum01.htm

The Great Bronze Age of China. http://afe.easia.columbia.edu/special/ china_4000bce_bronze.htm

The History of Zhou Dynasty. http://www.hceis.com/chinabasic/history/zhou%20dynasty%20history.htm

The Kushan Empire. http://depts.washington.edu/silkroad/exhibit/kushans/essay.html

The Magna Carta. http://www.fordham.edu/halsall/source/magnacarta.asp

The Mongols after Genghis Khan. http://www.chinaahistoryofwarfare.com/blog/626001-the-mongols-after-genghis-khan/

The Mongols. https://www.uwgh.edu/dutchs/WestTech/xmongol.htm

The Neo-Confucian, Zhu Xi. http://www.fsmitha.com/h3/phil-asia02.htm

The Origins of Universities. http://www.cwrl.utexas.edu/~bump/OriginUniversities.html

The Renaissance of Neo-Confucianism. http://www.chinaknowledge.de/Literature/Classics/neoconfucianism.html

The Shang Dynasty, 1600–1050 BCE. The Spice Digest. Freeman Spogli Institute for International Studies. Stanford University. http://iis-db.stanford.edu. Fall2007.

The Silk Road. http://ess.uci.edu/~oliver/silk.html

The Spanish and Portuguese Reconquest, 1095–1492. http://libro.uca.edu/bishko/spr1.htm

"The Steppe." *Encyclopedia Britannica.* http://www.britannica.com/EBchecked/topic/565551/the-Steppe

The Sui Dynasty (581–618). http://www.warriortours.com/into/history/sui/

Tzu, Hsün. *Basic Writings.* Translated by Burton Watson (New York: Columbia University Press, 1963).

Ursin, Aisin Gioro and Shi, Jin. *Manchuria from the Fall of the Yuan to the Rise of the Manchu State (1368–1636).* http://www.ritsumei.ac.jp

Vaissière, Étienne de la. "Huns et Xiongnu." *Central Asian Journal.* Volume 49, Number 1.

Van Leuven, John. *Tatian, His Works, and His Theology.* A paper submitted to the Pittsburg Presbytery of the Reformed Presbyterian Church of North America, November 7–8, 2008.

Wallech, Steven, Daryaee, Touraj, Hendricks, Craig, Negus, Anne Lynne, Wan, Peter P., and Bakken, Gordon Morris. *World History: A Concise Thematic Analysis.* Second edition (Malden, MA; Jogn Wiley and Sons, Inc.).

Weatherford, Jack. *Genghis Khan and the Making of the Modern World* (New York: Broadway Books, 2004).

Wergild. http://www.britannica.com/EBchecked/topic/639839/wergild

What is the Wergild? http://csis.pace.edu/grendel/projs2003a/Nikki&Sevag/wergild.htm

William of Ockham. http://plato.stanford.edu/entries/ockham/

Yuan, Jing. *Livestock in Ancient China: An Archaeological Perspective.* http://anthro.unige.ch

Zengtao, Zhao, Zhang Winting, and Zhou Dingzhi (trans). Mencius. Confucian *Classics: A Bilingual Edition* (Shangdong Friendship Press).

Zhu Xi's Views on Human Nature. http://www.iun.edu/~hisdcl/h425/zhuxi.htm

Index

Page numbers in *italics* refer to figures. This index is organized in letter-by-letter order, i.e. spaces and hyphens are ignored in the alphabetical sequence.

China and the West to 1600: Empire, Philosophy, and the Paradox of Culture,
First Edition. Steven Wallech.
© 2016 John Wiley & Sons, Inc. Published 2016 by John Wiley & Sons, Inc.